THE
TITANIC
DISASTER

Library of Congress Cataloging-in-Publication Data

Bryceson, Dave.
    The Titanic Disaster: as reported in the British national press
April–July 1912/Dave Bryceson. 1st American ed.
        p.   cm.

    1. Titanic (Steamship)   2. Shipwrecks – North Atlantic Ocean.
    I. Title.
    G530.T6B79   1997
    363.12'3'091631 – dc21   96-48325

ISBN 0-393-04108-5

Original edition published in Great Britain by Patrick Stephens Ltd.,
part of Haynes Publishing, Sparkford, Nr Yeovil, Somerset
BA22 7JJ, England.

W. W. Norton & Company, Inc., 500 Fifth Avenue, New York,
N.Y. 10110
http://www.wwnorton.com
W. W. Norton & Company Ltd., 10 Coptic Street, London
WC1A 1PU

5 6 7 8 9 0

THE TITANIC DISASTER

As reported in the British National Press
April – July 1912

DAVE BRYCESON

W · W · NORTON

NEW YORK · LONDON

DEDICATION

This book is dedicated to my parents, Eric and Julia Bryceson, who encouraged and supported me throughout the preparation stages. Sadly, both died prior to publication. My sister Anne and I will always be thankful that they lived their lives by stretching forth a loving hand.

★ ★ ★ ★

My grateful thanks go to the following organizations and individuals who kindly permitted use of their copyright material. Without their contributions the work could not have been undertaken:

Barnardos, Ilford
Ed and Karen Kamuda, 7C's Press, Massachusetts
Mr Harold W. G. Lowe, Australia
Mrs P. Maxwell-Scott OBE, Scotland
Reuters, London
The Solo Syndication and Literary Agency Ltd, London
Times Newspapers Limited, London
Madame Tussaud's, London

★ ★ ★ ★

I must also mention my many fellow Titanic enthusiasts and friends who were kind enough to help me with advice and proof-reading: Brian and Janet Ticehurst, Steve Rigby, Alice and Joanne Pickering, Jane Webb, and John Fry – all in UK – and Jerry Kaczmarczyk in the USA. 'Olly' Michael for his help with reproduction work. My special friend, Debbie Danson for copious cups of tea – yes, you can have the dining room table back now!

THE LOSS OF THE STEAMSHIP TITANIC

The Titanic wasn't the first or the last passenger ship to sink, so what was so special about this tragedy that countless books have been written about the events of the night of 14/15 April 1912, films have been produced, societies have been formed, and authentic memorabilia realises astronomical prices at auction? Even the word itself has now become common usage in the English language – my own Thesaurus lists twenty-three alternatives for the word Titanic including vast, enormous, massive, tremendous, mighty, colossal, gigantic and heroic. There perhaps lies our first clue, the Titanic was all of these things. At 46,328 tons she was not only the largest ship afloat but also the largest moving object ever made by man. She was the most luxurious, boasting many features unheard of before on ocean-going liners. But above all, she was new and the object of much admiration and curiosity. Like Concorde sixty-four years later, those with bookings were delighted to be travelling on the maiden crossing – what a story to relate to friends!

A magazine article printed before her departure described the Titanic, due to her construction with fifteen watertight bulkheads, as "Virtually Unsinkable" – and popular conversation, as is its habit, was to abbreviate this to just the word "Unsinkable". Everyone knew that man had reached the pinnacle of engineering design and had built the perfect ship: the Titanic could not go down. And yet, just five days out from Southampton on her maiden voyage the Titanic was to end her life lying, a sad and shattered wreck on the ocean floor – the ghastly tomb of 1,500 of her former passengers and crew. Her working life had lasted for just 110 hours and 5 minutes.

It is said that the whole world loves a hero, and there were many heroic acts played out that night. Yet the world had to wait to hear of their telling. Living as we do now in an age of rapidly progressing technology it is hard for us to imagine a time when there were no radio or television services. Had the Titanic tragedy happened today we could all have been aware of Captain Smith's initial distress signals within minutes. Long range Chinook helicopters sent out from Newfoundland could have reached her to drop inflatable life rafts. The final agony of her foundering would have been witnessed on television screens around the world. Reporters would have landed on the Carpathia all eager to secure the first eye-witness accounts of the tragedy.

Things of course weren't like that in the larger and slower world of 1912. The only two methods by which news was spread were by word of mouth and the daily newspapers. It was Spring in England and all was well. The British Empire spread its wings over one fifth of the world's population. The debated questions of the day were the introduction of the Irish Home Rule Bill and the issues raised by the forced feeding of imprisoned suffragettes. At Olympia the Daily Mail Ideal Homes Exhibition introduced the Broadwood-Hupfeld Player-Piano with prices from 40 guineas. On the 28th of March the annual Oxford and Cambridge Boat Race resulted, for the first time ever, in both boats sinking.

And on the morning of Wednesday 10th April, RMS Titanic, the Pride of the White Star Line, slowly began her journey into infamy.

On the evening of Monday 15th, strange, unbelievable rumours began their spread, chiefly around Belfast, Liverpool, Southampton and London – cities with links to the new, great and powerful, Atlantic liner. How could anything have gone wrong – surely it was impossible?

The headlines the following morning were to shake the whole of Britain, and indeed the world, with the news that tragedy had befallen the Titanic. The full story of the disaster was to slowly unfold in the subsequent editions. Man had received a sharp reminder that nature and the natural elements have their part to play in the control of life on earth and not just man himself.

Compiling this book – based primarily on reports from Britain's *Daily Sketch* and *The Times* newspapers – has been, for me, a complete labour of love. It is my fervent hope for those whose first contact it is with a Titanic publication, that you will be enthralled by the story that it tells, and will go on to study more comprehensive works. For those whose knowledge about the disaster is already advanced, I hope that there may lie in these pages the odd snippet of information that is new to you. I have added my own comments, in italics within a double asterix, on a number of pages where I consider them to be explanatory or necessary. I have attempted throughout to reproduce faithfully all articles as they originally appeared, and this is the reason the astute reader will notice a number of spelling errors, particularly of surnames, in a number of the reports. The years have taken their toll on the condition of the original 1912 newspapers from which my research was taken – it may be that some parts of photographs and captions are missing. My apologies where this is the case, but both the publishers and I felt they should be reproduced for their historic value. Likewise I have reproduced the stories as near as possible to the original – mistakes, punctuation and all – for better authenticity.

So, please, sit back and turn the pages of time, and learn, as the people of Britain did in 1912, of the sinking of the mighty Steamship

TITANIC . . .

Dave Bryceson
Folkestone, Kent
January 1997

A TWENTIETH CENTURY MARVEL AFLOAT

The launch. – The vessel, which displaces 24,000 tons, gliding into the scarcely disturbed water.

On the stocks. – A bow view showing the vessel's enormous height.

Afloat. – A broadside view showing the Titanic's great length (882 feet).
THE GREAT WHITE STAR LINER TITANIC – ONE OF THE TWO LARGEST VESSELS IN THE WORLD – LAUNCHED FROM THE YARD OF MESSRS. HARLAND AND WOLFF AT BELFAST. "Daily Graphic" photographs.

SENSATIONAL START TO LINER'S MAIDEN VOYAGE

A sensational incident occurred at Southampton yesterday, where a big crowd had assembled to see the giant White Star liner Titanic start her maiden trip to New York. As the screws of the world's biggest liner began to work, and she prepared to pass the Oceanic and New York, the latter's stern rope parted, and the suction swung her round into midstream. The Titanic's screws were stopped immediately, and what might have been a serious accident was happily averted. The photographs show – (1) The dangerous proximity of the two great ships, and (2) the Titanic proceeding down Southampton Water after the incident. Commander E.J. Smith, of the Titanic, is inset.

Daily Sketch **Photographs**

DAILY SKETCH.

No. 968.—TUESDAY, APRIL 16, 1912.   THE PREMIER PICTURE PAPER.   [Registered as a Newspaper.]   ONE HALFPENNY

DISASTER TO TITANIC ON HER MAIDEN VOYAGE.

The Titanic leaving Southampton on Wednesday last on her maiden voyage to New York. On Sunday night she struck an iceberg 280 miles south of Cape Race, Newfoundland, and in response to her wireless messages for assistance the Allan liner Virginian, her sister ship the Olympic, and the Baltic raced to her help.

Captain E. J. Smith in command of the Titanic, who was captain of the Olympic when she was in collision with the cruiser Hawke off Cowes. He has been a White Star commander for 25 years.—Daily Sketch Photographs

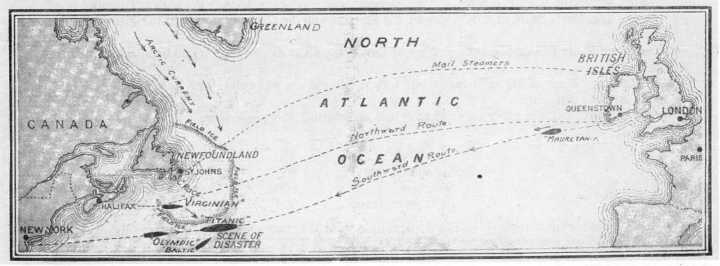

This map, drawn from the information contained in yesterday's wireless messages, shows the track of the great liner, and how the Virginian, which sailed on the homeward trip from Halifax on Saturday, was able to get to the Titanic first. The Olympic, which also sailed aboard the Parisian and Carpathia, which also got alongside yesterday. on Saturday, was able to steam towards the Titanic also when she picked up the wireless message. Many of the great liners traversing the ocean highway have been in communication with the White Star liner ever since her accident. The passengers were transhipped

TERRIBLE DISASTER TO TITANIC

Feared Loss of 1,700 Lives in Mid-Atlantic

655 KNOWN TO HAVE BEEN SAVED

Rush of Ocean Liners To The Rescue

On her maiden voyage the White Star liner Titanic, the largest ship afloat, met with a disaster as a result of which she sank.

Six hundred and fifty-five of the Titanic's passengers and crew are known to have been saved, says the Central News. It is feared that the others have been lost.

There were some 2,300 souls on board, and should the feared loss of life be proved true it will mean that about 1,700 human beings have perished.

The news of the sinking of the great ship was only received at an early hour this morning.

The intelligence was communicated by wireless to the New York office of the White Star Company by the captain of the Olympic.

In mid-Atlantic, shortly after ten o'clock on Sunday night (American time) she collided with an iceberg.

Wireless telegraphy messages were sent for assistance, and in a short time a number of liners were racing to her aid.

The wireless station at Cape Race first picked up the call for help, but very soon afterwards came the announcement that the Allan liner Virginian had received the same message, and was speeding towards the maimed Titanic.

Other great liners were reached by the same signals, and were soon hurrying over hundreds of miles of sea. Three of them, the Virginian, the Parisian and the Carpathia reached the Titanic almost together.

Meanwhile the Titanic had been sinking by the head, and an anxious night had been spent by those on board.

Passengers were put off in lifeboats, and fortunately the sea was calm. They were taken up by the liners without difficulty.

When she left Queenstown the Titanic had on board 2,358 passengers and crew, made up as follows:-

First Class	350
Second Class	305
Steerage	800
Officers and crew	903

This is the first disaster of such awful magnitude that has befallen a mammoth liner in the open sea.

CALLS FOR HELP

Many Great Liners Race to the Rescue

From Our Own Correspondent

MONTREAL Monday Night

Disaster has marked the maiden voyage of the gigantic White Star liner Titanic, for, while steaming through the night some 270 miles south-east of Newfoundland, she struck an iceberg, and is now crawling towards Halifax in imminent danger of sinking. Happily, so far as can be at present ascertained, no lives have been lost, and with plenty of help from other liners standing by, the passengers should be landed safely to-night or to-morrow.

The first notification of the disaster came from the wireless station at Cape Race, which about 10.30 last night picked up the Titanic's message for help. Shortly afterwards came another wireless message from the Allan liner Virginian, which left Halifax yesterday morning for England, stating that she had also picked up the message and was hastening to the liner's relief.

As the Titanic carried no fewer than 2,358 passengers and crew further news was awaited with anxiety. The next message received by the wireless station was even more alarming, for the Titanic's operator reported that the ship was sinking by the head and that the women and children were being put in to the lifeboats.

Then came a long pause, and at 12.27 the Virginian's operator said the last signals received from the Titanic were blurred and indistinct, and that the message had been broken off suddenly.

By this time no fewer than eleven great liners had picked up the despairing "S.O.S." signal and were heading full speed to the rescue. The Titanic's sister ship Olympic, which was herself in collision only a short time ago, was about three hundred miles away on her voyage from New York to Southampton, and while passing the message on she announced that she was racing to the scene.

Another boat comparatively near was the White Star liner Baltic, which will be remembered as the rescuing ship in the Republic disaster about two years ago. The Baltic, which left New York on Thursday, was east of the Titanic, but promptly put back. Of the other vessels, the Hamburg American liners Amerika and Cincinnati, the Allan liner Parisian bound for Glasgow, the Cunarder Carpathia, the North German Lloyd Prinz Friedrich Wilhelm and Prinz Adalbert, and the French liner La Provence sent wireless messages of encouragement and the news that they were hurrying to the rescue.

Four anxious hours passed, and then came a message from the Virginian that all the passengers had been got into the lifeboats by three-thirty this morning, and that the Titanic was still afloat, though badly damaged and low down by the head. Fortunately the sea was calm and there was apparently no fog.

The Virginian, the Parisian and the Carpathia appear to have reached the Titanic almost together, and although details are meagre, wireless messages received late this afternoon prove that the passengers have all been safely transhipped. The Allan Line officials here have not received any messages from the Parisian and the Virginian, but one transmitted by the Olympic, which was fast coming up with the wrecked liner at the time of despatch, says the majority of the passengers have been taken on board the Parisian, which will put back to Halifax with them.

Another message states that the Virginian is towing the Titanic, and while the Allan officials have no confirmation of this, they admit that it is highly probable. The Carpathia was apparently only able to stand by in case of necessity, for, owing to limited accommodation, she was unable to take many of the Titanic's passengers aboard. The Baltic, which according to last advices was nearing the scene, will also take some of the passengers, and Government steamers from Halifax and Cape Race will complete the rescue work.

Absolutely no details are to hand yet as to how the accident occurred, but messages received throughout the week-end prove that there is an unprecedented amount of ice south of Cape Race, and the Virginian had, in fact, warned several other ships.

ICEBERG DANGERS

Huge Field in the Track of Liners

The iceberg with which the Titanic collided was one of a huge field which has drifted into the track of west-bound steamers.

According to a Central News message from New York yesterday the liner Carmania has reported that many of the icebergs are mountain-like in size. The French liner Niagara and other vessels have been damaged by the ice.

Interviewed yesterday, a Manchester ship's officer who has made about 200 Atlantic voyages said:- "This is the worst period of the year for ice and fog in the North Atlantic, and icebergs are the one thing an officer dreads in these latitudes.

Rocks and islands we have charted, and know their whereabouts to a nicety, but when a big iceberg comes drifting into your path in the darkness, or in a fog, there is an element of fortune as well as careful seamanship if you avoid trouble.

The routes of liners are chosen so as to bring them as much as possible outside the paths along which winds and currents carry the great masses of ice from the Arctic seas, but icebergs are frequently sighted much further south than the most southerly of the two main routes to New York.

This period of the year is the worst for fog, and frequently there is fog near a big berg when neighbouring parts of the ocean are clear.

Sometimes the only indication that you are near an iceberg is the echo of the ship's whistle, and if you know there is no land near you may be satisfied, if you are anywhere south of the banks of Newfoundland, that you are unpleasantly near an iceberg.

About seven-eighths of a berg is submerged, and while some are almost perpendicular others have submerged ice stretching a great way from the part that is visible.

A ship with the power of the Titanic might rip herself to pieces if she struck a submerged berg this way.

THIRTY MILLIONAIRES

New York Excited by Peril of Wealthy Passengers

From Our Own Correspondent

NEW YORK Monday Night

The news transmitted this morning from Montreal of the disaster to the Titanic was received here with absolute consternation, for the passenger list includes many of the most prominent millionaires in this country.

Ships arriving here last week-end, notably the Cunarder Carmania, and the French liner Niagara, reported having encountered great ice packs. The latter had in fact sustained considerable damage and had been compelled to signal for assistance. The Olympic, which left here on Saturday, quickly reported that she was on the way to the rescue, as did the Baltic, the Carpathia, the Amerika, and Prinz Friedrich Wilhelm.

Anxious crowds gathered round the White Star office clamouring for news, but the officials had none to give until quite late in the day. Mr A. S. Franklin, vice-president of the International Mercantile Marine, made a reassuring statement to the effect that the vessel was absolutely unsinkable and that the watertight compartments would certainly keep her afloat.

Shortly before mid-day (New York time) the welcome news was received that twenty boatloads of the Titanic's passengers had been transhipped to the Allan liner Parisian, which seems to have been the first of the fleet of rescuers to arrive on the scene. The message came from the Olympic, which was then nearing the disabled liner, and later the same vessel reported that the Cunarder Carpathia had also taken off some passengers, while the Virginian was standing by.

Details are as yet fragmentary, but according to messages received from the Olympic, the Baltic, and the Virginian, the Titanic's commander Capt E. J. Smith, acted with commendable promptitude immediately after the disaster. Realizing the seriousness of the situation, he had the passengers put into the lifeboats, which were swung out ready to launch at a moment's notice, while his wireless operator was filling the air with appeals for help.

Fortunately the seemingly deserted ocean highway was unusually crowded with east and west bound liners and no fewer than twelve were within a radius from three hundred to seven hundred miles. The Parisian, Carpathia and Virginian arrived on the scene between nine and ten o'clock this morning, while the Olympic should have arrived there at two o'clock this afternoon. The passengers will be rushed either to Halifax or New York, and the mails will probably be taken by the Virginian.

The latest messages received here this evening confirm the news that the Titanic is proceeding to Halifax, partly under her own steam, partly in tow by the Virginian. No mention is made of any casualties, and there is every reason to hope that once more the Marconi wireless system has prevented an appalling disaster, and that, with the certainty of prompt assistance, the pluck and good seamanship of the Titanic's officers and crew have triumphed over terrifying conditions.

Apart from the immense value of the great liner and her cargo, the total wealth of her passengers would reach a record figure. There were fully thirty millionaires on board, including Mr G. D. Widener (son of Mr T. A. B. Widener, the Philadelphia millionaire), Colonel John Jacob, Mr J. Bruce Ismay (chairman of the White Star Line), Mr J. J. Astor and his young bride, Mr B. Guggenheim, the famous banker, Mr C. M. Hays, president of the Grand Trunk Railway, with his wife and daughter, Mr Isidor Straus, and Mr J. B. Thayer, president of the Pennsylvania Railway.

Other notable passengers included Mr W. T. Stead, Major Archibald Butt, President Taff's aide-de-camp, and the Countess of Rothes.

INSURED FOR £1,000,000

The value of the Titanic and her cargo is probably about a million and a half. It is stated that she is insured at Lloyds for £1,000,000 which does not extend to any valuables or specie that she might have been carrying at the time.

THE MAN AT THE WIRELESS

On enquiry at the Marconi headquarters in London yesterday the *Daily Sketch* was informed that the wireless installation on board the Titanic is an exceptionally powerful one. It is in charge of a first class operator, John George Phillips, of Farncombe, Godalming. His parents last night received the following message from their son:- "Titanic making slowly for Halifax Virginian standing by. Try not to worry."

For the explanation of this message see article on page 26.

"LIKE AN EGGSHELL"

Liner's Bows Crushed, Twisted and Broken In

SPLENDID BEHAVIOUR OF THE CREW

A graphic story of the disaster is told in a brief wireless message from the Carpathia which picked up the Titanic's signals when four days out on her voyage from New York to Gibraltar.

When she struck the iceberg the Titanic was running at reduced speed, presumably from the knowledge of the proximity of ice. Most of the passengers had retired to bed, but they were awakened and terrified by an impact which crushed and twisted the towering bows of the liner and broke them like an eggshell.

The behaviour of the crew was exemplary, and they were assisted by many of the male passengers, who calmed the women and children. The wireless was set going, and as a precaution the majority of the passengers were placed in the liner's boats, which were swung out ready to be lowered.

Though the sea was pouring into the vessel forward, her machinery had not been disabled. It was found that, with the pumps working and the watertight bulkheads holding well, there was a good chance of the liner making port, and the captain proceeded slowly and cautiously in the direction of Halifax, notifying his intention to the vessels already hurrying to his aid.

It would have been a long and trying wait until the Virginian could come up with the Titanic, but just before daylight the Cunard liner Carpathia arrived, and after an exchange of messages began preparations for the transference of passengers.

As soon as there was sufficient light the boats were lowered away and thirteen hundred of the fourteen hundred passengers on the Titanic were ferried over to the Carpathia without accident of any kind. While the transhipment was in progress the wind began to rise, and for a while the work had to be suspended, but fortunately the calm was renewed.

Altogether twenty boatloads of people were thus taken from the Titanic to the Carpathia. Presently the Virginian also arrived, and while the remainder of the passengers were being transferred to the Parisian the Virginian got ready to attempt the difficult task of towing the Titanic into Halifax.

By this time the Titanic was low in the water, and her foreholds were full, but the captain and crew were sanguine that she would be safely docked. The White Star Company is making special arrangements for the conveyance of the passengers from Halifax to New York. One special train, to carry six hundred, has already been ordered.

According to newspaper reports the Titanic carried something like five million dollar's worth of bonds and jewels, etc, all of which have, it is believed, been saved.

SAVED BY WIRELESS

Valuable Record of Service to Life and Shipping

Wireless telegraphy has a long record of valuable service in Life-saving at sea and the salving of distressed ships since it's adoption by the Merchantile Marine.

On March 3, 1899 the s.s. R. F. Matthews ran into the East Goodwin lightship. The accident was reported by wireless to the South Foreland lighthouse and lifeboats were promptly despatched.

On January 1, 1901 the barque Medora, of Stockholm, was waterlogged on the Ratal Bank. The mail steamer Princess Clementine notified the Marconi station near Ostend and a tug was sent out and towed the barque off. Some days later the Princess Clementine herself ran ashore at Mariakerke during a thick fog, intelligence of the accident being conveyed to Ostend by wireless.

Towards the end of 1903 the liner Kroonland disabled her steering-gear 130 miles W. of the Fastnet and had to be put back to Queenstown. The captain within an hour and a half of the receipt of the news by the agent at Antwerp had been instructed as to the measures to be taken. Passengers on board communicated with their friends in all parts of the world, and in some cases obtained money supplies from the purser on the authorities of the replies.

In 1904 two accidents – a stranding and a collision to the liner New York – were reported by wireless, and the Friesland was also located with a broken propeller shaft by the same means.

On January 23, 1909 the liner Republic sank after a collision. Communication was established with the Marconi station at Siasconset and the news was telegraphed to several other vessels, which immediately proceeded to the scene and the whole of the crew and passengers were saved.

On June 10, 1909 the whole of the passengers, numbering 410, and the crew of the Slavonia were saved. The vessel was wrecked on Flores Island, Azores, and was able to communicate with two liners which went to her assistance.

COMMANDER SMITH

The Titanic is under the command of Commander Edward J. Smith R.N.R. who had been transferred from the Olympic. Captain Smith was commander of the Olympic when, while in charge of a pilot, she collided with the Hawke. He is sixty years of age, and has been one of the White Star Company's commanders for about twenty-five years.

THE MAN WHO BROUGHT ASSISTANCE TO THE TITANIC

Mr Jack Phillips, the wireless telegraph operator, who flashed through the darkness the messages calling for assistance for the Titanic. The code "S.O.S." which is used now instead of "C.Q.D." was picked up by vessels within a radius of several hundred miles. Mr Phillips is a son of Mr and Mrs G. A. Phillips, of Farncombe, Godalming. He is 25 years of age, and served as a telegraphist in the Godalming Post Office, afterwards joining the Marconi School at Liverpool. His first wireless appointment was on the Teutonic, after which he was appointed to the Mauretania, Lusitania and Oceanic, being transferred to the Titanic for her maiden trip.

Students of the Titanic tragedy will be aware, whether they believe in them or not, that there were a number of premonitions and coincidences of a psychic nature surrounding the sinking of the ship. Devotees of that line of thought may take heart at the following short report in the same edition of the Daily Sketch. Liverpool was of course the port of registration for RMS Titanic.

LIVERPOOL IN DARKNESS

Shortly before nine o'clock last evening the entire electricity supply of Liverpool failed suddenly. The streets were plunged into darkness, electric cars came to a sudden standstill, and all social life was held up. It was fully three-quarters of an hour before normal conditions were restored.

BIGGEST BOAT IN THE WORLD COLLIDES WITH AN ICEBERG

The launch of the Titanic at Belfast.

The Olympic and Titanic alongside each other in Belfast Lough, during the time the Olympic undergoing repairs after her mishap with the Hawke. This photograph shows the two vessels alongside each other.

Mr. M. Hay.   Mr. W. T. Stead.   Mr. N. Craig, K.C., M.P.   Colonel May.   Countess of Rothes.   Mrs. Levison.   Mr. Bruce Ism

There were 2,358 persons on board the Titanic, comprising 350 first-class, 305 second-class, and 800 steerage passengers, and 903 of a crew. We reproduce portraits of some of th

The Parisian cafe on board the Titanic—an innovation in ocean travelling.

The luxurious sleeping accommodation in the first-class cabins.

HER MAIDEN VOYAGE FROM SOUTHAMPTON TO NEW YORK.

The incident at the sailing of the Titanic from Southampton. As the great new boat prepared to pass the Oceanic and New York her suction swung the latter from her moorings, and the stern ropes parted. The Titanic's screws were stopped and the New York was towed to another berth.

The Titanic sailing from Belfast for Southampton on April 2.

...n of White Star Line. Mrs. Figler. Mrs. Ettinger. Mr. J. Ridgeley Carter. Mr. George Eastman. Mr. W. K. Vanderbilt. Col. and Mrs. Astor.

people who were transferred to other liners to complete the voyage to New York. Photographs by Lafayette, Langfier and E.N.A. Mr. Bruce Ismay is reproduced from *The Syren*.

A private suite of apartments.

A private promenade deck, which may be reserved.

What an iceberg is like at sea. A British battleship meeting one of the monsters which reaches to nearly the top of the funnel.

FIRST TO RACE TO ASSISTANCE OF THE TITANIC

The Allan liner Virginian, the first vessel to go to the assistance of the Titanic.

All steamers of the undermentioned Lines will follow the NEW SOUTHERLY COURSE Eastbound and Westbound, thus avoiding all possibility of meeting ice, and each steamer will have BOAT AND LIFE RAFT capacity for every person on board, including both passengers and crew.

New 45,000 Ton **OLYMPIC** Sails from NEW YORK **MAY 25**
JUNE 15—JULY 6
JULY 27—AUG. 17

American Line
N.Y.—Plymouth—Cherbourg—Southampton
Philadelphia, May 11. New York, May 25
Philadelphia—Queenstown—Liverpool.
Haverford, May 4. Merion, May 18.

White Star Line
N.Y.—Plymouth—Cherbourg—Southampton
*Philadelphia, May 11. Oceanic, May 18.
*American Line Steamer.
New York—Queenstown—Liverpool
Baltic ....May 9 | Cedric, May......16
Boston—Queenstown—Liverpool
Arabic...May 7 | Cymric (2d class) May 22

FROM BOSTON TO THE **Mediterranean**
Cretic ......May 18 | Canopic ....June 8
ROBT. E. M. BAIN, S. W. Pass. Agt.

Red Star Line
N.Y.—London—Paris via Dover—Antwerp
Finland, May 4. Vaderland, May 11.

Atlantic Transport Line
New York—London Direct.
Minnetonka, May 4. Minnehaha, May 11.

WHITE STAR LINE CANADIAN SERVICE
LARGEST STEAMERS FROM CANADA
From Montreal via Quebec to Liverpool
MEGANTIC May 11, June 8, July 6
*TEUTONIC May 18, June 15, July 13
LAURENTIC May 25, June 22, July 20
*CANADA ....June 1, June 20, July 27
*Only One Class of Cabin (II) Passengers

Both Phones, 9th and Locust Sts., St. Louis, Mo.

The White Star Line, in common with all the major shipping companies, had contracts for block advertising in all the major papers in the countries to which their services extended. It is notable that in a number of the American papers on the morning of Tuesday 16th April 1912, while the headlines were reporting the initial news of the disaster, the White Star Line advertisements (above) had been amended to mention the more southerly route and the provision of lifeboat accommodation. In the British papers no such amendment had been made, presumably because of the time difference, and the advertisements still referred to the next scheduled sailing of the Titanic from Southampton on Wednesday 1st May (below). The necessary deletion had been carried out by the following morning's editions.

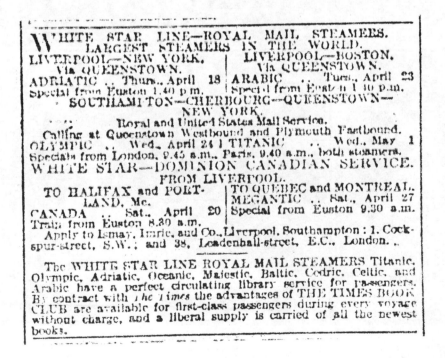

WHITE STAR LINE—ROYAL MAIL STEAMERS.
LARGEST STEAMERS IN THE WORLD.
LIVERPOOL—NEW YORK. | LIVERPOOL—BOSTON.
Via QUEENSTOWN. | Via QUEENSTOWN.
ADRIATIC .. Thurs., April 18 | ARABIC .. Tues., April 23
Special from Euston 1.40 p.m. | Special from Euston 1.40 p.m.
SOUTHAMPTON—CHERBOURG—QUEENSTOWN—
NEW YORK.
Royal and United States Mail Service.
Calling at Queenstown Westbound and Plymouth Eastbound.
OLYMPIC .. Wed., April 24 | TITANIC .. Wed., May 1
Specials from London, 9.45 a.m. Paris, 9.40 a.m., both steamers.
WHITE STAR—DOMINION CANADIAN SERVICE.
FROM LIVERPOOL.
TO HALIFAX and PORT- | TO QUEBEC and MONTREAL.
LAND, Me. | MEGANTIC .. Sat., April 27
CANADA .. Sat., April 20 | Special from Euston 9.30 a.m.
Train from Euston 8.30 a.m.
Apply to Ismay, Imrie, and Co., Liverpool, Southampton: 1. Cock-
spur-street, S.W.; and 38, Leadenhall-street, E.C., London.

The WHITE STAR LINE ROYAL MAIL STEAMERS Titanic,
Olympic, Adriatic, Oceanic, Majestic, Baltic, Cedric, Celtic, and
Arabic have a perfect circulating library service for passengers.
By contract with the Times the advantages of THE TIMES BOOK
CLUB are available for first-class passengers during every voyage
without charge, and a liberal supply is carried of all the newest
books.

DAILY SKETCH.

No. 969.—WEDNESDAY, APRIL 17, 1912.　　THE PREMIER PICTURE PAPER.　　[Registered as a Newspaper.]　ONE HALFPENNY.

THE FAREWELL CHEERS FROM THE DOOMED TITANIC.

The huge Titanic, which sailed away from Southampton on her maiden voyage under promising auspices a week to-day, will never be seen again. She lies deep down on the bed of the Atlantic Ocean beyond hope of salvage, and she carried 1,500 souls to their doom with her. The terrible news conveyed by the wireless messages flashed in the night from the sister ships which arrived too late impressed the whole civilised world, and had a stupefying effect in England and America. Our first picture shows the crew and passengers on the great vessel returning what has proved to be the last farewell to those they left behind at Southampton as the big vessel commenced her fatal voyage. Below are photographs taken outside and within the White Star offices, Oceanic House, Cockspur-street, London, yesterday. They show anxious relatives studying the lists and leaving the building.

NEARLY FIFTEEN HUNDRED PERISH WITH THE TITANIC

LINER SINKS IN THE NIGHT

Lifeboats Said to Have Been Swamped

SEARCH AMONG MASS OF WRECKAGE

The King and Queen Send Message of Sympathy

The foundering of the Titanic is the biggest shipping catastrophe in the world's history.

About two-thirds of the 2,358 persons stated to have been on board have perished.

The Cunarder Carpathia has 868 survivors mostly women and children on board, the remaining 1,490 are unaccounted for.

It had been hoped the Allan liners Virginian and Parisian had survivors on board, but wireless messages received from them yesterday said they had not.

The Leyland liner Californian searched the scene of the disaster, but there is little hope that any appreciable number of passengers beyond those on board the Carpathia have been rescued.

From a Marconigram sent by the Olympic to the White Star headquarters in Liverpool it appears that the Titanic had gone down some time before the Carpathia reached the scene. "Found boats and wreckage only" the message says.

The Titanic did not struggle far after colliding with the iceberg, and she seems to have sunk three or four hours afterwards in the middle of the night.

As the water in which she sank is about two miles deep there is no hope of salvaging her.

Commander Smith is reported to have gone down with his ship.

The Carpathia is having a perilous journey to New York. For a long time she was in the midst of the great field of ice which brought disaster to the Titanic.

The survivors on the Carpathia were picked up from lifeboats. They had been in the boats for the greater part of the night. Icebergs were all around them. Many well-known people, including a number of millionaires perished. Mr W.T. Stead and Colonel J.J. Astor are among the missing.

The disaster is a terrible blow to Southampton. Nearly all of the Officers and crew lived there, and very few of them can have been saved.

The King has sent a message of sympathy on behalf of the Queen and himself.

ONLY 868 PEOPLE SAVED

No Room For Hope That There Are More Survivors

From Our Own Correspondent

NEW YORK Tuesday Night

Messages received here this morning confirmed only too fully the appalling news that the Titanic sank yesterday morning while endeavouring to make her way to Halifax, and it is now clear that of her total complement nearly 1,500 have been drowned. Revised figures officially issued by the White Star line place the number of passengers at 316 first class, 279 second class and 698 steerage, while the crew numbered between eight and nine hundred.

Of these it is known that 868 persons have been saved by the Cunarder Carpathia but the messages during the day leave little ground for hope that there are any more survivors. The first grim message from the Carpathia said that she had only arrived on the scene after the Titanic had gone down and she had picked up all the survivors she could find.

For a long time there was no news of the Allan liners Virginian and Parisian, and there seemed every reason to believe that these vessels must have picked up some of the missing passengers and crew, but shortly after mid-day (Canadian time) wireless messages were received stating that neither of these vessels had arrived in time to effect rescues.

The lists of names of survivors came through in fragmentary messages from the Carpathia and are as yet incomplete. Two hundred and four first-class passengers and 115 second-class have been identified. It is certain, however, that none of those definitely stated to be missing are on board the Carpathia, and her commander's messages hold out no hope that they could have been saved.

CARPATHIA AMONG THE ICE

The Carpathia is now in the icefield which proved fatal to the Titanic, and in a message to his owners Captain Rostron says "I am proceeding to New York unless otherwise ordered with about 800 survivors. After consulting with Mr Bruce Ismay and considering the circumstances with so much ice around I consider New York to be the best port to make for. There are a large number of icebergs about and near us is a twenty-mile icefield containing many bergs."

Yesterday's message to the effect that the Virginian was towing the Titanic, and that the Parisian and Carpathia were standing by, proved to have been wholly inaccurate, and there is considerable mystery as to how they could have been dispatched. President Franklin, of the White Star Company, declares that the messages were certainly received by the Marconi system, and were believed to be genuine. There are, however, so many private and unauthorized wireless instruments in use along the Atlantic seaboard that it can only be surmised that they were the work of amateurs.

Frantic scenes were witnessed to-day outside the offices of the White Star line in New York, where thousands of distracted relatives and friends sought information about the missing passengers and crew.

The crowds at one time assumed a threatening aspect, and angry charges were made that the White Star company deliberately held up the details of the disaster all day yesterday. The police endeavoured to secure order, but the grief-stricken crowds were beyond control. The most pathetic feature about the disaster as revealed by the list of survivors is that husbands and wives, fathers and children, brothers and sisters have been parted, the men in most cases being drowned.

WOMEN AND CHILDREN FIRST

The old British rule "Women and children First" was strictly adhered to, and as a result, the Carpathia is bringing to port many widows who sailed on the Titanic as wives. Among the most prominent may be mentioned Mrs John Jacob Astor, the girl wife of the multi-millionaire, who was returning with her husband after a four months' honeymoon. Other wives who were separated from their husbands were Mrs Henry B. Harris and Mrs George D. Widener, and although some couples have been saved it is a splendid tribute to the Anglo-Saxon sense of duty that so far there is no record of a husband being saved without his wife.

Mr Thayer's wife and son were saved with him, and Mr Charles M. Hays, president of the Grand Trunk Railway, was rescued with his wife and daughter. Another prominent family saved were Mr and Mrs Washington Dodge with their son, and Mrs Walter M. Clark and Mrs Isidore Straus were rescued without their husbands.

The Carpathia is due here on Thursday evening or Friday morning, and until she arrives no detailed account of the disaster is likely to be obtained. The fragmentary messages received from the Carpathia and the Olympic indicate that the end must have come with awful suddenness. It has been suggested that some of the boats were swamped and dragged down by the suction, but this is negatived by the Carpathia's announcement that all the boats have been accounted for.

Later

On checking the list of survivors and those whose names have not been received from the Carpathia it has been established that of the saloon passengers saved 134 were women, six children and 63 men, while of the second class 88 were women, 10 children, and 16 men.

DISTRESSED MILLIONAIRES

NEW YORK Tuesday

Great excitement prevailed here throughout the night. Crowds watched the newspaper bulletin boards until long after midnight.

Millionaires and their wives, and friends, rushed from the theatre to the White Star offices to obtain the latest news.

In a leading article on the disaster the *New York World* says:- Nothing could exceed the sensational character of this appalling catastrophe. All the boasted wonderful progress made in the safety of ocean travel is turned into a mockery. The rivalry of the Transatlantic companies in giant construction has received a fearful check."

CARPATHIA IN PERIL

Cunarder in the Midst of Icefields

ABOUT 800 SURVIVORS ON BOARD

A delayed wireless message received this morning by the Cunard Line from Captain Rostron of the Carpathia, says:-

"We have about 800 survivors. Expect to proceed to New York. The ship at present is in the icefields."

Another message from Captain Rostron, timed 7.55 a.m. (New York Time), and sent from latitude 41.45 north, longitude 50.230 west, has been received at the offices of the Cunard Company, New York. It says:-

"Am proceeding to New York unless otherwise ordered with about 800 survivors, after consulting Ismay, and considering circumstances. With so much ice about considered New York best."

The message goes on to state that large numbers of icebergs are adrift in the vicinity of the disaster. The Carpathia has traversed 20 miles of icefields with large bergs embedded in them.

After the receipt of the foregoing message the following delayed wireless telegram came to hand from the Carpathia, via Cape Race:-

"Titanic struck iceberg and sank Monday, 3 a.m. in 41.46 north, 50.14 west. Carpathia picked up many passengers from boats. Will wire further particulars later. Proceeding New York."

The Carpathia is likely to arrive at New York on Thursday night or Friday morning. Late last night Mr Franklin, the head of the White Star line here, stated that no ship was by the Titanic when the vessel sank, and that it was impossible for the Virginian and the Parisian to be anywhere near the scene.

From the known character of Captain Smith, of the Titanic, it is believed that he went down with the ship, and also other officers.

The Titanic, Mr Franklin added, had sufficient lifeboats to take off the whole of the passengers and crew.

NEARLY ALL WOMEN AND CHILDREN

White Star Official on British Discipline

Mr James Parton, the London manager of the White Star Line, yesterday morning received the following message from the head office of the line in Liverpool:-

Have received the following Marconi from Olympic: Carpathia reached the Titanic position at daybreak.

Found boats and wreckage only. Titanic had foundered about 2.20 a.m. in 41deg. 16min N., 50deg. 14min. W.

All her boats accounted for; 675 souls saved of crew and passengers; latter nearly all women and children.

Leyland liner Californian remaining and searching position of disaster.

Carpathia returning to New York with survivors.

In conversation with a reporter, Mr Parton observed, "What discipline must have been maintained! The fact that nearly all those who are saved are women and children is, I think, evidence of that."

Asked if the figure 675 was to be regarded as representing the total number of those saved, Mr Parton said, "The object of the Leyland liner remaining on the spot is in the hope of picking up others. The 675 mentioned in the message are on board the Carpathia."

Of estimates of loss Mr Parton could say nothing. The fact of the Titanic having gone down in mid-ocean precluded of course all hope of salvage.

"It is a dreadful disaster," added the White Star manager. "Possibly the worst in the history of the mercantile marine" suggested the interviewer. "Yes, possibly: although disasters to pilgrim ships may have been on a larger scale but in regard to such cases I have no recollection of the precise losses.

MISSING AND SAVED

Many Millionaires Among The Lost

MR BRUCE ISMAY RESCUED

Until every ship that passed anywhere near the scene of the disaster has reached port there will still be some hope that the list of those saved may be augmented. That many may be saved is unlikely, but here and there it is possible that one or two may be picked up.

One of the saddest of the many sad stories which has to be told concerns the fate of Mr Daniel W. Marvin, a young American who was returning with his wife from the honeymoon trip spent in Europe. Mr Marvin is missing, but Mrs Marvin is reported to have been saved.

The husband was only 19 years of age, and the wife is a year younger. The Marvins are well known in New York society, and the young man himself was a friend of Edison.

AMONG THE MISSING

Among those who are not reported as saved are:-

COLONEL J. J. ASTOR, one of America's richest men. He is a cousin of Mr W. Waldorf Astor. He was a prominent figure during the American war with Spain.

MR W. T. STEAD, probably the best known journalist in the world. He has taken a great part in the movement which aims at world-wide peace.

MR BENJAMIN GUGGENHEIM, of the Copper Trust. He was very wealthy, and often worked in conjunction with Mr Pierpont Morgan.

MAJOR ARCHIBALD W. BUTT, President Taft's aide-de-camp, who was returning from a visit to the Pope.

MR JACQUES FUTRELLE, the well-known writer of detective stories.

MR WASHINGTON DODGE, a member of the American banking firm.

MR GEORGE D. WIDENER, son of the Philadelphia millionaire, who recently bought "The Mill" the picture which the Marquis of Lansdowne offered to the British nation.

MR CHRISTOPHER HEAD, of Chelsea, who took a leading part in the King Edward Memorial work.

MR F. D. MILLET, an American painter who has spent a great deal of time in London.

MR ISIDOR STRAUS, lately a member of the United States Legislature, and a millionaire.

COLONEL WASHINGTON ROEBLING, whose fortune is said to be £5,000,000.

Messrs. Harland and Wolff, of Belfast, who built the Titanic, announced yesterday that in addition to Mr Thomas Andrews, jun., one of the managing directors of the firm, eight members of their staff sailed on the Titanic.

REPORTED SAVED

The best known people who are reported as safe include:-

MR J. B. ISMAY, chairman and managing director of the White Star Line, and president of the International Mercantile Marine.

MR C. M. HAYS, president of the Grand Trunk Railway, one of the most powerful men in the railway world in America.

MRS J. J. ASTOR, wife of Colonel Astor, who is mentioned above.

MR J. B. THAYER, one of the least of America's millionaires. His fortune is computed at £2,000,000.

MRS GEORGE D. WIDENER, wife of the Mr Widener who is reported drowned.

THE COUNTESS OF ROTHES, who is on the way to join her husband in America. She is the only daughter of Mr Thomas Dyer-Edwardes.

SIR COSMO and LADY COSMO DUFF-GORDON. The latter is "Lucille" the West End and New York modiste. The two joined the vessel at Cherbourg.

COLONEL ALFONSO SIMONIUS, president of the Swiss Bankverein.

K. H. BEHR, the famous tennis player.

MR H. B. CASE, managing director of the Vacuum Oil Company.

WIRELESS CHAOS

Why Important Messages Have Been Delayed

An official of the White Star line stated yesterday that one of the reasons why it had been so difficult to obtain important information was that apparently a number of outside wireless telegraphists had been dispatching messages. Consequently messages containing news of the utmost importance was being delayed, whilst others of little or no importance are being expedited.

A great deal of chaotic information has been dispatched both to this country and to America.

SEARCHING THE LISTS

Distracted Crowds at White Star Offices

NATIONAL RELIEF FUND

Southampton Mourning For Relatives or Friends

From Our Own Correspondent

SOUTHAMPTON Tuesday Night

Southampton is a town of mourning. Ninety per cent of the crew of the Titanic were born or had residences in the port and its neighbourhood, and there is scarcely a house but is apprehensive for the safety of a relative or friend.

In the absence of definite news the White Star officials here are still hopeful, but the optimism is not shared by the townsfolk. The Mayor (Councillor H. Bowyer) a lieutenant in the R.N.R. has caused the blue ensign on the Town Hall to be placed at half-mast. Elsewhere on the public buildings and churches and at the quays flags are similarly flying.

Several shopkeepers have put up shutters, and there are many private houses in which blinds are drawn. The suspense is almost more wearing than the actual knowledge of death would be.

Down at the docks before dawn this morning a crowd waited at the White Star offices, which have been open since 2 a.m. and the numbers have been steadily increased throughout the day. Women with babies in their arms, their cheeks pale and drawn and their eyes red with weeping, have stood for hours reading and re-reading those vague messages of the disaster which the company had posted up.

FOR THE RELATIVES

The Mayor received me at the Town Hall and stated that, unable longer to doubt that a disaster had overtaken a portion of the crew at least, he was opening a national relief fund for the relatives.

"I have written to the Lord Mayor of London to-day" he said, "and shall visit him personally to-morrow. I have suspended the meeting of the Harbour Board, of which I am the chairman, sine die. Southampton has been plunged into grief and the sympathy of the country, of the whole world in fact, will go out to the town."

The Mayor inclines to the view that of the 700 passengers and crew reported saved only two per cent would be members of the crew. "That crew was the cream of the profession. Most of the men were members of the British Seafarers' Union, which is a new organisation started in October last. Mr T. Lewis, the President, told me that a few of the stewards came from Liverpool by process of promotion. The Titanic had absorbed the most capable officers of the White Star line.

One prominent officer is said to have been on the Oceana, which was sunk off Eastbourne recently. Not a few of the seamen and firemen joined because their vessels were detained in port by lack of coal. It is recalled as a bad omen that when leaving Southampton on Wednesday the Titanic nearly fouled the New York, which the suction caused to break her cable.

There are men in the town congratulating themselves that by fortuitous circumstances they did not sail in her. Six firemen who should have been on board by noon on Wednesday were a few minutes late, and were summarily dismissed in accordance with regulations. Another fireman left the Titanic when she reached Queenstown.

GREATEST DISASTERS

Appalling Record of Sea Tragedies

FAMOUS CATASTROPHES RECALLED

The sinking of the Titanic is the greatest disaster that has ever overtaken a liner in point of loss of life. Before this the unenviable record was held by the New York excursion steamer General Slocum, which caught fire in the East river on June 15, 1904 and 1,000 were burned or drowned.

To go no further back than 1850 reveals an appalling list of colossal sea tragedies. Here are the disasters in which not less than 300 people perished:-
Loss of life.
1,000 – General Slocum, New York 1904
600-700 – Princess Alice, the Thames 1878
569 – Great Queensland, blew up 1876
564 – Utopia in collision Gibraltar 1891
560 – Atlantic, White Star Liner 1873
483 – H.M.S. Captain, foundered 1870
480 – City of Glasgow, disappeared 1854
471 – Austria Emigrant ship burnt in mid-Atlantic 1858
470 – Cospatrick, Emigrant ship, burnt 1874
454 – Birkenhead, troopship, off Capetown 1854
400 – Royal Adelaide, off Margate 1850
400 – Lady Nugget, troopship, foundered in hurricane 1854
380 – Tayleur, Emigrant ship, on Irish coast 1854
359 – H.M.S. Victoria, rammed 1893
348 – Annie Jane, emigrant ship, on the Hebrides 1853
300 – Northfleet, off Dungeness 1873
300 – H.M.S. Eurydice near Ventnor 1878
300 – La Liberte, French Warship blown up at Toulon 1911
300 – Waratah, disappeared in Indian Ocean 1909

Notable disasters earlier than 1850 were the loss of H.M.S. Association with Sir Cloudesley Shovel and 800 men at the Scilly Isles in 1707, the sinking of the Royal George with 600 on board in 1782, and the burning of the Queen Charlotte in 1800, when 673 perished. The most serious blow to the British Navy, in terms of men, was the stranding of the St. George, Defence and Hero on the coast of Jutland in 1811. Admiral Reynolds and 2,000 crew were lost.

"BEST TRADITIONS OF THE SEA"

PREMIER'S STATEMENT IN THE COMMONS

In making a statement to the House of Commons yesterday the Prime Minister (**Mr Herbert Henry Asquith M.P.**), referring to the fact that the majority of the Titanic's survivors were women and children, remarked that "the best traditions of the sea seem to have been maintained." He said:- "I am afraid we must brace ourselves to face one of those terrible events which baffle foresight, which hold the imagination, which make us realize the inadequacy of words to do justice to what we feel.

We cannot say more at this moment than to give necessarily imperfect expression to our sense of admiration that the best traditions of the sea seem to have been observed in the willing sacrifices which were offered to give first chance of safety to those least able to help themselves, and to the warm heartfelt sympathy of the whole nation to those who have found themselves suddenly bereaved of their nearest and dearest in desolated homes."

There was a murmur of applause as the Prime Minister sat down.

NOT FROM WIRELESS MAN

It was stated yesterday that the message received by Mr and Mrs Phillips, of Godalming, the parents of Mr J. G. Phillips, the wireless operator on board the Titanic, was not from the liner, but from another son in London. The message read:- "Making slowly for Halifax: practically unsinkable; don't worry." In the excitement of the moment it was mistakenly concluded to have come from the son on the Titanic.

"MAN THE BOATS"

Safety Devices Have Not Kept Pace With Size of Liners

By a Shipbuilding Engineer

Why have so many lives been lost?

That is the question men are asking one another to-day.

Here is the greatest ship in the world, as nearly unsinkable as her designers could make her, down among the ooze two miles below the surface of the Atlantic. Obviously the crash into the iceberg must have been so terrific as to shake the vessel almost to pieces. One may imagine the many feet of the steel bows crumpled up like so much cardboard, and the great longitudinal girders so twisted that the water-tight doors in the bulkheads would not work. The best ship building science cannot guard against such an appalling catastrophe.

Four hours would seem to have passed between the moment of collision and the time of sinking – four hours in which to get the boats out.

Here we touch the very crux of the matter. By law every passenger carrying vessel is compelled to carry as many lifeboats as may be required to take in safety every person on board. The White Star liners, and indeed all Transatlantic liners, are well found in this respect. They have plenty of boats. But the boats these liners carry have not developed in size and efficiency as rapidly as the liners themselves.

Forty or fifty small boats take a long time to man and swing overboard. Ten large motor-driven lifeboats with the same total capacity could have been lowered in a quarter of the time.

And there is this important point – every boat fewer means less risk of panic and accident.

The law as it stands at present is obeyed to the letter – the Board of Trade officials see to that.

What is needed is a revision of the law.

ROYAL SYMPATHY

The King and Queen Send An Affecting Message

The King, in a telegram to the managing director of the White Star line says:-

The Queen and I are horrified at the appalling disaster which has happened to the Titanic, and at the terrible loss of life. We deeply sympathise with the bereaved relatives, and feel for them in their great sorrow with all our hearts – GEORGE R. and I.

Queen Alexandra telegraphed:-

It is with feelings of the deepest sorrow that I hear of this terrible disaster to the Titanic, and of the awful loss of life. My heart is full of grief and sympathy for the bereaved families of those who have perished.

The directors of the company, in acknowledging the gracious messages, expressed their deep gratitude for the Royal sympathy, which, they said, would be cherished by all who had suffered bereavement.

SIX MEN OWNING £90,000,000

The aggregate wealth of half a dozen of the millionaires who are reported to be missing may be roughly estimated at about £90,000,000. Colonel J. J. Astor's estate is reckoned to be worth £30,000,000. Mr Benjamin Guggenheim, of the family of bankers and gold mine owners, is worth about £20,000,000. Mr Alfred Vanderbilt's wealth has been computed at £14,5000,000. Mr George Widener's at £11,000,000. Mr Isidor Straus' at £10,000,000 and Colonel Washington Roebling's at £5,000,000.

THE FEARFUL FATE OF THE TITANIC AND THE 1,500

The White Star flag at half-mast at Oceanic House.

Mr. and Mrs. Daniel Marvin, related to well-known New Yorkers, who were returning from their honeymoon. Young Marvin, who was associated with T. A. Edison in business, was drowned, and his girl wife survives as a widow at 18.—Dover-street Studios.

Mr. B. Guggenheim, New York banker. Mr. W. T. Sloper, business man of Seattle. Mrs. E. M. York Soci

Captain E. J. Smith, of the Titanic, with his dog.

Major Butt, aide-de-camp to President Taft.

Mr. Christopher Head, formerly Mayor of Chelsea.

A map of the north-west coast of the Atlantic, showing the the Atlantic ferry traffic. The position of the Titanic when

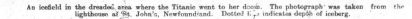

An icefield in the dreaded area where the Titanic went to her doom. The photograph was taken from the lighthouse at St. John's, Newfoundland. Dotted line indicates depth of iceberg.

Mr. J. H. Ross, Professor Wisconsin Univ Mrs. John J. Astor, wife of millionaire. Mr. J. J. B

S ABOARD WHO WERE SWALLOWED IN THE ATLANTIC.

F. M. Hoyt, New k Society hostess.

Mr. P. Marechal, a Washington resident.

Mr. Carter, former Senator (Montana).

Lady Duff-Gordon, the famous modiste (saved).

Colonel J. J. Astor. (Body reported picked up.)

Mr. Jack Phillips, the Marconi operator on the Titanic, whose messages became blurred after sending out the "S.O.S."

current and the drift of the ice from the north to the track of ed is indicated, as also the spot where she is said to have sunk.

Karl H. Behr, famous tennis player. (Saved.)

Charlie Williams, English racquets champion.

The interior of a wireless telegraphist's cabin on a great liner.

cotton

Mrs. J. Snyder, New York Society woman.

Mr. H. Widener, of great American family.

The news of the catastrophe fell on Southampton yesterday morning with terrible effect. The crew, numbering nearly 1,000, all had their homes in the town. This picture shows the early morning crowd round the offices in quest of news.

MEMBERS OF THE TITANIC'S CREW
WHO HAVE PERISHED

A group of White Star Line engineers photographed on the Olympic. Most of them had been transferred to the Titanic, and have perished in her. The victims are the 2nd, 3rd, 9th, and 10th in the top row, 2nd, 3rd, 4th, 5th, 6th, 7th, 8th, and 11th in the second, and the 5th and 6th in the third row.

AMERICAN CONAN DOYLE

Jacques Futrelle With His Wife

Jacques Futrelle, the American Conan Doyle, known to many thousands of readers in this country as the author of "The Professor on the Case" and "The Thinking Machine," was a passenger in the Titanic with his wife. She also is a successful novelist, and her book "A Secretary of Frivolous Affairs," published in this country by Gay and Hancock about a fortnight ago, had a large sale in America last year.

A pathetic story is told of Mr Futrelle by his literary agent, Mr Hughes Massie, of Curtis Brown and Massie, Henrietta-street. Mr Futrelle had booked his passage to New York for to-day, but turned homesick, and when paying a visit to Mr Massie on April 3 expressed a desire to return at an earlier date. Mr Massie wanted him to be present at the Savage Club on Saturday night for one of the famous evenings, but finding the American impervious to the most urgent invitation suggested that he should leave on Saturday, April 6. This idea appealed to Mr Futrelle, and Mr Massie departed for a holiday in Devonshire under the impression that his guest would leave on the day proposed. But, unfortunately, that could not be managed, and so Mr and Mrs Futrelle had to take their passage on the ill-fated Titanic.

It was three years since Mr Futrelle finished the last series of "The Thinking Machine" tales, and he was so tired of them that he declared then that they would be the last he would write dealing with the marvellous Professor. But he received the most dazzling offers from several publishers to write just one more, and yielded. He had, in fact, finished a new series during his stay in England. The tales were for an American magazine, and for them he was to receive a royal recompense.

Mr Jacques Futrelle

MONEY MATTERS

Titanic Disaster Has a Depressing Affect on Markets

6 BIRCHIN-LANE E.C. Tuesday

The Stock Exchange had a gloomy appearance to-day, for which the appalling disaster to the Titanic was responsible. In all directions the calamity was the chief topic of conversation, and the sympathetic as well as the financial aspect of the loss had a marked effect on the House. In nearly every section there was a heavy tone, the dullness most of the day extending from Consols at one end of the list to Marconis among Miscellaneous issues . . .

VIGIL OF THE BEREAVED AT SOUTHAMPTON

Relatives of the crew of the Titanic waiting for news at the White Star offices at Southampton. Later in the day the scenes near the docks were painfully pathetic. Hundreds of families were torn with hope and fears at the report that 200 out of 900 of the crew were saved.

PLAN OF LOWER DECK OF THE TITANIC SHOWING HOW SHE WAS SUBDIVIDED BY WATERTIGHT COMPARTMENTS

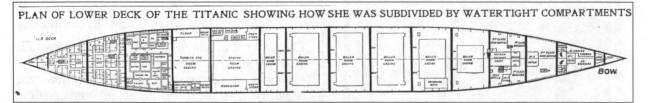

The Titanic was subdivided by 15 transverse watertight bulkheads. The first, a broken double bulkhead, went to the top deck, the second to the second deck, but the succeeding ones, up to the fore end of the engine-room, did not go so high. From the engine-room aft the bulkheads went to the second deck. There were 29 boilers, having 159 furnaces, arranged in six watertight compartments, the first of which was about 200 feet from the bows of the vessel. The reciprocating engine-room was the longest compartment in the ship, being 69 feet long, the turbine-room being 57 feet. It was calculated that any two compartments could be flooded without imperilling the safety of the ship, though the bulkheads were rather more broken both in section and by doors than is usual.

The Iceberg

To most of us icebergs have always seemed to be merely extravagant details in the fairy tales of science. We were as little concerned with them as with the glass mountains of Grimm or the flying horses of the Arabian Nights. So distant and unfamiliar they were that their pictures figured in the school books alongside the hot geysers, the volcanoes, and the other jokes and threats of the universe which only our dreamiest children and our wisest scientists have time to consider, except in the most casual fashion. But now our generation will have different and enduring thoughts. The iceberg will not settle back into the oblivion of the school book picture for a lifetime at least.

Popular imagination rushes first round the idea of might and wealth afloat luxuriously. The Titanic, like some monstrous siren, had by her beauty and ease, by her splendour and confidence, lured down to the sea men and women to whom life itself almost seemed subservient and obedient. Places ever in the sun might be theirs. They could follow spring's smiling all round the world. The arts poured treasures at their feet: for them Pavlova might have been dancing, Caruso might have been making rapture. But instead they went to meet the frozen monster.

If we think of the others less quickly, they stay longer in our minds. The Titanic took with her to the distant shadowy floor of the Atlantic a townful of breadwinners, a host of husbands, fathers and brothers. Her servants were legion, and she keeps them nearly all.

She sailed with her miniature world of men and women, but the ice-monster, drifting southward, must have a clear path, and the rest is a story too overwhelmingly tragic to forget, too intolerable to be dwelt on. The hundreds sailed in all degrees of splendour from stoker to millionaire, but in the majesty of one of the most wonderful sepulchres in all history they share alike.

E.S

SOCIAL & PERSONAL

Gossip About Prominent People

A Countess on the Titanic

Young Lady Rothes, who was among the passengers on the Titanic, being on the way to meet her husband in America, is an only child. Her father, Mr Thomas Dywer Edwardes, is the owner of Prinknash Park, in Gloucestershire, Prinknash Park being not only the name of a seat but also the name of a parish, a parish with but three houses in it. Mr Edwardes seat is on a slope of the Cotswolds. Dating from the year 1530, it began as the country seat of the Abbots of Gloucester. The ancient chapel and other portions of the house were restored in the year 1847 – in the time of the late Mr James Ackers, M.P. for Ludlow, a former owner – and after he came into possession Mr Edwardes again enlarged the chapel and restored the house. Miss Edwardes married the Earl of Rothes twelve years ago, and now has two sons. Lord Leslie, the elder, entered on his eleventh year a month or two ago, while the younger son will not be three till the end of this year.

DAILY SKETCH.

No. 970.—THURSDAY, APRIL 18, 1912.   THE PREMIER PICTURE PAPER.   [Registered as a Newspaper.]   ONE HALFPENNY.

FIRST UNCLOUDED HOURS OF TITANIC'S FATAL VOYAGE

We have received from a gentleman who sailed on the Titanic from Southampton last Wednesday and landed at Queenstown on Thursday a series of exclusive photographs he secured on the trip, which have a pathetic interest in view of the terrible fate which awaited the great liner and those on board less than four days after our contributor came ashore at Queenstown. In the first photograph a little boy (probably one of those subsequently dropped into the open boats in the middle of the night and at this moment being carried to New York on board the Carpathia) is seen spinning his top on the saloon deck on Thursday morning, whilst men, now buried in the Atlantic, look on. The second snapshot was taken under the bridge as the Titanic steamed out to sea down the Solent.

CARPATHIA IN ROUGH WEATHER

US Cruisers Journey To Meet Her

ONLY FIVE OFFICERS OF THE TITANIC SAVED

Steamers Sent To Search For Bodies

Official messages received yesterday hold out no hope that there are any survivors of the Titanic disaster beyond those on board the Carpathia.

According to the latest compilation there were on board:-

316	first-class passengers
279	second-class
698	steerage
1,293	
850	crew
2,143	total

It is stated that there are 705 survivors, so that the death roll is 1,438.

The following cablegram was received by the White Star Line last evening from their New York office: "Carpathia now in communication with Siasconset reports 705 survivors aboard."

It is reported that the Carpathia has encountered rough weather, which put her out of wireless touch with other vessels for a long time.

She is expected to arrive at New York this evening, and until then full details of the disaster will not be available.

The principal officers of the Titanic went down with the ship, and only five of them (including a wireless operator) are reported to be among the saved.

The steamer Mackay Bennett has been sent from Halifax to search the scene of the disaster for bodies. Just prior to sailing she took on board 600 roughly constructed pine-wood coffins, and her passengers include an undertaker and a clergyman. It is believed that bodies will be given proper sea-burial as they are recovered.

The question of the provision of adequate safeguards against disaster on all passenger carrying steamers is being discussed in America, where important legislation is foreshadowed.

In the matter of the precautions taken to minimise the risk of loss of life on big liners, questions are also being addressed in the English Parliament to the President of the Board of Trade.

NO OTHER SURVIVORS

Worst Fears Confirmed

At a quarter to eleven yesterday morning the White Star Line in London received the following telegram from their head offices in Liverpool:-

Have received following from Captain Haddock, of Olympic, via Celtic:

"Please allay rumours that Virginian has any Titanic passengers. Neither has the Tunisian. Believe only survivors on Carpathia. Second, third, fourth, fifth officers and second Marconi operator only officers reported saved."

The worst fears have now received official confirmation, and it is known definitely that the Carpathia is the only ship to pick up survivors.

The following telegram, timed 7.56 a.m. yesterday, was received from Southampton at the offices of the White Star Line in London:-

"Titanic: Have been pressing New York for names of crew survivors. Following cable just received:-

Referring to your telegram of 16th we have been pressing Olympic for this information but regret so far have been unable to secure names of crew survivors."

From this we conclude that previous messages were coming from Carpathia through Olympic, and that the two ships have now got out of touch with each other.

The Olympic is due at Plymouth on Saturday morning, and the Carpathia is expected in New York to-day or to-morrow.

STRICKEN FAMILIES

Pathetic Scenes Among The Southampton Poor

SOME HARD CASES

From Our Own Correspondent

SOUTHAMPTON Wednesday Night

A big hoarding has been erected outside the White Star offices, and on this the names of the survivors among the crew will be posted. At the moment of writing no list has been published, but the huge number of men and women which it first attracted has not sensibly diminished, and they wait on in the sunshine, apathetic in their suspense. The names of four officers have been received here, but only one of these afforded local interest, and he came from Netley, some miles distant.

I have visited the Northam district, a suburb of Southampton whence most of the trimmers and firemen on the Titanic were drawn. Children swarm in the drab streets, and an occasional exotic parrot, warming in the sun in his polished cage, adds his shriek to the general clamour; but at the doors sad-eyed women congregate and discuss their own and their neighbours' woes. They all agree that the saddest case is that of Mrs May, of York Street.

TEN DEPENDANTS

If Mrs May's "man" is not a survivor there will be a family of ten dependant upon her. She faces the problem with calm fortitude. A thin, pale-faced woman with neatly arranged hair and dark eyes, into which the tears continually came and were as continually forced back, Mrs May told me that her husband and eldest son, who has been married for just a year, and has a child a few weeks old, were both on the Titanic, the former as firemens' messman, and the other as fireman.

"This was the first time they had sailed together," she said, "and that was because my son could not get work ashore owing to the coal strike. My husband really belonged to another boat, and both of them intended to leave the Titanic when she returned to Southampton." One son, a delicate lad of 19 is in casual occupation, but the others are earning nothing, and Mrs May has a child six months old.

In this district there are many families for whom the spectre of want is in ambush if the bread-winner has sunk with the Titanic. A rumour is persistent that a young mother who had given birth to twins and whose husband was a fireman, has died of shock.

AT CAPT SMITH'S HOUSE

At the other end of Southampton, in the wealthy quarter near the New Forest, grief has fallen not less heavily than in the poorer neighbourhoods. At Capt Smith's house the garden is full of spring flowers, but the blinds are half drawn as if to show that the fate of the captain is still in doubt. When I called this morning I was told by the maid that Mrs Smith was prostrated with grief. No communication has been received from the captain since he sailed from Southampton.

A family named Hickman at Fritham, in the New Forest, are in a pitiful plight. There were eleven of them, and three of the brothers, one of whom had his wife with him, were on the Titanic, as they decided to settle out West. The coal strike prevented them from making the journey earlier. Their names are not among the survivors, and a sister, stricken at the disaster, has not spoken since the news reached Fritham.

CARGO OF DIAMONDS AND FURS
From Our Own Correspondent

BERLIN Wednesday

A dispatch from Antwerp states that a large quantity of diamonds belonging to merchants of that town were on board the Titanic. They were insured. Several diamond merchants from Antwerp were among the passengers, but there is no news concerning their safety.

In addition to the diamonds there were on board, says a telegram from Leipsic, furs valued at £150,000.

CARGO OF COFFINS

Gruesome Preparation For Burial of Victims

From Our Own Correspondent

MONTREAL Wednesday

Tremendous excitement was caused here this afternoon by a Halifax message, stating that the Government cable ship Minia, which has returned there, reported having received a wireless message, stating that the White Star liner Baltic had rescued 250 of the Titanic's passengers, while the Carpathia was stated to have rescued 760.

The commander of the Minia, however, threw cold water on the hopes raised by stating that he had not been in direct communication with the Baltic, and that owing to the many conflicting wireless messages picked up by his operator he could not vouch for the accuracy of the message.

Officials of the White Star line have no knowledge of such a message, and as it was stated yesterday that the Baltic was resuming her voyage to Liverpool it is feared that very little reliance can be placed on this report. Earlier reports that the Ultonia had seen fishing-boats near the scene of the wreck, and that there was a possibility of these having rescued a few survivors, are also discredited.

The Dominion Government has ordered lighthouse keepers and patrol boats to keep a sharp look-out for bodies of the victims of the Titanic, and the cable ship Mackay-Bennett is preparing to proceed to the scene of the wreck in the hopes of picking up bodies. A gruesome feature of her preparations is that she is taking coffins, undertakers and embalmers.

MYSTERIOUS MESSAGES

Contradictory "Wireless" Reports To Be Investigated

Many of the wireless messages circulated from the Canadian and American receiving stations proved of a conflicting nature, and in some cases entirely removed from the truth.

They were, however, for the most part optimistic, but they were reported to have come from the liners which were hurrying to the scene of disaster. The wireless apparatus of the Titanic was one of the most powerful that has been installed on any liner, but it was rendered useless within a short time after the impact with the iceberg. The wireless system is consequently facing a torrent of criticism, emanating from all quarters, and the authorities are asked to explain why so many false rumours managed to reach London and New York.

Mr Turnbull, of the Marconi Wireless Telegraphic Company, told the *Daily Sketch* that several of the unfounded statements cannot be traced to any wireless operator.

"For example," he said, "we are accused of stating that all the passengers had been saved, and that the Titanic was proceeding under her own steam to Halifax.

This report was not issued by any wireless operator, but was the result of a telegram sent from London by the brother of the Titanic's senior operator to his father.

Many of these messages will be the subject of inquiry," added Mr Turnbull. "Some of them may have been founded on rumours, because the occasions where mistakes are made in the process of transmission are very rare."

UNITED IN MOURNING

The King's Message To President of US

The King has sent the following telegram to the President of the United States:-

"The Queen and I are anxious to assure you and the American nation of the great sorrow which we experience at the terrible loss of life that has occurred among the American citizens and my own subjects by the foundering of the Titanic. Our two countries are so intimately allied by ties of friendship and brotherhood that any misfortune which affects the one must necessarily affect the other, and on the present heartrendering occasion they are both equal sufferers.

"Signed" GEORGE R. and I.

THE VOYAGE OF DISASTER: EXCLUSIVE PHOTOGRAPHS BY

The Titanic dropping the Southampton pilot off Portsmouth last Wednesday. He was taken ashore by an Isle of Wight boat. In the distance are the Channel forts. This photograph was taken from the upper promenade deck.

The last photograph of the lost liner, the Titanic leaving Queenstown Harbour on

BUSINESS HELD UP BY THE ECLIPSE OF THE SUN.

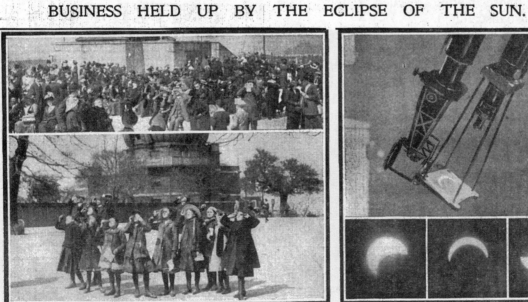

Everybody paused in their daily toil yesterday to watch the eclipse of the sun. Leisured folk took it quite comfortably by accepting the invitation to make their observations from Selfridge's roof garden. Below is a photograph of children looking at the eclipse under the shadow of the dome at Greenwich Observatory.

Taking a photograph at the West Kensington Observatory at the moment of the greatest obscuration.

The eclipse, which comm photographed

Photographs of the eclipse at 11.40 noon and 12.50

ENGER WHO LEFT THE DOOMED TITANIC AT QUEENSTOWN.

g after taking on board the mails. The decks are crowded with passengers waving a   Good-bye to Southampton. A photograph taken from the top deck as the Titanic cast off and commenced her first and last voyage.

EVERYBODY SUN-GAZING AT NOON YESTERDAY.

and ended at 1.31 p.m. of Parliament.

The old way and the new—a naval officer using a sextant alongside a man gazing through smoked glass. Below is Mr. Hawke examining the radiator at the Scientific Society's Observatory at Hampstead Heath.

A motor-car party provided with glasses on Hampstead Heath.
An adjournment at the Law Courts whilst judge, jury and counsel go outside to view the eclipse.

Daily Sketch Photograph.

OUT OF TOUCH

Long Period of Waiting for News of the Carpathia

THE STEERAGE PASSENGERS

NEW YORK Wednesday Night

To-day brought little fresh news of the survivors from the ill-fated Titanic, and the American continent is waiting with the most intense interest for the arrival of the Carpathia. According to an official statement issued by the Cunard Company the Carpathia is due here at eight o'clock to-morrow night, and not until her un-looked for passengers have landed will it be possible to obtain reliable information as to how the great liner met her end.

Various imaginative stories have been printed here only to be contradicted or disproved by the shipping companies and the Marconi Company, who have been able to show that no such wireless messages have been received. The only real news to-day was of a negative character, and further emphasised that there can be no hope for anyone who is not on board the Carpathia.

For some time there was considerable anxiety felt for the Cunarder's safety, for after yesterday's message from her commander, saying that he was groping his way cautiously through icefloes and bergs, communication with the ship ceased.

This proved to be due, however, to atmospheric disturbances and the fact that the Olympic, which had been acting as a relaying station between the Carpathia and the shore, had got out of wireless range. Eventually a reassuring message was received from the Sable Island wireless station stating that they had been in communication with the Carpathia, and later the White Star Line Company received the following message: "East of Ambrose 596 miles 11 p.m. Tuesday, all well."

THE NUMBER OF THE SAVED

Ambrose, of course, means the Ambrose Channel lightship off New York harbour, and already a large fleet of vessels has been chartered by the newspaper men and friends and relatives of the survivors, who intend going down the bay to meet the Carpathia at quarantine. Some confusion was caused this afternoon by the receipt of a wireless message from a passenger on the liner Franconia stating that the Carpathia had reported by wireless that she had only 705 of the Titanic passengers on board.

After the definite report from Captain Rostron issued by the White Star Company that he had aboard 868 survivors the statement of the Franconia's passenger, a Mr Wingfield Thompson, must be received with considerable reserve, unless indeed it is intended to mean that only 705 of the survivors were passengers. Even then, it is pointed out, it is hardly likely that so many as 163 of the crew would be saved.

Another wireless message received here to-day appears to be worthy of more consideration. This is one sent by a passenger on the Olympic, Mr Roy W. Howard, general news manager of the United Press. He explains that the passengers of the Olympic were not allowed to use the ship's wireless until all official messages and reports from the Carpathia had been dealt with.

In his message, which was addressed to the United Press, Mr Howard says that wireless messages to the Olympic indicate that the Leyland liner Californian has picked up some bodies near the scene of the wreck, and is conveying them to Boston.

OLYMPIC AS A WIRELESS STATION

Mr Howard goes on to say that the receipt of the Titanic's wireless appeal for help caused tremendous excitement on the Olympic, and her passengers and crew are saddened that, despite the fact that the liner raced at full speed all the way, she was unable to be of any assistance to her sister ship. The Carpathia sent the appalling news by wireless, and from that time the Olympic constituted herself a relaying station for the smaller vessel.

All day Tuesday the great liner remained practically stationary, flashing the names of the survivors to the land station as fast as she received them from the Carpathia. The sympathetic interest of the passengers had to remain unsatisfied until the Olympic received instructions to continue her voyage to England. Then the list was published for the benefit of inquirers, and the embargo on the private use of the ship's wireless instrument was removed. The Olympic's passengers immediately opened a fund for the benefit of the families of the victims of the Titanic, and handsome donations were at once received.

Heartrendering scenes are being witnessed at the White Star offices here, as relatives of the victims, who refuse to abandon hope, continue to beg the officials to give them news. Mr Henry W. Taft, brother of the President, has paid several visits to the offices to inquire whether there is any news of Major Butt and Mrs Benjamin Guggenheim, and distracted ladies haunt the building frantically upbraiding the officials for not keeping the rescuing ships on the scene of the wreck.

Meanwhile relatives of the steerage passengers, very few of whose names have been published, are pitifully pleading with the White Star officials for a full list of those steerage passengers saved. The United States cruiser Chester, which was sent out to meet the Carpathia, has reported to the Navy Department at Washington that the Carpathia has already transmitted a full list of the first and second class passengers saved, and this is taken to mean that the 560 survivors as yet unaccounted for are all steerage passengers or members of the crew.

Elaborate preparations are being made here for the accommodation of the shipwrecked people, and a committee of thirteen New York Society leaders, under the chairmanship of Mrs Nelson Henry, has been formed to take care of the Titanic's surviving steerage passengers, who will, of course, be landed here practically destitute.

DAILY MAIL
THURSDAY 18 APRIL 1912

SAVED BY A DREAM

CAUSE OF A CANCELLED PASSAGE

A confession that a dream prevented him from sailing in the Titanic was made yesterday by the Hon. J.C. Middleton, vice-president of the Akron-Canton Railway of Ohio. Mr Middleton told the dream to his friends ten days before the tragedy, and this fact is vouched for by several well-known people, one of whom gave Mr Middleton a signed "affidavit" to that effect.

Mr Middleton says: "I booked a cabin in the Titanic on March 23. I felt unaccountably depressed at the time, and on April 3 I dreamt that I saw the Titanic capsized in mid-ocean and a lot of the passengers struggling in the water. The following night I dreamt exactly the same dream. The next day I told my wife and several of my friends, and afterwards, on receiving cable advice from America that my business did not necessitate my crossing at once, I decided to cancel my passage."

Both Mr J. H. Curling, the pigeon-shooting champion, and Mr Feddon, to whom Mr Middleton told his dream, confirmed his statement yesterday.

FATE OF A FAMILY

PARENTS AND NINE CHILDREN IN TITANIC

On board the Titanic were eleven residents of Peterborough, Mr and Mrs John Sage, of Gladstone-street, and their nine children, whose ages range from twenty-two to five years.

Mr Sage, who is a Londoner, went to Peterborough from Lynn about two years ago and for a time had a shop at the corner of Gladstone-street and Hankey-street. He, however, disposed of the business, and with his eldest son George went to Canada and spent some time on a farm in Saskatchewan. He returned to England about three months ago, and, intending to go in for fruit farming, purchased a farm at Jacksonville, Florida. He was proceeding to his new home with his family on the Titanic. On Saturday a postcard was received in Peterborough with the Queenstown postmark from Mr Sage, who stated that they were getting on well. Mr Sage is about fifty years of age, and his relatives are practically all in London. Three of his sons were at work, his eldest daughter Stella was at home, and the other two sons and three daughters were still at school.

A photograph of the unfortunate Sage family appears on page 225.

41

MANSION HOUSE FUND

Sir Thomas Crosby's Appeal for the Widows and Orphans

A letter from The Lord Mayor of London:

Sir, I desire, by your courtesy, to intimate that I have today opened a fund at the Mansion House for the immediate aid and permanent relief of the widows, orphans and dependant relatives of those – whether they be crew or passengers – who have lost their lives in this great national calamity, and to invite the ever-generous assistance of the benevolent public, in attempting to relieve, in some degree, the distress which has been occasioned in many hundreds of families by a disaster fortunately unparalleled in the history of ocean navigation.

In taking this step I feel sure that I am promptly responding to the wishes of those who urge that the keen sympathy universally and unstintedly entertained for those who have thus suddenly been plunged into misery and distress should assume some practical shape for the future advantage of the bereaved families. Some time must necessarily elapse before information can be obtained as to the number of those lost, their wives and families, and their circumstances, but sufficient is known to make it evident that a very large sum will be required to provide adequately for those in distress apart from their claims under the Workmen's Compensation Act.

In raising a Mansion House Fund I am assured of the hearty and active co-operation of the Mayor of Southampton, to whose town the great bulk of the crew and their families belonged, and of others who are raising subscriptions, and I should especially welcome the assistance of the Press in making known the existence of the Fund, and, if possible, in collecting, acknowledging and remitting donations in response to this appeal.

Donations may be sent to the Mansion House or to the Bank of England, where an account, "The Titanic Disaster Fund" has been opened.

I am, Sir, your obedient servant.

THOMAS BOOR CROSBY Lord Mayor
The Mansion House, April 17th, 1912

Send On Shillings
Relief Fund Opened By "Daily Sketch"

APPEAL TO READERS

Lord Mayor's Help for Titanic Sufferers

The sinking of the Titanic was a national calamity; the task of assisting the relatives is a national duty. From all parts of the British Empire have come manifestations of sympathy for the relatives of those who perished; now is the time to give that sympathy tangible shape. We can best honour the dead by remembering the living.

The Lord Mayor of London announces that he will this morning open a fund on behalf of the relatives of the victims of the Titanic disaster. This fund will not only be for relatives of the crew, but for all in distress through the loss of those who have gone down on the ill-fated vessel.

At the Lord Mayor's request the *Daily Sketch* will receive contributions for one week, remitting the total at the end of that time to him. The minimum subscription has been fixed at ONE SHILLING, but this need not prevent anybody subscribing. TWELVE PENNIES may be collected to make one subscription.

Send your cheques and postal orders to:-

The Cashier,
Daily Sketch
17, Tudor-street
London, E.C.

and mark the envelope "Titanic Fund"

We understand that the City Corporation will give a substantial sum towards the fund, and the proprietors of the *Daily Sketch* have started the collection with a contribution of 1,000 shillings.

The memory of the awful calamity will long remain with us, but it will be softened by the knowledge that the relatives of those who died were not forgotten.

We feel sure that the S.O.S. signal of the *Daily Sketch* will be answered as promptly as was the wireless message from the doomed Titanic.

"HIS NAME IS NOT ON THE LIST"

Hoping Against Hope for More Rescues

LADY'S ALL-NIGHT VIGIL

Yesterday was the third day of suspense, and as soon as the City offices of the White Star Line were opened, the telephone bell began ringing and the clerks' voices repeated again and again the sad and, by now, monotonous phrase "His name is not on the list."

On the desks were prepaid telegraph forms, already filled in, which the officials, who throughout have shown the utmost sympathy with inquirers, have undertaken to dispatch directly the required name was received as that of a survivor.

In the morning the names of only 330 or 340 survivors had filtered through, and there remained more than 500 to come.

Some of the women feared to enter the office, hesitating to ask lest the names of their dear ones were not included in the list. One pale young woman, on whose face anxiety and sleeplessness have left their traces, has made constant enquiries, hoping against hope, and her figure has become so familiar to the officials that she only has to ask "Is there any news?" Each time the answer is "Not yet, but there are many more names to come."

The crowd fluctuated considerably during the day. Sometimes it was impossible to get near the notice-boards for the crush. Ten minutes later the public hall would be untenanted save for a heavily veiled woman who had waited patiently since mid-night for the next dispatch from the other side of the Atlantic.

One elderly lady, dressed in black, who had not left the offices since six o'clock last night, dozed quietly in a corner seat.

A young man in a steward's uniform who also had scarcely left the building since yesterday afternoon told a Press representative that he was waiting for news of his father and brother, who had long been in the service of the White Star Line as stewards, and were transferred to the Titanic last week.

LUCKY STEWARD'S HOLIDAY

"I only missed the boat myself by a fluke," he said. "I had come back from a trip on the Oceanic, and although my father asked me to sign on with him for the Titanic's maiden voyage, I told him I wanted a holiday. What surprised me was the large number of first trippers among the stewards, who were nearly all from London. This is my brother's second shipwreck. He was on the Republic when she was wrecked, and was only rescued after several hours."

Crowds waited all night in the vicinity of the White Star Line offices at Southampton Docks for news of the survivors of the Titanic's crew. At noon yesterday they were still without definite information.

The name of the Marconi operator reported to be saved is Mr Harold Sidney Bride, of Bromley. He has been with the Marconi Company for twelve months, and is 22 years of age and unmarried.

An official of the Marconi Company told the *Daily Sketch* yesterday that Bride was a fully qualified man, and that since becoming associated with the company he had acted as operator on the liners Haverford, Lusitania, and the Lanfrane and Anselm, of the Booth line. He left the Anselm to act as assistant to the chief operator Phillips on the Titanic.

Mr Lawrence Beesley, who is among the missing, was a science master at Dulwich College. He resigned his position to go for a holiday in the States, and to visit his brother at Toronto. He is a widower, and leaves a young son.

MEMBERS OF THE TITANIC'S CREW WHO HAVE PERISHED IN THE DISASTER

Mr W Ennis
CHIEF
BATHMAN

Mr J Rieran
CHIEF
STEWARD

Mr Joughin
CHIEF BAKER

Mr H. W. Brook
SMOKEROOM
STEWARD

Mr Proctor
CHIEF 1st
CLASS

Mr C S Ricks
STOREKEEPER

Mr Nichols
SHIPS
BOATSWAIN

Mr J T Wheat
ASST 2nd
STEWARD

Mr AH Whiteman
BARBER

Mr G Dodd
STEWARD 1st
CLASS

Mr Freeman
STEWARD

Mr Maytum
BUTCHER

Mr Walpole
BUTCHER

Mr T Hardy
C/STEWARD 2nd
CLASS

THE LIFEBOATS

Questions for Board of Trade to Answer

An indication that the recent disasters to big liners will have the effect of compelling searching inquiry into the question whether greater precautions should be taken to minimise the risk of loss of life is afforded by the questions which are being addressed to the President of the Board of Trade (Mr Sydney Buxton) in Parliament.

Mr Bottomley will ask Mr Buxton whether he can state the exact lifeboat accommodation that was provided on the Titanic, and what proportion it bore to the authorised number of passengers and crew. He will ask also whether Mr Buxton will consider the propriety of framing a regulation for the purpose of preventing British passenger liners for New York, during the spring season, taking the northern Atlantic route, with a view to establishing crossing records.

Mr Fred Hall (Dulwich) will ask whether the President will take steps that regulations may be made to compel all steamers to carry boats, rafts, or other life-saving apparatus sufficient to accommodate the whole of those on board.

The White Star Line yesterday stated officially that the Titanic carried a number of boats in excess of the official requirements.

Mr Taft and the members of the Cabinet are, says a Central News telegram from Washington, taking a personal interest in the determination of the leaders in Congress to impose upon the steamship companies regulations calling for the provision of further safeguards for the lives of passengers. Government officials are also bent on obtaining legislation restricting the operations of amateur wireless telegraph operators. It is stated that Congress will be able to provide for the refusal of clearance papers to foreign vessels failing to comply with the new and more stringent rules.

AMONGST THE MISSING PASSENGERS

Mr Herbert Parsons, Mrs C. E. H. Stengel, and Miss Margaret Graham, three saloon passengers on the ill-fated Titanic. Mr Parsons is a former Congressman of New York City, and Miss Graham a well-known Californian actress. They are amongst the missing.

APPARATUS THAT SENT OUT THE DREADED SIGNAL

Photograph of the actual Marconi wireless apparatus used by Mr Jack Phillips and Mr Harold Bride to send out the code of distress "S.O.S." from the Titanic. While Mr Phillips met his death, his assistant Mr Bride (inset), was saved together with four officers, who are now on the Carpathia. Mr Bride, whose parents reside at Bromley, was formerly with the Booth Line.

WARNED AGAINST BERGS?

Titanic Said to Have Message From the Amerika

According to the *New York Herald* the Titanic had been warned by the German steamer Amerika that there were icebergs in the neighbourhood.

A message from Baltimore to this paper states that the United States Hydrographic Office received the following wireless message from the Titanic:-

"Sunday, 9 p.m. – German steamer Amerika reports passing two large icebergs, latitude 41.27, longitude 50.8."

This message is timed about an hour and a half before the Titanic collided with an iceberg. The position of the icebergs as reported by the Amerika is not many miles from the spot where the Titanic was struck – latitude 41.46, longitude 50.14.

The White Star Line announce that all their steamers, and indeed all steamers belonging to the International Maritime Company, are taking a track unusually far south to avoid ice on both the westward and eastward journeys.

MAKING THE MARCONI MACHINES

Secluded Essex Factory that Supplies The World

WORKING DAY AND NIGHT

The Marconi machines on the Titanic, to which alone are due the fact that not all the mighty ship's company was lost, were made in a secluded patch of a quiet Essex town. Here, on the premises of a disused soap factory, Marconi wireless instruments are made for all quarters of the globe. Nowhere else are Marconi wireless instruments made.

Cross the river bridge at the bottom of the placid High-street of Chelmsford, turn up a lane that promises nothing, and you are suddenly surprised by sight of a mighty aerial mast that dwarfs the low buildings clustered at its foot almost out of significance.

Enter one of these buildings, and you are in a long low room humming with lathes. Still, this place has no definite character of its own; it might be a cycle factory. But upstairs are a hundred or so deft-fingered, bright-eyed girls pasting sheets of tinfoil on three-inch squares of glass, dipping glass tubes into pungent shellac, winding unending lengths of blue-cased wire on wooden cores, engraving name-plates, flinging together the prepared sides of interesting polished wooden boxes, all at a rapid nervous speed; here, too, are long baize-covered tables at which a rather larger number of men are fitting together the parts prepared by the women into "sets."

You may see a sub-manager handing out sticks of platinum a foot long to many of the men; metal far more valuable than gold. No other factory has a room like this. To a one-stored building lying across the quiet country road the "sets" are taken and tested on the dynamos. The wires are attached, an operator touches a key, the room is lit up with a piercing blue flame and filled with vital crackling noise. The "waves" thus set up are carried by cable to the top of the aerial mast, travelling thence everywhere over England. For the last two years the little factory has worked day and night without intermission.

TESTING THE INSTRUMENTS

TO TAKE TITANIC'S PLACE

It is officially arranged that the Majestic will take the place of the Titanic on the Southampton–New York service. If the Olympic does not arrive at Southampton in time, the Majestic will sail on Wednesday next.

MANSION HOUSE FUND

The Lord Mayor of London has accepted Mr Oscar Hammerstein's offer of the London Opera House for a performance in aid of the Mansion House Fund. He suggests that a matinee concert would be appropriate.

DONATIONS FROM THE ROYAL FAMILY

At the Easter Banquet held last night at the Mansion House, the Lord Mayor announced that the King had sent him 500 guineas, the Queen 250 guineas, and Queen Alexandra £200.

Following the announcement of the setting up of the Mansion House Fund to aid the sufferers of the Titanic Disaster, many of the national newspapers instituted their own funds to help the main appeal. The Daily Mail addressed their particular appeal to the women of this country with this touching poem.

TO THE WOMEN OF ENGLAND

Women of England! Mothers and daughters of England's sons,

Are you proud, in the hour of mourning, of the glory so dearly bought?

Proud of the simple heroes who died for the helpless ones,

Calm in the hour of danger, counting their lives as nought?

These, though they made no bargain, have left you a debt to pay,

A debt of duty and honour to those that they leave behind,

The care of the stricken and lonely, who else might fall by the way,

And it shall be yours to welcome the trust that is here assigned.

Be sure that the bitterest anguish that those who have perished knew,

Was the thought of the widow and orphan alone in a distant land;

But in that dark hour of their trial, O! doubt not they looked to you,

Mothers and daughters of England, to stretch forth a loving hand!

TOUCHSTONE

An Afterthought

Presently, of course, we shall forget. The time will certainly come when the memory will cease to trouble us – but when will it come? It is not wonderful that many are longing to-day for some swift oblivion which would rid us of the remembrance of things too terrible to be faced.

The realisation came slowly. The thing was too vast to be understood at once, the meaning of it too tremendous to be grasped. But the days have gone by; little details have been made known, gradually much of the story has been unfolded and made plain, and the truth has been brought home to us, the bitter truth of disaster and of death, and of a shattered, broken pride added to the breaking of human hearts.

So proud we were, so quick with our praise of the skill of man who had made so vast a thing, who had flung so mighty a challenge in the face of Nature. This was the last and greatest triumph over the storms that rage and the billows that toss upwards as to the very skies. This was man's most recent statement of his power and of his dominion. But the old forces awoke and answered the challenge: death came to very many hundreds of the children of men, and the great ship sank to rest where no human hand may touch her any more for ever.

Once more defeat has overtaken us, once more our boasting has died away, drowned in a flood of tears. As we are greater in act than our fore-fathers, so is our suffering greater. As we reach out to triumphs beyond their furthest imagining, so do we pay penalties heavier than all their dreaming. Our great works serve only to bring us to great disasters. The proportion stands unaltered.

When first man made a little boat to carry him upon the face of the waters, death if it came took him and him only. When the old heroes of our race began first to cross the Atlantic they went in small ships with small crews. But now, now that we have exalted ourselves so greatly, we have to pay on an equal scale.

That is the thought that comes, rising above the thought even of those who are facing now in many lands the fact of swift and terrible bereavement. And, indeed, it is well that it should come, for who is there that can bear to think of those sufferers? Easier it is to call to the mind the picture of that last hour on the great ship, when the fact of the approach of death came home to the people she bore, when they knew that they stood before the wide gate of Eternity. One can think and speak of them, but for those whom they have left there can be no adequate tribute but silence – silence and a little turning of the head away that they may be left alone with their grief.

And as we turn we come face to face with that other burden of which I have spoken, the burden which we and all our race have to bear. Our pride is broken, and brought low. Our mightiest work has testified against us; the triumphant thing that we made has served only to glorify the power of those forces we made it to overcome. What is there for us in this hour of the knowledge of defeat?

There is, waiting behind all the horror and the pity and sadness, the fact of the unconquerable heart of man. We are defeated? Then we will fight again and fight better for our defeat. If this ship has failed us we will make another, and another after that; we will reach forever towards final triumph.

And – ponder this carefully, for it is the conclusion of the whole matter – there are many of us who hope, trust and believe, that neither we nor our children's children shall live to see that final triumph. H.L.

The Astor Fortunes

The founder of the Astor fortunes, which seem likely to undergo some redistribution owing to the loss of the Titanic, was John Jacob Astor, who was born, the son of a butcher, in a small German town near Heidelberg. He worked in London for a time, but when only twenty-one went to America, made money in a furrier's business and purchased the land about New York which is now of an almost fabulous value owing to the expansion of that city. Colonel John Jacob Astor, who now figures in the terrible disaster, is his name-sake and great-grandson.

AMERICAN ACTION

INVESTIGATION BY THE HOUSE OF REPRESENTATIVES

WASHINGTON Wednesday

The Chairman of the Merchant Marine Committee of the House of Representatives states that on arriving at New York some of the survivors of the Titanic will be summoned to Washington to relate to that Committee the facts concerning the inability of the steamship officers to save the lives of all aboard.

The Senate has adopted without discussion a Bill calling for a comprehensive investigation of the Titanic disaster. The resolution empowers the committee to summon witnesses and to take any necessary steps to secure their attendance.

Meanwhile, back in Britain concerns were also being expressed in the House of Commons.

M.P.'S QUESTIONS

RETICENCE OF SHIPPING OFFICIALS

A quite unwarrantable mystery has been created as to the number of lifeboats carried by the Titanic, their capacity, and the extent of the life-saving appliances in the vessel.

At the London offices of the White Star Company the reply to inquiries is that the metropolitan department is concerned only with the passenger side of the traffic. At Liverpool the officials will say no more than that the Titanic had "full boat accommodation," and carried a greater provision of lifeboats than the regulations of the Board of Trade demand. At the Board of Trade, where all the figures are kept, information for the Press is politely declined.

The facts will, presumably, be made known in the House of Commons to-day, for a question on the paper runs:

"To ask the President of the Board of Trade whether he can state the exact lifeboat accommodation which was provided in the Titanic, and what proportion it bore to the authorised number of passengers and crew."

The answer to this may be surmised. The Titanic was a sister ship of the Olympic. In the House of Commons about eighteen months ago the Under Secretary of the Board of Trade announced that the Olympic was provided with fourteen lifeboats and two ordinary boats, with an aggregate capacity of 9,752 cubic feet. As ten cubic feet are demanded for each passenger that would mean boat provision for 975 persons. The Titanic lifeboats and cutters, we understand, numbered twenty.

There were certainly lifebelts, more than sufficient to go round, but these can never take the place of lifeboats. As to "approved life rafts", no information can be obtained.

A strange secrecy is maintained as to the life-saving appliances, not only in the Titanic but in other passenger vessels of the North Atlantic service. Officials say it would be "impudent," and possibly mischievous, to make any statements before the inquiry as to the cause of the wreck is held.

In the House of Commons to-day the President of the Board of Trade will be asked by Mr Martin if there is any law which gives his Board power to compel the owners of passenger steamers to provide sufficient lifeboats to give a place in them to every human being in the boat in case of a disaster like the loss of the Titanic; whether, as often alleged, there is no passenger steamer leaving a British port with lifeboats sufficient for that purpose; whether in many cases the lifeboat accommodation is only about one-third of that required; and, if there is no such law, will the Government introduce a Bill for that purpose?

The White Star Line state that Mrs Ismay was not on board the Titanic.

Mr J.H. Ismay (brother of Mr J Bruce Ismay) who is ill with pneumonia at Iwerne Minster, Blandford, Dorset was slightly improved yesterday. He has not yet been told of the loss of the Titanic.

Mr W.T. Stead's son, who is at Johannesburg, while still hoping that his father may be saved, is confident that he would have been among the last to leave the ship.

WORLD'S SYMPATHY

THE KAISER'S MESSAGE TO THE KING

The Kaiser has sent a telegram from Corfu to the King expressing his sympathy in connection with the Titanic disaster. His Majesty has charged the German Ambassador to express his sympathy to the British Government. His majesty has also telegraphed to the White Star Line as follows:

I am deeply grieved at the news of the terrible disaster which has befallen your line. I send an expression of deepest sympathy with all those who mourn the loss of relatives and friends.

THE DUKE OF CONNAUGHT The Duke of Connaught, Governor-General of Canada, has expressed "deepest and heartfelt sympathy with the relatives of all those lost in the terrible catastrophe."

RUSSIAN MINISTER OF TRADE The Russian Minister of Trade and Industry has telegraphed to the Secretary of the Board of Trade to express his sorrow and sympathy.

PREMIER OF CANADA Mr Foster, Acting Premier of Canada: "The heart of all Canada beats in deep sympathy."

GENERAL BOTHA In the South African Union House of Assembly yesterday General Botha, in proposing a vote of sympathy, said he felt sure that the British sailors had done their duty now as always in the hour of danger.

LORD MAYOR OF SYDNEY The Lord Mayor of Sydney has telegraphed to the Lord Mayor of London saying: "Although separated by distance, Sydney is united with London in grief and sorrow."

GOVERNOR OF NEW ZEALAND The Governor of New Zealand, Lord Islington, has telegraphed to the Colonial Secretary expressing the sympathy of that Dominion.

THE MAYOR OF ROME The Mayor of Rome, Signor Nathan, has expressed the sympathy of the city to the British and American Ambassadors.

FOREIGN PARLIAMENTS The Danish, Swedish, Belgian and Hungarian Parliaments yesterday expressed their sympathy with Britain's loss.

LLOYD'S £500,000 LOSS

The losses which members of Lloyd's, apart from the ordinary insurance companies, will have to meet in connection with the sinking of the Titanic are stated to be a little over £500,000.

In order to provide ready cash promptly to meet their obligations the members concerned realised securities on the Stock Exchange yesterday. The Preferred shares in the International Mercantile Marine Company, which owns all the share capital of the Oceanic Steam Navigation Company, the owners of the White Star Line, which stood at 26½ before the disaster, were yesterday quoted at 21¾ on the Stock Exchange.

When the Oceana sank off Beachy Head on March 16 with £750,000 worth of specie, Lloyd's members and the insurance companies paid up their losses on this head within three or four days.

THE LOST LETTERS

The Titanic carried the whole of the British letter mails for the United States and Canada, and for certain places in Central and South America. There were about 3,418 mail bags, containing some 400,000 ordinary letters and 200,000 newspapers and magazines.

Among the British mails there were rather more than 3,000 registered letters, but as the values are not declared on registration the authorities have no means of knowing the total amount of the loss.

The Post Office does not undertake any insurance on letters for either America or Canada.

There was no special chivalry attached to it, said Miss Sylvia Pankhurst, questioned yesterday as to the large proportion of women and children among the Titanic survivors. It was the universal rule in shipwrecks that women and children should be saved first.

MILLIONAIRE'S SACRIFICE ON THE TITANIC

Senator William B. Allison, of Iowa, one of the millionaire Americans on the Titanic, who is said to have perished in the disaster with his wife. They are said to have sacrificed their lives to save their little son.

Mrs W. E. Carter, a well-known American Society lady, who was a passenger on the Titanic, and who is said to be amongst the rescued, on her way to New York on the Carpathia. – Photograph by Lallie Charles.

ON THE EVE OF HIS MARRIAGE

Mr Hughes, assistant second steward; who was engaged to be married shortly to Miss Porritt, a young lady living at Hoylake, Cheshire.

DAILY SKETCH.

No. 971.—FRIDAY, APRIL 19, 1912. THE PREMIER PICTURE PAPER. [Registered as a Newspaper.] ONE HALFPENNY.

COLD & TREACHEROUS SEA WHERE THE TITANIC WAS LOST.

The ice floes drifting in the Atlantic, south of Cape Race. The first photograph was taken a few weeks ago by a photographer on a French liner, and the second was obtained from the deck of the Canadian Pacific liner Empress of Ireland, and shows the emigrant passengers looking out over the floating ice as their vessel crept through the treacherous sea. It was in such a sea as this that the Titanic met her doom last Sunday night.

CARPATHIA ARRIVES AT LAST

Commander Sends Message To New York

FLAGS AT HALF-MAST

Coffins Taken to the Dock for Victims' Bodies

The Carpathia, carrying the survivors of the Titanic disaster, arrived at New York at 1.30 this morning.

She arrived off the lightship at the mouth of New York Bay at 11.30 last night, and previously a wireless message had been received in New York from her commander.

It was a wild night outside the harbour, and there was a heavy fog over the bay. Rain was falling, and there was lightning at intervals. Despite the heavy weather, says an Exchange message, the Carpathia maintained a limited speed of 13 knots per hour. When she passed the quarantine station doctors went aboard.

At half-past one (8.30 p.m. American time) the Carpathia arrived off the dock, where an immense crowd awaited her arrival. President Taft ordered that all flags should be hoisted half-mast high.

The following wireless dispatch was received from Captain Rostron of the Carpathia, at New York, via Sagaponack, just before 11 o'clock last night:-

"Weather very hazy since eight a.m. About 96 miles east Ambrose noon. Two ambulances are required. Mr Victor Penasco, Mr Benjamin Guggenheim, Mr Vincent Giglic are not on board. Mrs Thomas McNamee also is not on board. Margaret Hays and Mr Penasco are both here. The wireless apparatus is working satisfactorily."

The Cunard Line, says an Exchange message, ordered an undertaker to take a number of coffins to the dock where the Carpathia will berth this morning, as it is believed she has the bodies of some of the victims of the disaster on board.

The White Star Line last night received at Liverpool the following wireless message from the ss Baltic, which is eloquent in meaning:-

"11.8 (New York time), Sunday, received wireless C.Q.D. from Titanic, 253 miles east of her position. Immediately turned back, and steamed 134 miles in her direction, when hearing from Carpathia assistance was no longer required continued our course for Liverpool."

Elaborate arrangements for the reception of the Carpathia have been made by the United States Government, and the following cablegram from the Exchange Telegraph Company's correspondent at New York is significant:-

"The White Star Company have accepted the offer of St Luke's Hospital to set aside accommodation for sixty of the survivors of the Titanic. This confirms the fears which have been entertained here that many of the rescued passengers will be suffering from physical or mental breakdown."

There is still no official information as to the number of the rescued, but no denial has been received of the statement that the Carpathia is carrying only 705. Of the dead 698 were third-class passengers, made up as follows:-

Men	486
Women	134
Children	78
Total.	698

THE SHIP OF SORROW

Expected at New York at Nine o'clock This Morning

From Our Own Correspondent

NEW YORK Thursday

As the time approaches when the Carpathia with her sorrowful load of survivors from the Titanic will arrive here public excitement is reaching fever heat. A bulletin posted by the White Star officials at 2.45 p.m. states that the Carpathia has been delayed, but should arrive off Sandy

Hook about nine o'clock, and be docked by 11 o'clock to-night (4 a.m. English time).

Many more or less authentic messages concerning the Carpathia have been published here to-day, and all emphasise the point that the Cunarder is a ship of sorrow, with her company almost mad with grief. Mr A. S. Franklin, Vice-President of the White Star Line, protested at mid-day that definite information was absolutely unavailable. The shipowner, who is quite broken down by the shock, declared with considerable emotion, "I have received absolutely no details. We know nothing about what happened, and all on board the Carpathia are so overcome by the memory of the disaster that they are unable to tell connected stories. I have had a code message from Mr Bruce Ismay, but it throws no light on the tragedy."

Messages printed here to-day, apparently emanating from Mr Ismay, gave the impression that the White Star chairman intended to return to England immediately, on the Cedric, which should have sailed to-day, but which was held up by orders from the White Star Company to take the survivors of the Titanic's crew home to-morrow. Mr Franklin, however declared that he had no knowledge of any intention on the part of Mr Ismay to return by the Cedric, and that he would come right up to New York on the Carpathia.

Another message, presumably also from Mr Ismay, gave instructions to the White Star Company to send competent officers and men down to quarantine to take over thirteen lifeboats saved from the Titanic, and the general opinion was that the members of the Titanic's crew were to be taken off the Carpathia with the lifeboats at the quarantine station and sent straight back to England.

GOVERNMENT INVESTIGATION

Whether the White Star Company ever had any intention of doing such a thing is immaterial, for this afternoon an official intimation was received from Washington to the effect that a special sub-committee consisting of seven members of the Senate Committee of Commerce were on their way to New York for the purpose of commencing the investigations into the circumstances of the disaster

A revenue cutter has been placed at the disposal of the Senators. With the Customs officials they will board the Carpathia at quarantine and personally examine the officers and crew of the vessel and such of the Titanic's survivors as are well enough to be questioned. Nobody will be allowed to leave New York until the evidence has been taken by the commission. Those wishing to leave for Europe immediately will be questioned closely, and it is evident that the United States Government intends taking the most stringent measures to ensure a thorough inquiry being held. In order that the destitute survivors shall be spared the delay of examination by the immigration officials, Mr Charles Nagel, Secretary for Commerce and Labour, has personally taken charge of the arrangements for their arrival.

Public feeling has been particularly exasperated by the apparent censorship which is being placed on the Carpathia and other vessels, for, although the Cunarder has been in wireless touch with land stations all day, absolutely no information concerning the disaster is obtainable. Even a personal inquiry from President Taft remained unanswered, though it was transmitted by the United States scout cruisers Salem and Chester.

AMERICAN FEARS

The commanders of these vessels reported that while the Carpathia undoubtably received their messages no answer was given. The commander of the Salem, who relayed a message from President Taft, sent a laconic report: "Can read the Carpathia but he won't take any business from me."

The American public is convinced that the silence which has been maintained means that a ghastly tale will be unfolded when the survivors are landed. Many of the rescued must be nearly crazed with grief and weak from exhaustion and exposure.

The preparations that have been made for the reception tend to confirm this belief, for a large number of doctors, nurses and ambulances will be in readiness on the pier. All outsiders will be barred from the dock, and no photographers will be permitted to snapshot the arrival. Some of these precautions are, of course, necessary and wise for the protection of the distressed passengers and crew, but the opinion is general that secrecy is being carried to too great an extreme.

The correction of the number of rescued from 868 to 705 has given rise to all sorts of conjectures, and a ghastly explanation put forward in some quarters is that the 163 who have been taken from the original official total were really rescued, but have died on board the Carpathia as the result of exposure or injuries received in the disaster. There is no confirmation of such a suggestion, but it represents fairly accurately the state of mind to which people have been brought by the disaster and the lack of information.

THE FIRST MESSAGE

All day the wireless stations along the coast have been trying to secure information from the Carpathia, but atmospheric conditions were at their worst. The Government eventually temporarily closed down all land stations in order to keep the air clear for official communications, but the first direct communication from the Carpathia reached New York shortly after eleven, when Captain Rostron reported that he expected to dock some time to-night.

Later a message was posted up in Wall Street which purported to be from the Carpathia, saying that none had been saved from the Titanic except those on board the Carpathia. The message also stated that Mr John Jacob Astor's body was not on board, and that Mrs Astor was seriously ill, while 100 survivors were also in a dangerous condition.

STILL HOPING

Night Vigils at Southampton Offices
STORY OF STRANGE PRESENTIMENT

"No further names yet" was the response given to the inquirers at the White Star offices in London yesterday. The numbers had fallen off considerably from the previous day, but groups of eager-eyed people scanned the lists posted up. Silently they tip-toed from list to list, ever expecting the realisation of faint hopes.

Many people had gone into full mourning, while others wore a black tie or a piece of crepe round the arm. The aristocrat rubbed shoulders with the democrat in the sorrowful search, and

here and there haggard faces told only too plainly the tragedy of sleepless nights.

The gloom which hangs over Southampton is intensified daily, and the agonising scene at the docks would move the hardest heart to compassion.

The shadow of death lurks everywhere, but most insistently in the mean streets of Northam and other districts where many homes have lost all the bread-winners of the family. Round the offices of the White Star Line and outside the main dock gates, where fateful notices are being posted, the patient crowd maintains its mournful vigil. The all-night watches in the chilly air have exhausted many, and with the dawn of a new day that brings no more hopeful tiding the common sorrow is deepening.

HAGGARD FACES

It was pitiful to watch the haggard faces of men and women alike as they strained their eyes to read the latest news affixed to the big black boards on the railings of the shipping office. They were all prepared for the worst now, and most of them had reached that stunned condition where grief finds no possible outlet.

Here and there a woman strove ineffectually to choke back a sob, but for the most part the grief was dry-eyed. Men tried to smoke, but somehow pipes would not draw, and giving up the attempt in despair they walked aimlessly up and down the road.

In the midst of the horror the waiting women find consolation in the heroism and courage of their men-folk.

Among the restaurant staff of the crew of the Titanic were ten cousins of the manager, Mr L. Gatti, whose name is among the missing. The majority belonged to Italy, and this was their first voyage as part of a ship's crew.

Mr Gatti lived with his wife and child at Southampton. On Sunday night, at about the hour when disaster befell the liner, Mrs Gatti had a strange presentiment of danger, and throughout the night she was unable to sleep. This feeling had such an effect upon her that the next morning she came to London and remained with a sister. Mr Gatti held a similar position on the Olympic at the time of her collision with the Hawk to that he occupied on the Titanic.

The Southampton officials last evening received a list of third-class passengers of the

Titanic who are aboard the Carpathia, but the names had already been published. No names of the surviving members of the crew are to hand.

———————————

The White Star Line announce that they are prepared to settle legal payments to the relatives of the crew as soon as possible.

———————————

ONE OF THE OFFICERS SAVED

Mr C. H. Lightoller, the second officer on the Titanic, who is one of those saved by the Carpathia.

———————————

S.O.S.
(SEND ON SHILLINGS)

This is an appeal to every reader of the Daily Sketch to help those who suffer by the loss of the Titanic – the fatherless and the widows.

The Lord Mayor of London has opened a relief fund, and has asked for the co-operation of the *Daily Sketch* in raising money for the dependants of the crew and of the poorer passengers, who will starve unless prompt aid is given.

Much money is needed. During the next few days some pitiable cases will undoubtably come to light, and to the sufferings which are certain there must not be added that of want. It is certain that many of the third-class passengers who were crossing had all their worldly belongings with them. It is equally certain that nothing of value has been saved.

In many of our seaports, in Southampton in particular, there are widows and fatherless children who must be helped. Probably half the families in England are interested, directly or indirectly, in some man whose work is on the sea. News of a shipping disaster brings dread into thousands of English homes until further news comes that some man or other is safe. Then there is a fervent "Thank God." Remember there are many hundreds of people who cannot say that to-day. We want you to help them.

So we have started a Shilling Fund. The proprietors of the *Daily Sketch* contribute a thousand shillings, and we invite our readers in every part of the British Isles to do their share. If you can send no more, send a shilling. If you can afford more, or collect more, all the better. Every contribution, small or large, will be acknowledged in our columns.

All contributions should be addressed to:-
The Cashier
Daily Sketch
17, Tudor-street
London, E.C.
Mark the envelope "Titanic Fund."

DAILY SKETCH S.O.S. FUND

	Shillings
Proprietors of the *Daily Sketch*	1,000
Sunshine and Peter	21
Mr and Mrs Turner	2
G.H.H.	3
J.H.	5
Kilburn, Sympathy, C.H., J.H.H., E.S.H., H.G.L., F.G.S., E.W., A.M., S.H.O., J.P., T.M., W.H.A., J.F.W., E.S., F.J.D., H.H., W.S., R.R., C.B., R.L., E.H., T.E.E., B.J., W.B., W.G.K., G.A.B., J.W., J.C., J.L., C.S., C.F.M., P., W.G.M., S.M., M., R., E.G., A.S., R.R., G., C., M., F.H., W.W., S.A., J.F.A., F.S., A.F., C.F., R., B.E.S., B.B., J.B., G.M., G.M., G.M., H., F., and F.W. – 1s. each	58
Total.	1,089

More subscriptions have been received and will be acknowledged to-morrow.

SECTIONAL DIAGRAM OF THE TITANIC: THE BOATS O

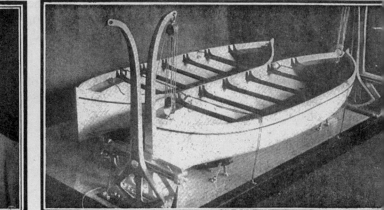

How two boats are carried side by side.

Mr. Harold Cottam, the wireless operator on the Carpathia, of Southwell, Nottinghamshire, who has transmitted all the list of survivors, but steadily refused all yesterday to give details of disaster.

Mr. Thomas Andrews, son of the Right Hon. Thomas Andrews, one of the directors of Messrs. Harland and Wolff, Ltd., who was making a business voyage in the Titanic.

Although the Titanic was fitted with davits to carry two boats, only one was fitted to each from the original models of the actual davits fitted to the Titanic. Mr. A. Welin, at a meeti Olympic and also on the Titanic this double-acting type of dav

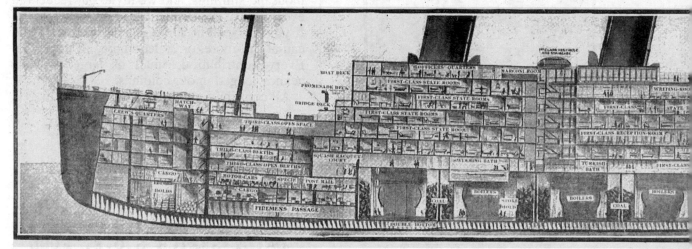

A sectional plan of the magnificent structure which has been sent a shapeless mass to the bottom of the Atlantic. The Titanic was divided into thirty water-tight compartments, and the ironbulkhe Parliar

AMERICA'S DARBY AND JOAN PREFER TO GO DOWN TOGETHER.

THE ACTUAL LIFEBOATS SWUNG FROM

Mr. and Mrs. Isidor Straus, who went down together. On account of her age Mrs. Straus was entitled to precedence in the boats, but her friends believe she preferred to stay beside her husband. The couple were greatly devoted to each other, and were known as the Darby and Joan of American Society people.

Photographs of the actual boats which were used to take off the survivors from th

HE GREAT LINER: SHOULD MORE HAVE BEEN CARRIED?

How one boat is lowered with the other ready for lowering immediately.

nal plan was undoubtedly for two or three boats to each davit. The pictures have been taken
ion of Naval Architects just before Easter, said :—"On the boat deck of the White Star liner
throughout in view of coming changes in official regulations."

Mrs. F. J. Swift, a well-known New York
hostess.

Mr. E. W. Ring, chief clerk to the Titanic's
purser.

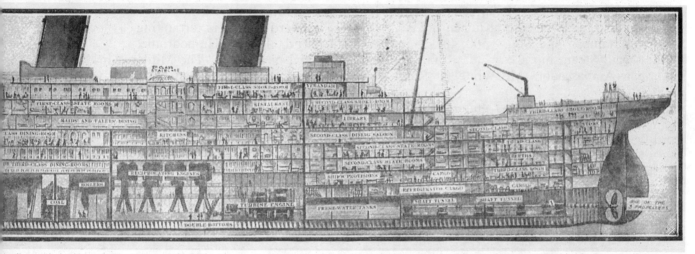

he diagram by the thickened black vertical lines. The Titanic had nine steel decks, and she carried 16 boats on the davits and four other boats, which, accor ding to a statement in
forded accommodation for 1,178.

ITS ON THE TITANIC'S HIGHEST DECK.

SOUTHAMPTON COUNCILLOR'S WIFE AND DAUGHTER RESCUED.

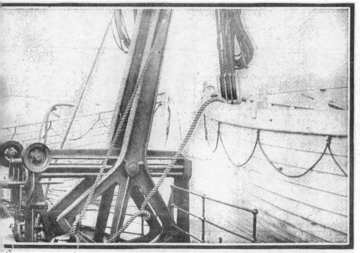

anruck. Only one boat was swung from each davit, although she was fitted for pairs.

Miss Elsie Doling, daughter of Mr. Doling,
of Shirley Warren, Southampton, who was
accompanying Mrs. Doling across the
Atlantic.

Mrs. Doling, wife of Mr. J. T. Doling (cou
cillor), of 33, Canute-road, Southampton, a
a passenger by the Titanic, who was save

MANSION HOUSE FUND

It was announced last night that the Mansion House Fund amounted to over £25,000. Among the donations received were:- Her Royal Highness the Princess Royal, £100; the Corporation of London, £1,050; Lord Mount-Stephen, £1,000; Sir William Nelson, £1,000; the Canadian Agency Ltd, £525; J. Henry Schroder and Co., £525; Lazard Bros. and Co., £525; Sperling and Co., £525; Stocken and Concanon, £525; the Partners of Donald Currie and Co., £525; Baker, Mason and Co., £500; Brown, Shipley and Co., £500; Emile Erlanger and Co., £500; Glyn, Mills, Currie and Co., £500; George Kitchen and Co., £500; C. Hambro and Son, £500; the Union Castle Mail Steamship Co., Ltd., £500; the American Ambassador (Mr Whitelaw Reid), £500.

In addition to the thousand guineas sent by the White Star Line for the relief of sufferers, Lord Derby (the Lord Mayor of Liverpool) has also received the following sums:- Mr Harold A. Sanderson, of the White Star Line, £500; Mrs Ismay, £200; Miss Lottie Ismay, £100; and Mr John Temple, 50 guineas. Lord Derby is contributing £50 and Lady Derby £20.

HELP FROM THEATRES

Several theatrical performances are to be given in aid of the Titanic Fund.

Mr Oscar Hammerstein has placed the London Opera House at the disposal of the Lord Mayor for a matinee concert. This will be held next week, and Mr Hammerstein is hoping to get the services of Paderewski and a number of other prominent artistes have been asked to assist. Miss Felice Lyne may be mentioned as a certainty.

Mr Dennis Eadie and Mr J. E. Vedrenne have undertaken to give a special matinee performance of "Milestones" at the Royalty Theatre on May 1.

Sir Edward Moss is arranging a special matinee at the London Hippodrome.

A special matinee of "The Military Girl" by Charles and Muriel Scott-Gatty will be given in the Savoy Theatre to-morrow at 2.30, in aid of the relief fund. Tickets can be obtained at the box office.

The directors of the Alhambra Theatre have also decided to organise a matinee. A special programme is being arranged for the performance, which is to take place on Monday, when the Lord Mayor and Sheriffs have promised to attend.

MEMBERS OF TITANIC'S CREW & PASSENGERS

Mrs G. M. Stone
New York Society
Lady, on board.

J. P. Moody
Survivor,
Grimsby,
Sixth Mate

Mr Barker
Purser on
the Titanic

Mr Beesley
Dulwich

TITANIC'S BOATS

More Than Board of Trade Required
BUT NOT ENOUGH FOR ALL

Important Statement in the Commons by Mr Buxton

"The Titanic carried 16 boats on the davits, giving accommodation for 990, and four other boats with accommodation for 188, a total accommodation of 1,178. There were also 3,560 lifebelts. The total number of passengers and crew certified to be carried was 3,500. The number actually on board the vessel was 2,208 when the vessel left Southampton".

This statement, made by Mr Buxton in the House of Commons yesterday, removes all doubt as to the life-saving apparatus on board the lost Titanic.

The President of the Board of Trade had been asked a number of questions arising out of the Titanic disaster, and the important announcement given above was part of a long statement on the rules of the Board of Trade now in force.

These rules, said Mr Buxton, were originally drawn up in 1890, and subsequently revised. In view of the increased size of modern passenger vessels the Board of Trade last year referred to an advisory committee the question of the revision of these rules, especially with regard to the life-saving provisions to be required in case of vessels of the largest size, and in view of the public interest aroused by this lamentable disaster the report of this committee would be published.

After considering this report the Board of Trade were not satisfied the increased provision recommended by the Advisory Committee was adequate, and within the last few days referred the matter back to the committee for re-examination.

Before this terrible disaster occurred the Board had been carefully considering the question of the revision of the scale of lifeboat accommodation prescribed by the rules for large vessels.

Up to the present it had been considered that division by watertight compartments was a safe-guard, and that had been taken into consideration in fixing the minimum number of lifeboats to be carried.

The present disaster created a new situation which must be most carefully considered, but not in a panic. (Hear, hear.) The present scale of the Board of Trade in the case of a ship of 10,000 tons and upwards required a minimum lifeboat accommodation of 9,625 cubic feet – or 16 boats on the davits, and 75 per cent in the shape of other boats. This would provide for 960 persons.

With regard to the question of preventing liners taking the northern route, he was not prepared at the moment to express an opinion. These and other relevant matters would be subjected to a searching inquiry.

Mr Bottomley asked whether in view of Rule D. Clause 1., requiring three-fourths increase in the boats if the specified tonnage were exceeded, the Titanic ought not to have carried twenty-eight lifeboats?

MORE THAN THE RULE REQUIRED

Mr Buxton replied that, as he had already explained, the Titanic carried more lifeboats than the rule required. The hon. member had misread the rule, which required sixteen boats should be carried, with a cubic capacity of 5,500. In addition, if that were not sufficient, they had to provide 75 per cent additional boats, but not necessarily on the davits. The Titanic actually carried more than she was required to carry under the existing Board of Trade regulations.

Mr Ashley asked if the case of small steamers would not also be taken into consideration, and said one cross-Channel steamer with 400 people on board had only six lifeboats.

Mr Buxton: Certainly, small as well as large vessels will be considered.

Mr O'Brien: Cannot the Board of Trade do some thing to discourage racing to set up time records?

Mr Buxton: I am afraid we have no power, but, no doubt, time will lead to some alteration.

The Right Hon. T. Lough: Having regard to the rapid growth of vessels between the years 1894 and 1911, have not the Board of Trade been slow in making regulations for vessels over 10,000 tons?

Mr Buxton did not reply to the question.

FAMOUS PAINTING BY ARTIST WHO IS AMONGST THOSE MISSING FROM TITANIC

"Between Two Fires" – a popular painting by Mr Francis Davis Millet, the well-known American artist, who was a passenger on the Titanic and is amongst the missing. Mr Millet served as a drummer-boy in the Civil War and studied at the Royal Academy of Fine Art, Antwerp, in the seventies. He was a newspaper correspondent in the Turkish War of 1877, and in the Spanish-American War acted as Times correspondent. "Between Two Fires" is in the Tate Gallery.

The painting is still owned by the Tate Gallery but is not currently on display.

SPIRITUALISTS' HOPE

Looking Forward to a Message From Mr Stead

Spiritualists are looking forward with some confidence to receiving communications from the "Beyond" from Mr Stead. They feel that so confirmed a believer in Spiritualism as the founder of "Julia's Bureau" would not pass to the other side without communicating with his friends on earth.

Inquiries made among spiritualists yesterday show that so far as is known no tidings of Mr Stead communicated by supernatural means have been received by any of those numerous friends in London with whom he engaged so diligently in psychic research.

At the offices of the London Spiritualist Alliance Mr Godfrey told a representative of the *Daily Sketch* that it was very possible that some message had been received from Mr Stead, although up to the present they had not been able to get into touch with anyone who had been thus favoured.

"I am quite certain that in the course of time messages will be received from him," said Mr Godfrey "although it must not be expected that they will be of an extraordinary character or very long. In that respect many disappointments have been experienced after the death of some of the most notable spiritualists of the time."

"Sooner or later communications have come from them, but they have not been the circumstantial and elaborate narratives that a lot of people have looked forward to."

"WIRELESS" EXPANSION

Under a new working agreement the Marconi Wireless Telegraph Company and the Marconi Wireless Telegraph Company of America are to have the full benefit of the land line stations of the Western Union Telegraph Company of New York State and the Great North Western Telegraph Company of Canada for the receipt and delivery of their messages throughout America and Canada.

The Marconi companies are about to erect new long-distance wireless stations providing direct communication between New York and London.

£10,000 FILM LOST

Record of "The Miracle" Goes Down With Titanic

"I had dozens of close friends on the Titanic," Mr Hammerstein told a Press representative yesterday. "There was Mr Guggenheim, Mr Harris, and Colonel Astor, whom I knew intimately. He was a fine man and very democratic. They all came to see me here when they were in London. Only the day before he sailed Mr Harris leant back in that chair and we arranged to meet in the autumn, when I am going over to America to transact business.

"He told me he was taking back with him the moving picture films of 'The Miracle' which he had secured for £10,000 and a royalty. Those have all been lost now."

For further mention of 'The Miracle' see page 296.*

BOARD OF TRADE'S REPORT

In the report of the Committee on Lifeboats, published yesterday by the President of the Board of Trade, they recommend that the minimum number of boats to be placed under davits should be 16 for vessels of 10,000 tons and upwards, and that the minimum number of boats to be readily available for attachment to davits should be for boats of 12,000 and under 20,000 tons, 2; for boats of 20,000 and under 35,000 tons, 4; for boats of 35,000 and under 45,000 tons, 6; and of 45,000 tons and upward, 8.

DAILY SKETCH.

No. 972.—SATURDAY, APRIL 20, 1912. THE PREMIER PICTURE PAPER. [Registered as a Newspaper.] ONE HALFPENNY.

WHERE THE BRITISH CAPTAIN STOOD TILL DEATH.

"I saw Captain Smith while I was in the water. He was standing on the deck all alone. Once he was swept down by a wave, but managed to get to his feet again. Then, as the boat sank, he was again knocked down by a wave, and then disappeared from view."—Mr. G. A. BRADEN, of the Union Trust Building, Los Angeles, California.

"Captain Smith was the biggest hero I ever saw. He stood on the bridge, shouting through the megaphone, trying to make himself heard." —Mr. ROBERT DANIEL, of Philadelphia.

"The captain stood on the bridge and continued directing his men right up to the moment when the bridge on which he stood became level with the water. He then calmly climbed over the rail and dropped into the sea."—Mr. LAURENCE BEESLEY, of London.

It is evident that the disgraceful story circulated in some newspapers yesterday that Captain Smith shot himself are hysterical inventions, as is evidenced by the statements reproduced above.
Our photograph of Captain Smith was taken on the bridge of the Titanic the day before she sailed from Southampton.—*Daily Sketch* Photograph.

CAPTAIN SMITH DIES LIKE A BRITISH SAILOR

Captain Smith (on right) chatting with Lord Pirrie at Southampton.

HOW THE TITANIC HEROES WENT TO THEIR DOOM

THE TRUTH AT LAST

Stories of Heroism and Horror

CAPTAIN SMITH DIES AT HIS POST

Many Women Refuse to Leave Their Husbands

At last the veil is lifted from this terrible drama of Death.

To the waiting world, at whose heart-strings a tense anxiety has been tugging through these breathless days and sleepless nights, there flashed across the deep sea cables yesterday's tragic story in all its naked, sombre horror. It is a story that burns into every brain, that sears all humankind with a common sorrow and an all-mastering pity, a tragedy of the sea without parallel in history.

"Women and children first!" No one had doubted it, but now we know the quiet courage, the silent heroism with which Death, in its terrible shape, came to those who waited for the only end.

In the hush of an awful stillness, peopled by bareheaded men and weeping women, there glided to the Cunard quay in New York harbour the ship of a whole world's woes. Slowly, painfully, with eyes still stricken with the tragedy of that night of darkness and death, these who are survivors step once more to shore.

Heartrendering is the tale they have to tell. From one broken narrative and another it is now possible to piece together the truth of the Titanic's end.

There is a crash upon an unseen reef of knife-edged ice. The engines cease their roar down in the depths of the mighty ship. The vibrant motion that every sea traveller knows is suddenly stilled. There is the interrupted game of cards, the questioning of people who feel that something is wrong, yet cannot imagine the deadly worst so near.

Then the quick-voiced orders ringing from fore to aft, from deck to deck, the lifebelts hastily grasped, the boats swinging loose in the davits. "Women and children first!" There is no murmuring. The law of the Sea prevails.

Hardly knowing it is the long farewell, the words are said as the women step silently into the boats. A kiss here, a hand clasp there – it is all there is time for now.

Slowly, steadily, but always, the ship is sinking at the bows. One after another the boats fill with their human freights and slip away into the dark. Wives who refuse to go are thrown, with tender roughness, to their only chance of life. But some there were who insisted on staying, and they waited with the men for Death.

Out on the open waters, under the starlit sky, are boatfuls adrift, with cooks at the oars and stokers at the tillers, and men freezing to a wakeless sleep.

High up on the bridge, at his post to the last, is the liner's captain. Waves sweep him off his feet, but he rises. And when the Titanic sinks beneath the waste of waters Captain Smith dies like a simple hero, as a British sea-captain should.

Of all the cruelly heartless fabrications which the sensation-mongers have woven about this tragedy of the Titanic, the most stupid and senselessly false is the tale that Captain Smith killed himself on the bridge.

The full story, in all its terrible truth, tells us what we had guessed to be true – that Death came honourably and nobly to all.

HOW THE MEN DIED

Tributes to Captain Smith and His Officers

COLONEL ASTOR'S LAST MOMENTS

From Our Own Correspondent

NEW YORK Friday

Flags are flying half-mast all over the American continent to-day in memory of the victims of the disaster to the gigantic White Star liner Titanic. The stories printed in the papers here have caused the most profound impression, for even after analysing the conflicting reports given by survivors, and admitting that there may have been something of a panic and a fight for the boats when the liner first struck, it is impossible not to realise the magnificent heroism and sense of duty displayed by officers and crew.

The most sensational reports printed here do not suggest for one moment that Captain Smith and his subordinates failed in their duty, and, in fact, all survivors speak in the highest terms of the coolness and courage they displayed from the moment when the ship struck to the time she disappeared below the waves. The reports that Captain Smith committed suicide are quite discredited by the overwhelming volume of evidence volunteered by the survivors, while the alternative suggestion that it was the first officer, Mr Murdock, who shot himself on the bridge is disproved in an equally emphatic manner by the quartermaster at the wheel, Robert Hitchens, who declares that Mr Murdock was in charge of the vessel at the time of the accident and that he acted in the coolest possible manner, closing the water-tight doors and stopping the engines.

THE STORY OF A SHOT

Lady Duff-Gordon declares that she saw an officer shoot one of the male passengers who endeavoured to force his way into a boat, and others agree that there was a shooting, but it appears to have been more for the purpose of restoring order and frightening "panicky" passengers than with the intention or necessity of killing stampeding cowards.

The survivors' stories justify the inclusion in the list of the world's great heroes of the names of Captain Smith, Colonel John Jacob Astor, Major Archibald Butt, Mr Howard Case, and the two wireless operators (Jack Philips and Harold Bride).

Of Major Butt President Taft's eulogy perhaps best covers the situation. When details of his aide-de-camp's end were conveyed to him to-day, Mr Taft said "I never really had any hope of seeing him again. Archie was a soldier, and he was always where he was wanted. When I heard that 1,200 people had gone down in the Titanic I knew Archie would be among them. He would be on deck doing his duty to the end."

Of Colonel Astor's conduct there can be no two opinions. The fact that he asked the officer in charge of the boats whether he might accompany his wife on account of her delicate condition was seized upon by casual observers as an indication of cowardice, but there is convincing evidence that on being told that no men would be allowed in the boats until the women had been got off, he at once joined the officers and crew in their efforts to save the remainder of the passengers. His last act was to place a baby in the last boat, the occupants of which declare that he stood gazing after them for a few moments before raising his hand to his head in a military salute. He then made his way to the bridge and joined Major Butt.

MR STEAD AMONG THE HEROES

According to the statements of other passengers, Mr W. T. Stead and Mr Jacques Futrelle, the novelist, were most courageous in assisting in the preparation of the boats and helping the women.

Colonel J. J. Astor and Major Archibald Butt, Mr Taft's aide-de-camp, died together on the bridge of the sinking liner.

Dr Washington Dodge, of Washington, describing their heroic death, said that when he last saw them they were standing on the bridge with their arms extended to each other's shoulders. Throughout the whole of the panic and during the loading of the boats these two officers assisted the ship's officers. Some of the survivors say that Colonel Astor held his wife in his arms for a moment and kissed her before placing her in the lifeboat.

"LIFEBOATS NOT FULL"

Passenger Confidence in the Great Liner

Dr Washington Dodge, of Washington, said: "I am confident that the Titanic broke in two, and that is why she sank. I remember that, after she struck, she rocked fearfully several times. Many of the lifeboats were not completely filled. One, I think, had only five persons on board."

The reason for the lifeboats not being filled was, he believed, due to the fact that many of the passengers did not think the Titanic would go down.

The Carpathia sailed for the Mediterranean on Friday afternoon.

DARBY AND JOAN

Millionaire's Wife Died With Husband

SAILORS COULD NOT WRENCH HER AWAY

Mr and Mrs Isidor Straus were drowned together. Mrs Straus refused to leave her husband's side.

According to the descriptions given by fellow passengers the noted New York millionaire and his wife went to their deaths together standing arm in arm on the first cabin deck, Mr Straus quietly and tenderly reassuring his wife so far as he could.

As the lifeboats were leaving the scene of the disaster the couple were seen calmly awaiting their fate.

Their devotion to each other was described by a passenger, Mr Stengel. Mr Stengel himself jumped into the sea and rose to the surface close enough to catch hold of the gunwale of a lifeboat, and was dragged to safety. He said "I can never forget Mr and Mrs Straus, who have been Darby and Joan in my life, and who were not separated by death.

"The sailors of the Titanic, in their endeavours to save Mrs Straus, tried to wrench her away from her husband, but she refused to leave his side. Finally the sailors had to abandon their task.

Then the boat began to sink, and as the lifeboats drew away from her we could see the pair standing together arm in arm, Mr Straus bending towards his wife."

Mr Straus was a social reformer and a friend of the late President Cleveland. He was noted for his philanthropy.

LAST MAN SAVED

Colonel Rescued Many With a Raft

The last man to be saved was Colonel Archibald Gracie, of the United States Army, who is also a large cotton grower in Jefferson Co., Arkansas.

Colonel Gracie said that when the ship plunged he was swirled around for what seemed an interminable time, but he eventually came to the surface amidst a quantity of wreckage. Fortunately he discovered among the debris a life-raft of canvas and cork, which had floated up.

Another man clambered on to the raft, and the pair of them began to pick up some of those who were struggling in the water.

"When dawn broke," Colonel Gracie said, "there were thirty of us on this raft knee-deep in the icy water, and afraid to move for fear we should capsize it. The hours that elapsed before we were picked up were the longest and most terrible that I have ever spent.

HELP YOUR COMRADES

The general secretary of the Seamen's Union in London has received the following telegram from Mr Havelock Wilson, at Rotorua, New Zealand:- "I appeal to the seamen of the world to give two days' pay each to the relations of sailors, firemen, cooks and stewards of Titanic. I give £10. I will ask seamen of Australia, New Zealand.:- HAVELOCK WILSON."

The Mansion House Fund for the relief of the relatives of the victims of the disaster reached over £40,000 yesterday.

A matinee will be held at the Coliseum on Wednesday, May 1, in aid of the fund. It will be under the patronage of the Lord Mayor.

Messrs. Stedman's will hold a benefit performance at the Savoy Theatre on May 18 in aid of the orphans of the seamen who lost their lives in the disaster. The programme will be given by 100 of the cleverest child actors and actresses in London.

Dr Barnardo's Homes have intimated that they are ready to admit any number of really destitute children who have become orphans through the sinking of the Titanic.

MUSICIAN HERO

Man Who Led the Band on the Sinking Liner

Mr Wallace Hartley, the central figure of the wonderful scene on the Titanic, when the band went down at their posts, doing their best to save a panic. Mr Hartley was a native of Dewsbury, Yorkshire, and was well known and popular in many parts of the country. He had just been promoted from the Mauretania to be the musical director of the Titanic. He had conducted orchestras at Harrogate and Bridlington, and was well known in Leeds where he was a member of the Savage Club. He was engaged to be married to a lady in Boston Spa, near Wetherby, and was with her in the little Yorkshire village only a week ago.

Here is a full list of the Titanic's band:-

W. Hartley (bandmaster), Surreyside, West Park-street, Dewsbury.
J. Hume, 42, George-street, Dumfries.
C. Taylor, 9, Fentiman-road, Clapham.
J. W. Woodward, The Firs, Windmill-road, Headington, Oxon.
R. Bricoux, 5, Place du Lion d'Or, Lille.
F. Clarke, 22, Tunstall-street, Smithdown-road, Liverpool.
G. Krins, 10, Villa-road, Brixton.
W. T. Brailey, 71, Lancaster-road, Ladbroke-grove, London.

MUSICIAN LEAVES CARPATHIA TO JOIN TITANIC

W. T. BRAILEY   **PERCY C. TAYLOR**   **G. KRINS**

Three of the missing musicians who reside in London. Mr Brailey is an only son. The pianist on the Titanic, he filled a similar capacity on the Carpathia – the rescue ship – leaving the vessel to join the Titanic's orchestra.

SAVED ONLY BY ACCIDENT

How the Carpathia Got the Titanic's Signals

CAPTAIN ROSTRON'S STORY

It was only by accident that the wireless operator on the Carpathia picked up the "S.O.S." signal sent out by the Titanic. In another few minutes he would have been in bed and the Carpathia would not have known of the accident.

This statement was given in evidence by Capt Rostron, of the Carpathia, at the inquiry opened by the Committee of the Senate in New York yesterday. The meeting was open to the public. Mr Bruce Ismay, the four officers of the Titanic, and Captain Rostron, of the Carpathia, were subpoenaed to attend, and Senator Smith presided.

Before the meeting (says a Central News message from New York) Mr Smith said that his heart swelled with pride at the conduct of both British and Americans.

After summoning Mr Ismay to appear, Mr Smith said: "We will not fail to give the public all the facts of the case. We are going to get at the truth."

Mr Bruce Ismay, giving evidence, declared that at no time during the trip was the Titanic put at full speed. He was asleep at the time of her impact with the iceberg, but he rose and went up to the bridge, where he learned from Captain Smith that the damage was serious. When the order was given he helped to launch the boats. He believed the ship's speed on Saturday last was twenty-one knots. He saw three boats lowered, the women and children being taken first.

Questioned as to his departure from the sinking vessel, Mr Ismay said an officer asked the question "Are there any more women or children?" There being no response witness got into the boat. He did not see the Titanic sink, and heard no explosions. He was rowing at the time, and had his back to the vessel, as he did not wish to see the end. The Titanic had her full complement of boats. She could have floated with two compartments full of water if the impact had been head-on, and in all

probability would have been in port to-day.

As it was, he understood that the blow was a glancing one, between the forecastle and the Captain's bridge.

Captain Rostron, of the Carpathia, who followed, declared that the Titanic was on the right course, i.e., she was on the course which was the proved one for this time of year. The Carpathia's wireless operator was in his cabin at the time of the picking up of the "S.O.S." signal on purely unofficial business, and was only listening by accident. In another ten minutes he would have been in bed, and the ship would have known nothing of the disaster.

"SNOWBALLING"

Passengers Played With Bits of the Berg

DANGER NOT REALISED FOR SOME TIME

NEW YORK Friday

One of the most coherent narratives is that given by Dr Kemp, registrar of Manila University, who is on a tour of the world, and was a passenger on the Carpathia. He said:- "The wireless operator of the Carpathia received the distress signals from the Titanic when he was making his final call for the night before turning in. The vessel at once made for the scene at full speed, and we first sighted the lights of the lifeboats about 3.30, when three or four came into sight on the horizon.

"By five o'clock we had picked up ten or twelve boats, and the last boat-load was rescued about 9 a.m. The condition of the survivors was terrible, and many collapsed when they were brought into the warm air on the Carpathia. The women had been rowing in several boats and were in a state of exhaustion when rescued.

I learned from passengers that the crash made the vessel shiver, but at first caused little alarm. The collision threw great quantities of ice and snow on to the upper decks, and some of the passengers were actually amusing themselves by throwing snowballs.

It was sometime before the danger was realised, and then the liner gradually sank deck by deck. The lights did not fail until a few minutes before the final plunge.

"BOAT ALMOST FILLED WITH MEN"

"One of the boats was almost filled with men, most of them stokers. After picking up the boats we proceeded to the actual scene of the disaster, but discovered no bodies and very little wreckage. There were just a few tables and broken chairs.

The scene of the disaster was a vast icefield at least 35 miles across and containing many bergs.

Several first-class passengers told me that they did not want to enter the boats, and told the officers that they would willingly have gone back for an hour or so.

They say that the Titanic was making about 20 knots at the time of the crash, and that they suddenly saw an immense pinnacle of ice towering up."

Dr J. F. Kemp told of a funeral service held on board the Carpathia for the victims of the disaster. This service was attended by thirty women: twenty of them were under 23 years of age, and had been made widows. Although their husbands were missing, few of them realised that the service was being held for their dead husbands, whom they thought had been rescued.

MRS ASTOR'S GRIEF

Mrs Astor was almost fully dressed when she came aboard the Carpathia.

She went straight to a cabin, where she was attended by the ship's surgeon, and did not re-appear until we reached New York.

I saw Mr Bruce Ismay once or twice. He seemed terribly worried, but was otherwise well."

WIRELESS MAN'S ACCOUNT

How Phillips Stuck to His Post to the Last

STOKER TRIED TO ROB HIM OF LIFEBELT

A narrative of the disaster by Mr Harold Bride, the surviving wireless operator of the Titanic, is reported by the *New York Times*.

Mr Bride says he was just relieving Mr Phillips, the chief operator, when Captain Smith came into the cabin and said:-

"We have struck an iceberg. You had better get ready to send out a call for assistance, but don't send it until I tell you." The Captain came back ten minutes later and said "Send the call out." "What call should I send?" asked Phillips. "The regulation international call for help – just that" was the reply.

Phillips then began to send the signal, joking while doing so. "We all made light of the disaster," said Mr Bride, "and it was some time before we realised its seriousness. Phillips was a brave man, and I shall never forget his work during the last awful 15 minutes. I strapped a lifebelt on him while he worked. Phillips clung on sending messages until after the last boat but one had been launched.

While I was in my room getting Phillips' money for him I saw a stoker or someone from below leaning over Phillips and trying to slip off his lifebelt. I did my duty, and I hope I finished him. I left him lying on the floor of the wireless cabin, and Phillips ran aft. That was the last I saw of him.

At that time the band was playing a rag time tune. I saw a collapsible boat on deck and a number of men trying to push it out. I went to help them when a big wave swept it off, carrying me with it. The boat was overturned and I was beneath it, but I managed to get clear.

I saw men all around – hundreds of them – depending on lifebelts. I swam with all my might and I suppose I was 150 feet away when the Titanic, with her after quarter sticking straight up, began to settle.

After a time I managed to board the collapsible boat. The sight all round was terrible. Men were swimming and men were sinking. All of us in the collapsible boat recited the Lord's Prayer.

After a time we were taken on board lifeboats, although they were already full. When I was dragged on board the Carpathia I went into hospital and stayed there for ten hours.

Then someone said the Carpathia's wireless operator was getting queer from pressure of work, and asked if I could help. I couldn't walk – both feet broken or something – but I went on crutches, took the key, and never left the wireless cabin.

I come from Nunhead and my age is 23."

WOMEN'S HARROWING TALES

Stories of Shots and a Scrabble

LAST STRAINS OF THE HYMN

Miss Bounell, of Youngstown, Ohio, stated (according to an Exchange telegram) that the orchestra belonging to the first cabin assembled on deck as the liner was going down and played "Nearer my God to Thee."

"By that time most of the lifeboats were some distance away and only a faint sound of the strains of the hymn could be heard.

As we pulled away from the ship we noticed that she was hog-backed, showing she was already breaking in two.

She was not telescoped, the force of the impact being sustained on the keel more than the bows. We were in the small boats for more than four hours before we were rescued by the Carpathia.

There were ice-fields and ice-floes all around us. They were constantly grinding and crashing together, and our boats were in danger of being dashed to pieces. The weather was extremely cold, and we suffered intensely. The men in the boats showed splendid heroism. There was no panic among the steerage or second-class passengers, though it is alleged that there was a wild scramble among the first-class passengers, and I am informed shots were fired."

MANY WOMEN INSANE

Mrs Andrews, an elderly lady, said to an Exchange reporter, "Many women are insane. We did not know until daybreak whether we would be rescued. We were in the open boats for eight hours, and the suffering of all was indescribable."

Mrs Henry Stengel, of Newark, N.J., who was much upset said "I witnessed terrible scenes. Chinamen and stokers hid in the bottoms of the boats before they were launched. There were no lights; the boats were without provisions – it was horrible. The collision was terrific, but nobody seemed to realise the seriousness of its effects. We were over confident that the boat was unsinkable. I am sure that more might have been saved but for this false confidence. The boats were undermanned."

Mrs Lucy Ridsdale, of London, who was on her way to Marietta, Ohio, to make a home with her sister, was saved with the few clothes she wore. She had written in advance letters to her friends telling them of her safe arrival and the pleasant voyage, but those letters went down with the ship.

RETURNING FROM HONEYMOON

Mrs Dickinson Bishop, of Detroit, Michigan, said – "I was the first woman in the first boat, and I was in the boat for four hours before we were picked up by the Carpathia. I was in my bed when the crash came. I got up and dressed quickly, but, being assured that there was no danger, I went back to bed. There were few people on deck when I got there, and there was little or no panic. The behaviour of the crew was perfect. My husband, thank God is also saved. We were returning from our honeymoon."

BRAVERY OF THE CREW

Mr Paul Cheveret, a well-known Canadian sculptor, said that neither he nor the other passengers believed that the vessel would sink. He did not want to get in to the boat, but was forced to do so. He saw no cowardice among the passengers or crew.

"I take off my hat," he said, "to the English seamen who went down with the ship and to the men who manned the lifeboats. Every man of them was a hero."

PASSENGER'S REVOLVER

Mrs D.W. Marvin, of New York, said she saw one passenger with a revolver fight his way to a boat, and threaten to shoot anybody who interfered.

Mr Robert Daniel, a Philadelphia cotton broker, is stated to have told the Central News:- "There was some shooting among the passengers, but only on the part of those who had become frenzied."

73

HOW MR. STEAD MET HIS DEATH.

THE LAST DRE
TITANIC

Impressionist picture specially drawn by Charles E. Dawson for the
Beesley, late of Dulwich C

Mr. W. T. Stead died as he lived—courageous and fearing nothing. He was foremost in the work of helping to get the women and children into the boats, and when the last boat had pushed off Mr. Stead jumped into the sea. During the dinner he talked much of Spiritualism, thought transference and the occult.

HEROIC FAITHFULNESS OF ENGLISH TELEGRAPHISTS.

Jack Phillips, of Godalming.   Harold Bride, of Bromley.

A dramatic story is told by the rescued assistant wireless man Bride, who speaks of his senior, Phillips, sticking to his post amid all the confusion, and of another man trying to steal the operator's lifebelt whilst he worked.

SHIPBUILDER LOST.   SURVIVOR WITH A STORY.

Mr. Thomas Andrews, managing director Messrs. Harland and Wolff, went down with the boat his firm built. He did all he could to help the passengers.

Mr. Laurence Beesley, the former science master at Dulwich College whose long story is accepted as the true description in this country.

"It was now one o'clock in the morning. The starlit night was be but as there was no moon it was not very light. The sea was as ca pond. It was an ideal night, except for the bitter cold. In the dista Titanic looked enormous. Her length and her great bulk were outl black against the starry sky. Every porthole and saloon was blazir light. It was impossible to think that anything could be wrong wi a leviathan were it not for that ominous tilt downwards in the bows, the water was by now up to the lowest row of portholes. At abo o'clock we observed her settling very rapidly, with the bows and the brid pletely under water. She slowly tilted straight on end, with th

Beesley told Reuter's Agency that he owed his escape to an officer who bundled him ove ladies?" and Mr. Beesley

~SCENE AS THE ~UNDERED.

~from the descriptive details of the last scene, provided by Mr. Laurence
~nger who is among the saved.

~ally upwards; as she did so the lights in the cabins and the saloons,
~ch had not flickered for a moment since we left, died out, flashed once more,
~ then went out altogether. At the same time the machinery roared down
~ugh the vessel with a groaning rattle that could have been heard for
~s. It was the weirdest sound surely that could have been heard in the
~le of the ocean. It was not yet quite the end. To our amazement, she
~ted in that upright position for a time, which I estimate as five
~es. It was certainly for some minutes that we watched at least 150ft.
~e Titanic towering up above the level of the sea, looming black against
~ky. Then, with a quiet, slanting dive, she disappeared beneath the waters."

~t which was short of its full complement. There was no response to the cry "Any more
~y cried "Lower away."

MILLIONAIRE HELPED THE CHILDREN.

COLONEL ASTOR.   MRS. ASTOR.

Colonel J. J. Astor is reported to have kissed his wife and turned aside when offered a
place in a boat. He handed in the children and then went back to the bridge.

DEVOTED COUPLE GO DOWN TOGETHER.

The pathetically beautiful story of the death in each other's arms of Mr. and Mrs. Isidor
Straus is confirmed. Mr. Straus joined with the officers in entreating his aged wife to take
her place in the boats, but she declined, and when last seen the couple were embracing
each other as they went down to their watery grave, in death not divided.

HELPED THE WOMEN AND CHILDREN INTO THE BOATS

Major Butt, aide-de-camp to President Taft, and Mr. Howard ~ Case ~ also took a prominent
part in getting the women and children into the boats. Major Butt took charge of a section
of the ship, and Mr. Case instituted a system to get the women off.

BLEST DEPARTED

Solemn Memorial Service in St. Paul's Cathedral

MULTITUDE AT PRAYER

For them that sleep in the great waters a multitude met to pray in a service that was perhaps the most solemn and deeply touching in all the history of St. Paul's.

It was to voice from welling hearts the aching sorrow of two hemispheres that this multitude of people of high and low degree were met yesterday within the walls of the domed Cathedral where England's heroes rest.

To pray, while the reeds of the organ quivered, while the clear, pure notes of the singing-boys soared tremulously through the air and the massed drums of the Guards rolled out a requiem.

To the service came the ambassadors of kings and nations – Mr Whitelaw Reid, of the United States, M Cambon of France, the representatives of Russia, Spain, and Turkey, and a score of other diplomats.

High Ministers of State were there in person or by proxy. Mr Sydney Buxton and Mr John Burns were present, and the Prime Minister, Sir Edward Grey, and Mr Winston Churchill, were represented. Colonel Sir Edward Ward came on behalf of Lord Haldane and the War Office. The King was not officially represented. The Lord Mayor (Sir Thomas Crosby) and the Sheriffs attended in states to represent the sympathy of the city.

A MOURNING MULTITUDE

Far up in the crowd were places reserved for the kinsfolk of the dead, and far down the nave and shadowy aisles stretched the mourning multitude of women who could not hide their tears and of men whose pale, set faces indexed the profound emotion of the moment.

Long before eleven o'clock – the service was fixed for noon – every seat in the vast Cathedral that was available to the public had been taken, and crowds were standing about the pillars. Long before the Lord Mayor's gilded carriage drove up to the steps at the great west doors the authorities had had to display big black-lettered placards that told of "Church full."

All round the churchyard thousands waited through the service, many wearing black clothes and carrying open prayer books. Among the mourners who passed into the Cathedral were Mr Herbert Stead, the brother of Mr W.T. Stead, accompanied by Miss Hetherington, representing the *Review of Reviews*, as well as the Right Hon. Alexander Carlisle, the designer of the Titanic, and Mr James Parton, the London manager of the White Star Line. Altogether there could hardly have been less than 10,000 persons present at this impressive memorial service.

The clergy conducting the service included Canon Newbolt, Canon Simpson, and Archdeacon Holmes, and Sir George Martin was at the organ. The Kneller Hall military school band were placed just under the pulpit and played the Dead March in "Saul" and Beethoven's Funeral March.

On all the service made a moving and memorable impression, and one, at any rate, in that vast congregation it touched with pathetic poignancy. This was Mr Carlisle, who was so overcome that he fainted and had to be carried out of the building. He was taken to the police ambulance, and medically attended, and was subsequently able to be sent home in a carriage.

RACQUETS CHAMPION SAVED

Mr Peterman, hon. secretary of the Racquets Association, stated last night that he had received a cable from Williams, the professional racquets champion, who was on board the Titanic. Williams was to have played a match in New York against G. Standing on April 29 for the championship of the world. The cable reads: "Match postponed; return next week. Williams."

AMBASSADORS AND CABINET MINISTERS JOIN THE HUGE MULTITUDE AT MEMORIAL SERVICE.

The intense feeling created by the awful disaster to the Titanic was reflected by the enormous congregation that gathered at St. Paul's Cathedral to attend the memorial service yesterday. The diplomatic corps was fully represented, and many members of the Cabinet attended. Long before the Lord Mayor drove up in his state coach the doors had to be closed to the general public, thousands of whom waited outside during the entire service. The photograph shows the scene outside the Cathedral. Inset: The American Ambassador, Mr. Whitelaw Reid, and Mrs. Whitelaw Reid leaving the service.

The Lord Mayor descending the steps of St. Paul's to enter his carriage. Among the congregation were the brother of Mr. W. T. Stead and the Right Hon. Alexander Carlisle, the designer of the Titanic. A painful incident occurred during the service. Mr. Carlisle, who has been deeply affected by the disaster ever since the receipt of the first news, was so overcome that he fainted, and had to be carried out of the building.

BAND PLAYED SOLEMN HYMN AS GREAT SHIP SANK

ORCHESTRA PLAYED ON

Till The Water Closed Over Them

THEN – "NEARER MY GOD TO THEE"

Edward Wheelton, the chief steward on the Titanic, gave the following account of the disaster to an Exchange reporter:-

"It was about 11.45 on Sunday night when the disaster occurred. It had been a beautifully clear spring night, but fog was just commencing to descend.

There had been dancing and music on board, and many of the passengers were still on deck and in the saloon. There was a sudden crash amidships, but no immediate commotion. The passengers were somewhat startled, but they did not at first realise the extent of the disaster.

The officers of the ship reassured the passengers, but at that time they themselves did not know that anything serious had happened.

It was fully half an hour before the full realisation of the effect of what had happened dawned upon both officers and passengers. The ship began to fill and settle down by the head. The wireless operators began sending out signals of distress, and these were kept up for at least two hours. In fact the wireless apparatus was not out of commission until just before the ship sank.

When the vessel began to settle down we thought it advisable to begin lowering the lifeboats. The nearest ship was seventy miles away, and we knew it would be morning before any rescue vessel could arrive.

As the liner began to settle down rapidly all the lifeboats were lowered from the starboard side. The men were only permitted to join their wives on the starboard side to say good-bye, as the order had been given that women and children were to be placed in the boats. Even then no one seemed to realise that the situation was so serious.

HUNDREDS DIED FROM EXPOSURE

Major Butt, President Taft's aide-de-camp, was very calm. He gave orders and pacified the men, who were inclined to be 'panicky.'

The last I saw of him he was standing against the rail looking into the water. All the lifeboats reached the water safely.

As the boats were being lowered the orchestra was playing operatic selections and some of the latest popular melodies of Europe and America.

It was only just before the liner made her final plunge that the character of the programme was changed, and then they struck up 'Nearer, My God, To Thee.'

I should think we were in the lifeboats for about two hours when we saw the Titanic give a lurch upwards and then disappear.

Mr Wheelton declared that there were many women who refused to leave their husbands, and remaining on board, went down with them. Several hundred people were in the water, and most of them died from exposure.

Bodies could be seen floating about when day-light broke, and then the women became frightened.

RESCUED OPERATOR'S MESSAGE

The parents of Harold Bride, the assistant wireless operator on the Titanic, who reside at Shortlands, Bromley, Kent, have received a cable from New York stating: "Safe. Two pounds Mayor's Fund – Harold."

ELOQUENT FIGURES

Percentage of 1st class passengers saved......63
                      2nd...39
                      3rd..27
                      crew 22

These percentages are based on the latest available figures.

GRIEF-STRICKEN SOUTHAMPTON: ANXIOUS CROWDS

Crowd outside the White Star offices at Southampton anxious to read the list of names posted up yesterday. It is estimated that there are 2,000 dependants of the crew in the town, and many sad scenes were witnessed.

TITANIC'S SURGEON AND CHEF DROWN

Dr. J. Ernest Simpson, M.B., junior surgeon, who went down with the Titanic. He was well known in Belfast, his home.

Mr P. Rosseau, the Titanic's chief-chef formerly chef in the North British Station Hotel, Edinburgh.

THE TITANIC LESSONS OF THE DISASTER

A SURVIVOR'S TELEGRAM TO THE EDITOR OF THE TIMES

Sir, – As one of the few surviving Englishmen from the steamship Titanic which sank in mid-Atlantic on Monday morning last, I am asking you to lay before your readers a few facts concerning the disaster in the hope that something may be done in the near future to ensure the safety of that portion of the travelling public who use the Atlantic highway for business or pleasure.

I wish to disassociate myself entirely from any report that would seek to fix the responsibility of any person or persons or body of people, and by simply calling attention to matters of fact, the authenticity of which is, I think, beyond question and can be established in any Court of Inquiry, to allow your readers to draw their own conclusions as to the responsibility for the collision.

First, that it was known to those in charge of the Titanic that we were in the iceberg region; that the atmospheric and temperature conditions suggested the near presence of icebergs; that a wireless message was received from a ship ahead of us warning us that they had been seen in the locality of which latitude and longitude were given.

Second, that at the time of the collision the Titanic was running at a high rate of speed.

Third, that the accommodation for saving passengers and crew was totally inadequate, being sufficient only for a total of about 950. This gave, with the highest possible complement of 3,400, a less than one in three chance of being saved in the case of accident.

Fourth, that the number landed in the Carpathia, approximately 700, is a big percentage of the possible 955 and bears excellent testimony to the courage, resource, and devotion to duty of the officers and crew of the vessel; many instances of their nobility and personal self-sacrifice are within our possession, and we know that they did all they could with the means at their disposal.

Fifth, that the practice of running mail and passenger vessels through fog and iceberg regions at a high speed is a common one; they are timed to run almost as an express train is run, and they cannot, therefore, slow down more than a few knots in time of possible danger.

I have neither knowledge or experience to say what remedies I consider should be applied; but, perhaps, the following suggestions may serve as a help:-

First, that no vessel should be allowed to leave a British port without sufficient boat and other accommodation to allow each passenger and member of the crew a seat; and that at the time of booking this fact should be pointed out to a passenger and the number of the seat in the particular boat allotted to him then.

Second, that as soon as is practicable after sailing each passenger should go through boat drill in company with the crew assigned to his boat.

Third, that each passenger boat engaged in the Transatlantic service should be instructed to slow down a few knots when in the iceberg region, and should be fitted with an efficient searchlight.

I am, Sir, Yours faithfully,
LAWRENCE BEESLEY
Cornell University Club
New York   April 19

FRENCHMEN'S ACCOUNT

PASSENGERS' FAITH IN THE SHIP

In a special edition the *Matin* published the following narrative signed by three French survivors of the disaster, – M. Pierre Marechal, an aviator; M. Omont, a manufacturer of Havre; and M. Chevre, a sculptor:-

We were quietly playing auction bridge with a Mr Smith from Philadelphia, when we heard a violent noise similar to that produced by the screw racing. We were startled and looked at one another under the impression that a serious accident had happened. We did not, however, think for a catastrophe, but through the portholes we saw ice rubbing against the ship's sides. We rushed on deck and saw that the Titanic had a tremendous list. There was everywhere a momentary panic, but it speedily subsided. To the inquiries of a lady one of the ship's officers caustically replied, "Don't be afraid, we are only cutting a whale in two." Confidence was quickly restored, all being convinced that the Titanic could not founder. Captain Smith nevertheless appeared nervous; he came down on deck chewing a toothpick. "Let everyone," he said "put on a lifebelt, it is more prudent." He then ordered the boats to be got out. The band continued to play popular airs in order to reassure the passengers. Nobody wanted to go in the boats, everyone saying "What's the use?" and firmly believing there was no risk in remaining on board. In these circumstances some of the boats went away with very few passengers; we saw boats with only about 15 persons in them. Disregarding the advice of the officers many of the passengers continued to cling to the ship. When our boat had rowed about half a mile from the vessel the spectacle was quite fairylike. The Titanic, which was illuminated from stem to stern, was perfectly stationary, like some fantastic piece of stage scenery. The night was clear and the sea perfectly smooth, but it was intensely cold. Presently the gigantic ship began to sink by the bows, and then those who had remained on board realised to the full the horror of their situation. Suddenly the lights went out, and an immense clamour filled the air. Little by little the Titanic settled down, and for three hours cries were heard. At moments the cries were lulled, and we thought it was all over, but the next instant they were renewed in still keener accents. As for us we did nothing but row, row, row to escape from the obsession of the heartrendering cries. One by one the voices were stilled.

Strange to say, the Titanic sank without noise and, contrary to expectations, the suction was very feeble. There was a great backwash and that was all. In the final spasm the stern of the leviathan stood in the air and then the vessel finally disappeared – completely lost. In our little boat we were frozen with cold, having left the ship without overcoats or rugs. We shouted from time to time to attract the attention of the other boats, but obtained no reply. With the same object a German baron who was with us fired off all the cartridges in his revolver. This agonizing suspense lasted for many hours, until at last the Carpathia appeared. We shouted "Hurrah" and all the boats scattered on the sea made towards her. For us it was like coming back to life.

A particularly painful episode occurred on board the Titanic after all the boats had left. Some of the passengers who had remained on the ship, realising too late that she was lost, tried to launch a collapsible boat which they had great difficulty in getting into shape. Nevertheless they succeeded in lowering it. The frail boat was soon half full of water and the occupants one after the other either were drowned or perished with cold, the bodies of those who died being thrown out. Of the original 50 only 15 were picked up by the Carpathia, on board which we joined them.

We cannot praise too highly the conduct of the officers and men of the Carpathia. All her passengers gave up their cabins to the rescued women and the sick, and we were received with every possible kindness. Similarly we bear sorrowful tribute to the brave dead of the Titanic. Colonel Astor and the others were admirable in their heroism and the crew fulfilled with sublime self-sacrifice all the dictates of humanity. Much useless sacrifice of life would have been avoided but for the blind faith in the unsinkableness of the ship and if all the places in the boats had been taken in time. What have we saved from the wreck? Omont has a hair-brush, Marechal a book "Sherlock Holmes" and Chevre nothing. We all three send to our families resurrection greetings, and it is with immense joy that we cry from this side of the Atlantic "A bientot."

© **Times Newspapers Limited 1912**

OTHER STATEMENTS BY SURVIVORS

NEW YORK April 19

Mr A. H. Barkworth, of Tranby House, East Yorkshire, said he was sitting in the smoking-room when the boat struck the iceberg. He saw Mr W. T. Stead on deck. He described how the forecastle was full of powered ice. He noted the foremast was listing heavily to starboard. As Captain Smith was telling the women to put on their lifebelts he went down to his cabin and changed his clothes. All the boats had left his deck. He put on his lifebelt and fur coat and jumped overboard. While he was swimming hard to get away he was struck by wreckage and a huge wave passed over his head. Swimming about, he found a boat which was rather crowded. He clutched at it and was helped on board. After that they helped another man in. Two men died after being helped into the small boat.

George Rheims, of New York, who was on the Titanic with his brother-in-law, Mr Joseph Holland, a London resident, said that none seemed to know for 20 minutes after the boat struck that anything had happened. Many of the passengers stood round for hours with their lifebelts on. He saw the people getting into the boats. When all the boats had gone he shook hands with his brother-in-law, who would not jump, and leaped over the side of the boat. He swam for a quarter of an hour and reached a lifeboat. It had 18 occupants and was half under water. The people were in the water up to their knees. Seven of them died during the night. Only those who stood all the time remained alive.

Many people seem to have slept through the shock of the collision, and the tale told by Emilio Portaluppi, a second cabin passenger, shows that he was first awakened by the explosion of one of the ship's boilers. He hurried up to deck one and strapped on a lifebelt. Following the example of others, he then leapt into the sea, and held on to an icefloe, with the help of which he managed to keep afloat until he was seen by those in the lifeboats and rescued.

Mrs Churchill Candee, of Washington, was taken from the Carpathia with both her legs broken and hurried off in an ambulance to the hospital. She received her injuries while getting into the lifeboat. Most of the men saved, she declared, were picked up from the water, having plunged overboard after the lifeboats had been launched.

Mrs Edgar J. Meyer, of New York, highly praised the officers and men of the Titanic. Her husband was among those who went down with the ship. She said:- "We were well away from the steamer when it sank, but we heard the screams of the people left on board. There were about 70 of us widows on board the Carpathia. The captain and the passengers of the Carpathia did all they could for us."

Mrs W. D. Marvin, of New York, who was on her honeymoon trip, was almost prostrated when she learned on reaching the dock that her husband had not been picked up by some other boat:- As I was put into the boat he cried to me "It's alright, little girl. You go. I will stay." As our boat shoved off he threw me a kiss, and that was the last I saw of him.

Mr Edward Beane, of Glasgow, who, with his wife, occupied a second-class state room, declares that 15 minutes after the Titanic hit the iceberg there was an explosion in the engine-room which was followed a few minutes afterwards by a second explosion.

Mr Robert E. Daniel, a young cotton broker, of Philadelphia, said:- "I was in my cabin dictating to the stenographer when the ship struck the berg. The shock was not violent. The officers who survived told me afterwards the Titanic slipped up on the iceberg and tore her bottom out. I went on dictating until somebody knocked at my door and cried out that the ship was sinking. I grabbed a life preserver and went to the deck. The 16 boats were filled with passengers, most of them women. Twelve of the boats pulled away from the port side and four from the starboard. There was no panic. Had there been sufficient lifeboats it is my opinion that practically all the passengers would have been saved."

Mr Daniel leaped overboard when he discovered that the ship was sinking, and was picked up by one of the boats.

Mr Jacques Futrelle was one of those who parted from his wife and steadfastly refused to accept a chance to enter a lifeboat when he knew that the Titanic was sinking under him.

How he met his death is told by Mrs Futrelle, who said:- "Jacques is dead, but he died like a hero, that I know. Three or four times after the crash I rushed up to him and clasped him in my arms begging him to get into one of the lifeboats. 'For God's sake go,' he fairly screamed, and tried to push me towards the lifeboat. I could see how he suffered. 'It's your last chance, go', he pleaded. Then one of the ship's officers forced me into a lifeboat and I gave up all hope that he could be saved."

Mr Simon Sencal, a Montreal merchant, who was a passenger on the Carpathia said:- After his vessel had rescued boatloads of women he saw a life-raft upon which were about 24 persons. Half of these were dead. Several of the Carpathia's boats went to the raft and took off the living, leaving the dead behind. The water was thick with the bodies of the drowned. The crew of the Carpathia in their work of rescue came across numerous bodies floating in the water.

Mr Charles Williams, the racket player of Harrow, who was on his way to New York to defend his title of world's champion, said he left the squash court in the Titanic at 10.30. He was in the smoking-room when he first felt the shock. He rushed out and saw an iceberg which seemed to loom over a hundred feet above the deck. It broke up amidships and floated away. Eventually he jumped from the boat deck on the starboard side into the sea, getting as far away from the steamer as possible. He was nine hours in a small boat standing with water up to his knees before he was picked up. Mr Williams said that the sailors conducted themselves admirably.

Mr August Wennerstrom, of Sweden, said he found a collapsible boat behind one of the smoke stacks as the vessel was sinking. With three other men he managed to tear it from its lashings and the four jumped overboard with it. The boat turned over four times, but each time they managed to right it. While drifting about Mr Wennerstrom said he saw at least 200 men in the water who were drowned. Finally, he and his three companions were all picked up by the Carpathia.

Mr Taylor, another survivor, jumped into the sea just three minutes before the boat sank. He said he was eating when the boat struck the iceberg. He did not realize for some time what had happened, and no one seemed to know the extent of the accident. They were told that an iceberg had been struck by the ship, and they felt the boat rise. It seemed as though she were riding over ice. He ran on deck and then he could see the ice, a veritable sea of it. He should say that parts of the iceberg were 80ft. high, but it had been broken into sections probably by the ship. He jumped into the sea and was picked up by one of the boats. He never expected to see land again. He waited on board the ship until the lights went out. It seemed to him the discipline maintained was wonderful.

Mr George Brayton, of California, related how he was standing beside Mr Henry B. Harris when the latter bade his wife good-bye. Both started towards the side where the lifeboat was being lowered. Mr Harris was told of the rule that the women should leave first. "Yes, I know," he replied "I will stay." Shortly after the lifeboat left a man jumped overboard and the other men followed. It was like sheep following their leader. Captain Smith was washed from the bridge into the ocean. Shortly before the ship sank there was an explosion which made the ship tremble from stem to stern. Mr Brayton also said that he saw one of the stewards shoot a foreigner who tried to press past a number of women in order to gain a place in the lifeboats.

Ellen Shine, a girl from County Cork. said that when the accident happened they rushed to the upper deck where they were met by members of the crew who endeavoured to keep them in the steerage quarters. The women, however, rushed past these men and finally reached the upper deck. When they were informed that the boat was sinking most of them fell on their knees and began to pray. She saw one of the lifeboats and made for it. In it were already four men from the steerage who refused to obey an officer who ordered them out. They were, however, finally turned out.- Reuter.

SURVIVORS' STORIES
MR BEESLEY'S GRAPHIC ACCOUNT

The Scene When the Vessel Went Down

NEW YORK APRIL 18 11.45 PM

The following account of the disaster is given by Mr Beesley, who till lately was a master at Dulwich College:-

The voyage from Queenstown was quiet and successful. We had met with very fine weather. The sea was calm and the wind was westerly to south-westerly the whole way. The temperature was very cold, particularly on the last day. In fact, after dinner on Sunday evening it was almost too cold to be on the deck at all. I had been in my berth about ten minutes when at about a quarter past 10 I felt a slight jar. Then soon afterwards there was a second shock, but it was not sufficiently large to cause any anxiety to any one, however nervous they may have been. The engines, however, stopped immediately afterwards. At first I thought that the ship had lost a propeller. I went up on deck in my dressing gown and I found only a few people there who had come up in the same way to inquire why we had stopped, but there was no sort of anxiety in the mind of any one. We saw through the smoking-room window that a game of cards was going on, and I went in to ask if they knew anything. They had noticed the jar a little more and looking through the window had seen a huge iceberg go by close to the side of the boat. They thought that we had just grazed it with a glancing blow and they had been to see if any damage had been done.

None of us, of course, had any conception that she had been pierced below by part of a submerged iceberg. The game of cards was resumed, and without any thought of disaster I retired to my cabin to read until we started again. I never saw any of the players or the onlookers again.

A little later, hearing people going upstairs, I went out again and found that everybody wanted to know why the engines had stopped. No doubt many of them had been awakened from their sleep by the sudden stopping of the vibration to which they had become accustomed during the four days we had been on board. Going up on the deck again, I saw that there was an unmistakable list downwards from the stern to the bows, but knowing nothing of what had happened, I concluded that some of the front compartments had filled and had weighed her down. Again I went down to my cabin, where I put on some warmer clothing. As I dressed I heard the order shouted, "All the passengers on deck with lifebelts on." We all walked up slowly with the lifebelts tied on over our clothing, but even then we presumed that this was merely a wise precaution the captain was taking, and that we should return in a short time to go to bed. There was a total absence of any panic or expression of alarm. I suppose this must be accounted for by the exceeding calmness of the night and the absence of any signs of an accident. The ship was absolutely still, and except for the gentle tilt downwards, which I do not think one person in ten would have noticed at the time, there were no visible signs of the approaching disaster. She just lay as if waiting for the order to go on again when some trifling matter had been adjusted. But in a few moments we saw the covers being lifted from the boats and the crews allotted to them standing by and uncoiling the ropes which were to lower them. We then began to realize that it was a more serious matter than we had at first supposed.

My first thought was to go down to get more clothing and some money, but, seeing people pouring up the stairs, I decided that it was better to cause no confusion to people coming up by attempting to get to my cabin.

PREPARATIONS FOR LEAVING

Presently we heard the order, "All men stand back away from the boats. All ladies retire to the next deck below," which was the smoking-room or B deck. The men all stood away and waited in absolute silence, some leaning against the end railings of the deck, others pacing slowly up and down. The boats were then swung out and lowered from A deck. When they were level with B deck, where all the women were collected, the women got in quietly with the exception of some, who refused to leave their husbands. In some cases they were torn from their husbands and pushed into the boats, but in many instances they were allowed to remain, since there was no one to insist that they should go.

Looking over the side, one saw the boats from

aft already in the water slipping quietly away into the darkness. Presently the boats near me were lowered with much creaking, as the new rope slipped through the pulleys and blocks down the 90 feet which separated them from the water. An officer in uniform came up as one boat went down and shouted out, "When you're afloat, row round to the companion ladder and stand by with other boats for orders." "Aye, aye, Sir," came up the reply, but I do not think any boat was able to obey the order, for when they were afloat and had their oars at work the condition of the rapidly settling liner was much more apparent. In common prudence the sailors saw that they could do nothing but row from the sinking ship, and so save, at any rate, some lives. They, no doubt, anticipated that the suction from such an enormous vessel would be more than usually dangerous to the crowded boat, which was mostly filled with women.

NO TRACE OF DISORDER

All this time there was no trace of any disorder. There was no panic, or rush to the boats, and there were no scenes of women sobbing hysterically, such as one generally pictures happening at such times. Every one seemed to realize so slowly that there was imminent danger that when it was realized that we might all be presently in the sea, with nothing but our lifebelts to support us until we were picked up by passing steamers, it was extraordinary how calm every one was, how completely self-controlled we were, as one by one the boats filled with women and children were lowered and rowed away into the night. Presently word went round among us that men were to be put in boats on the starboard side. I was on the port side. Most of the men walked across the deck to see if this was true. I remained where I was and shortly afterwards I heard the call, "Any more ladies?" Looking over the side of the ship I saw boat No 13 swinging level with B deck. It was half full of women. Again the call was repeated, "Any more ladies?" I saw none coming. Then one of the crew looked up and said "Any ladies on your deck, Sir?" "No" I replied. "Then you'd better jump," said he. I dropped and fell into the bottom of the boat as they cried, "Lower Away" As the boat began to descend two ladies were pushed hurriedly through the crowd on B deck, and a baby ten months old was passed down

after them. Then down we went, the crew shouting out directions to those lowering us – "Level" "Aft" "Stern" "Both together" until we were some 10ft. from the water. Here occurred the only anxious moment we had during the whole of our experience from the time of our leaving the deck to our reaching the Carpathia.

A LIFEBOAT IN DANGER

Immediately below our boat was the exhaust of the condensers, and a huge stream of water was pouring all the time from the ship's side just above the water line. It was plain that we ought to be smart away from it if we were to escape swamping when we touched the water. We had no officers on board, and no petty officer or member of the crew to take charge, so one of the stokers shouted, "Some one find the pin which releases the boat from the ropes and pull it up." No one knew where it was. We felt as well as we could on the floor and along the sides, but found nothing. It was difficult to move among so many people. We had 60 or 70 on board. Down we went, and presently we floated with our ropes still holding us, and the stream of water from the exhaust washing us away from the side of the vessel, while the swell of the sea urged us back against the side again. The resultant of all these forces was that we were carried parallel to the ship's side and directly under boat No 14, which had filled rapidly with men and was coming down on us in a way that threatened to submerge our boat "Stop lowering 14," our crew shouted, and the crew of No 14, now only 20ft. above, cried out the same. The distance to the top, however, was some 70ft. and the creaking of the pulleys must have deadened all sound to those above, for down she came 15ft. 10ft. 5ft., and a stoker and I reached up and touched the bottom of the swinging boat above our heads. The next drop would have brought her on our heads. Just before she dropped, another stoker sprang to the ropes with his knife open in his hand. "One," I heard him say and then "Two," as the knife cut through the pulley rope. The next moment the exhaust stream carried us clear, while boat No 14 dropped into the water, taking the space we had occupied a moment before. Our gunwales were almost touching. We drifted away easily, and when our oars were got out we headed directly away from the ship. The crew seemed to me to be mostly cooks. They sat in their white jackets two to an oar, with a stoker at the tiller. There was a certain amount of shouting from one end of the boat to the other, and the discussion as to which way we should go was finally decided by our electing as captain the stoker who was steering and by all agreeing to obey his orders. He set to work at once to get into touch with the other boats, calling upon them and getting as close to them as seemed wise, so that when search boats came in the morning to look for us there would be more chance that all would be rescued.

THE SINKING OF THE VESSEL

It was now 1 o'clock in the morning. The starlit night was beautiful, but as there was no moon, it was not very light. The sea was as calm as a pond. There was just a gentle heave as the boat dipped up and down in the swell. It was an ideal night, except for the bitter cold. In the distance the Titanic looked enormous. Her length and her great bulk were outlined in black against the starry sky. Every porthole and saloon was blazing with light. It was impossible to think that anything could be wrong with such a leviathan were it not for that ominous tilt downward in the bows, where the water was by now up to the lowest row of portholes.

At about 2 o'clock we observed her settling very rapidly with the bows and the bridge completely under water. She slowly tilted straight on end with the stern vertically upwards; as she did so the lights in the cabins and the saloons which had not flickered for a moment since we left died out, flashed once more, and then went out altogether. At the same time the machinery roared down through the vessel with a groaning rattle that could have been heard for miles. It was the weirdest sound surely that could have been heard in the middle of the ocean. It was not yet quite the end. To our amazement she remained in that upright for a time which I estimate as five minutes. It was certainly some minutes that we watched at least 150ft. of the Titanic towering up above the level of the sea looming black against the sky. Then with a quiet slanting dive she disappeared beneath the waters. Our eyes had looked for the last time on the gigantic vessel in which we set out from Southampton.

Then there fell on our ears the most appalling noise that human beings ever heard – the cries of hundreds of our fellow beings struggling in the icy water, crying for help with a cry that we knew could not be answered. We longed to return to pick up some of those who were swimming, but this would have meant the swamping of our boat and the loss of all of us. – *Reuter.*

Mr Lawrence Beesley went to Dulwich College as a science master in 1904, after having had two years' experience in teaching at Wirksworth Grammar School. He was educated first at Derby School, where he took a scholarship, and afterwards at Caius College, Cambridge, of which he was a scholar and prizeman. He took a first-class in the Natural Science Tripos in 1903.

AN OFFICER'S ADVENTURES

Sucked Down With Titanic

Colonel Gracie, of the United States Army, jumped from the topmost deck of the Titanic when she sank, and was sucked down with her. On reaching the surface again he swam until he found a cork raft and then helped to rescue others. He gives the exact time of the sinking of the Titanic as 2.22 a.m. which was the hour at which his watch was stopped by his leap into the sea. He said:-

After sinking with the ship it appeared to me as if I was propelled by some great force through the water. This might have been occasioned by explosions under the water, and I remembered fearful stories of people being boiled to death. The second officer has told me that he has had a similar experience. I thought of those at home as if my spirit might go to them and say "Good-bye" for ever. Again and again I prayed for deliverance, although I felt sure that the end had come. I had the greatest difficulty in holding my breath until I came to the surface. I knew that once I inhaled, the water would suffocate me. When I got under water I struck out with all my strength for the surface. I got to the air again after a time which seemed to me to be unending. There was nothing in sight save the ocean, dotted with ice and strewn with large masses of wreckage. Dying men and women all about me groaning and crying piteously.

NO MORE ROOM ON THE RAFT

The second officer and Mr J. B. Thayer, jun., who were swimming near me, told me that just before my head appeared above the water one of the Titanic's funnels separated and fell apart near me, scattering the bodies in the water. I saw wreckage everywhere and all that came within reach I clung to. At last by moving from one piece of wreckage to another I reached a raft. Soon the raft became so full that it seemed as if she would sink if more came on board her. The crew, for self preservation, had, therefore, to refuse to permit any others to climb on board. This was the most pathetic and horrible scene of all. The piteous cries of those around us ring in my ears, and I shall remember them to my dying day. "Hold on to what you have, old boy," we shouted to each man who tried to get on board. "One more of you would sink us all." Many of those whom we refused answered, as they went to their death, "Good luck, God bless you!" All the time we were buoyed up and sustained by the hope of rescue. We saw lights in all directions. Particularly frequent were some green lights which, as we later learned, were rockets fired in the air by one of the Titanic's boats. So we passed the night with the waves washing over and burying the raft deep in water. We prayed all through the weary night and there was never a moment when our prayers did not rise above the waves. Men who seemed long ago to have forgotten how to address their Creator recalled the prayers of their childhood and murmured them over and over again. Together we said the Lord's Prayer again and again. – *Reuter.*

ON BOARD THE CARPATHIA

How The Passengers Were Received

A passenger on board the Carpathia made the following statement:-

I was awakened at 12.30 in the morning by a commotion on the decks which seemed unusual. There was no excitement, however, as the ship was still moving. I paid but little attention to the disturbance and went to sleep again. About 3 o'clock, I was again awakened and I noticed that the Carpathia had stopped. I went up on the deck and found that our vessel had changed her course. The lifeboats had been sighted and began to arrive one by one. There were 16 of them in all.

The transfer of the passengers was soon being carried out. It was a pitiable sight. Ropes were tied round the waists of the adults to help them in climbing the rope ladders. The little children and babies were hoisted on to our deck in bags. Some of the boats were crowded, but a few were not half full. This I could not understand. Some of the people were in evening dress, while others were in their night clothes or wrapped in blankets. They were all hurried into the saloon at once for hot breakfast, of which they were in great need, as they had been in open boats for four or five hours in the most biting air I have ever experienced.

There were husbands without their wives, wives without their husbands, parents without their children and children without their parents, but there was no demonstration and not a sob was heard. They spoke scarcely a word and seemed to be stunned by the shock of their experiences. One of the women and three of the others taken from the lifeboats died soon after reaching our deck and their bodies were lowered into the sea at 5 o'clock in the afternoon. The rescued had no clothing other than that they were wearing and a relief committee was formed; our passengers contributing enough to meet their immediate needs. The survivors were so close to the sinking steamer that they feared that the lifeboats would be sucked down into the vortex. On our way back to New York we steamed along the edge of the ice-field which stretched as far as the eye could see. To the north there was no blue water to be seen at all. At one time I counted 13 icebergs.

One of the Carpathia's stewards in an account of how the first boatload of passengers was rescued said:-

Just as it was about half day we came upon a boat with 18 men in it but no women. It was not more than a third filled. All the men were able to climb up a Jacob's ladder which we threw over the port side. Between 8.15 and 8.30 we got the last two boats, crowded to the gunwale, almost all the occupants of which were women. After we had got the last load on board the Californian came alongside. The captains arranged that we should make straight for New York, while the Californian looked around for more boats. We circled round and round and saw all kinds of wreckage. While we were pulling in the boatloads the women were quiet enough, but, when it seemed sure that we should not find any more persons alive, then bedlam came. I hope never to go through it again. The way those women took on for the folk they had lost was awful. We could not do anything to quiet them until they cried themselves out.

The refusal of the operators on board the Carpathia to answer questions concerning the disaster is now explained. It was due to the physical exhaustion of both the men. They sent a large number of personal messages from survivors to friends ashore and received replies from the latter. This work was deemed to be more important than the answering of questions from the shore.

THE RESCUE BY THE CARPATHIA

John Kuhl, of Nebraska, said:-

It was almost 4 o'clock in the morning, dawn was just breaking, when the Carpathia's passengers were awakened by the excitement occasioned by coming upon a fleet of life-saving boats. At that hour the whole sea was one mass of whitened ice. The work of getting the passengers over the side of the Carpathia was attended by the most heartrendering scenes. The babies were crying. Many of the women were hysterical, while the men were stolid and speechless.

Some of the women were barefooted and without any headgear. The impression of those saved was that the Titanic had run across the projecting shelf of the iceberg, which was probably buried in the water, and that the entire bottom of the Titanic had been torn off. Shortly afterwards she doubled up in the middle and went down. Most of the passengers did not believe that the boat was going to sink. According to their stories it was fully half an hour before a lifeboat was launched from the vessel. In fact, some of the passengers keenly questioned the wisdom of Captain Smith's orders that they should leave the big ship.

Dr J. F. Kemp, the Carpathia's physician, says that their wireless operator happened by chance to have delayed turning in on Sunday night for ten minutes. Thus it was that he was at his post and got the Titanic's call for help. Had he gone to rest as usual there would have been no survivors. Dr Kemp describes the iceberg which sank the Titanic as being 400ft. long and 90ft. high. The Carpathia cruised twice through the icefield in the vicinity of the spot and picked up the bodies of three men and a baby. These bodies were committed to the deep on Monday evening. Among the congregation at the funeral service were 30 widows, 20 of whom were under 23 years of age, most of them being brides of only a few weeks or months.

DAILY SKETCH.

No. 973.—MONDAY, APRIL 22, 1912. THE PREMIER PICTURE PAPER. [Registered as a Newspaper.] ONE HALFPENNY.

THE TRAGEDY PASSES BUT THE SORROW AND GRIEF REMAIN

The full story of the heroism and horror of the wreck of the Titanic is now fully known, but the sorrow and grief remain. To lighten the burden of the bereaved is the task of the nation, and all classes are responding to the call. How urgently monetary assistance is required the first photograph proves. Here is a family group over which the shadow of death hangs heavily. It represents the home circle at the house of Mrs. May, of 75, York-street, Southampton, who has suffered as great a bereavement as any one in the grief-stricken town. The mother of eight children—six of whom are seen in the photograph—she has lost her hus-band and also her eldest son, both firemen on the Titanic. On the extreme right is Mrs. May, junior, the widowed daughter-in-law of Mrs. May. In the young widow's arms is her twelve weeks old baby, who will never know a father's care. It is for such sad cases that the *Daily Sketch* appeals to you for help. On the wall is a portrait of the father, and inset is a picture of the son when a lad. The second picture shows a street in Northam, the district of Southampton where most of the Titanic's crew lived. Every other house contains bereaved families.—*Daily Sketch* Photographs.

PROBING THE CATASTROPHE

Senate Committee Show Determined Hand

WIRELESS OPERATOR'S EVIDENCE

Was the Frankfurt Closer Than the Carpathia?

The Senatorial Committee that is inquiring into the Titanic disaster seems to be determined to make a thorough and complete investigation.

Mr Bruce Ismay, the ship's officers and a number of the crew are to remain in New York for the purposes of the inquiry.

The wireless operators on the Carpathia and the Titanic were called on Saturday.

Mr Harold Bride, who was the second operator on the sunken liner, was wheeled into Court on a chair.

In his evidence he said the German steamer Frankfurt replied to the Titanic's distress signal before the Carpathia.

After a while communication with the Frankfurt was discontinued. Bride is reported as saying that he thought it was believed the Carpathia could render more assistance than the German boat, although the Frankfurt apparently was the nearer.

"KEEP OFF, YOU FOOL"

Marconi Man's Curt Reply to a German Vessel

NEW YORK Saturday

When the Senatorial Committee resumed the inquiry into the Titanic wreck to-day Mr Bruce Ismay, Mr Franklin and Mr Marconi were among those present.

Harold Bride, the second wireless operator of the Titanic, was wheeled into Court on a chair. The first witness heard was Cottam, the Carpathia's wireless operator.

Closely questioned by Mr Smith, the Chairman of the Titanic Inquiry Commission, Cottam said he informed the Baltic of the disaster and the rescues at 10 a.m. on Monday.

He did not send a message which could be construed as reading that all the passengers were safe and that the Titanic was being towed to Halifax by the Virginian.

From Sunday he worked without relief until Wednesday when he obtained Bride's help.

Harold Bride, the surviving wireless operator of the Titanic, was the second witness.

On Sunday afternoon, he told the commision, he received from the Californian a message intimating the presence of icebergs, and he communicated that report to the officer on the Titanic's bridge. He received no message regarding icebergs from the liner Amerika.

At the time of the collision, Bride continued, he was asleep, the other operator, Phillips, then being on duty. At midnight Bride relieved Phillips, who then told him that something had happened. Phillips said the ship was damaged, and probably would have to be sent back to the builders. Then Phillips retired to rest.

Afterwards the captain came into the room and gave instructions to call for assistance to be sent out. Phillips re-entered the operating room and sent the C.Q.D. signal.

FIRST REPLY TO THE SIGNAL

Continuing his evidence, Bride said the Norddeutscher Lloyd boat Frankfurt replied to the Titanic's first C.Q.D. signal, the Carpathia answering the second.

Twenty minutes afterwards the Frankfurt asked, "What's the matter?" and Phillips replied: "You're a fool. Keep off." The Titanic heard nothing further from the Frankfurt.

Bride explained as the reason for Phillips' answer to the Frankfurt query his belief that the Carpathia could render more assistance than the German boat, although the latter was apparently the nearer.

Answering the chairman, Bride said he did not give the Frankfurt details regarding the condition of things because he thought it better to keep that information for the Carpathia rather than chance any interference with the wireless service by attempting further communication with the Frankfurt.

Speaking of the final moments of the disaster, Bride said he saw Captain Smith jump into the sea just before the liner sank. So far as Bride could see there was practically not one person dragged down by the vessel's suction.

TITANIC'S SPEED

Officer Believes It Was About 23 Knots

NEW YORK Saturday

Second Officer Lightholder, the senior surviving officer of the Titanic, who gave evidence during the sitting of the Senate Investigation Committee, expressed the belief that the speed of the Titanic at the moment of impact was between 22½ and 23 Knots.

He said that the precaution of doubling the lookout while the vessel was in the ice zone was not taken.

All the inquiries which have been made so far bring out the remarkable faith which Captain Smith and his officers had in the unsinkable character of the Titanic.

Captain Rostron, of the Carpathia, is the subject of universal congratulation and admiration.

When the proceedings of the Senatorial Commission were adjourned this evening it was intimated that the next sitting would be held at Washington on Monday.

Twenty members of the Titanic's crew have been subpoenaed to attend, in addition to Mr Ismay, Mr Franklin, and the surviving officers of the liner.

CAPTAIN'S WIDOW

Attends Memorial Service at Southampton

Mrs Smith, the widow of Captain Smith, attended the memorial service at St Mary's Church, Southampton, on Saturday.

The Bishop of Winchester, who preached the sermon, said the disaster was a mighty lesson against our security and confidence and trust in the strength of machinery and money. The name Titanic would stand as a monument of warning against human presumption.

Members of public bodies attended the service in state with the civic insignia draped with crape. The crews of the American and White Star Line vessels lying in dock went in their uniforms. A pathetic interest attached to the presence of the Gordon Boys, as the names of only two of the eight old Gordon Boys on the Titanic have appeared on the survivor's lists.

"NEARER, MY GOD, TO THEE"

Band Conductor's Favourite Hymn

HIS PRESENTIMENT OF THE FINAL SCENE

Mr Wallace Hartley, the conductor of the Titanic's orchestra, was well known in Leeds, where for several years he was connected with local orchestras.

"A splendid musician he was," said one of his former colleagues to the *Daily Sketch*, "and a better fellow you could not meet in a day's march. He was one of the best."

Apparently Mr Hartley had a presentiment that one day he would meet his end at sea, and it may have been no sudden inspiration that led him at the last moment to direct his orchestra to play "Nearer, My God, To Thee."

On one occasion he discussed the subject with Mr E. Moody, of Leeds, who played in the orchestra conducted by Mr Hartley on the Mauretania.

"I do not know what made me say it," said Mr Moody, "but one night when Hartley and I were walking round the Mauretania's deck together I suddenly asked, 'What would you do, old chap, if you were on board a liner that was rapidly sinking?'

'I'd get my men together and play,' he replied without hesitation.

'What would you play?' I asked.

'Well, he said, I don't think I could do better than play 'Oh God our help in ages past' or 'Nearer, My God, To Thee.' They are both favourite hymns of mine, and they would be very suitable to the occasion.'"

SWEETHEART'S FEARS

It is stated that a Newport (Mon.) young woman who fell in front of an express train and was seriously injured, had feared that her lover had been lost in the Titanic disaster.

Her fear was strengthened when a man of the same name appeared in a list of the missing. It turns out, however, that the girl's lover is engaged on another boat.

91

THE HEROIC ENGINEERS.

A NATION IN MOURNING : IMPRESSIVE

The Mayor and Corporation of Southampton, preceded by the mace bearers carrying draped halberds, on the way impressive memorial service at St. Mary's Church. Amongst those present were the Marquis of Winchester (Lord

Mr. Arthur Ward, one of the Titanic's engineers. In all the messages received no mention is made of what happened in the engine-room, of the gallant engineers sticking to their post with the water pouring into the bowels of the ship. That not one was saved is a tribute to the devotion and heroism of the men buried deep in the engine-room of the mighty vessel.

The disaster is a mighty lesson against machinery and money. The name Titanic presumption.—The Bishop of

Mr. Dyer, another engineer.   Mr. Young, fireman. (Missing.)

Robert Hitchens, one of the Titanic's quartermasters, who was the last man at the wheel.

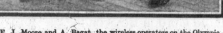

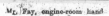

Mr. Taylor, fireman. (Saved.)   Mr. Fay, engine-room hand.

E. J. Moore and A. Bagat, the wireless operators on the Olympic, photographed on board the vessel yesterday at Southampton.

Officers and sailors of the White Star Line proceeding by t

IAL SERVICE IN GRIEF-STRICKEN TOWN.

IN THE SHADOW OF DEATH.

Counter) and Mrs. Smith (widow of the commander of the ill-fated vessel). Similar services were held all over the Anglo-world yesterday, and impressive scenes were witnessed.

confidence and trust in the strength of a monument of warning against human emorial Service at Southampton.

Little Percy Sawyer, the three-years-old child of Mrs. Sawyer, 25, Bervois-street, whose husband, a window-cleaner, is among the missing.

Senator Smith, who is presiding at the inquiry into the loss of the liner.

Mrs. Barrett, of 26, Bervois-street, Southampton, who is hoping against hope that her husband, a fireman, is saved. Four weeks ago

Southampton. The procession was watched raphs.

Collapsible lifeboats on the quay at Southampton ready to be shipped aboard the Olympic when she

Children playing in York-street, Southampton—a thoroughfare which mourns many of the victims—all unconscious of the dread gloom that —Daily Sketch Photographs.

"NOTHING I AM SORRY FOR"

Mr Ismay's Statement to Press

SILENCE OF THE CREW

"We Have Our Orders"
Some of Them Say

The importance attached to the American Senatorial inquiry into the Titanic disaster is shown by the statement which is reported to have been made on Saturday by the Chairman, Senator William Alden Smith.

According to an Exchange telegram Mr Smith said:-

"Mr Bruce Ismay sent a wireless message to General Manager Franklin, in which he urged that the outward bound liner Cedric should be stopped to take himself and the survivors of the crew of the Titanic back to England.

This message, however, was picked up by the wireless apparatus on a U.S. Government boat. Washington was at once communicated with. That is why the Senate Committee was so prompt in arriving in New York.

I was on the pier when the Carpathia put in. Not only was Mr Ismay eager to return to England on the Cedric, but he has been eager to get away on the Lapland since his arrival in New York.

We require Mr Ismay to remain here, however, as I have not concluded his examination. The crew will also be detained here for a time and a number of them will be questioned.

Though (it was afterwards learned) a large number of the crew had been allowed to leave New York on the Lapland, some of them, along with the four officers, have been detained for the purposes of the inquiry.

Mr Bruce Ismay said, in an interview, he had not thought of leaving the country for the purpose of putting any stumbling block in the way of an investigation. He did not, however, want the crew hanging about New York for a week getting into trouble.

"HORRIBLY UNFAIR"

According to the *Observer* correspondent Mr Ismay informed the reporters that there was absolutely no foundation for the allegations attributed to Major A. Peuchen, of Montreal, that he laughingly told a lady passenger that the ice warning, so far from keeping the Titanic back, would only cause her to increase her speed, so as to get more quickly out of the icefield.

To the question if there were any women and children on deck when he went into the lifeboat Mr Ismay replied:

"What kind of man do you think I am? Certainly there were no women and children around. I thought they had all been saved. I think it was the last boat that was lowered I went into. I did then just what any other passenger would do. And tell me how I was different from any other passenger? I was not running the ship. If they say I was president of the company that owns the ship then I want to know where you will draw the line.

As I lay in my stateroom on board the Carpathia I went over every detail of the affair. There was nothing that I did that I am sorry for. I can truthfully say that my conscience is clear.

This whole thing seems unfair, horribly unfair. I cannot understand it. I mean the Senatorial inquiry. They are going at it in a manner that seems unjust, and the injustice lies heaviest upon me. Why, I cannot even protect myself by having my counsel to ask questions. Do not misunderstand me by thinking that I mean questions calculated to twist witnesses up; on the contrary – questions intended to simplify involved meanings."

Members of the rescued crew were not favourable to interviewers.

"We have our orders," some of them said, "and know what's best, as we don't propose to lose the chance of a job."

One of them said that after all the lifeboats had gone he heard Captain Smith say, "Well, boys, it's every man for himself now."

MYSTERY OF A MESSAGE

Olympic Captain Denies "Virginian" Story
NOT SENT BY HIM

Were Two Communications Merged?

From Our Own Correspondent

SOUTHAMPTON Sunday

When asked to-day if he were responsible for the message attributed to him, that the Titanic had been taken in tow by the Virginian, and that all the foundered liner's passengers had been rescued, Captain Haddock, of the Olympic, said the story was an invention.

The Olympic arrived at Plymouth on Saturday with her flags at half-mast, and yesterday she landed her passengers at Southampton. Before their arrival the passengers had organised a Titanic Relief Fund, and nearly £1,400 had been collected before they dispersed.

Captain Haddock was indignant at the suggestion that he was responsible for the story of the Virginian. He warmly denied that it had emanated from the Olympic or that it was re-transmitted from his ship.

His own story is a plain and straightforward one. About twenty minutes after the accident occurred he received the news, but not directly from the Titanic. It came to him via the Celtic.

At the time Captain Haddock was 500 miles from the scene of the disaster, but he lost no time with his preparations for a dash to the rescue. The Captain's urgent orders to the engine-rooms were responded to with a speed of 23 to 24 knots an hour, and for thirteen or fourteen hours he maintained that speed as he ploughed towards the Titanic. Yet there was no great alarm until the startling news came from the Carpathia that all was over – that the Titanic had gone to the bottom and that all the survivors were aboard the Cunard liner.

The mystery concerning the much debated message is not dissipated as a result of the *Daily Sketch* chat with Captain Haddock.

THE CAPTAIN'S STATEMENT

"A message," he said, "was sent us on the Monday from an old lady – a veteran White Star traveller living in New York – asking: Are all passengers safe – or saved? I cannot say which. I at once began to get in touch with any vessels about, and got into conversation with the Asian. This vessel could tell me little, ending with a message that the words: Am towing an oil tank steamer to Halifax.

As I have told my owners in a letter of explanation I have written to them, I can only surmise that some other steamer chanced to pick up scraps of the message which came from the Asian, and misread her reference to herself as applying to the Titanic. I say most emphatically, and in this my two Marconi operators will bear me out, that I sent no message from the Olympic stating that all the passengers of the Titanic had been saved, and that she herself was proceeding under steam to Halifax.

The information, 'All the Titanic passengers safe' which had come to us in error, was posted up at the inquiry office, but nothing whatever was added with any reference to any vessel proceeding to Halifax. That message from the Asian was never transmitted by us to any other vessel; that I can declare positively.

The brief sentence from the lady's message, 'all Titanic passengers safe,' with the word 'are' omitted, together with the tail of the Asian's message, 'towing steamer to Halifax' must have become connected in some manner, caught up by some other boat and thus given out to the world."

The leading fireman on the Olympic told the *Daily Sketch* that he was awakened from his sleep by "C.Q.D." call.

"We went below and from a speed of 19 knots we soon increased to 23. To say we worked like niggers inadequately describes the position. Men worked as they had never worked before, even to the verge of breaking down. After 4 o'clock on Monday came the awful message. I knew then how hopeless our efforts were. I have lost myself over fifty close friends, many of them old school mates."

All entertainments stopped on board when news of the disaster was received.

AMONG THE TITANIC'S CREW

Haines, the bosun's mate (saved).

T. Ford, first-class seaman (missing).

Harder, a window cleaner (saved).

F. Wright, rackets court attendant (missing).

BIG HERO OF THE DISASTER

Mr Howard B. Case, whom one of the survivors has described as "the big hero of the disaster." He was a well-known American resident in England. He leaves a widow, two sons, and two daughters. He was managing director of the Vacuum Oil Company, Limited, Caxton House, Westminster, and resided at Coombe Grange, Ascot. He was forty-eight years of age, and originally came from Rochester, New York. First coming to England in 1886, he returned to the United States in 1891, but came back to England in 1899 to take the sole charge of the company's interests here, and had resided on this side ever since.

MORE LIFEBOATS

Canadian Pacific Take Prompt Measures

Interviewed with reference to the report that the Canadian Pacific Railway have decided to increase the number of lifeboats on their steamers without waiting for Board of Trade instructions Mr McL. Brown, their European manager, in an interview said:-

"Yes, we have received a cable from Montreal directing that all our steamers not already so supplied shall be immediately equipped with sufficient lifeboats for the maximum number of passengers and crew carried.

"As a matter of fact, our equipment for life-saving is already greatly in excess of Board of Trade requirements, and we have always been pioneers in adopting saving appliances.

VIRGINIAN CAPTAIN

Cannot Account for Messages About Titanic In Tow

Captain Gamble, of the Virginian, which arrived at Liverpool yesterday, reports having received a wireless message from Cape Race at 12.40 last Monday morning, stating that the Titanic had struck an iceberg and wanted immediate assistance. He altered his course to go to her assistance. At 3.45 a.m. he was in communication by wireless with the Russian steamer Berma, which was then 55 miles from the Titanic.

"At 5.45 a.m.," Captain Gambell said, "I was in touch with the Leyland liner Californian, which was seventeen miles north of the Titanic and had not then heard anything of the disaster. I Marconied her that she was in urgent need of assistance."

The Virginian was also in communication with the Frankfurt, the Carpathia, and the Baltic.

The Virginian's captain states that he can throw no light on the message that the Virginian had the Titanic in tow, and that other steamers were standing by.

MESSAGE THAT BROKE OFF

The White Star liner Baltic reached Liverpool on Saturday, and reported having received a message from the Titanic appealing for help. The message broke off abruptly. The Baltic steamed towards the scene of the disaster for nine hours, when a Marconigram was received from the Carpathia that all boats had been picked up, and that further assistance was not required. Thereupon the Baltic resumed her voyage.

A LADY'S DREAM

A dream story of the Titanic comes from Ellesmere Port.

Mrs Shrubsall, the wife of a draughtsman, is said to have dreamt last Sunday night that the Titanic was sinking. She woke her husband, to tell him her dream, but he dismissed it as a fancy, saying that no doubt the fact that she had relatives on board had made her anxious. Mrs Shrubsall's sister, a member of the staff of the vessel, is among the drowned.

THE SEARCH FOR THE DEAD

The following wireless message, dated April 20, was received this morning from the cable ship Mackay Bennett, which sailed from Halifax on Wednesday last to search for bodies of victims of the Titanic disaster:-

"Cableship Mackay Bennett off Cape Race. Steamer Rehia reports passing wreckage, bodies in 42.1 North, 49.13 East, eight miles east of three big icebergs. Now making for that position. Expect reach about midnight. Mackay Bennett."

A further message from the Mackay Bennett received by Mr Ismay states the vessel has arrived on the ground and starts operations to-morrow.

NAVY'S TRIBUTE

By Admiralty orders a memorial service was held yesterday on all warships in home ports. During the service flags were half-masted as mark of respect to the memory of the officers and men of all ranks and ratings of the British Mercantile Marine and others who were drowned and to their good and seamanlike behaviour after the accident had occurred.

PULPIT REFERENCES

Reference was made in most of the places of worship in London and the provinces yesterday to the loss of the Titanic, and in many the "Dead March" was played. A "hymn for the survivors," written by Mr Hall Caine, was sung at the evening service at the City Temple, and "Nearer, My God, To Thee" which was played as the liner sank, was sung by the congregation.

A memorial service at St Peter's, Liverpool, on Saturday was attended by representatives of every phase of public life.

A service was held at St John's Church, Isleworth, last night in memory of Mr Thomas Pears, of Messrs. Pears, the soap makers, who was among those who went down on the Titanic.

BIRKENHEAD DISASTER RECALLED

Speaking at a meeting of the Belfast Relief Fund on Saturday, Mr Kempster, managing director of Harland and Wolff, the builders of the Titanic, stated that before the ship left Belfast Captain Smith was asked if courage and fearlessness in face of death existed among seamen as of old. Captain Smith declared if any disaster like that to the Birkenhead happened they would go down as those men went down.

WENT DOWN TO HERO'S GRAVE

Mr J. F. P. Clarke, one of the heroic bandsmen who went down with the Titanic. He resided at 22, Tunstall-street, Liverpool, and was the only Liverpool man among the musicians.

CERTIFICATE OF HONOUR

According to a New York correspondent, an officer of the Queen's Own Rifles of Toronto has shown the following certificate:-

"Major Arthur Peuchen was ordered into the boat by me owing to the fact that I required a seaman, which he proved to be, as well as a brave man. – (Signed) C. W. Lightholder, second officer, late steamship Titanic."

Maj Peuchen was one of the survivors.

MANSION HOUSE RELIEF FUND

The Mansion House Fund now amounts to £72,000.

Among the donations received on Saturday were 250 guineas from the Prince of Wales, and £500 from the Gaekwar of Baroda. Mr W. W. Astor, cousin of Colonel Astor, sent £2,000.

Mr Vincent Astor, the son of Colonel Astor, has contributed £2,000 to the New York Relief Fund.

The Mayor of Southampton's Relief Fund amounts to about £10,000.

Nearly all the wives of the firemen and sailors who were aboard the Titanic are receiving by post from an anonymous source postal orders to the value of 13s. 6d.

AMONG THE SAVED

Mr Algernon H. Barkworth, J.P., of Tanby House, Hessle, near Hull.

Mrs Coutts, of Edinburgh, who with her two children was going to join her husband in New York.

SOME OF THOSE LOST

The Rev. T. R. D. Byles was a popular Roman Catholic priest at Ongar. He was born in Yorkshire, the son of a Congregational Minister, and educated at Rossall School and St. Edmund's College, Ware. He was a nephew of Sir W. P. Byles, and was on his way to America to officiate at the marriage of a brother. He has a sister, a missionary in China.

Dr John Edward Simpson, one of the surgeons on the Titanic, resided at Pakenham-road, Belfast, and Hillside-road, Sefton Park, Liverpool. He was formerly on the Cymric and the Olympic.

Richard Fry, Mr Bruce Ismay's valet in the Titanic, is amongst the missing. Fry had been in Mr Bruce Ismay's service for ten years as butler, and acted as Mr Ismay's personal attendant on his ocean voyages. He leaves a widow and two children.

Leslie Williams, Tonypandy, and David J. Bowen, Treherbert, were going to the United States to fulfil a 12 month's contract as boxers. Both are well known in the ring. Williams leaves a young widow and child. Bowen has a widowed mother. The two were originally booked for the Lusitania, but at the last moment Williams was unable to embark that day.

OTHER RELIEF FUNDS

At a meeting of Belfast citizens on Saturday it was decided to open a relief fund for the relatives of victims of the disaster. The speakers included Lord Londonderry and Lord Shaftesbury. Over £5,000 was subscribed, including 2,000 guineas from Lord and Lady Pirrie, 1,000 guineas from Messrs. Harland and Wolfe, and 100 guineas from Lord Londonderry.

The Mayor of Southampton's Relief Fund amounted on Saturday evening to £9,924. Nearly all the wives of the firemen and sailors who were aboard the Titanic are receiving by post from an anonymous donor postal orders to the value of 13s 6d.(**67½np**)

Mr Vincent Astor, the son of Colonel J.J. Astor, who went down in the Titanic, has contributed 10,000 dollars (£2,000) to the relief fund opened by the Mayor of N.Y.

CHARGE AGAINST A COLLECTOR

At Wimbledon on Saturday William Bagley, 19, described as a conjurer, of Homewood, Morden-road, Merton was remanded on bail on a charge of begging by means of a petition purporting to be for subscriptions for the Lord Mayor's Fund.

Police-sergeant Orchard said he found the prisoner calling from door to door in South Park-road, and ascertained that he had no authority to collect money. The name on the petition, William Nessle, was fictitious. The prisoner had 8s. 2d. in his possession, and, according to the subscription list, he had collected 6s. 4d. in sums of 6d., 3d., and 2d.

Inspector Morgan said the prisoner told him he was collecting for himself, and he did not intend sending the money to the Lord Mayor's Fund.

The prisoner, in evidence, stated that the name on the petition was his professional one – that which he used when giving charity concerts. He did not know he was doing wrong; he headed the list with 1s. and put his mother down for 6d. He thought he would collect more under his conjuring name.

At Villa Park, Birmingham, on Saturday, before the match between Aston Villa and Newcastle United, the band played the "Dead March" in *Saul*. During the interval, while a collection was being made for the sufferers, the band played the hymn "God be with you till we meet again."

A finely bound copy of Fitzgerald's "Omar Khayyam" containing Vedder's illustrations, has been lost in the Titanic. It was sold at Sotheby's on March 29 for £405, to Mr Isaacs, bookseller, of Piccadilly. The binding of the volume took two years to complete.

A service was held at St. John's Church, Isleworth, last night in memory of Mr Thomas Pears, a member of the soap making firm, who was a passenger in the Titanic. Between 300 and 400 of the employees attended with the whole of the staff and some of the principals of the firm.

MR. BRUCE ISMAY SENDS HOME A DEFENCE OF HIS ACTION.

I saw Captain Smith casually, as other passengers did. I was never in his room; I was never on the bridge until after the accident. I did not sit at his table in the saloon. I had not visited the engine-room. It is absolutely and unqualifiedly false that I ever said that I wished that the Titanic should make a speed record or should increase her daily runs.

I heard Captain Smith give the order to clear the boats. I helped in this work for nearly two hours as far as I can judge. I worked at the starboard boats, helping women and children into the boats and lowering them over the side. All the women that were on this deck were helped into the boat. They were all, I think, third class passengers.

As the boat was going over the side Mr. Carter, a passenger, and myself got in. At that time there was not a woman on the boat deck, nor any passenger of any class, so far as we could see or hear. The boat had between 35 and 40 in it; it was afterwards discovered that there were four Chinamen concealed under the thwarts in the bottom of the boat.

The boat would have accommodated certainly six or more passengers in addition, if there had been any on the boat deck to go. Neither Mr. Carter nor myself would, for one moment, have thought of getting into the boat if there had been any women there to go in it. Nor should I have done so if I had thought that by remaining on the ship I could have been of the slightest further assistance.

Mr. Bruce Ismay, who is in attendance at Washington with 28 officers and crew of the Titanic to answer the questions of the United States Senate Committee, has cabled a long statement to the *Times*, explaining his action in leaving the boat. Extracts are given above. Mr. Ismay complains that the American inquiry is not being fairly conducted.

Photograph by Ellis and Walery.

TITANIC INQUIRY

Mr Franklin's Remarkable Evidence

NEWS WITHHELD

Because He Believed It Was Unauthentic

WASHINGTON Monday

The United States Senate Committee, which is inquiring into the loss of the Titanic, resumed its sittings to-day.

Mr Franklin, vice-president of the International Mercantile Marine (the Morgan combine which includes the White Star Line), was the first witness called.

He admitted that the report circulated on Monday to the effect that the Titanic was safe might have originated in the White Star Office, but certainly no responsible officer ever made such a statement.

He said that he knew at noon on Monday that the Carpathia had picked up twenty boatloads of survivors from the Titanic.

This was not made public because he believed that it was unauthentic, although it came by a relayed wireless message via Cape Race.

Mr Franklin produced copies of wireless messages from Mr Ismay, asking for the liner Cedric to be held back to enable him and the crew of the Titanic to sail immediately for England without landing at New York. A message also asked for clothing to be provided for Mr Ismay. Mr Franklin replied, refusing to hold the Cedric back.

Further questioned, Mr Franklin denied sending to Congressman Hughes on Monday a message stating that the Titanic was still afloat and was being towed to Halifax. He had been unable to ascertain that any such message had been sent from the White Star offices.

FIRST NEWS OF THE DISASTER

The Chairman: When did you first learn that the Titanic had gone down? At twenty minutes past six in the evening. It was relayed from the Carpathia by the Virginian. We first heard at 2.20 from newspaper men of persistent reports that the Titanic had gone down, and we got into telephonic communication with Montreal, but we were unable to get confirmation. The message from the Virginian informed us that the Carpathia was alongside, and was doing everything that was possible.

What did you do after the receipt of that message? – It took us some time to pull ourselves together. There were two directors, Mr Steele and Mr J. P. Morgan, jun., with me. Then we read the message to the newspaper men, but we had only got as far as the foundering when they all rushed away.

Messages were received signed "Yamsi" (Ismay backwards) insisting that the crew of the Titanic should be returned as quickly as possible.

The Chairman: Has any effort been made by your company to spirit any member of the crew out of the country? – Not to my knowledge. As far as Mr Ismay and myself are concerned, it is our desire that every man needed shall appear in order to give the committee every opportunity to ascertain the facts.

In reply to further questions, Mr Franklin said he knew nothing of any censorship over the wireless messages.

SAILORS' WAGES

WASHINGTON Monday

A statement having been published to the effect that the wages of the sailors stopped with the sinking of the Titanic, a denial of the truth of the report is given by the men. They say Mr Ismay personally assured them to the contrary.

LADY READER'S OFFER

Dear Sir, – As there are so many orphans left without anyone to support them through the Titanic disaster, I should very much like to receive a little girl into my home to bring up as my sister. I am comfortably situated, and the child would be well cared-for and well educated.

I should prefer a little girl of about six years of age, who has lost both parents, or one of a large family whose mother would find it difficult to provide for at all. I should be much obliged if you could assist me in this matter. Yours faithfully,

DAISY F. TEAPE Victoria-road, Clapham.

HOPE DIAMOND AGAIN!

Was The Jewel of Ill-Luck on The Titanic?

ANOTHER SEA MYSTERY

Superstitious people are seeing in the awful circumstances that the Titanic never finished her maiden voyage a predestined doom, and are connecting it with strange suggestions of ill-luck aboard.

The strangest of them all is based on a belief that the Hope diamond was aboard the ill-fated ship and lived up to all the dread traditions of its name by casting the Titanic to the bottom of the sea.

It is a truly fantastic tale, but it will certainly find wide credence if by any chance the fact be ultimately established that the Hope diamond was really aboard. For a belief in good and ill luck is universal and the sanest and most matter-of-fact men own little superstitions which they would scarcely acknowledge even to themselves.

Ingrained in all human nature, however, is a very large element of superstition, and there are many travellers who would instantly feel misgivings if they learned that a jewel with so dire a history was aboard the ship on which they were voyaging.

The Hope diamond now belongs to a wealthy American lady, Mrs Evelyn McLean, who is a leading figure in Washington society. Some weeks ago, as the *Daily Sketch* recorded at the time, the diamond was worn by its fair possessor at a reception given by Mrs McLean in honour of the new Russian Ambassador to the United States.

HISTORY OF TRAGEDY

Some were recalled of the tragic happenings which have followed the famous diamond everywhere, for it is reputed to be an unlucky stone – the unluckiest in the world. From the days when it shone on the fair neck of Queen Marie Antoinette and brought its wearer to the horrors of the French Revolution, every owner of its maleficent is said to have been dogged by ill-fortune.

Mrs McLean wore the jewel in defiance of the Fates, wore it, too, in a costly setting composed of a magnificent circlet of pearls.

Now, every woman, knows that even pearls are linked with a tradition of tears. Many women are so superstitious on this point as to refuse to wear engagement or dress rings containing pearls, and shudder as much over pearls as others do at a gift of opals. Anyway, the setting was sufficient to emphasise rather than weaken the legend of the unlucky diamond, and rather than challenge the evil potentialities of the jewel a second time, so the story goes. Mrs McLean resolved to have her historic diamond reset. For this purpose "The Hope" was recently sent to Amsterdam for expert handling.

Rumour says that the Hope diamond was being secretly taken back to America in the care of a passenger on the Titanic. Inquiries have so far failed to confirm this, and, for the present it is a mystery whether the unlucky jewel was or was not really among the many costly gems which were certainly being carried by the Titanic.

Interesting theory but easily disproved: The Hope Diamond was owned by the MacLean family until 1948 when it was sold to Mr Harry Winston. It is now owned by the Smithsonian Institute in Washington. The Hope Diamond was not therefore being carried on the Titanic.

CAPTAIN'S WIDOW AS STEWARDESS

Mrs Lucy Violet Snape, daughter of Mr and Mrs Edward Lennard, of Witley, near Goldalming, a stewardess on the Titanic, whose name has not yet appeared among the list of survivors. Additional pathos attaches to the case from the fact that, bereaved only last July by the death of her husband – Captain Snape – the young widow, then only just in her twenties and left with a baby girl, obtained, in order to earn a living, the stewardess's position through the good offices of the local M.P.

She had until that time resided in Singapore.

"WIRELESS" AS A CAREER

How The Men Are Trained For Their Work

One effect of the calamitous events of the past few days has been to turn public attention to the possibilities of wireless telegraphy as a business career.

"At the present time there are several hundreds of wireless operators, and there is a growing demand for skilled men," said the general manager of the Marconi Company to the *Daily Sketch* yesterday. "Applicants for service on the staff should be not less than 21 or over 25 years of age. It is essential that they should be able to send and receive at the rate of not less than 25 words per minute on the ordinary Morse key and sounder.

After completing the course of instruction, which, by the way, may be done in a private school if desired, and passing the company's and the Government examinations, the operator is sent to sea, generally as second operator, before being placed alone in charge of a ship's installation.

A wireless operator on board ship is signed on the ship's articles as a member of the crew, generally in the honorary rank of a junior officer, and is subject to the disciplinary regulations of the ship.

NO ROOM FOR "SWELLED HEAD"

Every operator commences as a junior. The scale of pay is higher than that paid to telegraphists in the home Government and cable services, and much higher than that paid to railway telegraphists. Moreover, the pay is increased more rapidly. Operators have to serve some years at sea before qualifying for a shore appointment. The maximum scale of pay for a senior operator is 55s (**£2.75**) per week, and all found.

To the man who enters the service without an exaggerated notion of his own individual importance there are many opportunities of advancement provided he is capable and assiduous. The moment a man shows signs of suffering from 'swelled head' the company has no further use for his services.

ARE THERE ENOUGH MEN?

In respect of the accommodation provided for operators on our largest liners, by the way, we compare badly with Germany, where the shipping companies hire at least three operators to our two.

On our Dreadnoughts there are at least six wireless men but except in emergencies there is not sufficient work for more than two on any liner.

It is not true that both operators are asleep at nights. One of the two is always supposed to watch for a distress call.

One of the ugliest rumours in connection with the disaster is the accusation made against Mr Harold Bride, alleging that he refused to wire news from the Carpathia by collusion with a New York paper.

Mr Turnbull stated that Mr Marconi himself will deal with this imputation.

THE TRAGEDY WHICH HAS THRILLED THE WOR

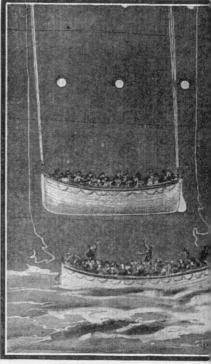

" We were carried under Boat No. 14, which was coming
threatened to submerge our boat. 'Stop lowering 14'
shouted. I reached up and touched the bottom of the swi
above. Just before the next drop a stoker sprang to the
his knife and cut us clear. We could not find the releasin
crew were mostly cooks."—Mr. LAWRENCE BEESLE

The Titanic disaster has sent a thrill throughout the world, and the newspapers in all countries devote great space to describing and illustrating the details of the calamity. We reproduce above a front page sketch of the final scene drawn by Paul
Theriat for the French daily illustrated paper Excelsior.

A full boat's crew in readiness ready to man the boat behi
the word of command from the officer. A cook is in

Last Portrait of Mr. Stead Before He Sailed to His Death on the T

, direct evidence has been forthcoming so far as to how the most famous Englishman on board the Titanic, Mr. W. T. Stead, met his death. Some survivors say that he took his chan
submitted himself to be "biofixed." The pictures were bound and sent to Mr. Stead wit

HE PROBLEM OF LIFEBOATS FOR GREAT VESSELS.

r the records of heroism the outstanding feature is the story of
boats. With a view to showing how the steamship companies do
e efforts to meet catastrophe our pictures, taken on the Kenilworth
le, at Southampton, illustrate the boat drill of the seamen of this
, and are typical of the drills that are held by the Union-Castle
Steamship Company on all their liners.

After the order to man the boats—fitting on the lifebelts.

The *Excelsior* artist's sketch illustrating the refusal of Mrs. Isidor Straus to leave her husband and take the place offered
her by the officers in a boat. The touching incident of the American philanthropist and his life-long helpmeet clinging to
each other in the face of death has been seized upon by the French artist for a dramatic picture.

ofix " Series of the Famous Veteran Journalist in Characteristic Gestures.

ea, ..d others that he was last seen helping the loading of the boats with women and children. A few days before he left this country Mr. Stead visited the Biofix offices, 56, Strand, and
ken of the famous journalist, who intended to use them in an article on novel photography.

LESSON TO SHIPOWNERS

Mr Ismay Says "There Must Be Boats For All"

This awful experience has taught the steamship owners of the world that too much reliance has been placed on water-tight compartments and on wireless telegraphy, and that they must equip every vessel with lifeboats and rafts sufficient to provide for every soul on board, and sufficient men to handle them.

So says Mr Bruce Ismay, the chairman of the White Star Line, in the course of a statement to the New York correspondent of *The Times*.

As for the Senatorial inquiry, Mr Ismay said; "I did not suppose the question of my personal conduct was the subject of the inquiry, although I was ready to tell everything I did on the night of the collision."

While, he said, he was under subpoena to attend the Court of Inquiry, he did not think courtesy required him to be silent in the face of the untrue statements made in some newspapers.

"During the voyage," he went on, "I was a passenger, and exercised no greater rights or privileges than any other passenger.

It is absolutely and unqualifiedly false that I ever said that I wished the Titanic should make a speed record or should increase her daily runs."

Mr Ismay said he was asleep when the collision occurred. He went on the bridge deck and asked Captain Smith what was the matter. He said we had struck ice. I asked him whether he thought it was serious, and he said he did. On returning to my room I met the chief engineer, and asked him whether he thought the damage serious, and he said he thought it was.

CONCEALED CHINAMEN

Mr Ismay said he returned to his room and put on a suit of clothes. He had been in his overcoat and pyjamas up to that time. He then went back to the boat-deck and helped to put the women and children into the starboard boats. He did nothing with regard to the boats on the port side.

After every wooden lifeboat on the starboard side had been lowered away (Mr Ismay said) he helped to get out the forward collapsible boat on the starboard side.

"As the boat was going over the side Mr Carter, a passenger, and myself got in. At that time there was not a woman on the boat deck, nor any passenger of any class, so far as we could see or hear. The boat had between 35 and 40 in it; I should think most of them were women.

There were, perhaps, four or five men, and it was afterwards discovered that there were four Chinamen concealed under the thwarts in the bottom of the boat.

All these facts can be substantiated by Mr W.E. Carter, of Philadelphia, who got in at the time that I did, and was rowing the boat with me. I hope I need not say that neither Mr Carter nor myself would, for one moment, have thought of getting into the boat if there had been any women there to go in it."

WORKED UNTIL DEATH CAME

Mr Peter Sloan, chief electrician, who went down with the Titanic. He had charge of all electric fittings, including, of course, the wireless installation. Lord Charles Beresford well eulogised the conduct of Mr Sloan and his company of brother heroes in a letter to *The Times* – "the fact that so many people were saved was because the dynamos were kept working and the lights burning."

BOARD OF TRADE ACTION

Commission of Inquiry Into Titanic Wreck

AMERICAN METHODS

Mr Will Crooks Admires the Conduct of the Senate

A sharp contrast between British official methods and American official methods of getting at the roots of a troublesome question was made in the House of Commons yesterday by Mr Will Crooks, who moved the adjournment of the House with the object of giving expression to the opinion of the public that not a moment should be lost in endeavouring to discover the cause of the Titanic disaster.

Perhaps Mr Crooks found justification for his action in the announcement made during the day that the Board of Trade had decided that the inquiry into the collision between the P. and O. liner Oceana and the German barque Pisagua in the English Channel on March 16 should be opened – on April 30, forty-five days after the disaster.

The anxiety of the House of Commons to come to close quarters with the question of the Titanic tragedy was shown at the commencement of the sitting in the afternoon.

A number of questions were asked regarding the detention of passengers and crew of the Titanic, so that they would be available to give evidence in England.

Mr Buxton said he had no powers to detain them, but the Court would be constituted almost immediately, and it would have full powers.

Lord Charles Beresford: "Will every passenger, officer or man that can give evidence be detained in this country, and will the hon. gentleman be careful that what occurred on the Oceana when the officers who manned the boats were allowed to leave the country before giving evidence, does not occur in this case?

Mr Buxton repeated his previous answer, that the court would have full powers.

Mr W. Crooks then intimated that he would move the adjournment of the House.

IN NO HURRY TO BLAME

When introducing his motion in the evening Mr Crooks said that he did not do so by way of a vote of censure upon the President of the Board of Trade. They had no right to blame anyone till they had heard the evidence. They asked that a commission should be set up at once and should begin immediately to ascertain the number of persons who could throw light on the disaster and to take steps to bring those persons before the proper tribunal.

The prompt action of the American Senate was referred to by Mr Crooks. That body, he said, did not wait to investigate the law as to capacity to deal with certain people. They at once sent a Commission out to intercept even the owners of the vessel, together with any others they desired as witnesses.

They had heard there was no law to enable them to do that, but they had done it, and England applauded them for doing it. Surely England was not to be behind. He asked for an assurance that a Commission would be set up at once, and that those who could give evidence would be subpoenaed, and that those who were not well enough to maintain themselves during the inquiry would be maintained by the Board of Trade.

The President of the Board of Trade, Mr Buxton, appeared to be fully sensible of the vital importance of the subject when he rose to reply, and he said so. He said he felt the weight of responsibility very heavily.

Further, he endorsed everything that had been said in reference to the courage, devotion, and heroism of the crew and passengers of the Titanic.

When he answered questions that afternoon he was not in a position to give information regarding the constitution of the Court of inquiry. The Board of Trade could appoint a stipendiary or, in certain instances, the President of the Board of Trade could request the Lord Chancellor to appoint a Wreck Commission. The latter course had not been resorted to for many years.

A STRONG COURT

It appeared to him in the existing circumstances it would be advisable to constitute the strongest possible Court under statute. The appointment of the Wreck Commission was in the discretion and under the authority of the Lord Chancellor, who would necessarily appoint a high judicial authority who would form an absolutely independent Court. He had communicated with the Lord Chancellor and had obtained his assent to such an appointment.

He was glad to announce that Lord Mersey, ex-President of the Admiralty Division of the High Court, had been good enough to undertake the responsibility. He would be assisted by assessors shortly.

The Court would thus be constituted in ample time for the duty that it would undertake, as the first batch of survivors could not arrive till Monday next.

Mr Buxton said there had been no delay whatsoever and the Court would have sufficient power to secure the attendance of witnesses it desired, and he anticipated that no difficulties would arise.

In reply to questions Mr Buxton said he thought it would be relevant for the Court to go into the questions of inaccurate telegrams and insurance.

Mr Crooks expressed satisfaction with the statement and withdrew his motion.

IN THE HEART OF THE HORROR

Lord Charles Beresford's Tribute to Engineers

All the Titanic engineers perished. The principal of them were:-

Chief Engineer – J. Bell	**Southampton**
Senior Second Engineer –	
W. Farquharson,	**Southampton**
Junior Second Engineers –	
J. H. Hesketh,	**Liverpool**
N. Harrison,	**Southampton**
Senior Third Engineer –	
G. F. Hosking,	**Itchen**
Junior Third Engineer –	
E. C. Dodd,	**Crewe**

In the *Daily Sketch* yesterday attention was called to the heroism that must have been displayed in the Titanic's engine-room.

Lord Charles Beresford points out in a letter to *The Times* that unintentionally the gallantry displayed below decks has not received adequate recognition in the comments on the disaster.

"It is stated," Lord Charles says, "that the lights were burning until a few minutes before the ship took her final plunge. This proves that the officers and men below remained at their posts when they must have known that a death – the most terrible and painful that it is possible to conceive – awaited them at any minute, either by the bursting of a steam-pipe or water rising in a compartment.

"That so many people were saved was due to the fact that those working below remained at their posts working the dynamos and kept the lights burning.

"It should be remembered that those below work in confined spaces, watertight doors closed, often in intolerable heat with a roar of machinery making orders difficult to understand.

"A man will face death with greater equanimity on deck than working below under the incidents I have mentioned.

BIRTHPLACE OF TITANIC'S CAPTAIN

The house in Well-street, Hanley, Staffordshire, where Captain Smith was born.

108

MISSING MONEY: Shillings That Have Not Been Sent

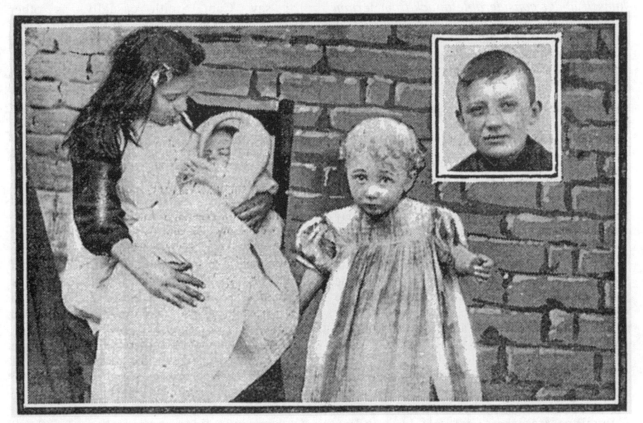

Why the *Daily Sketch* appeals to you. Here is a group of children whose father and breadwinner has been so ruthlessly snatched from them. From some homes father and son have been taken. To alleviate the misery and lighten the burden of the bereaved is the object of our "S O S" Fund.

Considerably more than a million people read the *Daily Sketch* every morning. We do not believe that a single one of these people fails to appreciate the true facts of the disaster to the Titanic.

Not a single one will withhold his admiration of the heroism which will be remembered as long as England has a history; not one would willingly withhold his sympathy from those who are suffering. If we could collect that shilling we have been telling you about personally we should have a million shillings to-day. But because we cannot there are a good few missing.

This is not a good enough reason. It is a matter of a two-minute visit to a post office and a failure to do that amounts to a refusal to help the people who are suffering. It is none the less a refusal because it is passive instead of active. To-morrow never comes. Do it now.

All contributions should be addressed:-
    The Cashier,
    Daily Sketch,
        17, Tudor-street, London, E.C.

LONDON AND LIVERPOOL HELP

The Mansion House Titanic Fund reached £100,000 yesterday. Included in the donations are the following:- The Marquis of Salisbury £100, Viscount Haldane £50, Lieutenant-Colonel Hope Edwardes £200, Earl of Dysart £100, Billett, Campbell and Grenfell £262 10s., Dunn Fischer and Co. £525, Mr J Lionel Dugdale £200, Mr H J Tennant, M.P., £100, Captain Spender Clay, M.P., £100, A. Keyser and Co. £105.

The Liverpool relief fund amounts to £3,270. Lord Derby has agreed to distribute the fund raised by the Philadelphia citizens.

Following the evidence he gave before the Senate Committee Mr Bruce Ismay found himself under considerable attack from certain sections of the American Press. Perhaps in the hope of preventing similar criticism back in England Mr Ismay cabled the following statement to the Editor of The Times:

MR BRUCE ISMAY AND THE WRECK

A Personal Statement

We have received the following statement by Mr Bruce Ismay. This was cabled by our New York Correspondent late on Sunday night and appeared in part of our issue of yesterday:-

When I appeared before the Senate Committee on Friday morning I supposed the purpose of the enquiry was to ascertain the cause of the sinking of the Titanic with a view to determining whether additional legislation was required to prevent the recurrence of so horrible a disaster.

I welcomed such an enquiry and appeared voluntarily without subpoena, and answered all questions put to me by the members of the Committee to the best of my ability, with complete frankness and without reserve. I did not suppose the question of my personal conduct was the subject of the enquiry, although I was ready to tell everything I did on the night of the collision. As I have been subpoenaed to attend before the Committee in Washington to-morrow I should prefer to make no public statement out of respect for the Committee, but I do not think that courtesy requires me to be silent in the face of the untrue statements made in some of the newspapers.

When I went on board the Titanic at Southampton on April 10 it was my intention to return by her. I had no intention of remaining in the United States at that time. I came merely to observe the new vessel as I had done in the case of other vessels of our lines. During the voyage I was a passenger and exercised no greater right or privileges than any other passenger. I was not consulted by the commander about the ship, her course, speed, navigation, or her conduct at sea. All these matters were under the exclusive control of the captain.

I saw Capt Smith casually, as other passengers did. I was never in his room; I was never on the bridge until after the accident. I did not sit at his table in the saloon. I had not visited the engine room, nor gone through the ship, and did not go, or attempt to go, to any part of the ship to which any other first-cabin passenger did not have access.

It is absolutely and unqualifiedly false that I ever said that I wished that the Titanic should make a speed record or should increase her daily runs. I deny absolutely having said to any person that we would increase our speed in order to get out of the ice zone, or any words to that effect. As I have already testified, at no time did the Titanic during the voyage attain her full speed. It was not expected that we would reach New York before Wednesday morning. If she had been pressed she could probably have arrived on Tuesday evening.

The statement that the White Star Line would receive an additional sum by way of bounty, or otherwise, for attaining a certain speed is absolutely untrue. The White Star Line received from the British Government a fixed compensation of £70,000 per annum for carrying mails without regard to the speed of any of its vessels, and no additional sum is paid on account of any increase in speed.

I was never consulted by Capt Smith, nor by any other person. Nor did I ever make any suggestion whatsoever to any human being about the course of the ship. The Titanic, as I am informed, was on the southern-most westbound track. The Transatlantic steamship tracks or lanes were designated many years ago by agreement on the part of all the important steamship lines and all the captains of the White Star Line are required to navigate their vessels as closely as possible on these tracks, subject to the following standing instructions:-

"Commanders must distinctly understand that the issue of these regulations does not in any way relieve them from responsibility for the safe and efficient navigation of their respective vessels, and they are also enjoined to remember that they must run no risks that might by any possibility result in accident to their ships. It is to be hoped that they will ever bear in mind that the safety of the lives and property entrusted to their care is the ruling principle that should govern them in the navigation of their vessels, and that no supposed gain in expedition or saving of time on the voyage is to be purchased at the risk of accident. The company desires to maintain for its vessels a reputation for safety, and only looks for such speed on the various voyages as is consistent with safe and prudent navigation.

Commanders are reminded that the steamers are to a great extend uninsured, and that their own livelihood, as well as the company's success, depends upon immunity from accident. No precaution which ensures safe navigation is to be considered excessive."

The only information I ever received in the ship that other vessels had sighted ice was by a wireless message received from the Baltic which I have already testified to. This was handed to me by Capt Smith, without any remarks, as he was passing me on the passenger deck on the afternoon of Sunday, April 14. I read the telegram casually, and put it in my pocket. At about ten minutes past 7, while I was sitting in the smoke room, Captain Smith came in and asked me to give him the message received from the Baltic in order to post it for the information of the officers. I handed it to him, and nothing further was said by either of us. I did not speak to any of the other officers on the subject.

If the information I had received had aroused any apprehension in my mind – which it did not – I should not have ventured to make any suggestion to a commander of Captain Smith's experience and responsibility, for the navigation of the ship rested solely with him.

It has been stated that Captain Smith and I were having a dinner party in one of the saloons from 7.30 to 10.30 on Sunday night, and that at the time of the collision Captain Smith was sitting with me in the saloon. Both of these statements are absolutely false. I did not dine with the Captain. Nor did I see him during the evening of April 14. The doctor dined with me in the restaurant at 7.30, and I went directly to my state-room and went to bed at about 10.30.

I was asleep when the collision occurred. I felt a jar, went out into the passage-way without dressing, met a steward, asked him what was the matter, and he said he did not know. I returned to my room. I felt the ship slow down. I put on an overcoat over my pyjamas and went up on the bridge deck, and on the bridge I asked Captain Smith what was the matter, and he said we had struck ice. I asked him whether he thought it serious, and he said he did.

On my way to my room I met the chief engineer, and asked him whether he thought the damage serious, and he said he thought it was.

I then returned to my room and put on a suit of clothes. I had been in my overcoat and pyjamas up to this time. I then went back to the boat deck and heard Captain Smith give the order to clear the boats. I helped in this work for nearly two hours as far as I can judge.

I worked at the starboard boats, helping women and children into the boats and lowering them over the side. I did nothing with regard to the boats on the port side. By that time every wooden lifeboat on the starboard side had been lowered away, and I found that they were engaged in getting out the forward collapsible boat on the starboard side. I assisted in this work, and all the women that were on this deck were helped into the boat. They were all, I think, third-class passengers.

As the boat was going over the side Mr Carter, a passenger, and myself got in. At that time there was not a woman on the boat deck, nor any passengers of any class, as far as we could see or hear. The boat had between 35 and 40 in it; I should think most of them women. There were, perhaps, four or five men, and it was afterwards discovered that there were four Chinamen concealed under the thwarts in the bottom of the boat. The distance that the boat had to be lowered into the water was, I should estimate, about 20ft. Mr Carter and I did not get into the boat until after they had begun to lower it away.

When the boat reached the water I helped to row it, pushing the oar from me as I sat. This is the explanation of the fact that my back was to the sinking steamer.

The boat would have accommodated

certainly six or more passengers in addition, if there had been any on the boat deck to go.

These facts can be substantiated by Mr W. E. Carter of Philadelphia, who got in at the time that I did, and was rowing the boat with me. I hope I need not say that neither Mr Carter nor myself would, for one moment, have thought of getting into the boat if there had been any women there to go in it. Nor should I have done so if I had thought that by remaining on the ship I could have been the slightest further assistance.

It is impossible for me to answer every false statement, rumour, or invention that has appeared in the newspapers. I am prepared to answer any questions that may be asked by the Committee of the Senate or any other responsible person. I shall, therefore, make no further statement of this kind, except to explain the messages that I sent from the Carpathia.

These messages have been completely misunderstood. An inference has been drawn from them that I was anxious to avoid the Senate Committee's inquiry, which it was intended to hold in New York. As a matter of fact, when despatching these messages I had not the slightest idea that any inquiry was contemplated, and I had no information regarding it until the arrival of the Carpathia at the Cunard dock in New York on Thursday night, when I was informed by Senators Smith and Newlands of the appointment of a Special Committee to hold an inquiry.

The only purpose I had in sending those messages was to express my desire to have the crew returned to their homes in England for their own benefit at the earliest possible moment, and I, also, was naturally anxious to return to my family, but I left this matter of my return entirely to our representatives in New York.

I deeply regret that I am compelled to make any personal statement when my whole thought is on the horror of the disaster. In building the Titanic it was the hope of my associates and myself that we had built a vessel which could not be destroyed by the perils of the sea or the dangers of navigation. The event has proved the futility of that hope. Present legal requirements have proved inadequate. They must be changed, but whether they are changed or not, this awful experience has taught the steamship owners of the world that too much reliance has been placed on watertight compartments and on wireless telegraphy, and that they must equip every vessel with lifeboats and rafts sufficient to provide for every soul on board, and sufficient men to handle them.

MR CARTER'S STATEMENT

(FROM OUR OWN CORRESPONDENT)

WASHINGTON April 22

Mr William E. Carter, a well-known Philadelphian, gives the following story of his departure and that of Mr Ismay from the Titanic. After seeing his wife and children into the boats on the port side of the vessel he went to the starboard side and there found Mr Ismay with several officers filling boats with women. As the last boat was being filled they looked around for more women. The women in the boat were mostly steerage passengers:-

Mr Ismay and myself and several officers walked up and down the deck crying "Are there any more women here?" We called for several minutes and got no answer. One of the officers then said that if we wanted to, we could get into the boat if we took the place of seamen. He gave us preference because we were among the first-class passengers. Mr Ismay called again, and after we had no reply we got into the lifeboat. We took oars and rowed with two seamen.

Here is a letter sent to The Times in which the author expresses a number of rather surprising views, the last of which must surely have placed him, universally, in a minority of one!

THE QUESTION OF BOATS

TO THE EDITOR OF THE TIMES

Sir, – The suggestion has been made that every ship should be compelled by the Board of Trade to supply sufficient boats to carry all on board. To assist in advising caution against panic legislation, may I offer a few facts for consideration?

1. The Titanic is the first of the Atlantic liners that has foundered by collision with an iceberg, although they make hundreds of voyages to and fro annually. Does such an exceptional case call for special legislation?

2. While attention is being riveted on a particular case, any rules of universal application are apt to be unsuitable – e.g., if a universal rule were now established that all steam boats should carry enough boats for all on board, this would prevent the sailing of excursion steamers. Such legislation, had it been proposed after the disaster to the Princess Alice, which was crowded, would have been condemned as impossible.

3. The Titanic would not have been able so successfully to lower her boats, swinging from a height of 70ft., had the wind been high and the sea rough. In that case had there been four times as many boats, as has been demanded, they would have been troublesome to deal with, and there might have been great confusion.

4. The Titanic was unsinkable by collision with a steamer or a derelict, or by stress of weather, or by direct impact upon an iceberg, or under the action of any forces other than the shearing, ripping stress that tore the plates over a great part of her length.

5. If the first officer, on seeing the ice on his starboard bow, had happened not to do the right thing, as he did in starboarding his helm, and had ported the helm, the ship would probably have struck the berg end-on, and would have arrived safely in New York with her bow crushed in, as did the Arizona some 30 years ago.

6. Lifeboats on the great Atlantic liners are not generally regarded by passengers as being required for safety. Personally, having crossed the Atlantic 33 times, having covered several hundred thousand miles at sea in all waters, and in all types of ship from battleships to tramps, and having been wrecked three times (though only once reduced to the straits of the Titanic passengers), and having carefully studied the art of navigation both in the theory and practice, I would feel perfectly at ease were I sailing to-morrow on any modern Atlantic liner totally unprovided with lifeboats. Few men would hesitate to risk the chance of such a misfortune happening a second time, as it is too small to be a practical consideration.

I am, Sir, your obedient servant,
GEORGE FORBES.
The Athenaeum April 20.

IN DEFENCE OF MR ISMAY

TO THE EDITOR OF THE TIMES

Sir,- As an old friend of Mr Bruce Ismay, I am anxious to protest against the ungenerous attacks which have been made upon his conduct in leaving the Titanic. At a moment of such deep tragedy and sorrow for Mr Ismay and his friends it seems incredible that he should be censured for doing what other men rightly did by accepting the last chance of saving his life after he had done everything in his power for others, it is unworthy of the traditions of a great country, that such criticism should be heard, and at such a sad moment.

It is gratifying to learn from to-day's paper that a protest has been made in the United States Senate against the manner in which Mr Bruce Ismay is being treated by the Committee.

I am yours faithfully,

JOSEPH C. MAXWELL SCOTT,
of Abbotsford.

Westside House.
Wimbledon Common
April 22

DAILY SKETCH.

No. 975.—WEDNESDAY, APRIL 24, 1912.   THE PREMIER PICTURE PAPER.   [Registered as a Newspaper.]   ONE HALFPENNY.

OLYMPIC WILL SAIL TO-DAY PACKED WITH LIFEBOATS.

Mr. Ismay's instructions that every passenger boat under his control shall be provided with boat accommodation for all on board in case of accident are being carried out on the Olympic, which leaves Southampton to-day for New York Our picture shows how boats are being crowded on the decks. A collapsible boat is seen in the foreground.

Miss Mabel Ludlow, an East Grinstead nurse, who is engaged to Harold Bride (inset), the rescued wireless operator on the Titanic, has received a cablegram from him that he is "safe and well."

Lord Mersey, known formerly as Mr. Justice Bigham, who has been selected as Chairman of the English Court of Inquiry into the Titanic disaster, was born and brought up in Liverpool, represented a Liverpool Division in Parliament, and was in the Probate, Divorce, and Admiralty Division when on the Bench.   Elliott and Fry.

Mr. and Mrs. T. W. Cavendish, passengers on the Titanic. Mr. Cavendish was a son of the Hon. Charles Cavendish, who was a grandson of Lord Waterpark. He was 30 years of age, and married Miss Julia Seigel, only child of Mr. Henry Seigel, a prominent wealthy American, Mr. Cavendish was drowned, and Mrs. Cavendish and her maid saved.

SOME SUFFERERS FOR WHOM WE ASK HELP

Why the *Daily Sketch* appeals to you. Here is a group of poor people whose breadwinner has been so ruthlessly snatched from them. From some homes father and son have been taken. To alleviate the misery and lighten the burden of the bereaved is the object of our Shilling Fund.

SIX CHILDREN – 6d.
Small Gifts That Mean Real Sacrifices

It is a very unromantic looking piece of paper. There is no crest on it, no printed address, no definite address of any kind indeed. Probably it started life as an envelope, and there are signs that the back has been cut away with infantile care if not with great precision.

It wandered into Tudor-street yesterday morning from Sydenham. It was wrapped carefully round a postal order for sixpence, and the whole enclosed in another envelope carefully addressed The Cashier.

"Sydenham. From 6 children" is all the information with which we are provided. Try to imagine the solemnity and importance of the occasion. One pen rejected because it could not spell, another because it had only one leg; the conference of six important people, all holding different opinions, as to the right way of spelling Sydenham, the distance one should

leave at the top of the paper, and the proper places to use capital letters. Then there was the journey to the post office, the financial transaction with the Government, and the throb of apprehension that perhaps after all everything was not quite in order as the letter disappeared through the hole in the red box.

It would take a long time, probably most of a spring evening; but it would be a joyful task. And now it is one of our most valued contributions.

If we knew how the disaster affected you personally we should know how to appeal to you, but as it is we have to leave it largely to yourself. One of our readers, for instance, finds it easy to sympathise because he was one of those rescued when the Princess Alice went down off Woolwich as long ago as 1878. Another contribution is worthy of consideration by those who "cannot afford" that shilling. It is sent by a cornet player who has often been on big liners, but is at present out of work.

SOCIETY LADIES' RUSH

Wild Scenes at the Titanic Inquiry

POLICE CORDON BROKEN

Mr Ismay's Order: Fill Boats With Women and Children

The Senatorial inquiry into the Titanic disaster was resumed to-day. Public interest in the investigation was greater than ever.

For some reason not fully explained the Commission did not sit in the caucus-room, the scene of yesterday's proceedings, but removed to a room of smaller dimensions.

The result was that only a very small proportion of those who made their way to the Senate buildings were able to obtain admission. The police had considerable difficulty in handling the crowds. Several rushes were made, in which hundreds of society women, many of whom had brought their lunch with them, made violent endeavours to get past the guards.

A number of them succeeded in breaking through. Only about one hundred and fifty persons, however, gained their way to the inquiry room.

The investigation is expected to last another fortnight, though in order that it may not be unduly protracted evening sittings will most likely be held.

Fourth Officer Boxhall was to-day too ill to resume his evidence, and Mr Pittman, the third officer was called.

Mr Pittman said that a notice was posted on the Titanic with reference to the presence of ice, but he himself saw no ice either on Saturday or Sunday.

In reply to questions he said he knew of no reliable test for ascertaining when a ship was in the vicinity of icebergs.

"TIME IS PRECIOUS"

Mr Pittman described how after the collision Mr Ismay came on deck in his dressing-gown and slippers and urged that the lifeboats should be lowered. Mr Ismay said "Time is precious. Fill them with women and children." Mr Pittman took charge of lifeboat No. 5, which had forty passengers, including six men.

The women did not like the idea of entering the boats, thinking they were better off on the ship. None of the women in his boat rowed, but several of them who were suffering severely from the cold wished to take an oar in order to keep themselves warm.

Describing the final scenes, Mr Pittman said he saw the ship go down perpendicularly, but he did not believe that the boilers exploded. He heard cries of distress.

Did you return in the direction of those cries? – No.

Your boat could have held twenty or thirty more people, couldn't it? – Yes, but I decided that it was better not to risk the boat swamped by the many people who would try and get into it if we went back.

Frederick Fleet said when he was engaged as look-out man in the crow's-nest of the liner he saw icebergs ahead some time before the collision, and he gave a warning to the bridge. He testified further that he had no marine glasses, although he had asked for them, and expressed the view that he could have seen the berg which caused the damage in time had he been using glasses. – Exchange.

WANTED . . . A THEATRE

For Matinee in Aid of Titanic Funds

A number of members of the Arts and Dramatic Club, in Prince's-street, Hanover-square, are organising a variety matinee in aid of those who have suffered through the Titanic disaster. Though they have already had many offers of help from numbers of entertainers they have not succeeded in obtaining the loan of a theatre or hall suitable for the performance.

Unless they succeed in doing this within the next day or two this opportunity of helping the relief funds will be wasted. With the exception of the arrangements about the hall the programme is, we understand, complete, and it is intended that the performance shall take place one afternoon next week. Anyone who can be of assistance to the promoters in their search for a theatre or hall is requested to communicate with Mr Ernest J. Lyon, at the club.

WHERE WERE THE WOMEN?

Mystery of the Last Moments on the Titanic

BOATS COULD HAVE HELD MORE

The number of women who went down with the Titanic will no doubt be the subject of searching inquiry.

So far as can be ascertained at present there were between seventy and a hundred.

It appears to be certain that some of them decided to die with their husbands.

Mrs Straus is a notable instance, and in her case there is authentic information that she deliberately sacrificed herself. The names of other women who also made that choice have been mentioned.

But even when full allowance has been made for the heroism shown by the women passengers in general – some of them, we know, had to be thrown into the boats – there remains much ground for investigation.

Here is a list (taken from the Times) of the women passengers, first and second class, whose names were not among the survivors.

FIRST CLASS

Davidson, Mrs. Thornton.
Allison, Mrs H. J.
Allison, Miss.
Fortune, Mrs C.
Goldenburg, Mrs E. L.
Compton, Miss S.R.
Stehli, Mrs Max Frolicher.
Isham, Miss A. E.
Evans, Miss E.
Straus, Mrs I.
Oatby, Miss H. R.

SECOND CLASS

Carbett, Mrs I. C.
Corey, Mrs C. P.
Chapman, Mrs E.
Carter, Mrs L.
del Carlo, Mrs.
Howard, Mrs E. T.
Kantor, Mrs S.
Karnes, Mrs F.
Kirliner, Mrs G. H.
Lahtinen, Mrs W.
Mack, Mrs M.
Nasser, Mrs N.
Tervan, Mrs A.T.
Wilkinson, Mrs S. G.
Funk, Miss A.
Harper, Miss N.
Hiltuner, Miss M.
Reynolds, Miss E.
Wilkinson, Miss A. C.
Yodis, Miss H.

It will be seen that there are twelve in the first class and twenty in the second.

The list of women in the third class who lost their lives is not yet available. Then there were a large number of stewardesses on board.

Doubtless the death-roll among the women is partly accounted for by their reluctance to enter the earlier boats – due in many cases to a belief that the liner was virtually unsinkable.

Mr Ismay has said – and his statement is confirmed – that there was not a woman to be seen on the boat deck when the boat into which he got was lowered. One passenger said that the call, "Any more women?" was repeated several times, but no woman was forthcoming.

Where were the remaining women? Many were with husbands and with male relatives. Others, with no male relatives to cheer them, must have huddled in groups, waiting their doom. With a ship the size of the Titanic some diligent searching might have been required to find them; and the task of the officers was a stupendous one.

What makes the tragedy of the women the more painful is the fact that – according to some survivors – the boats would have held many more.

MEMORIALS TO MR JACK PHILLIPS

A special meeting of the Godalming Town Council is to be held this week to pay tribute to the heroism of Mr Jack Phillips, the chief wireless operator on the Titanic, who was a native of the town, and to take steps to raise a permanent memorial to him. It has already been decided to place a memorial brass tablet in Farncombe Parish Church, at which Phillips was formerly a chorister.

ST. GEORGE PLAYS GOLF.

A MEMORIAL PICTURE O

Yesterday was St. George's Day, and in honour of the occasion an extraordinary golf match was played at Bushey Hall Golf Course between Mr. Harry Dearth, the well-known baritone, who takes the part of St. George in Sir Edward Elgar's masque at the Coliseum, and Mr. R. D. Margetson. Mr. Dearth, who played in a complete suit of armour, is seen in the photograph playing out of a bunker.

The statement has been made that no photograph is in existence of Captain Smith on the bridge of the Titanic. We are prepared to supply copies of the above photograph, which has been produced previously in the *Daily Sketch*, and was taken the day before the Titanic sailed by a *Daily Sketch* photo-
Fund for the widows and orpha

The golfing St. George snapped in various attitudes during the game. In one the knight is seen enjoying a cigarette and in another is starting a sprint to come up with his companion. Mr. Margetson won the match, but only by 2 up and 1 to play.—*Daily Sketch* Photographs.

ST. GEORGE FOR MERRIE ENGLAND : HUNDREI

The Bishop of Kensington addressing the huge assemblage that gathered yesterday at Tower Hill take part in a religious service held to commemorate St. George's Day—the revival of an old cust which was in vogue one hundred years ago. The Lord Mayor, with the Lady Mayoress and the Sher —the red cross on the white ground—l

HE TITANIC TRAGEDY.

FROM HENDON TO MURPHY'S FARM.

Mr. Corbett Wilson's aeroplane on the spot where he landed—at Mr. Murphy's farm at Crane, about three miles from Enniscorthy, after his successful flight from the Hendon aerodrome to Ireland. On approaching the Irish coast he experienced bad and foggy weather, which interfered with his course.

n the bridge, where Captain Smith remained until his death on the night of the dreadful ... Any of our readers who are anxious to obtain this as a memorial photograph will be supplied ...ge of 1s. 6d. for each print, and the proceeds will be devoted to the *Daily Sketch* Shilling ...ho perished.

OLD CUSTOM REVIVED ON TOWER HILL.

...on for many years on which the Lord Mayor has been present in ...nd. The Bishop, in an address, said that the day was a proud day ...f St. George which floated over the Tower, he said that that flag ...

(1) The young aviator setting off from Fishguard, where he descended before making his final dash to Ireland. (2) Seeing everything was in working trim before the flight across the Irish Sea. (3) Mr. Wilson in Enniscorthy.

BRINGING IN THE DEAD

Crowd of Relatives Journey to Halifax

The *New York Herald* has received a dispatch from St John's, Newfoundland, stating that more than 100 bodies have been picked up by the cable ship Mackay Bennett.

According to wireless messages received last night 27 of the bodies have been identified, and one of them is believed to be that of Mr Widener, the millionaire.

Many relatives and friends of the victims are now on their way to Halifax, there to await the arrival of the cable ship.

Captain Richard Roberts, master of the late Colonel Astor's yacht, is going to Halifax to represent the family.

Among the names of those picked up by the Mackay Bennett appears to be that of "W. H. Hambeck." This is evidently W. H. Harbeck, a cinematographer connected with the Canadian Pacific Railway, who was on a brief visit to Europe, and who told a friend the day before the Titanic sailed that he was planning to catch that steamer. As his name has not hitherto appeared in the published list of passengers, it was thought that he had missed the Titanic and sailed by some other boat.   Central News

LOUIS AND LOLO

Frenchwoman Claims Two Baby Survivors

The wife of a tailor, Mne Navratil, has declared (says the *Journal*'s Nice correspondent) that in the description of the two French children answering to the names of Louis and Lolo, who are among the survivors of the Titanic disaster, she recognises her own infants.

This woman says she was deserted by her husband, who disappeared with the children a month ago, telling friends he was going to America. Louis and Lolo travelled with Mme Hoffmann, a friend of the husband.

Mme Navratil has telegraphed to America for photographs of the children.

STRANGE SPIRITUALIST STORY

NEW YORK Tuesday

A telegram received here from Pittsburg, Pennsylvania, states that Mrs M. L. Feldman told the Convention of United States Spiritualists Association to-day that she talked with the spirit of the late Mr W. T. Stead yesterday. She was informed that Mr Stead was happy and was preparing to communicate with the Convention.

THE TITANIC'S SEAMEN

Our Liverpool correspondent says: The number of fully-qualified seamen on the Titanic, in addition to the captain and seven officers, was 58. It may be taken that all the men were of the best type. Many of them were naval reservists. A striking fact is that nearly a fourth of the whole number of people on board were stewards, their number being 494. Of these 23 were women.

IRISH CONVENTION'S TRIBUTE

When the convention of the United Irish League opened in Dublin yesterday Mr Redmond proposed a resolution expressing sorrow at the Titanic disaster. The whole convention stood up and the motion was passed in silence.

FOR BANDSMEN'S RELATIVES

The Amalgamated Musicians' Union, in conjunction with the Sunday League, are arranging for a concert to be held at the Queen's Hall on Sunday afternoon, May 5, in aid of the relatives of the heroic bandsmen who perished on the Titanic. There will be an orchestra of 500.

NEW PRODUCTION

"Arms and the Girl" a new operetta composed by Mr Richard Fall, will be produced at the Titanic matinee at the Hippodrome next Tuesday at a cost of £4,000.

It was originally intended for a later debut, but has been "speeded up" in view of the matinee.

BOATS FOR ALL

Decision of the Shipping Companies

STATEMENT IN THE COMMONS

In the House of Commons yesterday Mr Sydney Buxton announced the decision of the shipping companies with whom the Board of Trade was in consultation.

The companies, he said, had decided to provide boats and rafts sufficient to accommodate all on board.

There had been great difficulty to obtain a sufficient number of boats of the required kind owing to the great demand, but the vessels were to be equipped with an adequate number at the earliest possible moment.

This decision was come to voluntarily and not as a result of representations made by the Board of Trade.

The effect of the criticisms as to the inadequacy of boats carried by liners has led to an extraordinary boom in the building of lifeboats.

In Liverpool during the past two or three days orders have poured into boat builders from all the leading steamship companies in Liverpool, and day and night shifts are arranged in order to cope with the demand. None of the builders had any surplus stock, and considerably advanced prices are being obtained for boats.

THE RELIEF FUNDS

The Mansion House Fund last night totalled £115,000. Subscriptions received yesterday included 100 guineas from the Queen of Norway and £500 from the Allan Line.

In New York Mayor Gaynor's fund amounted to over £20,000, and the Mayor of Southampton's fund exceeded £14,700.

The Liverpool fund totalled £12,000 last night.

BIRTHPLACE OF THE LATE MR W. T. STEAD

The birthplace of the late Mr W. T. Stead, the veteran journalist who perished in the Titanic disaster. Situated in the parish of Embleton, 7 miles from North-East Alnwick, the building possessed much historic interest. It was here that the great scholar Duns Scotus was born.

DAILY SKETCH.

No. 976.—THURSDAY, APRIL 25, 1912.   THE PREMIER PICTURE PAPER.   [Registered as a Newspaper.]   ONE HALFPENNY.

FIREMEN REFUSE TO SAIL ON BOARD THE OLYMPIC.

Firemen leaving the Olympic with their bundles yesterday, five minutes before the liner was due to depart. According to one report as many as 200 men refused to sail owing to lives were as important as those of any their dissatisfaction with the collapsible boats provided. One of the strikers, a single man, said that he was ready to sail, but a number of his comrades were married men, and their first-class passenger on board.

(1) An official addressing the strikers on the quayside. (2) Some of the firemen photographed as they left with their kits. The firemen tried to persuade the deck hands to join them, but their attempts were frustrated by the removal of the gangways.

"TEDDY SMITH HERO"

Boyhood Recollections of Titanic's Captain

"A GENIAL SCHOOLFELLOW"

"Teddy Smith has gone down with his ship, and out of the six of us lads who used to be schoolmates together only one is now left – myself."

From every corner of England Mrs Smith, the widow of the gallant captain of the Titanic who went so bravely to his death in the icy waste of the North Atlantic, has received letters of sympathy and support in her time of trial. He was known to thousands who have crossed the Atlantic in vessels under his command – millionaires and princes of commerce, ambassadors and leaders of life in a hundred directions. But of his boyhood friends few remain to mourn his loss, and of those is Mr William Jones, of Edmund-street, Hanley, Stoke-on-Trent.

Ted Smith was a Hanley boy, and in the words of Mr Jones he was "a genial and good schoolfellow; one always ready to give a kind of helping hand in any way to his mates."

Something like 48 years ago he was a scholar at Etruria, the school which the great and good Wedgwood, the potter of world-wide fame, established and maintained in Staffordshire.

"My memory," says Mr Jones, "brings back many happy days spent with him at school, and also many happy hours before and after school-time. There were six of us in those days – six firm friends who stuck together, and Smith was the staunchest of us all. I remember how Vincent Simpson used to call on me first, and how we would call for Johnny Leonard. Then the three of us would knock at Ted Smith's door, and having collected the others we would run down Mill-street and Etruria-road to school.

ALWAYS READY TO HELP

"Four died peaceful deaths – I was at the bedside of three of them when they passed away. Ted Smith passed away just as he would have loved to do. To stand on the bridge of his vessel and go down with her was characteristic of all his actions when we were boys together.

He was a brave soul as a boy. He was always ready to help and give of his best. I have not seen him for some years; the last time was when he was on a visit here to his brother-in-law. He was then captain of the Majestic, and had been, I think he said, only two or three voyages with her. He was the same fine healthy spirit as in his schooldays.

I cannot express my contempt for those who so cowardly reported that he committed suicide before the Titanic sank. Ted Smith commit suicide in the face of danger? His whole life as I know it, and especially when he and I were boys together, gives the lie direct to such a report.

I think if any man had dared to predict face to face with Ted Smith that if at any time he should be faced with such an emergency as that with which he met his death and had suggested that he would take his life that man would be minus a few teeth before the words were well out of his mouth."

One of Mr Jones' most treasured possessions is a faded photograph of the group of the six lads who went daily to Etruria school, in which the bright, determined face of the boy who was to be the leading figure in the world's greatest maritime disaster stands out conspicuously.

MEMORIAL TO BANDMASTER

It was decided yesterday at a meeting held at Colne to open a fund for the purpose of erecting a memorial to Mr Wallace Hartley, bandmaster of the Titanic, who was a native of that town.

The Mansion House Fund last night amounted to £138,000.

LINER STRIKES PIER

Consternation Amongst Mauretania's Passengers

NEW YORK WEDNESDAY

The Liner Mauretania, in leaving the harbour to-day, struck the head of the pier, causing consternation among the passengers. Fortunately only very slight damage was done.

The liner carried a number of extra lifeboats and rafts.

STEWARDESSES SAVED FROM THE WRECK

Miss M. Sloan, of Belfast

Mrs K. Gold, of Woolwich

Two of the stewardesses who were saved from the Titanic. Miss Sloan was previously on the Olympic. This is Mrs Gold's third experience of shipping accidents. She was on the Suevic when that vessel was wrecked, next on the Olympic during the collision with the Hawke, and now she has been rescued from the greatest maritime disaster in history.

LOST AND SAVED ON THE TITANIC

The President of the Board of Trade has issued the following particulars showing the numbers saved, and percentages, of each class and sex of passengers on the Titanic:-

	FIRST CLASS PASSSENGERS.			SECOND CLASS PASSENGERS.			THIRD CLASS PASSENGERS.		
	CARRIED.	SAVED.	Per Cent. SAVED.	CARRIED.	SAVED	Per Cent. SAVED.	CARRIED.	SAVED.	Per Cent. SAVED.
Men	173	58	34	160	13	8	454	55	12
Women	144	139	97	93	78	84	179	98	55
Children	5	5	100	24	24	100	76	23	30
Total	322	202	63	277	115	42	709	176	25

	TOTAL PASSENGERS. FIRST, SECOND, and THIRD CLASSES.			CREW.			TOTAL PASSENGERS and CREW.		
	CARRIED.	SAVED.	Per Cent. SAVED.	CARRIED.	SAVED.	Per Cent. SAVED.	CARRIED.	SAVED.	Per Cent. SAVED.
Men	787	126	16	875	189	22	1,662	315	19
Women	416	315	76	23	21	91	439	336	77
Children	105	52	49	—	—	—	105	52	49
Total	1,308	493	38	898	210	23	2,206	703	32

FIFTH OFFICER'S ORDERS

Peremptory Advice to Mr Ismay

PECULIAR EVIDENCE

Difficult to Get Enough People to Fill Boats

"Get to hell out of this" was the advice peremptorily given to Mr Bruce Ismay by Mr G. Lowe, the fifth officer of the Titanic, when the Chairman of the White Star Line was repeatedly urging him to lower away the lifeboats before the liner sank.

In stating this in evidence yesterday before the Senatorial Commission at Washington, Mr Lowe admitted that at the time he did not know to whom he was talking, but Mr Ismay walked away and assisted at another boat.

The discipline on board was excellent, said Mr Lowe, for 19 boats were sent away together, but it was difficult to get enough people to fill them. Towards the last there were no women available, and three of the boats contained men and women in equal numbers.

DOORS STORMED

Society Women Overpower Inquiry Officials

Further remarkable scenes marked the resumption of the inquiry. The doors of the Senate building were stormed by a crowd of society women, attracted by a widely-spread report that Mr Bruce Ismay would be among the day's witnesses.

The door-keepers were overpowered, and the women poured into the inquiry room, where they quickly filled the seats reserved for the Press and even those set apart for the investigating committee. The services of ten policemen were required before the ladies could be moved from their positions.

Frederick Fleet, the look-out man, was first called to continue his evidence. Senator Burton asked him how soon the ship changed her course after he sounded the alarm. He replied that the course was not changed until after he had gone to the telephone.

That was about seven bells. The impact came a few minutes later, the vessel striking the berg at a spot about 50 feet from her bow. The collision was apparently underneath rather than at the side of the ship.

Mr Lowe then gave evidence, and, questioned as to the speed of the Titanic, declared that she could have travelled at 24 or 25 knots had she been required to do so. He was submitted to half an hour's detailed examination regarding the rules in force on the liner, and stated that there was no boat drill after the liner left Southampton.

Mr Lowe indignantly denied that he had been drinking on the night of the disaster. He was not a drinker. After the collision occurred he got out a revolver.

IN THE HEAT OF THE MOMENT

Why? – You never know when you will need it.

He took charge of the launching of lifeboat No 5, said Mr Lowe. Mr Ismay, whom he did not know at the time, was present, and seemed over-anxious and excited. Mr Ismay kept repeatedly urging him to "lower away." He resented Mr Ismay's interference, and in the heat of the moment exclaimed: "If you will get the hell out of this I shall be able to do so."

Mr Ismay made no reply, but walked away and assisted at boat No 3. He believed there were fifty people in the first boat lowered, including ten men. Five men were necessary to man it.

The discipline was excellent, nineteen boats being got away at the same time. He understood that the one collapsible boat which did not get away in time was cut away bottom side uppermost.

Replying to Senator Smith, witness admitted that all the sailors were not available at their stations when the order was given to clear the boats.

SEARCHING AMONG THE WRECKAGE

After the Titanic sank he transferred some of the passengers from his boat to another, and then returned to where the wreckage was floating. He picked up four persons alive. One of them was Mr Hoyt, of New York, who was bleeding from the nose and mouth and afterwards died.

Mr Lowe said he saw no females in the wreckage.

OLYMPIC HELD UP IN SOUTHAMPTON WATER: FIREMEN O

A remarkable development of the Titanic disaster occurred when the Olympic should have sailed from Southampton yesterday. The firemen filed off the boat by the only remaining gangway, and alleged that some of the new collapsible boats which had been provided were not seaworthy. In the morning the Board of Trade officials had inspected every detail, and Captain Clark, the Government Inspector (standing in the boat) is seen making his tour of the boats. He made several suggestions which were acted upon.

Inspection of the Olympic crew before sailing.

Adjusting the pulleys for lowering a boat.

Launching a lifeboat from the boat de
height from which the boats have to b
that would have to be exercise

TO THE BOATS AND LEAVE THE SHIP AT LAST MINUTE.

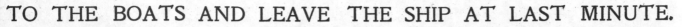

The Olympic crew at lifeboat drill yesterday morning in preparation for departure. They are seen wearing cork jackets while handling the tackle in a lifeboat.

er. The photograph shows the great Olympic, and gives an idea of the care the craft when full of passengers.

Seamen handing out lifebelts at the morning drill.

The collapsible boats to which exception was taken by the firemen.

At daybreak he took on board, from an overturned collapsible boat, twenty men and one woman. The woman was Mrs Henry B. Harris, of New York, one of whose arms was broken. Three people found clinging to the boat were dead.

"It would have been suicide," said Mr Lowe, "for us to go back into the zone where the 1,500 people, whose cries we heard, were drowning. I did my best, and went as near the scene as I dared. I am not ashamed of what I did."

"WOMEN WENT DOWN. I SHOULD"

The second officer, Mr Lightoller, said that Mr Ismay, when on board the Carpathia, had expressed his regret at having been saved, and added that he should have remained on board and gone down with the Titanic.

The second officer told the Committee that Mr Ismay's words were: "I ought to have gone down with the ship. Women went down. I should."

THE MYSTERY OF THE LIGHTS

Could They have Been Those of The Californian

It will be remembered that when he arrived at Liverpool on Saturday Captain Gambell of the Virginian said:-

"At 5.45 a.m. I was in communication with the Leyland liner Californian. She was 17 miles north of the Titanic, and had not heard anything of the disaster. I sent a Marconigram to her as follows: 'Titanic struck iceberg, wants assistance urgently, ship sinking, passengers in boats, her position lat. 41.46, long. 50.14.'

"At 6.10 a.m. I sent a Marconigram to the Californian 'Kindly let me know condition of affairs when you get to the Titanic.' She at once replied: 'Can now see Carpathia taking passengers on board from small boats. Titanic foundered about 2 a.m.'

"At 1.0 p.m. I saw a steamer to the eastward, presumably the Californian? at the position of the wreck, but the ice-field was between us and too heavy to take any ship through without incurring great risk of damage."

It will be noted that the Captain of the Californian says: "We saw no signals whatever." That being the case it is hardly likely that the lights seen on the Titanic were those of the Californian. If the Titanic could see the Californian's lights the Californian (it would be natural to assume) would see the Titanic's rockets.

HUNDREDS OF MILES AWAY

One suggestion is that the lights seen from the Titanic were those of the Hellig Olav, a Danish liner, which arrived in New York on April 17th. Senator Smith, who is presiding at the Senatorial inquiry, mentioned the name of this vessel in a question he put. However, her captain is said to have declared that he was hundreds of miles away from the Titanic when she sank.

The Hellig Olav is a passenger steamer of over 10,000 tons, plying between New York and Copenhagen. She was built at Glasgow, and is owned by Det Forenede Dampskibsselskab, of Copenhagen.

Their London agents are the United Shipping Company of 108, Fenchurch-street, but up to yesterday the directors had no news that would throw any light upon the exact position of the Helig Olav on the night of the disaster.

The Danish boat is equipped with an up-to-date Marconi wireless installation, and carries one operator.

CLASPING CHILDREN

Liner Sights Masses of Floating Corpses

NEW YORK Wednesday

The North German liner Bremen, which arrived here this morning, reports having passed seven icebergs on Saturday last in the locality where the Titanic disaster occurred.

Many bodies were seen floating in the water around the spot where the liner sank. All bore lifebelts.

Some of them are described as clasping the bodies of children, and others as still gripping deck chairs and other objects. The officers of the Bremen estimated that in one group there were two hundred corpses.

HELP NEAR ALL THE TIME

Californian Was In Icefield With Titanic

BUT WIRELESS COMMUNICATION HAD BEEN CUT OFF

We could not have been more than nineteen miles distant from the Titanic at half-past ten on the Sunday night. – Capt. Lord, of the Leyland liner Californian.

The good fortune that enabled the Carpathia to pick up the Titanic's distress signal – the Carpathia's wireless operator was off duty and had gone into the wireless room on unofficial business – is offset by the harrowing ill-luck which prevented the Californian from getting to the scene of the disaster before the liner sank.

Had the Californian caught one of the early distress signals everybody on the great White Star liner might have been saved.

Why Captain Lord did not hear of the Titanic's peril till it was too late is explained in a Central News message from New York yesterday. It said:-

"A telegram from Boston, Mass., states that the vessel whose lights loomed in the eyes of the hundreds perishing on board the Titanic was undoubtably the Leyland liner Californian.

The master, Captain Lord, who was interviewed on the arrival of the steamer, said:-

'We could not have been more than nineteen miles distant from the Titanic at half-past ten on the Sunday night. We had steamed into an immense icefield, and, in order to insure the safety of the vessel, the engines were shut off, and the wireless apparatus being cut off we thus knew nothing of the plight of the Titanic until we received wireless messages at daylight. We saw no signals whatever.'"

WHERE WERE THE WOMEN?

At the Titanic inquiry a passenger, Major Peuchen, made an observation which may partly answer the question: Where were the women and child victims when the last lifeboat left? Maj Peuchen suggested that they had not answered to the alarm in time to get on deck before the boats had gone.

PSYCHIC WARNINGS

Lady's Previous Description of Titanic Disaster

"It is easy to prophesy after the event" is the rather inaccurate but very common comment on "warnings" which are mentioned too late to be of any practical use. There have been a number of such premonitions mentioned since the Titanic went to the bottom of the Atlantic. Our postbag brings one or two every day. One more detailed than most, however, arrived yesterday, and as there is no reason for doubting the bona-fides of our correspondent – whose name and address we have – we give it for what it is worth.

"On Wednesday, April 3rd, a lady whom I will call Mrs A., who possesses remarkable psychic gifts, was at a lecture in this city. The lecturer, at the conclusion of his address, asked Mrs A. where she had been wandering during the time of his address, as he noticed her apparently disinterested. She replied, "I wish you had seen what I was seeing during the time you have been lecturing. I am sure that something dreadful will happen very shortly." Asked for particulars, Mrs A. then told some of her friends that she had seen a vision of a railway accident, then a mansion ablaze, thirdly a colliery explosion, and lastly a four-funnelled steamship in collision with a mountain of ice.

"The name of the vessel appeared as 'Tintac' and she distinctly heard Southampton called out, but had no idea that a vessel of that name was likely to sail in the near future; otherwise, she certainly would have made it known.

"It appeared to be dark, except that the ice shone brightly." She was interrupted by the meeting being brought to a close, otherwise no doubt more would have been given to her. After relating her experience to her friends, they made up their minds to watch the newspapers to see if anything like the incidents in the vision occurred.

I am informed by Mrs A. that it is quite a common experience to have visions of different incidents weeks and months before coming to pass. She related many incidents that she had had visions long before they had actually become facts. Three especially were the Berlin disaster, the Hawes Junction railway disaster at Christmas, and the outrage in connection with King Alfonso's wedding.

I asked her why she did not make it publicly known; she made the remark that the general public mind was not ready to accept these visions as genuine previous to them becoming facts. Mrs A. believes that both railway accidents, shipwrecks, etc., can be reduced to a minimum when people are willing to accept the warnings given.

WHAT MIGHT HAVE BEEN

The Hamburg-American steamer Ypiranga, which arrived at Plymouth yesterday from Mexico and West Indian ports, would have been within an hour or two hour's steaming from the Titanic when she went down, but for the receipt on the previous day of a wireless message from Cape Race that the German steamer Augsburg was drifting helplessly in mid-Atlantic. The Ypiranga went south searching for her, and on Sunday received the Titanic's call. She rushed at top speed to the aid of the sinking liner, but when within 50 miles heard she was too late.

LIFEBOAT STRIKE

Liner Olympic Held Up By Firemen

DRAMATIC SCENE

Dissatisfaction With Some of the "Collapsibles"

A dramatic strike of firemen and greasers held up the White Star liner Olympic – the Titanic's sister ship – at Southampton yesterday.

The cause of the trouble was a belief entertained by a number of the men that some of the collapsible boats on the liner were not seaworthy. It was denied there was any foundation for this belief, and it was pointed out that the boats had been passed by the Board of Trade.

However, the men were not reassured, and an attempt was made to call out the deck hands, but

before it had any chance of succeeding the gangways were removed, and the Olympic was taken to Cowes Roads, there to await the men she required.

The strikers numbered well over 200.

It will be remembered that, as a result of the Titanic disaster, the boat accommodation of the Olympic was greatly increased. A number of the additional boats were of the collapsible kind.

AMAZED PASSENGERS

The strike did not begin until a few moments before the liner was ready to sail.

All the passengers, 1,400 in number, among them the Duke of Sutherland, were on board; the gangways had been withdrawn with one exception; eight bells rang; and everything was in readiness for the vessel to depart.

Then, from the ship's forecastle, several of the firemen's kits were flung overboard. Everyone on the ship and on the shore wondered what the matter was.

A few moments later, to the amazement of everybody, a large number of firemen and stokers began to file down the only remaining gangway.

Asked why they had left the ship, they alleged that some of the collapsible boats that had been placed on the Olympic were not seaworthy. They declared that unless these boats were replaced by regulation lifeboats they would decline to sail.

Mr Curry, the local manager of the White Star Line, addressed the men. He pointed out that the boats carried by the Olympic were in excess of the requirements of the Board of Trade. Moreover, all the boats had been examined by the officials of the Board of Trade and passed.

Mr A. Cannon, secretary of the British Seafarer's Union, also addressed the men. He said he would leave the matter entirely in their hands.

"THUMB THROUGH THE CANVAS"

It is stated that after the men left the liner a deputation of five firemen and five greasers waited upon Mr Curry, the local manager of the White Star Line, and in the presence of Commander Blake, the emigration officer, said they were not satisfied with the collapsible boats. They alleged that a fireman, while examining the boats, put his thumb through the canvas of one of them.

Commander Blake said he had made an examination of the boats, and was perfectly satisfied with them.

He offered to take the Olympic down to Cowes, to let the men select any boats they pleased, and to give a demonstration of their seaworthiness. This offer the men refused to accept. One of their number expressed the fear that if they went on board again they would not be allowed to leave.

Mr Curry said he would then give the men five minutes to decide on their course of action. They thereupon held a meeting on the quay, with the result that they unanimously decided not to return to the ship.

The officials of the White Star Line called for volunteers for the stokehold from among the crowds of men on the quay, and about twenty men stepped forward and went on board. The whole of the deck hands remained on the ship.

After the delay of over an hour the Olympic was towed down Southampton Water, where she remained until other firemen could be secured to work her. The whole of the passengers remained on board.

After the vessel's departure the dissatisfied firemen left the dock in procession.

At nine o'clock last night a tug left Southampton with forty firemen on board for the Olympic.

In reply to a message from the seamen on the Olympic, "Shall crew proceed on Olympic? Sailors await your decision," the Southampton officials of the British Seafarer's Union wired last night: "No. Union will support you."

The Olympic firemen held a meeting last night and determined to continue the stand they had taken up for better lifeboat accommodation.

The Olympic was still at anchor off Spithead at a late hour.

LEADING STOKER'S VIEW

Leading Stoker Gregory, who was one of the men's spokesmen, told a reporter that for himself he didn't care, as he was unmarried; but many of the men had wives and families, and their lives were as valuable as those of the first-class passengers.

HOMES FOR ORPHANS

Lady Offers to Adopt Little Girl

One of the many children who has been rendered fatherless by the Titanic disaster has been offered a home. One of our readers is anxious to adopt a little girl, and we are glad to give publicity to her letter:-

"As there are so many orphans through the Titanic disaster, I should very much like to receive a little girl into my home to bring her up as my daughter. I am comfortably situated and the child would be well cared for and educated.

I should prefer one of about eight or ten years old who has lost both parents, or one of a large family whose mother would find it difficult to provide for all. I should be much obliged to you if you could kindly help me in getting one."

Our correspondent's name is Mrs Hastings, and her address, 249, Saffron-lane, Aylestone Park, Leicester.

Strange that this letter should be a virtual copy of a letter which appeared two days earlier (See page 101), but from a different writer and address. Most odd.

Mr Fegan, founder of "Mr Fegan's Homes" has written to the Lord Mayor offering on behalf of the council of these institutions to receive ten necessitous boys under 14 years of age into one of the orphanages in Buckinghamshire, and ten boys over 14 years of age on the training farm in Kent to be prepared for emigration to Canada next spring; and to the Lord Mayor of Southampton making a similar offer for the same number of orphan boys belonging to that town.

The shipwrecked Sailors and Families Gift Society makes a special appeal for suitable clothing of all kinds for the widows and orphans of the men who perished. Parcels should be sent to Mr J. E. Dawe, hon. agent, Shipwrecked Mariners Society, R. G. Artillery Drill Hall, St Mary's-road, Southampton.

WHY WE ASK FOR THE SHILLINGS OF THE PEOPLE

The picture appeals more eloquently than words to the sympathies of our readers. Here are a young mother and her five children, widowed and fatherless through the dreadful disaster to the greatest ship on earth. Mrs Warren is showing her brother, a postman, a message she has received confirming her loss. She lives at 71, St. Paul's-road, Southsea, and there and in Southampton and Portsmouth are many such families upon whom the icy hand of death lies heavily.

It is for the widows and the fatherless that we ask your aid. Their need is great and urgent. The Daily Sketch Shilling Fund was started to collect the shillings and pence of the people. When the Shilling Fund is closed the total will be sent to swell the Lord Mayor of London's fund for the relief of sufferers through the disaster.

Many rich men have given in a single subscription as much as our fund will raise, but their donations do not mean as much to them as a shilling does to the man with a pound a week. We are proud to say that the greater part of our Shilling Fund has been subscribed by people who could ill afford to give anything, but *did* give, because their hearts were full of compassion for their fellow-workers who perished in the dark Atlantic. If you have not yet subscribed to the Shilling Fund, will you please do so *to-day*? Address your contribution, large or small, to

The Cashier, "Titanic Fund" *Daily Sketch*, 17, Tudor-street. London. E.C.

TITANIC'S LOOK-OUT MEN ON NIGHT OF DISASTER

Frederick Fleet and G. Simonds, two of the Titanic's look-out men. Fleet, who was on duty at the time of the collision, told a remarkable story before the American Court that is investigating the disaster. He said that during his watch he reported a dark mass right ahead to the bridge, and sounded a warning by striking on a gong three times, but the ship was not stopped. The look-out men were not supplied with glasses, the witness added, although they asked for them. If they had had them they would have seen the ice sooner, and in time enough to get away from it.

"NOT A MOMENT'S DELAY"

President of Board of Trade and Titanic Inquiry

A large number of questions arising out of the Titanic inquiry were asked the President of the Board of Trade in the House of Commons yesterday, who, in reply, said the points raised would all be considered when the new regulations were framed.

"There will not," he added, "be a moment's delay in preparing and issuing revised regulations with regard to the number of boats and lifesaving appliances, but in so complicated a matter it is desirable to act in the light of the fullest information and the best expert advice. My expert advisers are at work on the subject, and I hope to receive a report from them and also from the Advisory Committee shortly. It will not be necessary to wait for the final report of the Advisory Committee before issuing regulations."

Asked whether, in view of the fact that only two-thirds of the lifeboat accommodation was used, it could be regarded as an established fact that a greater number of lifeboats would have saved more people, Mr Buxton said that was one of the facts on which further information was desired.

Mr W. Thorne: Is it imperative that lookout glasses should be supplied to the men on watch? The Speaker: That does not arise on this question.

Replying to another question Mr Buxton said according to information at present available the total number of women and children who perished was 156.

The Postmaster-General said he had called for reports relating to all wireless messages exchanged in connection with the Titanic disaster, and hoped to have them available by the end of the present week. Under the Berlin Convention all calls for distress had precedence of other messages.

Postcard: Author's collection

One of the many postcards issued in 1912 to raise funds for the relief of sufferers of the Titanic Disaster.

DAILY SKETCH.

No. 977.—FRIDAY, APRIL 26, 1912. THE PREMIER PICTURE PAPER. [Registered as a Newspaper.] ONE HALFPENNY.

THE FATAL ICEBERG: PHOTOGRAPH ON DAY OF DISASTER.

The gigantic iceberg believed to be that with which the Titanic collided. The photograph was taken at seven o'clock on the morning of the disaster by Mr. Nielsen, chief officer of the s.s. Birma, formerly the Arundel Castle, which was the first vessel to pick up the Titanic's wireless call for assistance. About daylight the Birma reached the position given them by the Titanic, after passing bergs of enormous size and steaming through fields of ice. It was then learned that the scene of the wreck was north of the floe, and the Birma steamed round to find the Carpathia taking on board survivors. As all offers of help were declined by the Carpathia the Birma resumed her interrupted voyage, but before doing so Chief Officer Nielsen took the above photograph from the bridge of his vessel.

SENATOR SMITH

In Disagreement With His Colleagues

TITANIC WITNESSES IN A PECULIAR POSITION

Mr Marconi Examined as to The Holding-Up of News

The proceedings of the Senatorial inquiry at Washington into the Titanic disaster threaten to come to a premature close, says an American telegram, owing to a disagreement which has arisen between Senator Smith and his colleagues over whom he is presiding.

The dispute has come about through the protests of Mr Ismay, the officers of the wrecked liner, and others against Senator Smith's expressed determination to keep all of them in America until the principal witnesses have been examined.

In respect of Quartermaster Hichens the other members of the Senate Committee have already overruled their chairman and the quartermaster is to be allowed to return to this country.

Mr Marconi was the first witness heard, and he was questioned very closely concerning the allegation that instructions had been sent to the Carpathia's wireless operator to hold up the news of the disaster.

While admitting that the operator had been ordered to keep back the "news story," Mr Marconi said these instructions referred only to a personal interview and not to the official account of the sinking of the liner.

Messrs. Harland and Wolff yesterday received a telegram announcing that one of their apprentices, whose name appeared in the list of survivors, has not been saved. Every member of their staff on board the Titanic lost his life.

S.O.S. This is the wireless signal for help that the sinking Titanic sent out. It also means Send On Shillings to the Daily Sketch Fund for the fatherless and widows.

500 DOLLARS

Price Paid for Mr Bride's Narrative

WASHINGTON Thursday

The Senatorial inquiry into the Titanic inquiry into the Titanic disaster threatens to come to grief owing to a disagreement which has arisen between the presiding Senator, Mr Smith, and his colleagues with regard to the detention of White Star officers and employees.

Senator Smith says he is determined to keep all of them in this country until the forty principal witnesses have been heard. Against this action Mr Ismay, Mr Franklin, and the officers, wireless operators; and sailors strongly protest, and the other members of the Senate Committee have already overruled Mr Smith in respect of Quartermaster Hichins, who is being allowed to return to England.

When the inquiry resumed this morning Mr Marconi took his place in the witness stand. He said the wireless station at Cape Race was capable of communication with ships having wireless installations similar to that on the Titanic and Olympic up to a distance of twelve to fifteen hundred miles.

Mr Marconi was closely questioned regarding the alleged instructions to the Carpathia's operator to hold up news of the disaster. He admitted that a wireless message was sent to Mr Cottam, the operator on the Carpathia, which read: "Hold news story disaster for four figures."

This telegram, however, was not sent until the Carpathia was off Sandy Hook, and it referred not to a general story of the disaster by wireless but to a personal interview.

Mr Marconi denied that he had authorised his operators to sell exclusive stories to newspapers.

He understood that Mr Bride, the surviving operator on the Titanic, was paid five hundred dollars for his narrative by a New York paper.

The Mansion House fund last night amounted to £147,000.

THE HEROIC ENGINEERS WHO WENT DOWN TO A MAN.

Back row—W. ...., junior fifth engineer, F. Parsons, senior fifth engineer.
Middle row—second F. Coy, junior assistant third engineer, B. Wilson, senior assistant second engineer, L. Hodgkinson, senior fourth engineer, A. Ward, junior assistant fourth engineer, J. Shepherd, junior assistant second engineer, H. Harrie, junior assistant second engineer, H. Dyer, senior assistant fourth engineer, R. Miller, junior fifth engineer.

P. Sloan, senior electrician, H. Jupe, assistant electrician.

Bottom row—J. Hesketh, second engineer, G. Hosking, second senior third engineer.

"Then, at the last, we'll get to port an' hoist their baggage clear—
The passengers, wi' g'oves and canes—an' this is what I'll hear:
'Well, thank ye for a pleasant voyage. The tender's comin' now,'
While I go testin' follower-bolts an' watch the skipper bow.
They've words for every one but me—shake hands wi' half the crew,
Except the dour Scots engineer, the man they never knew.
An' yet I like the wark, for all we've dam few pickin's here—
No pension an' the most we earn's four hunder pound a year." "McAndrew's Hymn," by Rudyard Kipling

The belated tribute to the heroism of the engineers who, far beneath the decks where the dramatic manning of the boats was taking place, were wrestling with the broken engines of the mighty Titanic when death came to them, has induced us to reproduce the group photograph of White Star engineers taken on board the Olympic a few months ago. All the men marked X had been transferred to the new boat, and none survive. Since publishing the photograph previously we have secured the names.

Captain Stanley Lord (with telescope), who has reported that on the night the Titanic foundered the Californian was only seventeen miles distant. Beside him is Mr. Stewart, chief officer, and standing behind are the second and third officers. Their Marconi apparatus was not working until dawn.

A deputation from the Olympic firemen who left the ship because they were dissatisfied with the collapsible lifeboats provided watching from a tug the boats being tested by the Board of Trade officials yesterday. The tests were made off Ryde, Isle of Wight, where the Olympic was held up owing to the strike.

Printed and Published by E. HULTON and CO., LIMITED, London and Manchester.—FRIDAY, APRIL 26, 1912.

THE FATAL BERG

Photographed by Officer of Russian Ship

We publish to-day a photograph of the iceberg which (there is every reason to believe) collided with the Titanic. It is suggested that the break in the middle of the berg was caused by the liner. The photograph was taken by First Officer Nielson, of the Russian liner Birma, which reached the scene of the catastrophe in the morning.

The Birma made a desperate attempt to reach the scene in time to be of assistance. She was in communication with the Titanic shortly before twelve o'clock, and was then about one hundred miles away. When, after daylight, they reached the position given them over the wireless, they found it was wrong. Then they heard that the Carpathia was picking up bodies.

The Birma is fitted with the De Forest system of wireless telegraphy, and her officers and her two wireless operators have put their signatures to a startling statement (published in the *Daily Telegraph*) as to the relations which sometimes obtain between vessels using this system and those using the Marconi apparatus.

According to this statement, when the Birma offered to help the Carpathia the reply "Stand by" was received. When provisions were offered the answer was "Shut up."

"This," the statement continues, "is vouched for by the two operators. Mr Ward is an experienced telegraphist who would make no mistake, and the same signal came to us many times in the subsequent attempts to gain or give information.

"It is a known fact that the Marconi Company will give no information to any ship not Marconi-manned, nor answer its calls, unless the ship is in distress. This may be a commercially fair system, but at the same time, while our ship was not in distress, we were trying to help. When it was found that our help was not needed, there came no word of thanks, no reply to our question as to whether more boats might be adrift, but only a salute from the flag at the stern of the Carpathia as she steamed on her way to the west.

"All day, and days following, we were refused any information. Every ship we spoke to replied: 'Are you a Marconi ship? If not we have orders to give you no information.' This after the energy of our officers and crew and the thirty hours' vigil day and night to help!

We firmly believe, and have convinced the officers of this ship, that the error lies not with the management of the Marconi Company, but with the employees on the ships. These men are in a more or less subordinate position, and tied by hard and fast rules, and it is even to an extent excusable that an operator, in the midst of the hustle and excitement – perhaps with the memory of the famed Jack Binns, of the Republic disaster, in mind – exceeded his authority or good judgement in forcing the rule of keeping other ships 'incommunicado' at a time when a man of riper judgement would have set rules aside in the common eagerness to help save life."

"DRESSED AS A SAILOR"

Extraordinary Story of One of the Survivors

VIENNA Thursday

Mme. Cardeza, whose husband and mother-in-law were among the survivors of the Titanic disaster, will go to New York to-day in order to accompany her husband on the homeward voyage.

She has received, it is stated, a letter from her husband in which he says that he bribed two sailors to give him sailor's clothing.

He and his secretary, dressed in these clothes, with his mother and her companion, succeeded in gaining the lifeboat, as they were supposed to be sailors.

LEEDS CHOIR TO SING TITANIC REQUIEM IN PARIS

The famous Leeds Choir (250) members travelled to London yesterday morning and left London Bridge station in the afternoon for Paris, where they are to give a series of concerts in the Fetes Hall of the Trocadero. This evening they will sing "Nearer, my God, to Thee," at the opening concert. Our pictures were taken as the special train left yesterday. In the centre of the group are Mr H.A. Fricker, chorus master, and Mr J. H. Green, secretary. *Daily Sketch* Photographs.

THE DOUBTING FIREMEN. WHERE THE TITANIC PLOUGHED ITS WA'

Members of the Olympic's crew waiting to board a special tug to take them to
their vessel should their deputation report favourably on the tests made of the
Olympic's lifeboats.

A break in the huge iceberg which it is suggested was made by the Titanic. Mr. Charles Edward Walte
American journalist on board the Birma, writes, in a description of the scene: "The icebergs such as we pa
the south-westerly side of the floe were photographed, but, owing to the distance, the picturé is not clear
largest bergs were on the south and north-easterly side, but, while a magnificent sight, they could have litt
ing on the tragedy, as the ice-floe lay between them and the course of the Titanic. Hence it is obvious that
the bergs we photographed on the easterly side must have caused the disaster. The ice-floe was larger th
boat at dawn, that field of ice

Mr. J. Cannon, the chief wireless operator on
the Birma, and his bride. He was married
just before he sailed. He is a London man,
and is making his first trip as an operator

At the memorial service on the Birma held on the Sunday following the wreck. The
captain and officers joined with the few Englishmen on board in honouring the dead. No
English flag being available, one was made by a member of the crew.

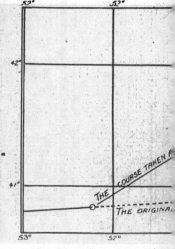

Track of the Birma after receiving the Tita
long and from three to twelve miles wide.
from 95 feet to 180 feet out of the water.
Birma steamed round the floe—dotted line—

APRIL 26, 1912.

OUGH BERG THAT SENT IT TO ITS DOOM.

TITANIC DEATH ROLL ANALYSED.

er been seen so early in the year in this part of the Atlantic, and the bergs extended as far south as 41deg."
e fatal berg was 140 feet high, 200 feet long, and it is estimated 980 feet under water. The photograph shows
e morning sun lighting up the grim relic in the lonely sea. The scene is thus described by Mrs. Brown, the wife
a Denver mineowner, who was one of the Titanic survivors: "The sun came up like a ball of red fire, lighting
the white peaks of the glassy bergs. Near us was open water, but on every side was ice ten feet high,
d to the right, left, back and front were icebergs. Imagine some artist able to picture what we saw from that
n playing on those giant icebergs."

First-Class Passengers.

173 MEN 58 Saved	*LOST*	Saved.
144 WOMEN 139 Saved	Saved.	
5 CHILDREN 5 Saved	Saved.	

Second-Class Passengers.

160 MEN 13 Saved	*LOST*	
93 WOMEN 78 Saved	*LOST*	Saved.
24 CHILDREN 24 Saved	Saved.	

Third-Class Passengers.

454 MEN 55 Saved	*LOST*	Saved
179 WOMEN 98 Saved	*LOST*	Saved.
76 CHILDREN 23 Saved	*LOST*	Saved.

Total Passengers.

785 MEN 126 Saved	*LOST*	Saved.
416 WOMEN 315 Saved	*LOST*	Saved.
105 CHILDREN 52 Saved	*LOST*	Saved.

Crew.

875 MEN 189 Saved	*LOST*	Saved.
23 WOMEN 21 Saved	*LOST*	Saved.

Total Passengers and Crew.

1 662 MEN 315 Saved	*LOST*	Saved.
439 WOMEN 336 Saved	*LOST*	Saved.
105 CHILDREN 52 Saved	*LOST*	Saved.

The number of women and children saved and lost in the Titanic disaster has been a subject of much discussion during the last few days. This striking diagram, based on the official returns, shows at a glance the proportion of men, women and children saved and lost in each class and among the crew.

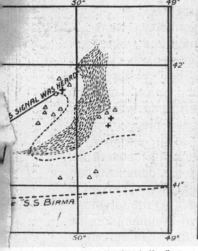

l. The ice floe shown in the chart is 69 miles
ngular marks represent icebergs ranging in height
e position indicated by the diagonal black line the
scene of the wreck, marked by two crosses.

The s.s. Birma, which is better known by her old name the Arundel Castle. She left New York
—bound for Rotterdam and Libau—three hours after the Carpathia. The photographs reproduced here and on page 1 were sent ashore off Dover when the vessel stopped specially for the
purpose.

The Seamen's Orphanage dog, a handsome St.
Bernard, familiar to ocean-going passengers
at Southampton, collecting for the Titanic
Relief Fund

"INSTANTANEOUS DEATH"

Surprising Report From Doctor On The Mackay Bennett

The following message has been received here by wireless from the cable ship Mackay Bennett:-

"Bodies are numerous in latitude 41.35 north, longitude 48.37 west, extending many miles both east and west. Mailships should give this region a wide berth.

"The medical opinion is that death has been instantaneous in all the cases, owing to the pressure when the bodies were drawn down in the vortex.

"We have been drifting in a dense fog since noon yesterday. The total number of bodies picked up is 205. We brought away all the embalming fluid in Halifax, which is enough for 70. With a week's fine weather we think we should pretty well clear up the relics of the disaster. In my opinion the majority of the bodies will never come to the surface."

The medical opinion (if correctly telegraphed) hardly coincides with the statement of Third Officer Pittman, that moans and cries were heard for an hour after the liner sank.

A Central News message says that the body identified as W. Vear is believed to be that of Mr W. T. Stead, and that reported as R. Butt is believed to be that of Major Butt.

THE INQUIRY'S LEGAL POSITION

In the House of Lords yesterday Lord Stanhope asked whether it was in accordance with the customs of International Law that an inquiry should be held in a foreign country into the loss of a vessel sailing under the British flag on the high seas, and whether the evidence which was being given in America would be admissible as evidence here.

Lord Morley, in reply, asked to be excused from discussing a situation so clearly unrivalled. There was no doubt that any State might institute an inquiry into the wreck of a foreign vessel in which the lives of its own subjects had been lost without a departure from International Law.

No communication had been made to the U.S. or to any other Government by England on the point on the admissibility of evidence. The Wreck Commissioner (Lord Mersey) would be able to receive any information that might be useful, and he would attach to it whatever weight he thought it deserved, quite independently of what might have happened elsewhere.

THE OLYMPIC STRIKE

Deputation Watch Test of Collapsible Boats

MEN ADVISED TO RETURN TO WORK

The "lifeboat strike" on the White Star liner Olympic is not yet over, but the firemen and stokers on strike have been recommended by a deputation from their union to return to the vessel this morning.

They will meet this morning to decide their course of action. The advice was tendered to the men after a demonstration of the seaworthiness of the collapsible boats taken on board since the Olympic's last voyage to America.

Complaining that the new boats were not seaworthy, nearly 300 firemen and stokers left the ship a few minutes before she was expected to sail on Wednesday, but yesterday a deputation from the Seafarers' Union visited the vessel as she lay at anchor off Ryde, waiting for additional firemen to take the place of those who had gone ashore, and in the company of Board of Trade officials watched lifeboat drills.

It was understood that if the demonstration was satisfactory to the deputation they would advise the strikers to go back to the Olympic. Last night on their return to Southampton the deputation announced that they had agreed to recommend the men return to work this morning, provided one of the collapsible boats, which they allege is unseaworthy, is replaced.

Mr P. E. Curry, the White Star manager at

Southampton, stated last night that the Berthon collapsible boats were all lowered, manned and rowed round to the satisfaction of the deputation, with the exception of one, which, after being in the water for two hours, was leaking a little. This boat was presumably slightly damaged in course of launching.

The White Star agent signed on a number of firemen at Portsmouth for the Olympic last night, and others have been obtained at Liverpool.

About 250 men left Sheffield last night to take service on the Olympic, if required, as stokers.

PASSENGERS' ALL-NIGHT WAIT

CHERBOURG Thursday

Several hundred passengers waited here yesterday evening to embark on the Olympic. They remained overnight, hoping for the vessel's arrival this morning.

LINERS CARRYING MORE BOATS

All Liverpool liners are being equipped with boats sufficient for all passengers and crew. The Baltic, with 1,343 passengers on board and the Lake Champlain with 800, sailed yesterday fully equipped with life-saving apparatus.

THE LATE MR STEAD

Eloquent Tribute At Memorial Service

An impressive memorial service for Mr W. T. Stead was held last night at Westminster Chapel, which was crowded in every part.

Queen Alexandra was represented by Major-General Brocklehurst, and among others present were Lord Haldane, Lord Esher, Lord Milner, Earl Grey, Mr Lloyd George, Mr John Burns, the Countess of Warwick, and Madame Novikoff. The Prime Minister was represented by Mr Eric Drummond.

The members of the family present were Dr Wilson (brother-in-law), representing the widow, Mr and Mrs Henry Stead, Mr Alfred Stead, Miss Pearl Stead, Dr J. E. Stead, and the Rev Herbert and Mrs Stead.

The service was conducted by Dr G. Campbell Morgan, and among the hymns sung was "Nearer, my God, to Thee."

Among the messages of sympathy which were read was one from Queen Alexandra, who telegraphed to Mrs Stead: "Do in my name let family know how much I grieve for them all."

Dr Clifford, who paid an eloquent tribute to the memory of a friend of a quarter of a century, was deeply affected. Many, he said, thought of Mr Stead as a journalist – brilliant, gifted, unconventional, rapid, accomplished, as a fountain of fresh and original ideas – yet to him Mr Stead was always a prophet.

A memorial service for Mr C. M. Hays, president of the Grand Trunk Railway, who was among the victims of the disaster, was held yesterday at the Church of St Edmund, Lombard-street, E.C.

BRITISH SEAMANSHIP

The importance of maintaining the supply of British seamen and the traditions of British seamanship is one of the most impressive reminders of the Titanic disaster.

In an article in the next number of the Sunday Chronicle Mr Frank T. Bullen, himself an old sailor, will discuss "The Decline of the Seaman Element in the Commercial Navy of Britain."

Miss Edna Lyall, a personal aquaintance of Mr Wallace Hartley, the Titanic bandmaster, will sing the hymn "Nearer, my God, to Thee" at the London Coliseum matinee on May 1.

HIPPODROME MATINEE

Amongst the fresh items on the programme of the Hippodrome Titanic matinee are the following:- Mr Cyril Maude, in "French as She is Spoke," and Mr Alfred Lester; Miss Clara Evelyn at the piano; Mr C. H. Workman and Mr Claude Fleming, in a duet from "Nightbirds"; Madame Alice Esty, Miss Mella Mars, Mr Herbert Sleath and Mr W. F. Grant, in "The Littlest Girl"; Mr Arthur Prince and Miss Constance Drever.

DAILY SKETCH.

No. 978.—SATURDAY, APRIL 27, 1912. THE PREMIER PICTURE PAPER. [Registered as a Newspaper.] ONE HALFPENNY.

OLYMPIC VOYAGE ABANDONED OWING TO MUTINY.

As a protest against the introduction of non-unionist firemen the Olympic's fifty seamen and quartermasters deserted and jumped into the tug which had brought the new firemen to the liner. Captain Haddock signalled to the cruiser Cochrane and the commander failed to persuade the deck hands to return to the Olympic. The shore police were sent for, and early yesterday the deserters were placed in custody and conveyed to Portsmouth, where they were remanded on bail. The first photograph shows the loyal firemen looking through the portholes of the great liner during the testing of one of the collapsible boats by the deputation. Below is a picture showing the position of the Olympic at Spithead, with the cruiser Cochrane to the right.—Photographs by Daily Sketch and Cribb.

CENTRAL FIGURE IN HISTORIC TRAGEDY

A hitherto unpublished portrait of Captain E. J. Smith, commander of the Titanic, who chose to share her fate.

OLYMPIC'S VOYAGE CANCELLED

Seamen's Dramatic Refusal To Sail

53 MEN ARRESTED

Appeal to Government for "Proper Punishment"

The revolt of the Olympic's "black squad" which arose out of dissatisfaction with some of the collapsible boats that were put on board after the loss of the Titanic, led to the liner's voyage being cancelled.

It will be remembered that nearly 300 firemen and greasers left the ship when she was about to sail from Southampton on Wednesday noon because, as they said, they considered some of the collapsible boats were not seaworthy.

A deputation from the firemen were taken out in a tug to witness a demonstration with the boats, and it was hoped that the men would be reassured.

However, as the dispute was not settled, batches of non-union firemen were taken aboard during Thursday night.

Soon afterwards a large number of deck hands and others jumped into the tug that had carried the firemen, and declared that they would not sail.

A dramatic incident followed. The Olympic signalled for assistance to the cruiser Cochrane.

Captain Goodenough, the commander of the cruiser, went on board the liner and told the strikers that their action was virtually a mutinous one.

This had no effect and police were fetched from Portsmouth. Over fifty seamen were taken into custody on a charge of refusing to obey orders.

When later in the day they were charged at the Police Court their counsel suggested that the men objected to sail with what was referred to as a "scratch crew." Counsel further implied that a number of the men were not satisfied with some of the lifeboats.

According to a statement by the White Star officials at Liverpool the passengers who booked berths on the Olympic will now have to be left to their own devices. It is believed that many will cross to Cherbourg and there join a German liner.

OFFICIAL STATEMENT

The managers of the White Star Line at Liverpool telegraphed to the Postmaster-General yesterday as follows:-

"Regret to inform you that, after shipping satisfactory engine-room crew, the deck and hitherto loyal men in the engine-room refused duty, asserting that they would not sail with substitute men.

Under these circumstances we have been compelled to order the Olympic back to Southampton and abandon voyage.

Earnestly hope you will secure for us official support in efforts we intend making, to secure the proper punishment of crew's mutinous behaviour, as unless firmness is shown now we despair of restoring discipline and maintain sailings."

A "SCRATCH CREW?"

Surprising Questions at the Police Court

The fifty-three men arrested on the Olympic were remanded at Portsmouth yesterday on a charge of unlawfully disobeying the commands of the master of the ship. They pleaded not guilty.

The majority of the men were seamen. Several of them were quartermasters. There were a few greasers and firemen and one storekeeper.

At first the defendants stood in two rows facing the magistrates, but they were afterwards provided with seats.

Mr C. Hiscock, of Southampton, appeared for the White Star Line. Mr C. A. Emanuel, barrister, on behalf of the British Seafarers' Union, represented the bulk of the defendants. Others of them were defended by Mr G. H. King, of Portsmouth.

Mr Hiscock explained that the men were charged under the Merchant Shipping Act, which provided that if any seaman was guilty of wilful disobedience to lawful command he should be liable to be imprisoned for a period not exceeding four weeks. Describing the circumstances of the case, he said that about 10.30 on Thursday night a number of men were taken from Portsmouth to fill the vacancies of those who had left at Southampton. When the defendants heard that the men who had been taken on board were non-union men they refused to remain on the Olympic unless the non-union men were sent off. Another lot of non-union men arrived on board just before midnight and completed the complement. The defendants then began to pack up their belongings and went to the tender alongside the Olympic. They remained there, although they were requested to go back on board the Olympic. In the morning they were handed over to the Portsmouth police.

Evidence was given by Mr John Edward Jarus Withers, Fifth Officer on board the Olympic. Mr Emanuel questioned the officer as to the cause of the dispute. "Was it," he asked, "because the men engaged did not know their work?" The officer replied, "The only reason I heard given was that non-union men were being employed."

Was not the sole reason why these men refused to sail that they objected to sail with a scratch crew who did not know how to stoke a fire or handle a boat? – No, I did not hear it.

Did you hear it said that the firemen refused to risk their lives with men in the stokehold who knew nothing about their work? – No.

STEWARDS AS STOKERS

Mr King: Were you not so badly off for a crew when you left Southampton that officers had to let go from the stern end of the ship? – Yes.

And that you had to send stewards down to help stoke the ship? – I heard so.

Mr King next asked: You set out to pick up anything with a suit of clothes on?

Mr Hiscock objected to the question, but the bench overruled the objection.

Mr King: Well, I suggest that the men complained about the very badly-manned ship. – Not personally to me. I heard it in conversation.

I will put it that three out of four of the boats were totally unseaworthy. – They only complained about one boat that I know of.

When the boats were opened out is it not a fact that they were stuck with paint about half an inch thick? – No.

Did it take 3½ hours to lower the boats? – Oh, no.

Will you swear that is not true? – I am not in a position to answer that correctly at the moment.

Mr King: I put it to you that broadly it was a scratch crew.

The Officer (smiling): Well, I don't know.

Is it true that of the 200 men taken on board only three were able to show discharges to prove that they had ever been to sea as stokers? – I can't say.

Do you know that Mr Curry had given instructions to take on as many French firemen as possible at Cherbourg, and complete the remainder at Queenstown? – The officer said he could not say.

Do you consider these boats absolutely seaworthy? – They were.

You had 24 Berton boats on board? – Yes.

I suggest to you that they were old Berton boats taken from a store, and that they had not been opened for years? – When I got them they were in a barge alongside.

The defendants were remanded on bail till Tuesday next.

HEAVY BLOW TO SOUTHAMPTON

Following upon the great blow inflicted on Southampton by the loss of hundreds of the Titanic's crew, the cancelling of the Olympic's voyage caused a great sensation in the town, and further developments are awaited with anxiety.

During the afternoon crowds of seamen and firemen congregated in the neighbourhood of the docks and discussed the situation. The events of the morning were deplored, all the more as a settlement of the dispute was so nearly reached on the previous night.

The distress in the port is great, and it will be rendered additionally so by yesterday's events.

PASSENGERS INDIGNANT

On the arrival of the Olympic at Southampton the passengers made a rush to the White Star offices in order to book berths on other boats.

They complained bitterly of the actions of the sailors, and many of them declared they would try to get back the cheques given in aid of the Titanic disaster fund.

It is stated that scores of the Olympic's passengers – first, second and third class – volunteered to act as firemen. The Commander, Captain Haddock, posted a notice, expressing the company's appreciation of the offer.

DUKE OF SUTHERLAND'S VIEWS

The Duke of Sutherland was interviewed on the Olympic yesterday by the *Daily Sketch*.

"I have to-day," said the Duke, "examined the collapsible boats on board the Olympic, and with reference to the boat about which so much has been said as regards leaking, I only found a cupful of water in it.

"The steamship company, in my opinion," his Grace added, "behaved admirably from beginning to end. Had more time been allowed them they could not only have got a full complement of stokers but a full crew."

"MEN BADLY ADVISED"

Opinion of Sailors' and Firemen's Union Official

At the London Headquarters of the Sailors' and Firemen's Union a reporter was officially informed yesterday that the Union could in no way be held responsible for the dispute which had arisen on board the Olympic.

"It is not our dispute," said an official, "but is being organised from the Seafarers' Union, an organisation which recently broke away from the National Sailors' and Firemen's Union, and has its headquarters at Southampton.

"We are afraid the men have been badly advised, for they must know perfectly well that, once they sign articles, they are subject to very heavy penalties under the Merchant Shipping Act should they refuse to join the ship or do anything that may be construed into an act of insubordination.

"Personally we regret the action of the firemen at Southampton, because it will leave a bad impression, and bring the whole case of the firemen into disrepute."

RULERS OF THE SEA

Marine Department and its Chief at Whitehall

DUTIES AND SALARIES

There are probably many people who have never even heard of the Marine Department of the Board of Trade.

Yet the department directed by Sir Walter J. Howell undertakes many important functions. How important will be better realised by the man in the street as its powers and responsibilities are unfolded during the coming inquiry into the loss of the Titanic.

The affairs of the Mercantile Marine are administered not in one, but in several buildings in London, while the Survey and Emigration Staff is distributed all over the coasts, from Aberdeen to Plymouth, with many English, four Scottish, and six Irish districts.

The headquarters, however, are in Whitehall-gardens, where Sir Walter Howell – whose official rank is that of an Assistant Secretary of the Board of Trade – presides over a numerous staff, whose salaries range from a hundred to a thousand pounds a year.

There are sea captains receiving four-figure salaries as "professional members" of the Department; a superintendent for wrecks; an inspector and a clerk in charge of life-saving apparatus; ship and tonnage surveyors, examiners of masters and mates, examiners of engineers, and even an inspector of ships' provisions.

The Marine Department has been in existence for many years, and besides having charge of the general administration of the Merchant Shipping Acts, grants certificates to navigators, which are their licenses upon the ocean highways.

Sir Walter Howell himself is a Londoner who has been in the Civil Service since he was 19 years of age, when he entered the Board of Trade offices after passing an open competitive examination.

He became private secretary to Sir Henry Calcraft when that well-remembered official held the Secretaryship to the Board of Trade, and filled a similar post to Lord St. Aldwyn when he was President of the Board.

SIR W. J. HOWELL

Called to the Bar at the Inner Temple in 1886, Sir Walter has been Marine Secretary since 1899, and besides being a Knight Commander of the Bath he holds the Royal Norwegian Order of St. Olaf.

He is a bachelor, and lives at Streatham-common, and counts yachting among his favourite recreations.

CREW DESERT THE OLYMPIC AND ARE ARRESTED

The sailors of the Olympic on board the tug Albert Edward as she made fast at Portsmouth on bringing the deserters from the   As each of the Olympic crew left the tug at Portsmou
Olympic. The seamen are seen leaving with their kits.   with non-union

TESTING THE COLLAPSIBLE BOATS.

The testing of the collapsible boats by the firemen's deputation. Captain Haddock says the alleged insecurity is pure nonsense. Forty collapsible boats from troopships are on board, and they have been tested and passed by the Board of Trade.

Hoping Against Hope: Painful Vigil of An:

One of the firemen pointing out a rent in a collapsible during the launching and trials of the boats. It was such discoveries that led the men to refuse to sail.

The scene outside the offices of the White Star Company in New York before the Carpathia brou
and stood for hours, filling the small Bowling Green Park, s

THEY COME ASHORE FOR DISOBEYING THE CAPTAIN.

n charge by a policeman. The sailors who refused to work
n coming off under arrest.

The seamen marching to the Portsmouth Town Hall under police escort from the Harbour Railway Station. The onlookers raised cries of encouragement, and the deserters seemed to be in excellent spirits. They sang sea songs in the cells and were remanded on bail.

elatives Before Survivors Arrived in New York.

THE SAILORS AND THE FIREMEN—A CONTRAST.

there last week. The offices were besieged by relatives and friends of the passengers, who sat
accurable news after the lists of the survivors had been given out.

The long file of Olympic deserters, accompanied by the police, walking along the road after coming ashore at Portsmouth.

The Olympic firemen who are on strike sitting about on their kits on the quayside yesterday awaiting developments. Some of the men, as will be seen, are enjoying a nap in the sunshine.

A MARCONI EXPLANATION

In view of the reports that the Marconi apparatus on the Californian was not in working order at the time of the disaster and that the failure to communicate was due to the fact that the ship's engines were stopped, Marconi's Wireless Telegraph Company Limited have issued a statement that the Californian is fitted with the usual emergency gear which is not directly dependant for its operation upon the running of engines. It is energised by a storage battery sufficiently large to enable working to be carried on for many hours after the engines are shut down. The value of this extra plant was demonstrated in the case of the wreck of the Republic, when communication was established and maintained with other ships solely by its means.

THE WRECK COMMISSION

The Lord Chancellor has appointed Lord Mersey to be a Wreck Commissioner of the United Kingdom and the Home Secretary has appointed the following gentlemen to act as assessors:- Rear-Admiral the Hon. S.A. Gough-Calthorpe, C.V.O., Captain A. W. Clarke, Commander F. C. Lyon, R.N.R., Professor J. H. Biles, LL.D; the name of the fifth assessor will be announced later. The secretary to the Commissioner is Captain the Hon. C. Bigham, to whom all communications on the business of the Court should be addressed at St. Ermin's Hotel, Caxton-street, S.W.

SEND IT TO-DAY!

Shillings Still Wanted for S.O.S. Fund

EVERY COIN HELPS RELATIVES OF TITANIC VICTIMS

The *Daily Sketch* S.O.S. Fund will be closed on Monday evening. At the time of writing over 11,000 shillings have been sent. Many thousands of our readers have no doubt contributed to other Titanic disaster funds raised locally, but it is probable there are still many who, for one reason or another have not helped.

It is to these people we are addressing ourselves. The sinking of the Titanic is the biggest disaster of modern times; it will take a place in history alongside the records of the "Birkenhead." It will be referred to years hence.

We cannot look back on all the records of heroism with unmixed pride. There is shame attached to some of them, for England has on more than one occasion thanked her heroes by letting them starve. Everybody says, when these matters come to light, that something should be done. It is often difficult for the individual to do anything, but in the case of the Titanic there is no difficulty. The way to help has been made easy; there will be no excuse if, in years to come, it is found that help was withheld.

THE TOLL OF GENIUS

Francis Davis Millet, artist, sculptor and designer, one of the distinguished passengers lost on the Titanic. Mr Millet was recently made president of the American Academy at Rome.

OLYMPIC SAILORS CHARGED WITH UNLAWFUL DISOBEDIENCE: SCENE IN COURT

The arrested Olympic Seamen in Court at Portsmouth yesterday afternoon, when they were charged with unlawfully disobeying the commands of the captain. The majority of the 53 men charged were seamen, but there were a few greasers and one storekeeper. Amongst the seamen were several quartermasters. All the defendants were remanded on bail till Tuesday next.

TAKING OFF THE OLYMPIC'S PASSENGERS

Owing to the revolt on the Olympic the voyage has had to be cancelled, and the passengers who were to have travelled by her will have to make their journey on some other vessel. In the photograph the Olympic's first-class passengers are seen leaving the Duchess of York, the boat on which they were conveyed from the Olympic to Southampton. In the inset seamen are seen transferring the passenger's baggage from the liner to the tender.

THE TITANIC'S SIGNALS

Sensational Statements at the Inquiry

LINER'S ROCKETS SEEN

Why Californian Waited for Daylight

More sensational evidence was given at the American inquiry into the Titanic disaster yesterday. A donkey engineman on the Californian spoke of seeing the lights on the great liner about ten miles off before her collision with the iceberg.

Then he saw the distress signals of the doomed vessel, but he did not tell the officers on the bridge because he presumed that they also had noticed the rockets that were being flung into the darkness.

This was happening while the Californian was drifting in the midst of a huge ice floe unable to continue her voyage, and she did not proceed to the scene of the disaster until daylight.

The man further asserted that he had overheard the officers saying that when the captain was informed that rockets had been sent up he said "Why the devil didn't they waken the wireless man?"

Other members of the crew, he declared, had refused to join him in protesting against the captain's conduct because they were afraid of losing their berths.

Captain Lord followed Gill on the witness stand and denied the truth of this story, declaring that he first heard of the Titanic from the Virginian when he awoke about six o'clock on the morning of the calamity.

TWENTY MILES AWAY

Another Vessel Held Up in the Ice-floe

Startling statements were made before the Senate Commission to-day by Ernest Gill, donkey engineman on the liner Californian.

Gill declared that he saw the lights of the Titanic at midnight on the Sunday and her distress signals half an hour later. The wireless installation on the Californian was not working at the time owing to the fact that the ship was among the ice and her engines had been stopped.

She did not proceed to the scene until daylight, the engines being started at 5 o'clock. Gill asserted that he heard conversations between the ship's officers in the course of which it was mentioned that when the captain was informed that rockets had been sent up he remarked: "Why the devil didn't they waken up the wireless man?"

Gill said he wanted other members of the crew to join him in protesting against the captain's conduct, but they refused owing to the fear that they would lose their jobs if they did so. The Titanic was less than 20 miles away.

Captain Stanley Lord, of the Californian, declared that there was no truth in the story told by Gill. He was asleep from half-past eleven on the Sunday night until ten minutes to six on the Monday morning, when he first heard of the Titanic from the Virginian.

Samuel Hemmings, a lamp trimmer on the Titanic, said he was told immediately after the crash that he had only one hour to live. This he was informed on the authority of Mr Andrews, the representative of the shipbuilders.

SENATOR SMITH'S METHODS

NEW YORK Friday

British criticisms of Senator Smith and his methods of investigation appear to be fully concurred in by the majority of Americans, and it would not be too much to say that the Senator is the laughing stock here, as he seems to be in England.

Members of the Senate are said to regret his having been placed in a position to bring down ridicule on United States methods, but it is none the less felt that the inquiry is doing much to bring out the salient facts concerning the disaster.

THE MANSION HOUSE FUND

The Mansion House Titanic Fund now amounts to £168,000.

DAILY SKETCH.

No. 979.—MONDAY, APRIL 29, 1912.   THE PREMIER PICTURE PAPER.   [Registered as a Newspaper.]   ONE HALFPENNY.

FIRST SURVIVORS OF TITANIC TO REACH ENGLAND.

The Lapland, the Red Star liner, arriving in Cawsand Bay, off Plymouth, yesterday morning with the Titanic survivors on board. The crew of the lost liner were not brought ashore against the taffrail of the immediately, but waited on the tender (Sir Richard Grenville) until the mails and passengers were got away from Plymouth. In the lower photograph the Titanic men are seen leaning tender.—*Daily Sketch* Photographs.

TITANIC SURVIVORS ARRIVE

Crew Tell Surprising Stories

MILLIONAIRE'S OFFER

Many Women Said to Have Disregarded the Alarm

A large number of the survivors of the Titanic's crew were landed at Plymouth yesterday by the Lapland.

Some of them had amazing stories to tell. One of them spoke of a millionaire who offered 5,000 dollars if he could be saved.

Another described the escape of a wealthy man and his wife in the emergency boat, and added that there was a distribution of cheques on the Carpathia.

It appears that great difficulty was experienced in getting some of the third-class passengers and crew to believe that the liner was in peril, and the survivors say that many perished through disregarding the warnings given.

Of the "black squad" on duty at the time of the disaster only very few were saved. They drew the fires to prevent the boilers exploding, and before they got out the water was above their waists.

TOLD THROUGH THE BARRIER

Men Waltz While Waiting for The Women

From Our Own Correspondent

On being put ashore the men whose depositions had been taken were free to roam about the dockyard, and many of them made for the gates outside which friends and townspeople were congregated. Many affectionate reunions took place in spite of the barrier between.

Comedy and tragedy went hand in hand. A pale youth from the stokehold leaning against the gates told his friends of the loss of his brother. "He was in the watch down below at the time we struck," he said. "I was in the watch which was to relieve him at midnight. As I started to go down I found the water rising in the stokehold. It being impossible for me to get below, I went on deck. I never saw my brother again."

A young steward said his chief memory of the disaster was the nonchalance that prevailed. "Lots of us who turned out when we felt the first shock of the collision went back to our bunks again, thinking nothing had happened," he said, "For some of them the sleep to which they returned proved to be the last sleep, I think."

Many of the New York stories that have been regarded as inventions found corroboration among the crew.

"I heard of one millionaire who was offering 5,000 dollars if he could be saved," one man told me. "I didn't hear him myself, but it was all the talk among our gang. Some of them heard it. To-day the American papers are printing the man's name in letters a foot long as a national hero."

"CHEQUES HANDED ROUND"

Another man, one of the firemen, spoke of a wealthy man who escaped in what is called the emergency boat – that is a boat which is kept ready for prompt lowering in case of "man overboard."

"He got his wife and family and some friends into that boat and got it lowered, promising the men who were rowing £5 apiece. The morning after we were picked up by the Carpathia the boat's crew was summoned to the saloon deck, and there received the money, in cheques."

Robert Williams, one of the firemen and an ex-Navy man, said the discipline of the crew was splendid. "I was in my bunk at the time of the collision, and was awakened, but lots of my mates were never disturbed. I ran aft, and a store-keeper told me how the water was rising below, and I hurried back to my quarters to tell my mates. Some of them laughed at me, and wouldn't get up.

They were taking the covers off the boats, and I helped them, and after that I went down below into the steerage to help to get the women and children up. They wouldn't believe there was any danger, and we had to fairly punch some of them up. A lot who were left below couldn't be persuaded at any cost to leave their quarters.

On deck I heard them shouting repeatedly for the women, but none appeared. The band was playing, and while we were waiting for the women several of us were waltzing round with one another, and smoking cigarettes.

Out of a watch of about a hundred firemen, trimmers and greasers, only ten were saved. The men drew the fires in the fore stokehold to prevent the boilers exploding, and before they got out the water was above their waists."

"I suppose I was dreaming, but my first impression of the collision was that I was in a tram which had run off the rails", Fireman Henry Senior told me. "Going on deck I saw a lot of ice about.

'It's nothing; we've struck an iceberg,' I said to one of my mates. 'We'll get back and turn in.' I went back to my bunk, and was dozing for a half hour before the order 'Man boats' roused me."

He went on to describe how the boats were lowered, and said that after all the ordinary boats had been launched he and others ascended to the hurricane deck and threw down a number of collapsible boats.

"While we were preparing to lower these," he went on, "we heard the captain shout 'Every man for himself.' I had seen the captain on the bridge. He was walking up and down, and giving orders. When he shouted his last command the ship was sinking fast.

I dived over the side, and by good luck I found myself in the water near one of the collapsible boats. It had either been thrown or had fallen over the side, and was floating bottom upwards.

Thirty-five of us scrambled on to the keel of that boat. One of them was the second officer Lightoller, and another was the wireless operator Bride. The second officer called to the men in the lifeboats, and they came and rescued us, some of us going into one boat, and some into another.

Just before I dived one of the forward boilers burst, and the fore funnel fell. It was at that moment that I sprang off.

While the boats were being loaded I saw the first officer produce a revolver and fire at two or three men who were trying to rush the boats. I don't think he killed anyone, for as far as I could see he fired over their heads. When I was in the water I picked up an Italian baby, but it died in my arms."

CAPTAIN WITH A BABY IN HIS ARM

The captain was swimming close alongside me, and he, too, had a baby in his arms. I saw him swim to one of the boats and hand the baby to someone, and the last I saw of him he was heading back towards the ship."

An extraordinary story was told by one member of the Titanic's crew. He was looking dazed, and his first words when I approached him were, "I can't remember anything." Asked if he had suffered any injury he volunteered the following statement: "When I was standing on the boat deck I was felled by a blow from an iron bar, and I fell forward into a boat. When I came to I was told I was on the Carpathia. I have not the remotest idea who hit me."

It is definitely established, according to the evidence of one witness before the Board of Trade officials, that Mr Bruce Ismay repeatedly called for women and children to take their places in the lifeboats, but there were no answers, and it was only after he had worked very hard to get the other boats filled and the last boat was on the point of being launched that he could be induced to leave the Titanic. He frequently urged those around him to "Be British."

In the course of the afternoon many of the men were allowed into the town, and in the evening a number of them were dispatched by special train to their homes in Southampton. The remainder will leave Plymouth to-morrow after the preliminary investigation has been concluded.

WHOSE SIGNALS?

Rockets from "Mysterious Stranger"

Captain Moore, of the Canadian Pacific liner Mount Temple, gave evidence to-day before the Senate Committee of the Titanic disaster. He said that he received the signal "C Q D" from the Titanic when his ship was about forty nine miles away, and he immediately proceeded to the scene of the disaster.

Captain Moore declared that he did not see the lights of the Titanic or any rockets.

Captain Lord, of the Californian, gave evidence that he saw rockets which came from

THE SURVIVORS ALLOWED TO RETURN: MEN WHO ESCAPED

A rescued steward and stewardess, photographed after coming ashore from the Lapland—Mr. J. Whitter and Mrs. Robinson.

The survivors of the crew of the Titanic who were not required for the American Senatorial inquiry and allowed to return by the Lapland shores of the Old Country again when day broke on Sunday morning and they sailed quietly into Cawsand Bay, Plymouth. They were kept

(1) Greetings through the guarded gate at Plymouth. One of the Titanic firemen clasping the hand of a woman relation. (2) The first three survivors to leave the docks—Threlfall, McGough and Cannon. (3) How the seamen were cared for when they came ashore at Plymouth.—Daily Sketch and Newspaper Illustrations Photographs.

The survivors of the crew of the Titanic having given their depositions to the Board of wards they were released to stroll through the town.

H WITH THE TITANIC THANKFUL TO SEE ENGLAND AGAIN.

Sir Richard Grenville, for some time, and this photograph shows the men gazing eagerly over the rails. Afterwards the men were sodated on the dock premises, for the purposes of the forthcoming official inquiry, by the Board of Trade and the White Star Company

A fireman, S. Hunt, lighting his brother's cigarette through the guarded dock gates. One of the first questions was, "How's the Plymouth Argyle gone on?"

men allowed to converse with friends and relations at the dockyard gates. Shortly after-ards left for Southampton.—*Daily Sketch* Photograph.

The combined Territorial parade on West Marlands Common, Southampton, yesterday, in aid of the Mayor's fund. (1) Procession of hospital nurses. (2) Service being conducted by Rev. J. W. Neister, of Bournemouth. Handel's "Dead March" was played by the massed bands.— *Daily Sketch* Photographs.

a mysterious stranger, and that these rockets were not distress signals.

Mr Evans, the wireless operator aboard the Californian, said the fourth officer awakened him at half-past three, saying that a vessel had been firing rockets. He went to the wireless instrument and then learned of the sinking of the Titanic.

Stewards of the Titanic lauded Mr Ismay's bravery and presence of mind, stating that he assisted women to the boats, and only entered a collapsible a few moments before the liner sank.

OFFICIALS CRITICISED

Men Refuse to Speak Until Leaders Come Aboard

PLYMOUTH Sunday

It was between seven and eight o'clock in the morning when the liner Lapland was sighted beyond the breakwater, and within half an hour she had come round under Penlee Point and dropped anchor within the sheltering arms of Cawsand Bay.

Presently a gangway was run out between the tender Sir Richard Grenville and the vessel, and then came the first glimpse of the survivors of the greatest disaster in the history of the sea. Very slowly they dribbled aboard the tender, silently and without emotion. No cheer was raised. The behaviour of these plain, homely British seamen, finding themselves once again safe home in port, was a typical example of British stolidity.

Having taken aboard her complement of survivors, the Sir Richard Grenville immediately steamed off beyond the breakwater, there to lie to – well out of the reach of inquisitive newspaper men – until the other two tenders should complete their share of the disembarkation.

The manoeuvre of the Sir Richard Grenville was all a part of a very elaborate scheme of "compounding" the survivors on their arrival at Plymouth until the Board of Trade officials had had an opportunity of interrogating them preparatory to selecting witnesses for the inquiry to be held this week at the dock station of the Great Western Railway.

WAITING ROOM AS DORMITORY

Extensive preparations had been made for keeping the men under surveillance from the moments they set foot on shore to the time when they should be released from this preliminary inquiry. All unauthorised persons were rigorously excluded from the dock, where the waiting rooms had been rigged up as dormitories and a huge store of cold provisions had been laid in.

This procedure of "coralling" the men gave rise to a great deal of criticism, both here and at Southampton, and it was freely asserted that the authorities were exercising unusual, if not unauthorised, powers in holding the men under lock and key in this fashion.

After cruising about in the Sound for four hours the Sir Richard Grenville put into dock at noon.

An amusing comedy had been enacted during the time they were in the Sound. Mr Lewis and the other officials of the Seafarer's Union had hailed the tender and demanded to be put on board. They were refused, whereupon they shouted to the men, urging them to refuse to furnish any information to the Board of Trade. This hint was acted upon. The work of taking depositions of the men had started, but, after this, they closed their mouths, and before their tongues could be loosened again their two trade union representatives had to be received on board.

SOS FUND CLOSING

Last Appeal to Our Readers

The *Daily Sketch* S.O.S. Fund will be closed to-morrow morning, when the last subscriptions which have been received during the week-end will be published.

Those of our readers who have not already contributed have one more opportunity to do so. Money is still wanted. The men who landed in England yesterday represent but a part of the crew who sailed away so proudly and hopefully on the Titanic. The widows and children of the other men must be helped. Nobody can question even the bare justice of this.

Our fund has been specially started with the small amounts in view. It is a shilling fund to which everyone may contribute, and we look for a last effort which will make it still more use to the sufferers from this overwhelming disaster.

The total amount received up to Saturday evening was 11,916 Shillings and 10 Pence.

The Mansion House Titanic Fund has reached £177,000.

SEAMEN'S DEMANDS

Right to Inspect the Ship's Lifeboats

STARTLING TRADE UNION MOVE AT LIVERPOOL

An important development of the lifeboat strike on the Olympic is reported from Liverpool.

The local branch of the Seamen and Firemen's Union have decided that on and after to-day the seamen and firemen of every ship leaving Liverpool shall insist upon the following conditions:-

The right of inspection of lifeboat accommodation by the accredited representatives of the Union.

An increase of wages, seamen's wages to be raised to £4 10s. per month and firemen's wages to £5 per month.

The proposals are to be discussed in detail at a meeting in Liverpool to-day, and it is considered likely that a course of action will be determined upon that will have far reaching results.

When the Cunard liner Lusitania left Liverpool on Saturday night for New York she carried the Olympic's mails. According to a statement made by the Cunard Company none of the Olympic's passengers had booked berths.

EMBARKING ON OTHER LINERS

Four hundred people have been waiting at Cherbourg for the arrival of the Olympic for some days, and on Saturday the White Star Company's agent at Cherbourg was advised that the saloon passengers would be transferred to the North German liner Prinz Friedrich Wilhelm, which called at Cherbourg yesterday, while the steerage passengers would leave on Wednesday on the Philadelphia.

A number of passengers whose business is urgent cancelled their passages, and proceeded to Havre to embark on the French liner Provence, which left for America on Saturday. About sixty of the passengers, including the Duke of Sutherland, left Southampton by special tender yesterday to join the Prinz Friedrich Wilhelm, which called in Southampton Water to pick up passengers for New York.

ATLANTIC PERIL

Another Liner Just Escapes Titanic's Fate

Another big liner has narrowly escaped the fate of the Titanic while crossing the Atlantic, according to an Exchange message from New York.

The Canadian Pacific liner Empress of Britain, which has arrived in Halifax, is reported to have just missed collision with an iceberg while crossing the Grand Banks on Wednesday morning during a dense fog.

At the time the ship was 240 miles east of the position where the Titanic disaster occurred.

The look-out man sighted a big berg directly ahead, and the engines were immediately reversed. The ship swung off, barely escaping.

The officers state that there was no collision. The ship was going dead slow. The captain reports that the ocean is dotted in all directions with hundreds of bergs.

BRINGING 189 BODIES ASHORE

HALIFAX Sunday

The Mackay Bennett is expected to arrive here to-morrow morning with 189 bodies of the victims of the Titanic disaster. Among the bodies is that of Mr F. D. Millet, the American artist.

APPOINTED ASSESSORS FOR THE TITANIC INQUIRY

Capt A. W. Clarke, Professor J. H. Biles, and Rear-Admiral the Hon. S. A. Gough-Calthorpe, whom the Home Secretary has appointed to act as assessors at the Titanic Inquiry, over which Lord Mersey will preside.

FOOTBALLERS HELP OUR SHILLING FUND

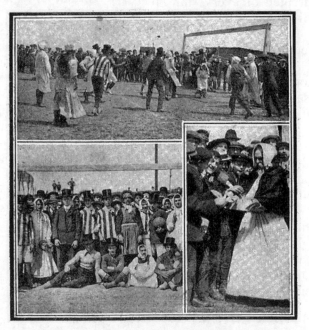

Scenes at the married and single men's charity football match played by the Anglesey Football Club at Shepherd's Bush on Saturday in aid of the Daily Sketch S O S Fund for the relief of sufferers from the Titanic disaster. The photographs show (1) First goal for the married men. (2) The teams in the mouth of the goal. (3) One of the collectors at work.

DAILY SKETCH.

No. 980.—TUESDAY, APRIL 30, 1912.   THE PREMIER PICTURE PAPER.   [Registered as a Newspaper.]   ONE HALFPENNY.

TITANIC SURVIVORS IN COLLAPSIBLE LIFEBOAT.

Photograph of a Boatload of Women and Children Making for the s.s. Carpathia.

One of a remarkable series of photographs taken from the deck of the Carpathia by Mr. J. W. Barker, a passenger. It shows women, children and sailors—all wearing lifebelts—making their way slowly towards the resuming steamer Carpathia. (Other photographs on pages 8 and 9.)

THE STORY OF THE BOATS

Titanic Survivors Say They Were Not Full

PASSENGERS SAY OFFICER FIRED AT AN ITALIAN

Stories told by the survivors of the Titanic disaster confirm the impression gained from earlier messages that there was considerable confusion at the launching of the boats.

In an interview at Plymouth yesterday two stewardesses on the Titanic, Mrs Gold and Mrs Martin, said that the first boat to leave was full of firemen. That was because the women were unwilling to leave the ship.

Another stewardess said that the night of terror in the boats so changed the appearance of some of the women that they were not recognised by their friends.

It is certain that many of the boats could have held more people than were in them when they left the ship.

Explanations of this vary, but the chief reason, to judge from the many statements that have been made, was that the passengers believed the Titanic to be unsinkable.

That many men got away in the boats while women and children still remained on board is now a matter of history, and not until the Court of Inquiry has finished its investigations shall we know why the women were not got into the boats.

One of the survivors interviewed by the *Daily Sketch* yesterday said one boat which could have carried 60 only held 13.

It is stated that after he went on board the Carpathia Mr Bruce Ismay kept to his room, refused food for two days.

HEROIC WORK

Passenger's Tribute to First Officer Murdock

A thrilling account of the last scene on the Titanic was given to the *Daily Sketch* yesterday by one of the survivors now at Southampton.

Describing his experiences he said: "I came up on deck about 11.45 and saw an iceberg half the size of the Titanic. I, with others, was ordered off the boat deck, and with my own eyes saw a trimmer kicked off it by one of the officers. We went on the lower deck and watched the water creep higher and higher. Among the lifeboats which were leaving the ship in rapid succession I noticed one in which were two American millionaires. This boat which could have carried sixty people, only contained thirteen, made up of the two Americans, one lady and daughter, five firemen, a trimmer, two sailors, and an officer. On that boat were provisions, bread, biscuits, etc., sufficient for a week.

The captain asked that this boat should return, but it did not. I saw Mr Murdock shoot down an Italian. This officer performed heroic work all through.

While seeing one of the last boats filled, and just after he had given directions about the men making way for women, someone shouted sarcastically, 'What about yourself, sir?' 'I'm going back to the ship in a minute or two,' replied Mr Murdock.

Just before the Titanic went down her stern was high up out the water, and I could plainly see the propellers and the bottom of the ship.

"WOULD HAVE HELD MORE"

Statements By Officers of the Lost Liner

Below we publish some of the statements given in evidence at the American enquiry and in interviews by those who escaped.

"As the boat was going over the side, Mr Carter, a passenger and myself got in. At that time there was not a woman on the boat deck, nor any passenger of any class, so far as we could see or hear. The boat had between 35 and 40 in it . . . The boat would have accommodated certainly six or more passengers in addition, if there had been any on the boat deck to go." – Mr Bruce Ismay.

"Nobody wanted to go in the boats, believing there was no risk. We saw boats with only about 15 persons in them." – M. Pierre Marechal, aviator.

"There were 35 in my boat, including Countess Rothes." – A Seaman.

"There were five members of the crew in the lifeboat commanded by me and 40 passengers. The boat would have carried 60 at a tight fit. Both my boat and boat No. 7 would have held more people. There were no more women about when my boat was lowered. There may have been some men about, but I thought I had enough when my boat was lowered. I think some of the boats had 60 in them when we reached the Carpathia." – Third Officer Pittman.

"The official capacity of the lifeboats is 65.5. That is the floating capacity. If you load from the deck to lower, I should not like to put more than 50 in." – Fifth Officer Lowe.

The Mansion House Fund now amounts to £182,000.

HOW CAPTAIN SMITH DIED

His Last Act Was to Save a Child's Life

Of all the wild and irresponsible messages that were sent to this country in the first few hours following the sinking of the Titanic the one that caused the greatest grief to Englishmen was the statement that Captain Smith had committed suicide on the bridge of his ship. That statement was quickly contradicted. It was proved that Captain Smith died like a sailor, but the exact manner of his death was not described. Many eye-witnesses have testified to seeing the captain on the bridge as the great liner was engulfed, and others say they saw the officer dive from the bridge just before the ship sank, but according to an interview published in the *New York World* Captain Smith died the greatest of all deaths. His last act was to save the life of a child.

The story is told by Charles Williams, coach of the Harrow Racquets Club, who was one of those saved from the Titanic.

Mr Williams is the guest of Mr George E. Standing, and the latter gave the *New York World* reporter the account as told to him by Mr Williams.

"He is a good swimmer," said Mr Standing, "and went overboard with a life preserver when he couldn't stay on deck any longer. He was in the icy water over two hours before he was finally hauled into one of the lifeboats. He says that he saw Captain Smith swimming around in the icy water with an infant in his arms and a lifebelt. When the small boat went to his rescue Captain Smith handed them the child, but refused to get in himself.

Maynard, the steward who took the baby from Captain Smith's arms.

He did ask what had become of First Officer Murdock. We told him Murdock had blown his brains out with a revolver. Then Captain Smith pushed himself away from the lifeboat, threw his lifebelt from him and slowly sank from sight. He did not come to the surface again."

It may be stated that there is no official confirmation that Mr Murdock shot himself: we give the whole account as it appeared in the *New York World*.

Mr Williams's story as to Captain Smith's death is borne out by statements made by Harry Senior, the Titanic fireman, and others, who, as reported in the *Daily Sketch* yesterday, said they saw the captain rescue the child.

RESCUED PASSENGERS AT NEW YORK

A flashlight photograph on the Cunard wharf, New York, showing first-class passengers being helped ashore by friends. According to the reports of the scenes on arrival many of the rescued women were in a state of collapse when they set foot on shore again. Their fortitude gave way when they were received by their relatives.

NIGHT OF TERROR

Women Whom Friends Could Not Recognise

FIRST BOAT WAS FULL OF FIREMEN

At Plymouth yesterday, two first-class stewardesses on the Titanic, Mrs Gold and Mrs Martin, related their experiences.

They were old shipmates, they said, having sailed together in the Olympic, the Adriatic and the Cedric. There were 74 people in their boat, and 62 of them were women.

The stewardesses said they laughed at the first warning of the disaster, ignoring for a time the advice to get up and put their lifebelts on, but Mr Andrews, the designer of the ship, came to them and told them to hurry on deck. When the stewardesses were putting on their belts they were joking about it.

The first boat to leave was full of firemen. That, said Mrs Gold and Mrs Martin, was due to the fact that none of the ladies were willing to go, and it was necessary to fill the boats.

Many more could have been rescued if the imminence of the danger had been realised earlier. In the early stages the lady passengers preferred to remain on the ship, as the getting down into the boats for them was a terrifying experience.

"ONLY STEWARDESSES"

Mr Bruce Ismay was helping to get the women into boats. He went to a group of stewardesses and asked them to take their places with the others.

They said: "But we are only stewardesses, sir." "You are women" replied Mr Ismay, and insisted upon them taking their places.

Later they saw Mr Ismay sitting on the gunwale of one of the last boats to leave. He had nothing on but his pyjamas and an overcoat, and he looked blue with cold.

Describing their adventures in the boat, Mrs Gold said "We did not talk very much, and the only sounds that reached us were the cries of the babies.

Among our people in the boat were Mrs A. Ryerson, of Philadelphia, and her two daughters. Mr Ryerson drowned. The family were going home because they had received a cable that Mr Ryerson's son had been killed in a motor accident.

Another lady was a Portuguese bride on her honeymoon tour. She lost her husband. It was a pathetic spectacle next morning to see her joy at the sight of what she thought to be the Titanic. When she was told it was the Carpathia, and that the Titanic had gone down, her grief was awful.

"THE PLUCKY LITTLE COUNTESS"

The stewardess-matron, Mrs Wallis, refused to leave her room. Her remark was "I am not going on deck; I am going back where I am safe."

Another one who refused to move was a second-cabin stewardess, Mrs Snape, a widow, 21 years of age with a little girl. As she fastened the lifebelts on her passengers she wished them good-bye.

Later she told some of the stewardesses that she did not expect to see them again. On the Carpathia the stewardesses had to sleep on deck.

A first-class stewardess said that Mrs Sloan, one of the stewardesses, was nearly left behind because she stayed on deck trying to persuade a lady passenger to go instead of herself.

All the women who were in the boats spoke with great admiration of Lady Rothes, who rowed all night in one of the boats and devoted herself during the whole time she was on the Carpathia to the care of the steerage women, and children.

Her ladyship helped to make clothes for the babies, and became known amongst all of the crew as "the plucky little Countess."

The stewardess said to her, "You have made yourself famous by rowing in the boat," and Lady Rothes replied, "I hope not; I have done nothing."

The night of terror in the boats so changed the appearance of some of the women that they were not recognised by their best friends.

EMPRESS OF BRITAIN'S TRIP

The Canadian Pacific Railway Company deny that the Empress of Britain had a narrow escape from colliding with an iceberg while crossing the Atlantic.

MANY MORE MIGHT HAVE BEEN SAVED: THE TIT

The first of the Titanic lifeboats picked up by the Carpathia. The passengers were being hoisted aboard when this photograph was taken from above. They were in a pitiable condition.

One of the boats drawing alongside the Carpathia. The occupants are chiefly women, some of w hours when this photograph was taken from the deck of the Carpathia, and must have suffered Apparently this was one of th

WIRELESS HERO WITH THE CRUSHED FEET.

"Somebody said the Carpathia's wireless operator, was getting queer from pressure of work, and asked if I could help. I couldn t walk—both feet broken or something—but I went on crutches, took the key, and never left the wireless cabin."—Harold Bride, the rescued assistant Marconi operator being carried ashore with frost-bitten feet. He was rescued in a collapsible boat.

The Titanic Lifeboats Waiting for the C

The boats of the Titanic roped as the Carpathia found them. The surviving ship's officers had in being picked up when help came. These snapshots

NIC'S LIFEBOATS PHOTOGRAPHED IN THE OPEN SEA.

(on the right) holding infants in their arms. They had been exposed in the open sea for five or six e of the women is scantily clad, showing she had made a hurried departure from the doomed liner. ch there was room for more passengers.

The lifeboat commanded by Mr. Lowe, the fifth officer of the Titanic, who rigged a sail and transferred passengers so that at daybreak he took on board from an overturned collapsible boat 20 men and one woman.

of the Carpathia after the Night of Horror.

THE WAIFS OF THE TITANIC.

er and done all they could to keep close to each other for the sake of company and greater certainty rom the Carpathia as she approached the shipwrecked people.

Louis and Lolo, the little French children who were thrown naked into one of the Titanic's boats. They were cared for by a lady passenger until they reached New York, where they were lionised and overwhelmed with attentions. This photograph has been sent to their mother in France, and if she identifies them they will be restored to her. Their father was drowned.

COLONEL ASTOR'S WILL

Estate Valued at Eighty Million Dollars

NEW YORK Monday

The *American* states that under the will of the late Colonel J. J. Astor, who perished on the Titanic, Mr Vincent Astor, his son, inherits sixty million dollars, and Miss Muriel Astor, daughter, fifteen million dollars.

The birth of a child by his second marriage is provided for; the fifteen million dollars bequeathed to Muriel being in that event divided into half, the child receiving one portion and Muriel the other.

As far as can be ascertained nothing is left to the present Mrs Astor, but (says the *American*) the will making the above bequests to his children by his first marriage was made before the late Colonel's second marriage.

The total estate is valued at eighty million dollars.

FALSE WIRELESS NEWS

P.M.G. Questioned in the House of Commons

Further questions regarding the Titanic disaster were asked in the House of Commons yesterday.

Colonel Yate asked the Postmaster-General whether he was now in a position to state the origin of the false reports regarding the safety of the Titanic.

Mr Samuel replied he had received a promise of full assistance from the shipping companies concerned, and the Marconi Company, but the records of some of the ships which were westward of the point had not yet been received. The origin of the false report had not yet been traced to any ship.

Answering Mr McCallum Scott, Mr Acland said the American Senate Committee was within its rights in holding the inquiry and in requiring the attendance of witnesses. In view of the fact that there had been considerable loss of American life as well as British it was not unreasonable that the American authorities should hold an inquiry in order to decide for themselves what was necessary to ensure safety. It would however be undesirable that British subjects should be put to great inconvenience, but the latest information was that the proceedings were not likely to be prolonged, so far as British witnesses were concerned.

No communication had been made to the United States Government on the subject.

NO MORE BODIES

Search For Victims Stopped By Gale and Fog

HALIFAX (NOVA SCOTIA) Monday

The captain of the Minia reports that owing to gale and fog it has been found necessary to suspend the search for bodies, which are no longer to be seen in groups. Until better conditions prevail the Minia has been forced to steam clear of the area in which the disaster occurred. Remains of the wreckage are now visible to a few passing steamers. The captain of the Minia is of opinion that all the bodies obtainable have been recovered by the Mackay Bennett.

WELCOMING THE SURVIVORS

Great crowds assembled at Southampton last night to welcome about 90 Titanic survivors who arrived from Plymouth. Many affecting scenes were witnessed.

THE BLACK BERG

The Sunderland steamer Portland, which saw the Titanic six hours before the disaster, had encountered a few hours before a black iceberg about twelve feet out of the water.

Some of those on board the Portland think it was this berg that struck the Titanic. In explanation of its blackness they say it probably drifted on to the coast line, touched bottom, and then turned turtle and floated again. In the darkness it would be almost impossible to see it. It was travelling at a good rate.

It may be pointed out that the iceberg that struck the Titanic is said to have been much higher out of the water than the one seen by the Portland.

The captain of the Portland changed his course to avoid the ice floes.

TAKING THE EVIDENCE

The officers of the Board of Trade were busily engaged at Plymouth yesterday in receiving statements of the survivors of the Titanic disaster.

It is understood to be the intention of the Board of Trade to complete the preliminary investigation with the least possible delay. The distribution has been made by the White Star officials of the £300 cabled over by Mrs Nelson H. Shearman, of New York, to be divided among the survivors of the crew.

It has been apportioned in a ratio of £3 each to the stewardesses, £2 each to the stewards, and £1 each to the remaining hands.

MNE TETRAZZINI'S HELP

A concert held on board the Mauretania raised £650 for the Titanic Fund and the Seamen's Orphanage Fund. Mne Tetrazzini sang for the first time on an ocean liner and sold a number of photographs of herself.

BERTHON BOATS

To the Editor of the Daily Sketch

Sir, – Referring to your illustration depicting a fireman pointing out a rent in one of the Berthon boats of the Olympic, I should like to point out the value of the principle of double skins which is so important a feature in the Berthon boats. A Berthon filled with people will float if perforated, whereas a boat of one skin would sink.

If a hole is made there is only the loss of buoyancy in one compartment, and seven filled with air are left to keep the boat afloat. In addition to this, if you cut away the whole of the outer skin you have the inner one left, i.e., it is a boat within a boat. – Yours, etc.,

BERTHON BOAT CO., LTD.

THANK YOU!

Closing Efforts for Daily Sketch Shilling Fund

READERS READY RESPONSE

The *Daily Sketch* Shilling Fund is now closed, and we want to thank all those of our readers who have contributed.

The ready response which was made to our special appeal was as surprising as it was gratifying.

We set out to collect those small amounts which were in danger of being overlooked, and they have come in by the thousand.

Shillings and even smaller amounts have found their way to Tudor-street from sources where they could ill be spared. Such tributes are worth while.

They will serve to show those who are suffering that there is real sympathy for them in Britain.

We shall now hand the Shilling Fund over to the Lord Mayor's Mansion House Fund.

Some of the third-class passengers of the Titanic photographed on the foredeck of the Carpathia after her arrival in New York. They received every assistance in the way of wraps and clothing from the other passengers on the Carpathia.

SURVIVORS' BELTS ON THE CARPATHIA

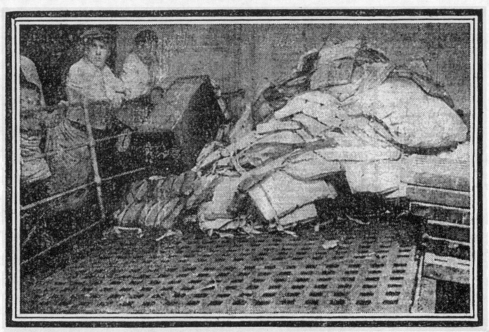

Life-preserving belts worn by the Titanic survivors lying in the hold of the Carpathia. Many a passenger owes his or her life to the possession of this apparatus.

MR BRUCE ISMAY AT TITANIC ENQUIRY

Mr J. Bruce Ismay, chairman of the White Star Line, giving evidence before the Special Senate Committee, meeting in New York to investigate the Titanic Disaster. Mr Ismay is seen in the centre of the photograph with his hand to his chin.

PATHETIC SCENES AS ANXIOUS RELATIVES GREET TITANIC SURVIVORS.

Joy and grief jostled each other in Southampton yesterday. Friends of survivors who arrived back by the Lapland were welcomed home by relieved friends, but their home-coming reminded those whose relatives had gone down of their sad loss. While happy meetings were taking place in different parts of the town the Mayor was surrounded by widows garbed in deepest mourning, to whom he was distributing much-needed financial aid. (1) Messrs. Hunt, Hebb, and Pragnell, three of the survivors, with their happy friends. (2) Quartermaster Wynn, who took charge of No. 9 lifeboat, containing 42 women and children—first, second and third class passengers. (3) The Mayor of Southampton (on left) distributing relief. (4) Seaman Gillow, who was four days in hospital after being rescued. (5) Seaman J. Pascoe, with his mother and three brothers. (6) Quartermaster Humphries, who has "heroism" written to his name now.

TITANIC DISASTER.

The Charter of

DR. BARNARDO'S HOMES

is " No Destitute Child Ever Refused Admission."

Under this rule the Homes are ready to admit any number of really destitute children who may be rendered orphans by this appalling disaster.

HEAD OFFICES : 18 to 26, Stepney Causeway, London, E.

DAILY SKETCH.

No. 981.—WEDNESDAY, MAY 1, 1912.   THE PREMIER PICTURE PAPER.   [Registered as a Newspaper.]   ONE HALFPENNY.

MR. BRUCE ISMAY TELLING HIS STORY OF THE WRECK.

Arrival at the Inquiry of Senator Smith, the Chairman, Who Asks Extraordinary Questions.

(1) Senator William Smith arriving at the Senate House, Washington, for the Titanic inquiry, over which he presides. (2) Mr. Bruce Ismay describing the disaster and answering questions as to how he reached the Carpathia. (3) Harold Cottam, the Carpathia operator, giving evidence. It is announced that the end of the A___ inquiry is now in sight,

RECOVERING THE DEAD

Upturned Boat on Scene of Titanic Disaster

MUTILATION CAUSED BY A TERRIFIC EXPLOSION

A surprising discovery was made on the scene of the Titanic disaster by the cable ship Mackay Bennett, which returned to Halifax yesterday from its search for bodies.

An Exchange telegram received yesterday, stated that a group of thirty bodies, including those of several women, was found alongside an upturned lifeboat. A woman's red skirt was attached to an oar, and had apparently been used as a distress signal. There were indications that the boat was afloat some time after the Titanic foundered.

It will be remembered that before the Carpathia reached New York the White Star Company received a wireless message from the Olympic reporting that all the Titanic's boats were accounted for. This message was read in the House of Commons by the Prime Minister.

The Mackay Bennett recovered 306 bodies, and 190 of them were taken to Halifax. One hundred and sixteen bodies were mutilated beyond recognition. Arms and legs were fractured, and the features in many cases were so terribly cut and bruised that (it is declared) the injuries could not have been caused by the sea or wreckage, but must have resulted from a terrific explosion.

The body of Colonel Astor, which has been embalmed, is to be conveyed on the journey to New York by special train to-day. His son, Mr Vincent Astor, will travel with the remains. At the sad landing yesterday the proceedings were conducted with impressive solemnity.

Cash to the extent of 16,000 dollars was found in the pockets of dead people. On Colonel Astor's body was found 2,500 dollars, and he was wearing a wire belt with a gold buckle, which is said to be a family heirloom. Many bodies were identified by papers, letters and cards. Most of the watches found had stopped between 2.10 and 2.15. The bodies of the first class passengers were found in groups.

CORPSES GUARDED BY BLUEJACKETS

The corpses taken to Halifax were landed at Government Dock and were guarded by Canadian bluejackets. All shipping was kept outside the Channel for the time being, and very few people besides Government officials were allowed in the dock premises.

Only one woman was admitted, and she was an undertaker. The rest of the undertakers, together with the mourners, gathered outside.

Captain Lardner, of the Mackay Bennett, reports that the bodies were recovered sixty miles north-east of the scene of the disaster in the waters of the Gulf Stream. The searchers swept a square of thirty miles, and the bodies found were all standing upright in the water.

Door, chairs, and wreckage were scattered all over the field of search. Several men found were in evening dress, but no one was found lashed to the doors or other wreckage. The first body discovered was supposed to be that of Mr Widener, but it was later established as that of Mr Widener's valet, Edward Keating, who had some of Mr Widener's papers on him.

The Captain believes that all the bodies buried at sea were those of the ship's crew. He is satisfied that the passengers were properly identified. The bodies of 18 women were found but none of them were those of first-class passengers.

Most of the bodies found were just on the edge of the Gulf Stream, and had they not been rescued at the time they were they would in all probability have floated for many miles in the current. One hundred bodies were in one group.

The White Star officials at New York yesterday morning received a wireless message from the Minia expressing the belief that if any more bodies of Titanic victims are floating they have been swept by the late northerly gales into the Gulf Stream and carried many miles to the east.

Fourteen bodies have been recovered by the Minia, of which two are unidentified, and these have been buried at sea.

"ONLY A SLIGHT SHOCK"

Steward's Story of the Sinking of the Titanic

ICEBERG MISTAKEN FOR A CLOUD

A simple but graphic account of the sinking of the Titanic was told to the *Daily Sketch* yesterday by Mr Jacob W. Gibbons, a second-class steward.

Mr Gibbons, who is a married man with five children, was on his maiden voyage and had taken the trip to improve his health.

Describing his experiences he said:-

"I had just turned in to the 'glory hole' – as our sleeping quarters are termed – and was hanging up my watch when I felt a sudden jar.

The shock was very slight, and to this fact I attribute the great loss of life, as many of those aboard must have gone to sleep again under the impression that nothing serious had happened.

When I got up on deck the boats were being lowered away, but many of the passengers seemed to prefer sticking to the ship. I helped some of the passengers into boat No 11, including two little children. Before doing this I had scanned the deck for others, but could see nobody about."

Mr Gibbons, commenting on the obstinate way in which passengers would go back to their cabins for nick-nacks:- "I saw one lady covered in furs complaining that she had several more left behind.

A LADIES MASCOT

She had a mascot in the shape of a little pig, which played a tune, and she would not leave the ship until she had secured her treasure. We drew away from the Titanic in charge of Mr Wheat, another steward, and when about half a mile away we saw her sink. The cries of those on board were terrible, and I doubt if the memory of them will ever leave me during my lifetime.

It has been denied by many that the band was playing, but it was doing so, and the strains of "Nearer, My God, to Thee," came clearly over the water with a solemnity so awful that words cannot express it."

Mr Gibbons mentioned a curious circumstance in connection with the iceberg that struck the Titanic. The berg, he said, was seen in the morning by the passengers, who mistook it for a cloud.

"HORRIBLE ACCUSATION"

Mr Ismay's Repudiation of a Sinister Suggestion

MORE SENSATIONAL STATEMENTS

WASHINGTON Tuesday

A sensation was caused to-day at the resumed Senate Inquiry into the loss of the Titanic by the testimony of Mr E. J. Dunn, of Beechurst, Long Island, to the effect that his father, a telegraphist in the service of the Western Union Company, told him a message announcing the sinking of the Titanic was delivered at the offices of the White Star Company on the Monday morning.

He was pressed to give the name of the person who gave his father this information, but refused to do so.

Mr Franklin, the vice-president of the International Merchantile Marine, interposed indignantly with a demand that this story should be thoroughly sifted.

Senator Burton stated that Mr Boxhall, the fourth officer of the Titanic, who gave evidence in private yesterday evening, declared that he heard Mr Andrews, the designer of the lost liner, inform Captain Smith, a few minutes after the collision, that the vessel would sink within an hour.

Mr Bruce Ismay was recalled and further examined at considerable length. He said he sent a wireless message to Mr Franklin on the Monday announcing that the Titanic had sunk, but it was not delivered until two days later.

Senator Smith:- Was any attempt made to re-insure the vessel after the accident? – Certainly not; it is a horrible accusation.

Mr Ismay went on to say that he courted the fullest inquiry into his personal conduct. He did not complain of his treatment at the hands of the committee, but he desired to return to England as soon as possible.

The Allan Line have decided to carry two Marconi wireless operators on each of their vessels.

The Mansion House Fund now totals £187,000.

BERG WITH BLADE IN IT

The bodies are remarkably well preserved. Most of them had very little clothing on when found, and several women were in night attire. Among the corpses was that of a boy two years old.

It was on Saturday (about six days after the Titanic foundered) that the first bodies recovered were found. The same night a burial service was held amid the icebergs.

From the side of the iceberg projected a large wedge-shaped blade, evidently torn from the liner. The berg, say those who saw it, had evidently been shattered by some great impact.

Bodies which were not identified (although a large number were remarkably well preserved) were wrapped in canvas and buried at sea in batches. A service took place at each burial, the ship's bell was tolled, and the crew stood with bare heads while Canon Hind recited the Church of England burial service. The hymn, "Jesu, Lover of My Soul," was sung by the ship's company.

AS A MEMORIAL TO MARCONI

(To the Editor of the *Daily Sketch*)

Sir, – It is an undoubted fact that nobody would have been saved from the ill-fated Titanic had it not been for the great invention of Signor Marconi. I would therefore suggest that one of the big liners soon to be launched should be named Marconi. – Yours, LORENZO SALAZAR

Kingstown, co Dublin

WIDOW'S ACTION FOR DAMAGES

Mrs Robins, widow of Colonel J. J. Astor's valet, has brought an action for damages against the owners of the Titanic, alleging that her husband was drowned through their wrongful acts. Mr Bruce Ismay, S/Off Lightoller, F/Off Boxhall, Mr Fleet and Mr Bride have all been served with subpoenas in connection with the case, this may delay their departure for England.

OLYMPIC HOLD-UP

Charge of Disobedience Against Crew

The 53 members of the Olympic's crew who were arrested because they refused to sail were again before the Portsmouth Bench yesterday. They were charged with disobeying the commands of the captain. All pleaded not guilty.

Mr Raeburn, who prosecuted, said that when the defendants left the Olympic and boarded the tender alongside, Captain Haddock ordered them to return and do their duty. The men refused, though repeatedly asked, and the captain made an entry in the official log.

For the defence Mr Emanuel said the men were arrested and taken before the Court illegally. They were placed under arrest before any warrant was issued.

Sir Thomas Bramsdon, the presiding magistrate, said the Bench considered they had jurisdiction, but they would be prepared to state a case.

The Olympic's purser, George Claude Borradaile, was asked if he could identify any of the men in dock with the offenders listed in the ship's log.

He picked out one or two, but as they were about to reply Mr Emanuel rose hastily and said to the men: "Don't say anything at all. Take no notice whatever."

The purser then found himself facing a double row of smiling seamen's faces, but the men preserved silence.

The case was adjourned until Saturday

COUNTESS AS PROGRAMME SELLER

At the matinee performance given yesterday afternoon at the London Hippodrome in aid of the Titanic relief fund barely a seat in any part of the house was unoccupied, and the Countess Townshend was among the ladies engaged in the sale of programmes, etc.

The performance, which lasted about five hours, included the presentation of lantern slides showing the arrival of the Carpathia at New York, sent specially from America for the matinee.

THE AMERICAN COMMITTEE LISTENING TO THE TERRIBLE S

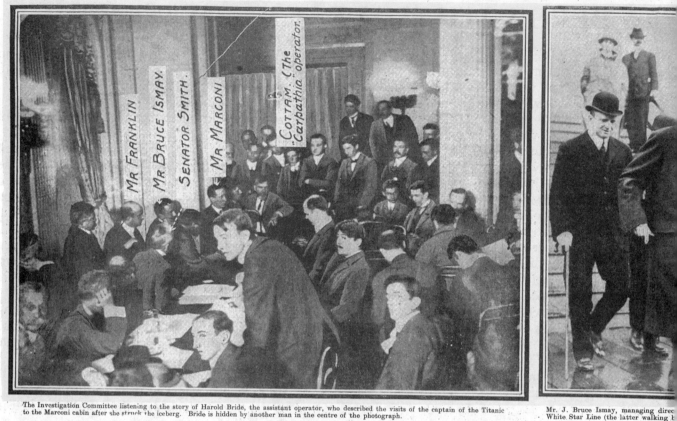

MR FRANKLIN

MR BRUCE ISMAY.

SENATOR SMITH.

MR MARCONI

COTTAM. (The "Carpathia" operator.

The Investigation Committee listening to the story of Harold Bride, the assistant operator, who described the visits of the captain of the Titanic to the Marconi cabin after she struck the iceberg. Bride is hidden by another man in the centre of the photograph.

Mr. J. Bruce Ismay, managing direc White Star Line (the latter walking b

THE PLIGHT OF THE SHIPWRECKED WOMEN.

Return of the Stewardesses

The Titanic survivors huddled together on the deck of the Carpathia as the latter turned back with them to New York. They had to borrow clothes, and were helped by the other passengers.

A group of the stewardesses of the Titanic photographed at Plym liner

Y OF THE TITANIC TRAGEDY FROM THE LIPS OF THE SAVED.

MR. FRANKLIN
GIVING EVIDENCE.

SENATOR SMITH
CHAIRMAN

A. S. Franklin, vice-president of the ‑ying umbrella) on their way to the

Mr. Franklin, the White Star Company's manager in New York, answering Senator Smith's questions in regard to the circulation of the false reports that several liners were standing by the Titanic and that she was in tow. A great number of fashionably dressed women crowded into the room where the investigation was held.

WE SLEPT ON THE CARPATHIA DECK EACH NIGHT.

Survived the Great Disaster.

them say they could not persuade the passengers to leave the big ‑ats.

The rescued passengers and stewardesses of the Titanic on board the Carpathia. The stewardesses say they slept on deck each night until they reached New York.

STILL COMING IN

Daily Sketch Shilling Fund Handed Over Today

We have, as announced yesterday, closed our S. O. S. Fund, and no more appeals will appear. Many of our readers sent us money yesterday, and this will, of course, be added to the fund. The total amount will be handed over to the Lord Mayor to-day.

It must not be understood that we cannot receive any more money. All that is sent will be acknowledged in our columns and duly handed over to the Mansion House Fund.

The little girl whose photograph appears is known best to her friends as Little Marzie. She collected 10s. for the fund at "The Queen of England," Goldhawk-road, Shepherd's Bush.

MAJOR PEUCHEN
A TITANIC SURVIVOR

Mr Arthur Peuchen, of Toronto, photographed with his wife and daughter after landing from the Carpathia. The Major was ordered into one of the Titanic boats by Officer Lightoller to act as a seaman, the Major being a skilled yachtsman, and he produced a certificate to this effect signed by the officer.

TITANIC MATINEE

Among the artistes who will positively appear at the Coliseum Titanic matinee to-day are Mr Arthur Bourchier and Miss Violet Vanbrugh, Mr Symour Hicks and Miss Ellaline Terriss, Miss Lydia Kyasht, Miss Constance Drever, Mr George Barrett and Miss Alice Russon, Mr C. H. Workman, Miss Esme Beringer and Co., Mlle Adeline Genee, Mr George Graves, Mr Arthur Prince, Little Tich, and most of the artistes appearing at the house this week. Mr Alfred Lester, as the Comedy Stage Director, will make continual appearances.

OLYMPIC CAPTAIN HEARS CASE AGAINST HIS MEN

Capt Haddock (x) listening to the charge at Portsmouth yesterday against the fifty-three Olympic sailors. The public portion of the Court was crowded.

The members of the crew waiting on the steps of Portsmouth Town Hall to surrender to their bail.

DAILY SKETCH.

No. 982.—THURSDAY, MAY 2, 1912.   THE PREMIER PICTURE PAPER.   [Registered as a Newspaper.]   ONE HALFPENNY.

BRITISH INQUIRY INTO THE TITANIC LOSS BEGINS TO-DAY.

The official inquiry ordered by the Board of Trade into the awful fate of the Titanic commences to-day at the Scottish Hall, Buckingham Gate. In the interior a big model of the lost liner and a large chart of the North Atlantic have been fixed. (1) Lord Mersey (formerly Mr. Justice Bigham), who will preside. (2) Professor J. H. Biles. (3) Rear-Admiral the Hon. S. A. Gough-Calthorpe. (4) Captain A. W. Clarke, Board of Trade Inspector and expert on boats. These are three of the assessors. (5) Mr. Raymond Asquith. (6) Mr. S. A. T. Rowlatt. (7) Mr. B. Aspinall, K.C., counsel for the Board of Trade.—Photographs by Daily Sketch, Elliott and Fry, and Lafayette.

LORD MAYOR'S THANKS

Cheque for 15,000 Shillings Handed Over

EVERY FARTHING WELCOME AS TOKENS OF SYMPATHY

(To the Editor of the *Daily Sketch*)

Mansion House, London E.C.
May 1, 1912

My dear Sir,

I sincerely thank you for so kindly remitting, for the Titanic Disaster Fund, the first instalment of £750 as the result of the appeal for shillings made to the readers of the *Daily Sketch*. To the 15,000 contributors of shillings which make up this large amount I beg you to convey my warmest thanks. It is very touching to observe the real sympathy felt, in this great calamity, by rich and poor, and I need hardly say that the offering of the farthing or shilling is as welcome to me, on behalf of the widows and orphans, as the very munificent contributions of the wealthy.

I am, my dear Sir,
Yours very truly,
Sir Thomas Crosby

BUSY DAYS AT THE MANSION HOUSE

The *Daily Sketch* called at the Mansion House yesterday to hand to the Lord Mayor of London a cheque for £750 (15,000 shillings) as a first instalment to the Titanic Relief Fund from *Daily Sketch* readers.

Unfortunately the Lord Mayor himself is still confined to his rooms by the effects of a chill contracted some days ago, and the cheque was received on his Lordship's behalf by his secretary, Sir William Soulsby.

The Lord Mayor (Alderman Sir Thomas Crosby) is greatly gratified by the prompt and generous response which has been made from all parts of the country to his appeal for assistance for the sufferers of the Titanic disaster. Every post brings fresh indications of the sympathy spontaneously evoked, and Sir William Soulsby, sitting in the sunny little workroom where the secretarial business of the Mansion House is daily transacted, is kept busy in penning acknowledgements of the practical help that is flowing in to the Lord Mayor's Fund.

THE REPLY TO OUR S.O.S. CALL

Immediately on the issue of the Lord Mayor's spirited appeal the *Daily Sketch* opened a subscription list, to which its readers, north, south, east and west, were invited to "Send On Shillings."

Nor have they been slow to answer to the call for help. The heart of the nation has been deeply touched, and all classes, from the highest to the lowest, have been eager to evince their appreciation of the spirit of true heroism shown in the hour of overwhelming calamity.

The *Daily Sketch* fund was specially started with the "widow's mite" in view, and it is expressed in terms of shillings which totalled to 15,000 in the cheque formally handed over yesterday to the Lord Mayor for the Mansion House Fund. It voices the ever-quick sympathy of many who, though poor maybe in this world's goods, are rich in the feelings of kinship and comradeship for them that mourn and suffer silently in deep distress.

FROM SCHOOLGIRLS AND SERVANTS

The very names under which many humble donors have elected to hide their identity are eloquent of this wonderful commonwealth of sorrow; and from the "Sailor's Widow," who offered her mite from a full heart that well knows the toll which the sea relentlessly takes of Britain's brave ones, to the "Happy Eight" of a single family sending their shillings in gratitude for their own freedom from all but a reflected sorrow, the fund is made up largely of small amounts freely given.

A schoolboy here and a schoolgirl there have dipped into their moneyboxes to help the fund. Servant girls with hearts immeasurably bigger than their purses, have given of their scanty savings. Workers who earn little themselves have spared their shillings that others might not want for the loss of them that went down with the Titanic. Even the workless have spared of their own small resources, as witness one offering in the name of "Got the Sack!"

"Old Traveller on the White Star Line," the "Old Black Horseman of Many Wars but Sorry to say no Scars," "One of God's Shut-ins," and "One on her way to China," are in their several ways typical of the call which the Titanic disaster has made to all humanity and of the humane answer nobly given.

TITANIC SUFFERERS' GRANTS

Official Trustee Willing to Administer Them

NECESSITY FOR CAUTION

In a short time the task of administering the various funds which have been subscribed for the relief of sufferers from the Titanic disaster will have to be undertaken, and the suggestion has been made that the interests of those who will benefit should be committed to the care of the Official Trustee.

Colonel Lockwood, from whom the suggestion comes, says: "I have had some knowledge of the benefits of this gentleman's experience in the past, both as regards public funds, and even such minor details as lower-class marriage settlements. I would suggest that his assistance should be sought from the earliest possible moment, both as regards the allocation and distribution of the fund."

Speaking yesterday to the *Daily Sketch*, the Public Trustee expressed his readiness to undertake the administration of the benefits on behalf of all or any of the beneficiaries.

"We acted as trustees to the English victims of the Messina disaster, who received grants from Mansion House Fund raised on that occasion," he said. "We were only called upon to administer 13 specific trusts in connection with that disaster, but we are quite prepared to deal with the more numerous cases which the Titanic disaster has brought in its train. We have all the machinery already at work, and could take up the task without confusion. All committees are ephemeral, but we go on forever.

If the interests of the widows and orphans were handed over to our care we should take the money allocated to them, invest it in safe securities, and administer it to the best advantage of the recipients. We have very wide powers of investment now, and can obtain very good returns for the moneys we invest.

In every case we get over 4 per cent.

It is very necessary that some responsible person should look after the interests of these poor folk. A very distressing case of hardship suffered through the injudicious investments of a trustee was brought to my notice recently. A man who had suffered a very serious injury received compensation to the amount of nearly £2,000. He was induced to invest the money in some small house property in London.

The property is in such a bad state of repair that a large sum will have to be spent to make it habitable, even if we can prevent the houses being closed altogether (I have only recently taken over the man's affairs). As a result of the difficulties into which he has got with the property it is very probable that he will lose some £800 or £900 of his capital."

A PERMANENT CHARITY

Lord Derby, Lord Mayor of Liverpool, yesterday announced that any surplus remaining in the Liverpool fund after the Titanic sufferers have been amply helped will be made the nucleus of a special and permanent fund for use in times of similar disaster.

TITANIC MATINEE AT COLISEUM

The Titanic matinee at the Coliseum was a magnificent success. The house was crowded, and the continuous entertainment provided by the company of stars was a treat the like of which comes very rarely.

It is impossible to individualise. Every turn was one of proved merit, and most of them have been favourably mentioned in the *Daily Sketch*.

Another point, and an important one, was that the advertised turns, with but one or two exceptions, made their appearance. That does not always happen at all star matinees.

TITANIC'S DEAD

£10,000 in Money and Jewellry Found on Bodies

Of the 190 Titanic bodies brought to Halifax by the cable ship Mackay Bennett, over 60 remain unidentified. Sixty of the corpses buried at sea were not identified.

According to the inventory made by Government officials the value of the money and jewellry found on the bodies amounts to 50,000 dollars (£10,000). A bag of gold was found on the body of a man who up to the present has not been identified.

According to a Central News telegram Captain Lardner, of the Mackay Bennett, said that they "came upon the bodies in packs, looking like swimmers asleep." There was no sign that any of the victims found had been shot.

The Senate Committee did not sit yesterday, Senator Smith arranged to proceed to New York last evening to take the testimony of some of the Titanic's rescued passengers.

LINERS RUNNING IN PAIRS

Mr Buxton, the President of the Board of Trade, stated last evening that he would consider the suggestion – although it appeared to him to be hardly feasible – of arranging with the United States Government that, during the period of danger from icebergs, it should be enacted that the great liners should travel two together, within easy reach. Mr Buxton also stated that lifebelts are tested by the officers of the Board of Trade in regard to their carrying properties, and the officers are instructed not to pass a belt that is not able to float in fresh water for 24 hours with 15lbs. of iron attached thereto. It is announced that full and authentic information as to the lost and saved will be submitted to the Court of Inquiry as early as possible.

BRITISH TITANIC INQUIRY

The British Inquiry into the loss of the Titanic will begin to-day at the Scottish Hall, Buckingham Gate. A large model of the liner has been installed.

FIRST INSTALMENT OF OUR SHILLING FUND PAID IN

On behalf of the Lord Mayor, his secretary, Sir William Soulsby, received yesterday from the *Daily Sketch* the first instalment of the shillings contributed by our readers for sufferers from the Titanic disaster. In the photograph a receipt is being made out for the cheque for 15,000 shillings, which was handed over to be added to the Mansion House Fund.

ALL THAT REMAINS OF THE TITANIC

The lifeboats of the Titanic lying in the Cunard Dock at New York after they were lowered from the Carpathia. According to New York papers the photographer who went out in a boat to take the pictures was shot at from one of the piers.

PROVING SEAWORTHINESS OF LINER'S LIFEBOATS

The Philadelphia which sailed yesterday from Southampton for New York with a full complement of passengers, including many from the Olympic, had all the lifeboats removed to the harbour basin and tested to prove to the crew their seaworthiness. The boats are seen lying in the water.

*A popular method of fund raising was the publication of books about the disaster. This rare example, 'THE FALLEN PILLAR' by Sylvanus (a term used to denote a number of different authors) was published in 1912 by "The New Life" Magazine, a religious periodical.**

The introduction to the verses reads:

"THE NEW LIFE" Magazine devotes this effort of its staff and readers to the cause of the afflicted. Each booklet sold will bring food to the "widow's cruse," and serve to perpetuate the memory of a great disaster that has brought nearer to all the truth of an old saying: "IN THE MID'ST OF LIFE WE ARE IN DEATH."

The profits from the sale of this booklet will be devoted to the succouring of the widows and orphans of the Titanic's crew, and all who engage in its sale and distribution, make of themselves servants of the Universal Soul.

*A number of illustrations from the booklet are reproduced throughout this book.**

DAILY SKETCH.

No. 983.—FRIDAY, MAY 3, 1912.   THE PREMIER PICTURE PAPER.   [Registered as a Newspaper.]   ONE HALFPENNY.

BRITISH INQUIRY OPENED INTO THE TITANIC DISASTER.

The scene inside the London Scottish Drill Hall, Buckingham Gate, yesterday, at the opening of the British inquiry into the loss of the Titanic. Lord Mersey himself constitutes the Court of Inquiry, but his lordship has the advice and assistance of a number of assessors, all experts. They are seated on the dais in the upper picture, models and charts occupying one side of the hall, and there is accommodation for a large number of people. Yesterday was largely occupied by the opening speech of Sir Rufus Isaacs.

THE TITANIC INQUIRY

Dispute Between Counsel and Lord Mersey

WIDOW'S APPLICATION

Will Passengers be Allowed to be represented

The opening of the inquiry into the Titanic disaster was marked by a dispute between Lord Mersey, who is presiding over the Court, and several barristers who had been instructed by clients desiring to be represented at the investigation.

Lord Mersey allowed the National Sailors' and Firemen's Union and the Chamber of Shipping to be represented from the outset.

As to the British Seafarers' Union (to whom many of the members of the White Star crews belong), the Imperial Merchant Service Guild (an organisation composed of ship's officers), the Dockers' Union, the Ship Constructors' and Shipwrights' Association, his Lordship decided that for the time being they should not be allowed to appear. But if during the inquiry it occurred to him that it was desirable they should be represented permission would be granted.

Lord Mersey said his ruling was subject to anything the Attorney-General (Sir Rufus Isaacs) might have to say. Sir Rufus Isaacs replied that he raised no objection.

To a barrister who asked to be allowed to appear for the widow of a first-class passenger Lord Mersey said: "I cannot listen to that at present." It is understood that several surviving passengers and relatives of passengers desire to be represented.

The inquiry opened in the Scottish Hall, Buckingham Gate, but it was found that the hall was unsuitable in that it was very difficult to hear what was said.

Owing, however, to the difficulty experienced in securing any suitable hall in the vicinity of Westminster, it is proposed to make the best of the Scottish Hall, and the *Daily Sketch* learns that large sounding-boards will be installed in order to improve the acoustics of the building.

LORD MERSEY ALMOST INAUDIBLE

From the back benches scarcely a word uttered by Lord Mersey was audible, and when Sir Robert Finlay (leading counsel for the White Star Line) drew attention to the matter, his Lordship remarked "I absolutely agree with you," and suggested that the Board of Trade solicitor should furnish other accommodation.

Beyond the fact that an immense model of the Olympic – sister ship to the Titanic, and therefore suitable for the purposes of the inquiry – was placed in one corner of the hall, with a chart of the North Atlantic nearby, and a sectional plan of the lost vessel over the way, the Court at first sight had nothing distinctly maritime about it.

Those who expected to see naval uniforms about were disappointed, for there was not a single uniform in the hall and only a pointed beard here and a sun-tanned face there betrayed the presence of men who have made the sea their profession.

The President of the Court and his five assessors sat upon a platform draped with plush curtains and furnished with desks and polished chairs.

At least fifty legal representatives of interest involved were ranged facing the bench.

The two chief counsel, Sir Rufus Isaacs for the Government, and Sir Robert Finlay for the White Star Line – the one youthful, the other silver-haired – were each precise in their methods. Sir John Simon sat next to Sir Rufus Isaacs, prompting and suggesting.

Farthest from his principal was Mr Raymond Asquith, the Premier's son, who was examining the section of the Titanic hung high above him.

It was curious to observe that while ordinarily the Court and counsel dispensed with glasses and spectacles, in the consultation of documents they were generally employed.

A special seat was reserved for Mrs Asquith.

About 300 witnesses have been summoned to attend the inquiry which was adjourned until to-day.

TITANIC'S BANDMASTER

Found With His Music Case Strapped To Him

HALIFAX, N.S. Thursday

The ship's surgeon of the Mackay Bennett has stated that after carefully examining the bodies recovered, he came to the conclusion that the majority died peacefully and without suffering, while the minority were instantaneously killed.

The body of Frederick Hartley, the heroic band-master of the Titanic, was identified last night. His music case was found strapped to the body. This will be forwarded to the White Star Company.

Many unclaimed dead will be buried here. A joint memorial service will be held on Friday at eleven o'clock. It will be conducted by the Evangelical Alliance, who express the hope that similar services will be held in England and the United States at the same hour.

THE MYSTERY SHIP

Reported Statement By British Captain

"HEARD PASSENGERS' VOICES"

PARIS Thursday

A telegram from Algiers to *Le Journal* suggests that the mysterious ship seen from the Titanic might have been the British steamer Kura, which arrived yesterday at Algiers from New York.

The Captain of the Kura remembers having had a glimpse of a large liner through the fog, and having heard the voices of passengers; but the dense mist prevented him from discovering anything abnormal concerning the liner. He concentrated his attention upon avoiding the icebergs. He did not hear of the catastrophe until he arrived at Algiers. The Kura left in the evening for Genoa.

THE MANSION HOUSE FUND

The Mansion House Fund has reached the sum of £217,000.

MR ISMAY LEAVES FOR HOME

NEW YORK Thursday

Mr Bruce Ismay, the officers Leightoller, Pittman, Lowe and Boxhall, and the thirty other survivors of the Titanic disaster, sailed for England to-day by the Adriatic.

Mr Ismay was pale, and looked worn out. Interviewed immediately before his departure, he said he did not complain of the conduct of the Senate inquiry, and would not comment for publication in the press on the treatment he had received.

"I am intensely thankful," he added "to be going home after the most tragic experience in my life, and I am prepared to assist to the utmost the further investigation of the disaster."

TITANIC'S CHIEF ENGINEER

Mr Joseph Bell, R.N.R., the chief engineer on the ill-fated Titanic. Mr Bell, it is said, was implored by some of the seamen to climb on a raft, but went to his death with a smile and the cry "No lads, my extra weight would sink it." 51 years of age, and leaving a widow and 4 children. He had worked on a score of the company's boats.

THE ASTOR INHERITANCE

The entrance hall and staircase of the Astor mansion on Fifth-avenue, New York. Inset are portraits of Mr Vincent Astor, who is now the head of the family, and Miss Muriel Astor, his sister, who inherits £3,000,000 under the will of their father, Colonel Astor.

SOCIAL AND PERSONAL

Gossip About Prominent People

The Astor Succession

The tragedy of the Titanic has changed things very considerably for Mr Vincent Astor. He may complete his course at Harvard, but there are infinitely more important matters to claim his consideration and engage his time, for Vincent Astor has become the head of his house, and possessor of one of the greatest fortunes in America.

No Astor has before succeeded to headship at so young an age as this boy, who will not be twenty-one until November 15 next. His father was twenty-eight before he succeeded, and his grandfather was sixty. His great-grandfather was fifty-three and his father was fifty-six.

An Invalid Childhood

Vincent Astor was born in the family mansion at Fifth-avenue and Thirty-fourth-street five months before his grandfather died and his father became head of the house. He was so frail a baby that only unremitting care kept him alive. He lived the loneliest of little-boyhoods because of this, and when other children romped in the open air he sat over a toy piano in a nursery to which no playmates ever came. Servants saved him every exertion; nurses were always with him; physicians awaited calls to him that had precedence over all others.

When he was twelve he almost died from appendicitis. In less than a year he was saved from death by another surgical operation, this time for a growth in the throat following an attack of mumps. He was taken every year then to the Riviera because of bronchial trouble, and his education was being directed by a tutor, who lived with him in a house taken for his exclusive use at Tuxedo.

His Chief Passion

Last autumn it was said that Vincent Astor had entered Harvard "with the distinction of having more clothes than any man at the university." Student correspondents sent forth tales of his "twenty suits for outdoor wear," of his "ten pairs of shoes, five of which are polished every morning," and of the six trunks that were filled with his "shirts, scarves, and neckwear."

Automobiling, however, has been young Astor's passion. He has had a long line of machines, each a bit more powerful than that which preceded it. Newport has not wholly recovered yet from the race he drove last August against Mr Hermann Oelrichs. They had come close to a speed of 110 miles an hour, when Oelrichs' machine burst into flames and Astor's machine wrenched itself from his control and plunged into the sea. Before he could recover himself a wave had broken over his head. It took four horses to drag the car from the grip of the sand that had packed about it.

At the Titanic Inquiry

Sir Rufus Isaacs, who is the principal counsel representing the Board of Trade at the Titanic inquiry, had considerable mercantile and commercial experience before he turned his attention to the Bar. He is a great friend of Mr Lloyd George, and it is generally believed that he will become Lord Chief Justice whenever Lord Alverstone retires. It is an open secret that his success as a Parliamentarian has not quite equalled his success as an advocate in the Courts, Sir John Simon, the Solicitor-General, being considered the ideal Parliamentarian as well as the profound lawyer.

One of Sir Rufus's brothers is a popular business man in the City, while another, Mr Godfrey Isaacs, is the managing director of the Marconi Wireless Telegraph Companies and a very able man of affairs. The Attorney-General is a connection by marriage of the distinguished Belgian author, Monsieur Maeterlinck, as well as another successful dramatist, Mr Alfred Sutro.

FIRST DAY OF THE BRITISH INQUIRY INTO THE LOSS (

Lord Mersey and his son, Captain Clive Bigham, who acts as secretary to the inquiry, on the way to the hall.

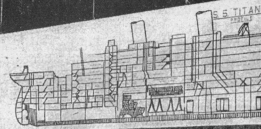

Sir Rufus Isaacs arriving.   Sir Robert Finlay, K.C., and his so for the

Profile section of the lost liner hung from the ladies' gallery. Lord Mersey has alrea

Revival of Ye Olde English Maye Daye : Clever Masque Perfor

The Right Hon. Ale Carlisle, designer of the tanic.

Teasing the unlucky occupant of the stocks—a sport that was greatly enjoyed.

The squire and his lady

E TITANIC, WHICH IS EXPECTED TO LAST MANY WEEKS.

iving. Sir Robert is retained   Rear-Admiral Gough-Calthorpe and Professor Biles.

Captain A. W. Clarke, Elder Brother of the Trinity, and Commander F. C. Lyon, R.N.R.
—two of the assessors.

r room, the acoustics of the Scottish Hall being imperfect for such a vital inquiry.

wich by Local Amateurs who Appeared in Costumes of the Period.

s to take part in the revels.

Another phase of the revels—joining in the Morris-dance.

Mr. Saunderson, managing director of the White
Star Line.

"FIRST OF JOURNALISTS"

Earl Grey's Tribute to the Late Mr W.T. Stead

An eloquent tribute to the memory of the late Mr W.T. Stead was paid by Earl Grey at the annual dinner of the Newspaper Press Fund at the Whitehall Rooms last night.

Mr Stead, Earl Grey said, embodied perhaps more fully than any other the characteristics of the journalistic crusader. He enjoyed the privilege of the late Mr Stead's acquaintance and friendship for over 30 years. He had visited him in gaol when he was paying the penalty of the law for journalistic indiscretions.

No danger ever appalled him. His stout spear was ever at the charge on behalf of a losing side, to the general detriment of his own interests.

To make, not to record, history, was ever the late gentleman's noble and disinterested ambition.

Although often profoundly differing from his views, Lord Grey had always regarded with affection and esteem Mr Stead's chivalrous and quixotic character, and had admired him, certainly during the early eighties as the "first of journalists."

A CHILD'S SYMPATHY

"I send you a shilling which I have saved to help some poor child who has lost its father. My own father died very suddenly two years ago, and I feel sorry for those children who have lost their friends in this terrible disaster."

This is the pathetic little letter which accompanies a remittance to our Shilling Fund.

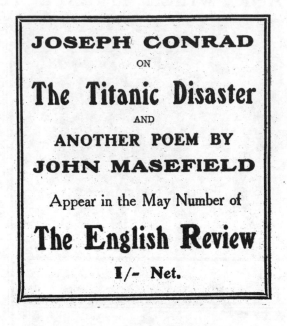

JOSEPH CONRAD ON

The Titanic Disaster

AND

ANOTHER POEM BY JOHN MASEFIELD

Appear in the May Number of

The English Review

I/- Net.

THINLY-CLAD WOMEN IN THE BOATS

Writing to the *Daily Sketch* Mr George Francis, of Saville-street, Marylebone, says:

"In your issue of the 30th ult. you produced some excellent photographs of the Titanic's boats bearing survivors of the terrible disaster alongside the Carpathia. In one you can discern a woman clad in her night attire. Does not this speak volumes for the modern selfish trend of manhood?

The poor woman had evidently sat for hours in that open boat, while the men occupants were all wearing coats. At least one of them should have given his coat to cover the semi-naked form of a woman, seeing that they had rowing exercise to keep their blood in circulation.

I suggest that if such an accident had happened a decade ago there would not have been such a spectacle – a woman sitting partially naked in a boat in an ice-chilled atmosphere, while strong men who were more physically fit to resist cold were warmly clad.

HOW THE TITANIC WAS WARNED

Lord Mersey on the Peril Of the Ice

"SPEED NOT REDUCED"

Look-Out Men Were Without Glasses

Sir Rufus Isaacs made his opening statement at the Titanic inquiry yesterday, and afterwards Able Seaman Joseph Scarrott and Archie Jewell, a look-out man, gave vivid accounts of the disaster.

During Sir Rufus Isaacs' opening statement Lord Mersey remarked that it would appear as if the Titanic made straight for the locality where ice had been reported; whereupon, Mr Laing, for the White Star Line, said there was some doubt as to the position of the ship when she struck.

An important point, said Sir Rufus Isaacs, was that the vessel did not reduce her speed from 21 knots after receiving the warnings about ice, although the temperature indicated the presence of ice.

The boats could carry 1,167 persons, and the number saved was 703.

Sir Rufus said the figures as to the number of survivors in each class were striking.

Scarrott described the ghastly appearance of those in a boat that went to the rescue after the Titanic sank.

So dense was the mass of corpses and wreckage that it took them half an hour to rescue a man who was only about fifteen yards away.

Some foreigners tried to rush a boat because they did not understand his orders, and he had to use "a little persuasion with the boat's tiller." It was at this time that Fifth Officer Lowe fired his revolver as a warning.

Scarrott gave the number of seamen on the ship as 42 or 43, and said that at least 64 skilled men were required to lower the boats.

Jewell said the look-out men were not provided with glasses.

Asked to describe the shape of the berg that struck the Titanic, Scarrott said it was like the Rock of Gibraltar.

On Monday Lord Mersey and the other members of the Commission will go to Southampton to inspect the Olympic, the Titanic's sister ship.

A sounding board has been put up in the Scottish Hall, and this effected such an improvement that it was decided to continue the inquiry there. The investigation will be resumed on Tuesday.

"GROWLERS IN THE TRACK"

Attorney-General's Opening Statement

When the Titanic inquiry was resumed yesterday Lord Mersey revised some of his rulings of the previous day and allowed the Merchant Service Guild (to which the officers of the ship belong), the Seafarers' Union, and the National Union of Stewards to be represented.

Asked if a passenger might be represented, Lord Mersey said, "I shall see about that later on."

Sir Rufus Isaacs then opened the case for the Government. The Titanic, he said "was certified to carry 3,547 persons all told. There were 1,316 passengers on board and 892 crew – 2,208 altogether. She carried fourteen lifeboats, two cutters and four collapsible boats; and the capacity of these was 1167. (The number saved was 703) There were 3360 life-belts or other approved similar articles and 48 lifebuoys.

She was designed on the principle that she would remain afloat in the event of any two adjoining compartments being flooded.

Her horse-power was sufficient to give a speed of at least 21 knots.

Coming to the voyage, Sir Rufus Isaacs said it was a quiet and successful one up to the collision. The weather was fine all the way and the sea was calm.

A STARRY NIGHT

The collision with the iceberg occurred about 12.40 p.m. It was a starry night, and the atmosphere was clear – some witnesses said it was particularly clear. There was no moon.

The vessel – beyond all question – up to the time of the casualty was going at a pace of 21 knots.

As far as he was able to gather from the evidence the speed was never reduced, and she continued at the speed during the whole of April 14, right up to the time of the collision with the iceberg, not-withstanding warnings that there were icebergs in the neighbourhood, and that in the track in which she was proceeding she would meet them, or would be likely to.

At the moment they were able to bring before the Court evidence of two vessels – the Caronia and the Baltic – having by means of telegraphy informed the Titanic during the day that icebergs, "growlers," and field ice were reported in the track along which the Titanic was proceeding.

The President: What is the description?

Sir Rufus Isaacs: Icebergs, "growler" and field ice. I think the distinction, so far as I follow it, between icebergs and "growlers" is that the "growler" is an iceberg with very little protruding above the water.

The messages from the Caronia and the Baltic were acknowledged by the Titanic.

Sir Rufus Isaacs then directed the President's attention to the fact that between January and August, on account of ice, there were more southerly tracks for vessels than at other periods of the year. The Titanic, he said, travelling along the track which was marked for her at that time of the year on the chart.

After consulting marked charts the President asked: Am I right in supposing she ran right into the locality where ice was after the warning that ice was there?

Sir Rufus Isaacs: Yes.

The President: That is what it comes to.

Mr Laing (for White Star Company) said there was some difference of opinion as to the exact spot where the collision occurred.

The President: It is not a question of the exact spot. According to the indications made by my colleagues on this chart it looks as if she, having had warning, made for ice.

Mr Laing said that there might be a substantial difference as to the place of the collision.

The President: If you say so I will wait.

Sir Rufus Isaacs said that undoubtedly during the Sunday the temperature was extremely cold.

Before the collision the cold had increased. That, Sir Rufus submitted, was an indication to those who were responsible for the Titanic navigation of the close proximity to ice, especially when taken in conjunction with the fact that she was then approaching the zone in respect to which she had received a warning that there were growlers, icebergs and fields of ice.

A GREAT RUSH AFT

The vessel sank by the head, and when she began to settle down a large number of people rushed aft and remained there until she foundered.

Sir Rufus Isaacs then analysed the list of survivors. He said:- "The striking figures which no doubt will engage the Court's attention are that 63 per cent. of the first-class passengers were saved, 42 per cent. of the second-class, but only 25 per cent. of the third-class, and 23 per cent. of the crew."

Sir Rufus mentioned another "striking figure" All except five of the first-class women passengers were saved. "If," he said, "you assume that those five refused to leave their husbands, the consequence is, one must take it, that all the women of the first class either were saved or had the opportunity of being saved and refused to avail themselves of it."

"RUSHED THE GATE"

Steerage Passenger's Story of How He Was Saved

The Senatorial inquiry into the Titanic disaster was resumed to-day, when a steerage passenger named Daniel Buckley, of Cork, told a dramatic story of his own and his fellow passengers' experiences. He said the first that was known of the disaster in the steerage quarters was when water began to pour in and a steward shouted to them:

"Get out, unless you want to be drowned like rats!"

Buckley ran up on deck, where he found a steward trying to lock the gate which separated the first and second decks. The steward knocked down a man who tried to prevent him fastening the gate, but eventually they all rushed the gate together.

Buckley saw five boats lowered on the starboard side of the liner. As the sixth was about to leave a number of men got in, but an officer ordered them out. Buckley was in this boat and Mrs Astor, who was also an occupant, covered him with her shawl, enabling him to lie hidden.

LOOK-OUT MAN

Says Crow's Nest Was
Warned About Ice

Archie Jewell, one of the look-out men on the Titanic, was the first witness called at the inquiry.

He said he was in the crow's nest from 8 to 10 on the Sunday night with another look-out man named Symons. The men on that duty took two hours each. When the weather was clear only two men were on the look-out. It was clear on the Sunday night.

At 9.30 a message was received on the telephone from the bridge: "Keep a sharp look-out for all ice, big and small." He thought it was the second officer who sent the message.

Up to that time they had seen no ice, and when he and Symons were relieved at ten o'clock by Fleet and Leigh he passed the message on to them, having seen no ice at all. Fleet and Leigh, he mentioned, "were being kept back in New York."

Jewell said that after he had turned in he was awakened by a crash. Rushing on deck he saw ice on the weather deck, and went below again, "because we did not think there was any harm. Later the bo'sun cried, All hands on deck!"

BOAT DRILL

Questioned about the boat drill at Southampton he said there were only two boats lowered away. Is that the practice? – Yes, Sir, that is the practice.

Continuing, Jewell said that all but four of those in his boat – the first to be lowered on the starboard side – were women and children. The boat might have held a few more. Three or four Frenchmen got into the boat. The Solicitor-General: Was there any excitement? – No, none

at all. It was very quiet. He thought a lifeboat was usually provided with a light.

The President: Whose business is it to look after the light? Jewell: The men at Southampton who come aboard the ship.

Jewell said his boat was lowered by the order of Mr Murdock.

When they thought the ship was sinking by the head they pulled clear a long distance away. That was about half an hour before she disappeared. They met Mr Pittman, the third officer, and he lashed his boat alongside theirs till the morning.

In answer to Mr Scanlon, who appeared for the National Sailors and Firemen's Union, Jewell said that no glasses were supplied.

"NOT IN A HURRY"

Mr Scanlan: Were you equipped with glasses on the Titanic? – We never had any glasses. On other boats on which you have been was it usual to supply glasses? – We had them on the Oceanic. Jewell added that he believed his mate on the Titanic had asked for glasses. Do you derive much help from glasses when you are on the look-out? – Yes, they are very useful. The President: How often have you used glasses? – Only on the Oceanic.

The Titanic and the Oceanic were the only liners on which he had sailed. There was a box for glasses in the crow's nest of the Titanic, but there were no glasses in the box. He had sailed seven or eight voyages in the Oceanic.

The President: And half a voyage on this one.

Jewell said he saw no searchlights on either the Oceanic or Titanic. It was generally the case that the men were called to the boats for drill on Sundays. But it was not done on the Titanic as there was a strong wind until sunset.

Jewell said he was rowing for seven hours and he had nothing to eat or drink. Biscuits and water were supposed to be put in the boats in port. There was water on board his boat, but he could not say whether there were any biscuits; he did not think anyone looked to see.

How long did the boat you were in take to prepare and lower? – Half an hour at least. We were not in a hurry.

The President complimented Jewell on the way he had given his evidence.

MAN WHO WAS PULLED BACK

Says Officer Shot Two Men Who Tried to Enter Boat

A graphic description of the scene on the Titanic after the boats had gone is given by an Athlone survivor, Mr Eugene Daly, in a letter to his sister.

He says he aroused two local lady passengers from his district and all three knelt down in the gangway and prayed.

"We afterwards went to the second cabin deck," he continues, "and the two girls and myself got into a boat. An officer called on me to go back, but I would not stir. They then got hold of me and pulled me out.

At the first cabin, when a boat was being lowered, an officer pointed a revolver and said if any man tried to get in he would shoot him on the spot. I saw the officer shoot two men dead because they tried to get into the boat. Afterwards there was another shot, and I saw the officer himself lying on the deck. They told me he shot himself, but I did not see him.

I was up to my knees in water at the time. Everyone was rushing around and there were no more boats. I then dived overboard and got in a boat."

Another survivor from the Athlone district, Miss Bertha Mulvehill, says she lost a picture of Robert Emmet, the Irish patriot, and as the ship went down all she said was "Good-bye, Robert."

A.B.'S STORY

"Ample Time to Rescue Third-Class Women"

Able Seaman Joseph Scarrott, the second witness at the Titanic inquiry, said that there was ample time for the third-class women and children to be got into the boats before the vessel sank.

The iceberg that struck the vessel resembled the Rock of Gibraltar, and it was about sixty feet out of the water – about as high as the boat deck.

He helped with four boats before he joined his own boat. There were 58 passengers in his boat – all women and children.

"There were some men," he said, "who tried to rush the boat, foreigners they were, because they could not understand the order I gave them and I had to use a little persuasion with the boat's tiller." (Laughter.) One man jumped in twice and Scarrott threw him out the last time. Mr Lowe, the fifth officer, was in his boat.

"I told him," Scarrott continued, "about the rushing business, and he said 'All right.' He pulled out his revolver and fired two shots between the ship and the boat's side and told them if any more rushing took place he would use it."

After the ship sank, his boat and four others that were under Mr Lowe's direction rowed to where she went down to see if they could pick up anybody.

After remaining until all hope of further rescue on the spot had to be abandoned Mr Lowe ordered all the boats to be tied together with the object he said of attracting the notice of any passing steamers.

"BODIES HANGING IN A CLUSTER"

"While that was going on," said Scarrott, "we heard cries coming from another direction. Mr Lowe decided to transfer our passengers among the other boats, and then make up the full crew of men to go in the direction of the cries. Then we went among the wreckage. When we got where these cries were we were among hundreds of dead bodies floating in lifebelts.

The wreckage and the bodies seemed to be hanging in one cluster. We pushed our way among the wreckage, and as we got towards the centre we saw a man – I have since found out he was a storekeeper – on the top of a staircase or a large piece of wreckage as if he was praying and at the same time calling for help.

When we saw him we were about as near as that wall (15 yards) from him, and the wreckage was so thick – I am sorry to say that there were more bodies than there was wreckage – that it took us quite half an hour to get that distance to that man. We could not row the boat through the bodies. We had to push them out the way, to force our way to the man. We could not get close enough to get him right off, only within reach of an oar. We pulled him off with that and he managed to hang on and get into the boat. We got four men into the boat and one died."

Just as they got clear of the wreckage they saw the Carpathia's lights. They took on board twenty people from a water-logged collapsible boat, two of whom were women, and took another collapsible boat in tow.

In further evidence Scarrott said the ship struck about 11.40 p.m., and it was about one o'clock when his boat got into the water. In the interval when they were getting the boats ready for lowering. Some time elapsed after the boats had been swung out before they had orders to take in passengers. It was 12.30 when they started putting the women into the boats. Apart from the rush by three or four foreigners there was no panic.

THIRD CLASS AND THE BOATS

Asked what were the means of summoning third-class passengers to the boats, he replied: "I do not know any special means. That would be in the stewards' department."

First and second class passengers would have a better chance of getting to the boats because they were always allowed to go on deck where they were lowered.

Is it not the case that from the time the collision happened until you were ready to take in passengers there was ample time for the women and children in the steerage to be brought to the boat deck? – Yes. There was ample time.

His boat was without its lamp. It was very important, he thought, that a lifeboat should be provided with a lamp.

Scarrott said that when they rowed back to the scene after the Titanic went down, eight men were rowing.

How many men are necessary for the proper handling of a boat that size? – Eight, and a man at the tiller in a storm certainly would be necessary to safely navigate a boat. When we left the Titanic, there was only one man on board who was a capable seaman. "That man was myself," added Scarrott, apparently as an afterthought, and the Court laughed.

There were not enough men when he got to the boat deck to lower the boats successfully.

It was difficult for the third-class passengers to get on the boat deck.

The President: In what sense? There was only one ladder leading to it. Afterwards Scarrott said that there was a ladder on both sides of the ship.

MRS ASTOR'S VIGIL

NEW YORK Friday

The funeral of Colonel Astor will take place to-morrow.

The young bride has remained alone by the side of the coffin almost continuously from the time it was taken to Rhineback Mansion.

GLAD HE WAS NOT IN THE TITANIC

Among the many men who count themselves fortunate that they did not sail in the Titanic is Mr F. H. R. Scheibner, a well-known West End restaurant manager, who was in expectation of being appointed to control the luxurious restaurant of the great floating hotel, but was, as he now sees, fortunately disappointed in that respect, to become manager of the new Blanchard's Restaurant which has risen on the site of the old establishment of that name in Beak-street, Regent-street.

Blanchard's, which is to be opened to the public on Monday, was given an auspicious send-off on Thursday evening, Sir Thomas Dewar presiding over a large gathering. For a "first night" in new premises everything went with wonderful smoothness, for which Mr Scheibner was deservedly congratulated.

Blanchard's is not a place of overwhelming luxuriousness, but there is elegant comfort, and the intention of the management is to provide good fare at reasonable charges.

THE MANSION HOUSE FUND

The Lord Mayor's Fund for the benefit of the Titanic sufferers amounted last night to £222,000.

SURVIVORS' GRATITUDE

Fund Opened on Board the Carpathia

GIFTS TO THE CREW

Steward's Story of Pathetic Scenes

A graphic account of the scenes on board the Carpathia after she received the S.O.S. signal from the Titanic was told by Mr J. W. Barker, of the Carpathia, in an interview with the *Daily Sketch* yesterday.

Captain Rostron had given orders for the ship to proceed at her utmost speed to the scene of the disaster when Mr Barker was called up from his bunk and found preparations being made for the reception of two thousand passengers from the sinking liner. So quietly were the arrangements made that not one of the thousand passengers on the Carpathia had been roused from their sleep.

For some time the wireless operator had been unable to get any reply to his messages and the rescuing ship was forging ahead, the engineers and firemen being unsparing in their efforts to obtain the utmost speed out of the vessel.

About 3.15 a blue flare was seen, and shortly afterwards the huge iceberg that was undoubtably the cause of the disaster loomed through the darkness in the distance.

It was frequently necessary to alter the Carpathia's course to avoid the icefield, and the first lifeboat was seen a little before 4 o'clock. Ten minutes afterwards she came alongside, half filled with women and children. Then it became known that the "unsinkable" Titanic had foundered after striking the iceberg. The survivors, many of them half-frozen in their scanty attire, were handed over to the medical staff and stewards.

Day was breaking and the other boats could all be seen within an area of about four miles. The scenes when the survivors were taken on board were heartrendering. One woman who had lost her husband had to be restrained from jumping overboard.

An Army officer had seen his mother thrown out of a collapsible boat which capsized and was unconscious as the result of a search for her in the ice-cold water.

At 8 o'clock all the boats had been picked up, but two survivors were so exhausted that they died while being taken on board. The bravery and self-possession of the saved, most of whom were women who had lost their husbands, was admirable. The Carpathia's passengers and officers gave up their cabins and the saloons, library and smoke-rooms were also used for sleeping quarters.

Mr J. W. Barker

On the Tuesday following the rescue a fund was inaugurated by the survivors to present a loving cup to Captain Rostron and the officers, a purse to the Carpathia's crew and a purse to the surviving officers and crew of the Titanic. In ten minutes 3,000 dollars had been subscribed, and other large sums had been promised. On the return voyage of the Carpathia to England the men were mustered by the Captain, who thanked them for their assistance and expressed his pride at being the commander of such a ship's company.

Later Captain Rostron presented the survivors' gift to the men, the average amount received being ten dollars each. It is proposed to entertain the men to a banquet and to present each with a suitably inscribed gold medal on their next arrival in New York.

AND·THE·SPIRIT·SHALL·RETURN
UNTO·GOD·WHO·GAVE·IT

"Down, down, and downwards, moves the giant dream,
Towards its last great anchorage."

LOOK-OUT MAN, THE FIRST WITNESS GIVING EVIDENCE AT

Jewell, the look-out man, photographed outside the hall where the inquiry is being held.—*Daily Sketch* Photograph.

The Titanic inquiry proper opened yesterday when after the statement by Sir Rufus Isaacs, the Attorney-General, evi was called. The first witness was Archie Jewell, who was in the crow's nest from 8 to 10 p.m. on the night of the disaster.

THE TAILORS' STRIKE: PICKETS WITH TAPE MEASURES AMONG THE SHOPS.

Tailors and tailoresses prepared for picket duty, and carrying their tape measures, stationed at Marlborough-street in connection with the present strike. The dispute, which hinges on a demand for higher wages, shorter hours, and better working accommodation on the part of the men, has come at the worst time for the public. It is estimated that 160 firms are severely affected by the trouble, whilst thousands of men's suits and several thousands of costumes for women have been stopped in the making.

Mr. Lewis, president of the National Seafarers' the detention at Plymouth of the members of hi who are witnesses at t

TITANIC INQUIRY, SAYS HE SAW NO ICE ON FATAL EVENING.

examined by the Solicitor-General, Sir John Simon, and said he saw no ice. Mr. Scanlan, M.P., is shown above questioning witness on behalf of the Seamen's Union. The assessors are on the dais on the right.—*Daily Sketch* Photograph.

Captain Haddock and Mr. Saunderson, managing director of the White Star Line. Inset—Mr. Scanlan.—*Daily Sketch* Photograph.

ccessfully pr   ted to the Board of Trade against
  among the survivors, with some of the seamen
      Sketch Photograph

ALARMING CARRIAGE ACCIDENT DUE TO HANDKERCHIEF WAVING.

The carriage containing the Mayor and Mayoress of Morecambe and the Mayor and Mayoress of Pudsey as it appeared after being overturned—due to the horses shying at some children's handkerchief waving at Blackpool at the opening of the new marine promenade by Princess Louise. Although at the time of the accident over 100,000 people were packed together in the vicinity nobody was seriously hurt.

ON BOARD THE RESCUE SHIP

Vivid Story of the Scenes on the Carpathia

GRIEF-STRICKEN WOMEN

The Saved Make Presents to their Rescuers

Below the *Daily Sketch* is able to give the first complete account of the scenes on the rescue ship that rushed to the aid of the doomed Titanic and carried her surviving passengers and crew on to New York.

The vivid narrative is told in the words of Mr J. W. Barker, of the victualling department of the Carpathia, in an interview with the *Daily Sketch* after his return to England, and it tells of the scenes on the vessel from the moment of the receipt of the Titanic's S.O.S. signal, through the long night when the vessel was fringing the huge icefield and steaming at her limit of speed past mighty icebergs until day was breaking.

Then as the darkness disappeared, the watchers on the Carpathia saw the lifeboats spread over a wide area of smooth sea and learned from the officer of the first to reach the rescuing vessel that the "unsinkable" Titanic had gone to her doom.

The scenes, as the survivors were taken aboard were heartrendering. The women were at first hysterical with grief, and one had to be restrained from jumping overboard. As the voyage to New York proceeded they gained control of their emotions, and before they reached port started a fund to show their gratitude to their gallant rescuers.

At a meeting held in the first-class saloon of the Carpathia on the day after they were taken on board the saved subscribed £600 in ten minutes, and many large sums had been promised. On the way to Gibraltar Mr Barker himself organised a pierrot entertainment to enable Captain Rostron to present cheques of reward from the survivors.

The concert, with its glees, choruses, etc., given in pierrot costumes made by one of the stewardesses, Mrs Quayle, was a welcome relief after the tension and misery of a few days before. The commander, who had already expressed his pride at being at the head of so fine a ship's company, presented sums ranging from ten to thirty dollars to the men of the crew.

On the next arrival of the vessel at New York it is proposed to entertain the men of the Carpathia at a banquet, at which each shall be presented with a suitably-inscribed gold medal. Many of the crew intend to frame the bills received from the Titanic survivors' fund as a memento of the greatest shipping disaster in history.

The Carpathia is now engaged on the broiling Mediterranean cruise, calling at Gibraltar, Naples, Trieste, Fiume, Messina and Palermo – the heat and the light-hearted pleasure on the Mediterranean trip forming the greatest contrast to the bitter cold and awful tragedy of her last voyage.

SLEEPING PASSENGERS

None Roused by the Liner's Preparations

"At midnight on Sunday, April 14," said Mr Barker, "I was promenading the deck of the Carpathia when, hearing eight bells strike, I went below to retire for the night. I had just turned in when an urgent summons came from the chief steward, and I learned that an urgent distress message had been received from the Titanic.

We were then about 58 miles to S.-E. of her, and Captain A. H. Rostron had already given orders for the Carpathia to be turned around and proceed at utmost speed in her direction. The heads of all departments were aroused and every preparation was quietly and quickly made to receive two thousand passengers.

Blankets were placed in readiness, tables laid up, hot soups and consommes, coffee and tea prepared, and the surgeries stocked and staffed. Men were mustered at the boats and given instruction to be in immediate readiness to launch and row to the Titanic and bring off all passengers and crew.

Within an hour every possible preparation had been made by the stewards' department, and, to their great credit be it recorded, not a single passenger of the 1,000 we were carrying had been aroused. It was now only possible to wait and look for any signals from the distressed vessel. Their wireless had failed some time. We were then forging ahead at the utmost speed that could be got out of our engines, making us about 18 knots per hour as against our usual 13 to 14. No words of praise can be too great for the unsparing efforts of the engineering department and the firemen.

THE FIRST LIFEBOAT

At about a quarter to three we got the first signal, a blue flare on our port bow. Shortly after we sighted our first iceberg, undoubtably the cause of the disaster, a huge ghostly mass of white looming up through the darkness a few miles distant. A little later we found ourselves in a field of icebergs, Large and small, and it became frequently necessary to alter our course.

It was a little before 4 o'clock when we came near enough to discern the first lifeboat, which came alongside at 4.10 a.m. She was not much more than half-filled with women and children, and was in charge of an officer, who reported that the 'unsinkable' Titanic had foundered a little more than an hour after striking the iceberg. The survivors were taken aboard and handed over to the care of the medical staff and the stewards, under the perfect control of Chief Steward Hughes.

Day was breaking, and over an area of four miles we were able to see the other boats. We were surrounded by icebergs of all sizes, and three miles to the north was a big field of drift ice dotted with bergs. During the next two or three hours we endured the most heartrendering experiences we have ever known. Some of the incidents were almost too pathetic for description.

One woman was heartbroken, and uncontrollable. She cried hysterically for her husband, and it was only with the greatest difficulty that she could be restrained from jumping into the sea to look for him. It was necessary to resort to the subterfuge of a lie, and tell her that her husband was safe before she could be calmed.

A Colonel was brought aboard unconscious. He had been swimming in the icy water for over two hours. His mother was placed in a collapsible boat which was launched only to capsize on reaching the water. Immediately he dived from the ship to his mother's rescue.

He was unable in the darkness to find her, and commenced a frantic search among the bodies and wreckage. One after another the lifeboats endeavoured to take him aboard, but he resisted until the coldness of the water overcame him. He was hauled into a boat just as he was about to sink and join his mother in death. It is doubtful if he will recover. He has spoken to no one. His mother was about to pay a visit to three other of her sons.

HER LIFE FOR A DOG

Another young woman went down with the Titanic rather than desert her dog – a huge St Bernard, and a great favourite on board. When the lifeboats were being launched a seat was prepared for her, but she demanded that the dog be taken also.

This was impossible, human lives being the first consideration, and she was urged to sacrifice the dog and save herself. She refused, and was last seen on the deck of the vessel, clasping her pet to her bosom. Her dead body was afterwards found floating by the side of her dog.

An old lady was bewailing to a steward that she had lost 'everything.' Indignantly he told her she should thank God that her life was spared, and not at such a time regret the loss of her property. Her reply was pathetic – Steward, I have lost everything – my dear husband – and she burst into tears.

About eight o'clock we had picked up the last boat, and got all the survivors aboard. Two were so exhausted from exposure that they died whilst being brought aboard. These, together with a sailor and steward who had perished at the oars, were buried at 4 o'clock.

The Carpathia's passengers behaved splendidly, giving up their cabins voluntarily, and supplying the distressed women with clothes. The captain, officers and crew also gave up their quarters, and did their utmost to alleviate the sufferings of the survivors. The saloons, library, and smokerooms were also utilised for sleeping quarters.

SURVIVORS' GRATITUDE

On the Tuesday following the rescue a meeting in the first-class saloon was attended by nearly all of the survivors. Mr Goldberg, the chairman, announced that it had been proposed to inaugurate a fund amongst those who had been spared from the

TITANIC SURVIVORS' GRATITUDE TO CAPTAIN AND CREW OF THE CA

Captain Rostron thanking the ship's company from the bridge of the Carpathia for the self-sacrificing manner in which they cared for the survivors of the Titanic. He expressed his pride at being the commander of such a fine crew. Later in the voyage he handed to his men monetary gifts subscribed by the rescued in gratitude for the kindness they received. The survivors also inaugurated a fund to present loving cup to Captain Rostron and his officers.

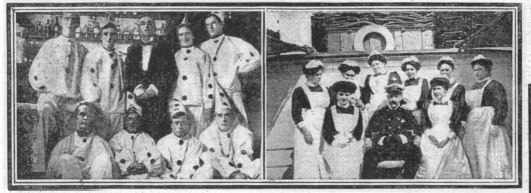

(1) Mr. J. W. Barker (in centre), who took the photographs, and his pierrot party specially organised for a concert on board on the return trip. At this concert the rewards were distributed. (2) Mrs. Quayle (X), who made the pierrot costumes with the chief steward and stewardesses.

THE NEW WING OF THE NAVY: BLUEJACKETS BUSY AND OFFICER IN AIR.

(1) Bluejackets bringing ashore from a lighter one of the Navy aeroplanes conveyed by H.M.S. Hibernia to Weymouth Bay for the manœuvres in which the aircraft are to play an important part. (2) Crowd watching Commander Samson arriving at Lodmoor, where hangars have been erected for the accommodation of naval officers' aeroplanes to form the air corps at the sham fight.

Several of the Titanic's crew who were Saturday from the White Star liner one of the men in the

Quartermaster Hichens, he man at the Upon arriving the men at once repo

: EXCLUSIVE PHOTOGRAPHS TAKEN ON BOARD THE RESCUING LINER.

ARRIVE IN ENGLAND.

the disaster arrived at Liverpool on came back was Fleet, the A.B. who was struck the fatal berg.

vn the gangway at the landing stage. the Receiver of Wrecks.—*Daily Sketch*

Captain Rostron and his officers on the deck of the Carpathia—Left to right (standing)—D. Colquhoun (7th engineer), W. T. Barton (steward), C. Bairnson (steward), P. R. Barnett (assistant purser), Roth Guntar (Hungarian officer), A. B. Johnson (chief engineer), T. W. Hankinson (chief officer), J. Deane (1st officer), W. G. Fairhurst (engineer), F. E. McGee (surgeon), E. G. F. Brown, R.N.R. (purser), V. Risicato (Italian doctor), R. Thomas (steward), A. Lengyet (Hungarian doctor), E. Harry Hughes (chief steward); (seated) T. Gould (boilermaker), G. V. Barnish (4th officer), Commander A. H. Rostron, R.D., R.N.R., J. E. Bisset (2nd officer) and J. Richardson (6th engineer).

(1) Watching the Titanic's boats arrive. (2) Some of the Carpathia's stewards who had everything in readiness for the shivering survivors when they scrambled on board. (3) Mr. E. G. F. Brown, the purser.

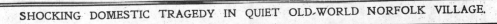

SHOCKING DOMESTIC TRAGEDY IN QUIET OLD-WORLD NORFOLK VILLAGE.

An inquest was held on Saturday at the quiet Norfolk village of Colby, near Aylsham, on William Joseph Barrett, a farm bailiff, who shot his wife and then turned the weapon on himself, falling over his victim's body. (1) Emily Gurford, in whose presence Barrett shot his wife. (2) Scene of the shooting. (3) George Daniels, who summoned the police.

disaster with a three-fold object:-

To present Captain Rostron and the officers with a loving cup.

To present a purse to the Carpathia's crew.

To present a purse to the surviving officers and crew of the Titanic.

This was agreed to unanimously. The response was immediate. In ten minutes 3,000 dollars had been subscribed, and many large sums had been promised.

A few days later the men were mustered on deck and addressed by Capt Rostron. He thanked them personally for their assistance and assured them that he was proud to be commander of such a ship's company."

CHEQUE FOR LIFEBOAT SERVICES RENDERED

Mr J. Horswell showing his sister-in-law the cheque handed to him by Sir Cosmo Duff-Gordon for services rendered in the boat which he and Lady Duff-Gordon were saved from the Titanic. Mr Horswell states that seven cheques were paid, and his is the only one that has not been cashed. Mr Horswell's evidence is likely to be sensational on the point of the number of passengers that were in his boat.

A memorial service to Captain Smith was held at St Mark's Church, Shelton, Hanley, yesterday morning. The commander of the Titanic was a Hanley boy, and many of his old school friends were present.

TITANIC WITNESSES

Two men who will be important witnesses at the Titanic inquiry – Robert Hichens, a quarter-master, and Frederick Fleet, a look-out man – arrived at Liverpool on Saturday by the Celtic.

Both were on duty at the time of the collision. Hichens was at the wheel; and Fleet, along with a man named Leigh, was in the crow's nest.

In his evidence at the American inquiry Fleet described how he reported to the bridge that there was ice ahead.

It was in his evidence that it first came out that the men in the crow's nest were without binoculars.

COLONEL ASTOR'S FUNERAL

A wireless message from the Minia reports the discoveries of the bodies of Mr C.M. Hays, the President of the Grand Trunk Railway, and sixteen other Titanic victims. The remains of Mr Astor were yesterday interred in Trinity Cemetery by the side of his mother. Mrs Astor, the widow, and Mr Astor's two children were the chief mourners. The Tribune says that at the suggestion of King George the Prince of Wales sent roses to the funeral.

ENGINEERS' MEMORIAL

It is suggested that the proposed Liverpool memorial to the Titanic Engineers should be a national one, and there is in contemplation a river-side scheme that would surpass, in architectural beauty, the Statue of Liberty at New York.

An influential committee has been formed with the approval of the Lord Mayor (the Earl of Derby).

All ranks of the Southampton postal staff attended a memorial service at St Peter's Church yesterday afternoon in memory of their colleagues, Messrs. Smith and Williamson, of the sea post service, who went down with the Titanic.

GUILTY – BUT LET OFF

Decision in Case Against Olympic Crew

'CRIMINALS' AS FIREMEN

Was the Ship's Speed to be Increased?

The 53 members of the Olympic's crew who were charged at Portsmouth with refusing to obey the captain's orders were found "guilty," but were allowed to go unpunished.

It will be remembered that the trouble began among the stokers, most of whom refused to sail because (they said) they were dissatisfied with some of the lifeboats. These men left the ship when she was ready to sail, and when men to replace them were taken on board a large proportion of the seamen refused to sail.

The seamen said that many of the men taken on as substitutes were unsuitable. On behalf of the company it was alleged that the ground of the seamen's objection was that the substitutes were non-union men.

Among the witnesses on Saturday was Charles William McKinnon, second engineer, who was one of the three officers to select 168 firemen from 200 sent from Yorkshire. He would not agree that they were "a miserable looking lot."

WISHED TO PICK UP TIME

Frederick John Blake, superintendent engineer of the White Star Line, said he picked out a hundred men, and they were all good men.

With the men selected from Yorkshire they would have had 70 men in excess of the ordinary number. The reason for the excess was that the ship was already a day and a-half late, and they wished to pick up that time on the round voyage.

Are you content to take on the Olympic criminals and people of that sort? – I am afraid we have to take them ordinarily.

Does it not strike you that in the event of any unfortunate disaster like the recent one they would be very undesirable people to have on board? – I don't think so.

Captain Steel, R.N.R., marine superintendent of the White Star Line at Southampton, said that the Berthon boats came from H.M. transport ships and other vessels. Some of them were about twelve months old, while ten were ten years old. The boat test proved satisfactory.

"THE SCALLYWAGS OF PORTSMOUTH"

George Martell, a quartermaster and an ex-Naval man was one of the witnesses for the defence. Martell said he and a man named Cox had a conversation with the captain, who said that if anybody wanted to go ashore they could go. They reported that to the men, who took a ballot, the result of which was that they decided they would all go ashore. They were later told by the captain that the firemen who left at Southampton were coming back, and a further ballot resulted in a decision not to go ashore.

Martell said he was thoroughly disgusted with the appearance of the men who were shipped to take the place of the firemen. "They were not the sort of shipmates for me," he said, "and that was why I went on the tender." (Laughter.) Martell said he described these men to Captain Goodenough of the cruiser Cochrane as the "scallywags of Portsmouth."

In announcing the decision of the Bench, Sir Thomas Bramsdon, the chairman, said the ship was seaworthy as required by law, and therefore the plea of justification did not arise. As to the question of punishment, the bench felt that the Titanic disaster was in the minds of the defendants, and that the men had done what on any other occasion they would not have done. Therefore, the Bench would take action under the Probation of Offenders Act, and dismiss the information without inflicting any punishment.

SOCIETY CHILDREN HELP TITANIC FUND

A number of artistic tableaux depicting the life and death of Joan of Arc were given in aid of the "Veronica and Patience Titanic Fund" at the residence of Mr and Mrs Leopold Albu at Hamilton-place on Saturday. Over £30 was made for the fund. (1) Miss Veronica Albu as Joan of Arc. (2) Miss Patience Lewis as St. Katherine.

DAILY SKETCH.

No. 986.—TUESDAY, MAY 7, 1912.   THE PREMIER PICTURE PAPER.   [Registered as a Newspaper.]   ONE HALFPENNY.

TITANIC COMMISSION INSPECT THE ILL-FATED LINER'S SISTER SHIP.

Lord Mersey (x) and his Assessors—Commander F. C. Lyon, Rear-Admiral S. A. Gough-Calthorpe, Captain A. W. Clarke, Professor Biles, and Mr. E. C. Chaston—watching a life-boat being lowered from the davits of the Olympic during a visit which the Titanic Wreck Commission paid yesterday to the sister ship of the ill-fated liner. The Commission made a special trip to Southampton to inspect the vessel, and spent nearly two hours on board.

All the bulkheads were inspected, and the Commission also visited the engine-room and the steerage quarters, in which they made a lengthy stay, evidently with reference to the means of access for third-class passengers to the boat deck. Mr. Saunderson, the general manager of the White Star Line, and Mr. Currie, their superintendent at Southampton, accompanied the party.—*Daily Sketch* Photograph.

CLOTHING THE TITANIC SURVIVORS

The officials of the Seamen's Home, New York, fitting out the surviving members of the ill-fated Titanic's crew with new clothing.

TITANIC PASSENGERS

Attorney-General will Support Claim to be Represented

The Attorney-General told the House of Commons yesterday that he would support an application for steerage passengers to be represented at the Titanic inquiry.

The Court's decision, he explained, was that individual passengers could not be represented.

The Court had not refused to allow a class of passengers to be represented.

Our photograph of Mr Joseph Bell, chief engineer of the Titanic, was reproduced by permission of the "Marine Engineer and Naval Architect."

OLYMPIC INSPECTED

Lord Mersey and the other members of the Titanic Commission yesterday inspected the Olympic. They were met at Southampton by Mr Harold Sanderson, of the White Star Line, and went to the dock in motor-cars.

The inspection was private and no pressmen were allowed on board.

The Mansion House Fund reached the sum of £230,000 last night.

An excellent model of Captain Smith, the brave captain of the Titanic, has just been added to Mme Tussaud's Exhibition. Mr John Tussaud has modelled the figure from a *Daily Sketch* photograph taken on the Titanic shortly before she started on her fatal voyage.

MAN AT THE WHEEL IN THE BOX

Tells What Was Done When Berg Was Seen

BRAVERY DOWN BELOW

How the Water Rushed Into the Stokehole

Robert Hitchens, the quartermaster who was at the wheel when the Titanic struck the iceberg, gave evidence at the inquiry yesterday.

He said that about half a minute after three gongs had been sounded by the look-out he was told to starboard the helm. Almost immediately after that had been done the vessel struck.

A thrilling account of the scene down below was given by Frederick Barratt, a leading stoker.

After the collision, he said, the water poured into his stokehole, and he and one of the engineers jumped into another section just before the watertight door closed. He did not know whether any more of the men in his stokehole were saved. When the fires had been drawn he noticed that there was no water in the boilers.

Able-Seaman William Lucas said that some of the boats would have held another 15 or 20 people.

Further applications were made to Lord Mersey for passengers to be represented at the inquiry, and he agreed to allow each class to be separately represented.

The President asked the Attorney-General to have some small models of the Titanic prepared to assist the Court.

STOKEHOLE SCENE

How the "Black Squad" Drew the Fires

Robert Hitchens, one of the Titanic's quartermasters, said in his evidence yesterday that the ship collided with the iceberg at 11.40. Before she struck Mr Murdock, the first officer, gave the order 'Hard a-starboard.'

Hitchens put the wheel hard over. The ship had swung two points when she struck.

Lord Mersey: The ship moved two points.

She did not move anymore, because, as I understand it, the crash came.

As near as Hitchens could tell, about half a minute elapsed between the sounding of three gongs – indicating that there was something ahead – from the crow's nest and the giving of the order 'Hard a-starboard.'

After the three gongs had been sounded Mr Moody received a telephone message and said to Mr Murdock: "Iceberg right ahead." Mr Murdock rushed to the telegraph and gave the order "Hard a-starboard." Almost immediately after Mr Moody reported to the first officer – as was his duty – that the helm was hard a-starboard the collision occurred. The ship stopped directly after the collision.

"45 KNOTS IN TWO HOURS"

According to the log, Hitchens said, the ship's speed was 45 knots in two hours. Up to the time the three gongs struck there was no change in speed.

About a minute after the collision Captain Smith rushed out of his room and asked Mr Murdock: "What was that?" Mr Murdock said: "An iceberg, sir." The Captain said: "Close the watertight doors." Mr Murdock said "They are already closed." The order from the bridge to close the watertight doors would refer only to the doors that closed automatically.

Orders for the ship's carpenter to sound the ship were then given. Those were the last orders Hitchens heard with the exception of the orders about the boats. He heard the captain say: "Get all the boats out and serve out the belts." That was after 12 o'clock. The captain then saw from the instrument that the ship had a list to starboard.

Hitchens said he was not aware that he had any boat station, and he never saw any list of boat stations, though it was usual for lists to be "printed for everyone to see."

THE MYSTERIOUS LIGHT

Hitchens was next asked about the mystery ship. Mr Lightoller, he said, told them to row to a light "about five miles off." He first saw the

217

light when they were putting people into the boat.

Two or three women helped to row his boat, and they steered for the light.

When they had gone about a mile the light disappeared. They at first thought it was a steamer, but afterwards inclined to the opinion that it was a schooner.

The Titanic sent up rockets "of all colours" and the rockets would be visible to the supposed ship. He saw no answering signals.

Hitchens thought that if there had been enough lifeboats there would have been time to rescue everybody.

At least four sailors, besides the man at the tiller, were required to man properly such a boat as his. The lifeboats would not have been of any use at all if there had been a rough sea.

In times of danger it was customary to double watches, but this was not done on the Titanic as far as he knew.

What method was adopted to keep the male passengers back? – All the officers had revolvers as far as I am aware of. Hitchens said he saw no ropes drawn across the deck. Were the revolvers used? – I heard several reports.

After the Titanic went down they heard faint cries.

Did you go in the direction of these cries? – I had no compass in the boat, and did not know what direction to take. Had I had a compass and known what direction I came from the ship I should have known what course to take back.

Lord Mersey: I should have thought your ears would have done it.

Hitchens replied that he could not have found his way back by that. Besides, the other boats were calling to each other, and he was a mile away.

Two of the "black squad" went into the box, and described what happened in the stokehole after the collision.

LEADING STOKER'S EVIDENCE

A graphic story was told by Frederick Barratt, a leading stoker.

He was in No. 6 section, and Mr Shephard was the engineer on duty.

"There is a clock face in the stokehole," Barratt said, "and a red light goes up for 'Stop.'

I was talking to Mr Hesketh (one of the engineers) when the red light came up, and I shouted, 'Shut all the dampers.' That order was obeyed, but the crash came before we had them all shut.

There was a rush of water into my stokehole. We were standing on plates about six feet above the tank tops, and the water came in about two feet above the plates.

Together with Mr Hesketh I jumped through the doorway into No.5 section. The watertight door between the section was then open, but it shut just as we jumped through. This door is worked from the bridge.

I do not know whether any more men in my stokehole were saved. The water was coming in fast enough through the side of the ship to flood the place.

ENGINEER'S BROKEN LEG

Shortly afterwards the order came from the engine room to send all the stokers up. "Most of them went up, but I was told to remain with the engineers to do any errands. Mr Harvey, Mr Wilson, Mr Shephard (of the engineers' staff) and I waited in No. 5 section.

Mr Harvey told me to send some firemen for some lamps. Just as we got the lamps the electric light came on again. They must have been changing the dynamos over.

Mr Harvey told me to fetch some firemen to draw the furnaces. I fetched about 15 firemen, and they drew the 30 furnaces in the section. That occupied about 20 minutes. I looked at the gauge and found there was no water in the boilers. The ship, in blowing off steam, had blown it out.

Mr Harvey told me, Barrett continued, to lift the man-hole plate, which I did, and then Mr Shephard, hurrying across to do something and not noticing the plate had been removed, fell down and broke his leg. We lifted him up and laid him in the pump-room. About a quarter of an hour after the fires were drawn there was a rush of water."

Did you see whether this water was coming through the bulkhead or over it? – I did not stop to look. Mr Shephard ordered me up the ladder. Barratt added that he thought something had given way when the rush of water came.

AWAY JUST IN TIME

A.B. Who Had Charge of Collapsible Boat

Able Seaman William Lucas, an ex-Navy man, another witness at the Titanic inquiry, said he was playing "nap" when the ship struck.

He got into a collapsible boat and they had only just got clear when the Titanic went down.

Lucas said he knew there was some ice "knocking about." The shock of the collision nearly knocked him off his feet.

After the collision what did you do? – I went down and put on an extra jersey. (Laughter)

Lucas said that as far as he knew the passengers on the boat deck were all of the first class. The boats lowered from that deck were not full by a long way. That was "because there were no women knocking about."

He got into the last boat to get away on the port side – a collapsible boat – but Mr Lightoller ordered him out.

He then went to the starboard side to see if there were any boats left there, but there were not, so he went back to the collapsible boat. A lady called out that there were "no sailors or plugs" in the boat, so he got in. The water was then up to the ship's bridge. With the rising of the water and the tilting of the Titanic the boat "floated off."

Lucas said the women were afraid of the collapsible boat when it had been lowered, and he transferred them to another boat. Afterwards his boat rescued 36 people clinging to an overturned collapsible boat. Two boats rowed back to the scene of the wreck, but they found nobody alive.

THE SAILOR'S "FINAL DRINK"

He said that after the boat drill at Southampton he went ashore. "It is a regular thing for the sailors to go ashore to have a final drink."

In the lowering of the boats was there sufficient interval to enable the female passengers from the steerage to get on to the boat deck? – They would have been able to if there had been anyone there to direct them to the boat deck. Lucas did not think there was anyone directing them.

There were two girls on deck when he left with the collapsible boat. "I said to them, Wait a minute, there is another collapsible boat being put down from the funnel. You had better get into that. I could not take them because my boat was full."

Lucas said that he and Mr Lightoller helped one elderly lady into the collapsible boat and then had to help her out again as she would not go without her husband. "There were several cases like that." he said.

The inquiry was adjourned.

The Lord Mayor's Fund for the relief of the sufferers in the Titanic disaster now amounts to £239,000.

COLONEL ASTOR'S WILL

Widow Will Forfeit £1,000,000 if She Marries Again

NEW YORK Tuesday

The latest will of the late Colonel J.J. Astor, which was made in September, has now been made public. The estate amounts to more than seventy-five million dollars (£15,000,000), and Mr Vincent Astor, the son, is the principal beneficiary.

Five million dollars (£1,000,000) each are left to the widow and to Colonel Astor's daughter Muriel by his first wife. In the event of the widow marrying again, her share will be forfeited.

Nothing is left to the first Mrs Astor, and the only charitable bequest is thirty thousand dollars (£6,000) to Mr Astor's old school.

Mrs Astor is nineteen years of age.

J. Ranger   Stoker Beechem   Lee, the look-out

Important witnesses at the inquiry into the loss of the Titanic, which was resumed at the London Scottish Drill Hall, Westminster, yesterday. George Beechem, who was a stoker on the Titanic, informed the Court that the watertight doors were closed five minutes after the collision. It took about a quarter of an hour to draw the fires when the order was given to do so. Asked if he heard any explosions when the ship went down Beechem said he heard a roar like thunder. There was no lamp, compass, water or provisions in the lifeboat of which he had charge.   *Daily Sketch* Photographs

TITANIC FIREMAN'S THRILLING STORY: NO PROVISIONS OR WATER ON LIFEBOAT UNDER HIS CHARGE

J. Gate   C. Hendrickson and S. Collins

LOOK-OUT MAN AND THE BERG

Says It Came Out of the Night

QUESTION OF EYESIGHT

"Night Glasses Certainly Better"

Seaman Lee, one of the men in the crow's nest when the Titanic collided with the iceberg, told the Court of Inquiry yesterday that when the berg was sighted it was "coming through the haze, perhaps half a mile ahead."

Although night glasses were "better than eyesight" none were provided for the Titanic's look-out men.

Able Seaman Poigndestre said that some of the foreign passengers tried to rush the boats.

He stated that the ship broke in two. After the forward part sank the after part righted itself and remained afloat for a couple of minutes.

Mr Farrell, M.P., told the Court that two Irish survivors had complained that while they were in the sea and trying to get on board a boat they were struck and pushed into the water again by members of the Titanic's crew. Lord Mersey said he could not turn himself into a criminal judge to hear charges of attempted manslaughter.

BLACK AND WHITE

"A Vast Mass that Came Through the Haze"

Reginald Robinson Lee, who was on the look-out with Fleet when the Titanic struck the iceberg, told his story at the inquiry yesterday. At times he showed much emotion.

There were no glasses provided for the look-out on the Titanic, though night glasses were certainly better than eyesight. One of the other look-out men asked for glasses, but was told there were none.

"It was a starlit night," he said, "but at the time of the accident there was a haze right ahead, extending more or less all round the horizon. It was freezing.

When we first came up the haze was not so distinct as it became later, but soon we had all our work cut out to pierce through it. My mate said 'If we can see through this we shall be lucky.'

About 11.40 Fleet, his companion in the crow's nest, struck three bells, meaning 'Something right ahead.' Immediately after that he telephoned to the bridge, "Iceberg right ahead, Sir." Someone replied from the bridge, "Thank you." Then the ship sheered, and it seemed at first as though she might clear the iceberg.

The iceberg was higher than the forecastle, which was about 55 feet out of the water.

It was just a dark mass that came through the haze, he said. As the boat moved away from it there was just a fringe of white on top. That was the only white to be seen about it until we passed it. Then one side seemed to be white and the other black.

He did not see the light of any other vessel when the ship struck. There was a light on the port bow of the Titanic as she went down, but it disappeared.

When you are going through a haze at night is it usual to slow up? – It is nothing to do with me. I am not on the bridge. I am the look-out.

But you have been in a fog? – I am in a fog now, retorted Lee smiling and scratching his head, and the Court laughed.

Lee said the crow's nest men talked among themselves about the absence of glasses for the look-outs. They asked each other what had become of the binoculars that were in the crow's nest on the trip from Belfast to Southampton.

Lee said he was medically examined before joining the Titanic, but not specially for his eyesight.

What sort of examination did the doctor make? – I suppose he pleased himself, as medical men generally do. (Laughter.)

"I believe my eyesight is good," Lee said to Lord Mersey.

Asked by Sir Robert Finlay (for the White Star Line) whether the haze was very bad, Lee said "It was so bad that you could not see an iceberg through it."

THE BUNKER FIRE

Had it Anything to Do With The Disaster?

Lord Mersey yesterday put a striking question to Frederick Barrett, a leading stoker on the Titanic.

After Barrett had described the outbreak of fire in one of the coal bunkers Lord Mersey asked if he thought the fire had anything to do with the disaster. Barrett replied that it would be hard to say.

On the previous day Barrett was asked whether the rush of water that drove him on deck was due to a bulkhead giving way, but he said he could not say. Yesterday he said that after the bunker where the fire occurred had been cleared the bulkhead that ran by that bunker was damaged, and he attributed that to the fire.

Barrett said that when he ran up to the promenade deck there were only two boats left.

Did you see any women? – The women were coming up from aft. I don't know where they were coming from.

His boat was not lowered until all the women had been taken off the deck.

"PUSHED BACK INTO THE SEA"

Grave Charge Against Some

At the Titanic inquiry yesterday Mr Farrell, M.P. for County Longford, stated that two Irish emigrants, survivors of the wreck, had alleged that while they were swimming in the sea after the wreck they attempted to board two of the lifeboats, and were struck over the head and hands and pushed back into the water by members of the Titanic's crew.

These men, Thomas McCormack and Bernard McCoy, were in America, but wished to be represented at the inquiry, and have the allegations investigated.

Lord Mersey replied that there might have been an attempt to commit manslaughter, but he could not try that.

There might be circumstances, Lord Mersey continued, that particularly affected third class passengers, and he should be glad to have evidence on such matters "But," he added, "don't turn me into a criminal judge to try charges of attempted manslaughter."

Lord Mersey decided to allow Mr Harbinson to represent all the third class passengers.

RUSH OF FOREIGNERS

Seaman Suggests That the Light Was an Imaginary One

Able Seaman John Poigndestre said the light seen by those in the boats might have been an imaginary light. He had seen imaginary lights at sea before. The light was low down on the horizon, he added, and might have been a star.

Poigndestre said that after helping to clear the boats he went to the forecastle, and while he was there the wooden bulkhead that separated the forecastle from the third-class cabin broke. He had to fight waist-deep through water to escape.

A number of foreigners – second and third class passengers – tried to rush the boats. He and two other sailors and Mr Lightoller (the second officer) kept them back as well as they could. They could not lower the boats as they ought to have done because of the men passengers crowding round.

The reason some of the boats did not have more passengers was that the second officer was afraid the falls would not carry any more. They heard cries after the ship sank, but there were not enough sailors in his boat to row to the spot where the cries came from in time.

Poigndestre declared that the vessel broke in two. The aft part remained afloat a couple of minutes after the forward part.

Asked about the facilities third-class passengers had for getting to the boat deck, he said that all the barriers were not down. If the barriers were not down the way was 'up the ladder from the after well deck and up through the second cabin.'

Lord Mersey: They had been able to find their way there somehow.

A STEWARD AT SEA

James Johnson, a steward in the first-class saloon, said his boat was not full; there were about 25 in it. Between 30 and 40 women, instead of getting into it, went back into the cabin. He thought they did not realize the seriousness of the position.

They rowed for a red light until it disappeared.

Was it at a right angle on the port bow? – A left angle I should think. (Laughter)

One of the witnesses said it was two points off? – I don't know a point sir, unless it's billiards. (Laughter)

THE MANSION HOUSE FUND

Additional receipts yesterday on behalf of the Mansion House Titanic Fund brought the total up to £242,000.

FOR THOSE IN PERIL

New Method of Launching Lifeboats

At a most opportune moment, when three shipping disasters, involving not only the loss of the vessels, but an appalling sacrifice of human life, have occurred within a period of twenty weeks, an attempt is being made to simplify the obsolete methods of getting a boat away from a sinking ship. It has been left to Major Sir Bryan Leighton to put forward a scheme which on the face of it at least bears the stamp of novelty.

Sir Bryan yesterday showed the *Daily Sketch* a model of an ocean-going liner with the appliance attached. Briefly, it is the introduction of a girder-like arrangement which, depending from the upper deck of the ship, rests when in use on a pontoon floating in the water. The boat slides down this chute into the water. The idea is to do away with the old fashioned system of launching boats from the davits. In the days of Elizabeth this system was in use, but, notwithstanding the enormous change in the methods of the sea, the same system is applied to-day.

Normally the girders, four in number, two on either side of the vessel, are lashed up to the gunwales with pontoons in position. In case of emergency the pontoon end is lowered to the water and at once provides a species of runaway or chute, down which the ship's boats, laden with passengers, may be slipped no matter what the state of the sea.

The idea is exceedingly ingenious but whether the Board of Trade would sanction its adoption is quite another matter. Its great drawback appears to be its complexity. Apart from the difficulty of launching the pontoons in rough weather with a ship under way would be enormous.

However, whether the apparatus is a success or not in its present stage Sir Bryan Leighton is entitled to the thanks of the community for taking what is undoubtably a pioneer step in solving the problem of life-saving at sea.

MORE HERO FUNDS

Dr Ross of Dunfermline has intimated that it is Mr Carnegie's intention to establish hero funds all over Europe.

MR MARCONI IN LONDON

Mr Marconi (on right) and Mr Godfrey Isaacs (brother of Sir Rufus Isaacs, K.C., M.P.) photographed in London yesterday as they were leaving a meeting of directors of the Marconi Company.

NORFOLK FAMILY OF ELEVEN WHO WERE WIPED OUT IN TITANIC DISASTER

The first photograph published of the Sage family, all the eleven members of which went down in the Titanic. The group shows the father and mother with their five boys and four girls – Stella, Ada, George, Douglas, Dorothy, Frederick, William (the baby), Constance, and Thomas. Mr and Mrs Sage kept an inn at Gaywood, near King's Lynn, on the main road to Sandringham, and afterwards moved to Peterborough, where they had a business in Gladstone-street. Some time ago Mr Sage decided to emigrate to Jacksonville, Florida, where he intended to start fruit-farming, and the family were on the way to the land of their adoption.

BOAT THAT DID NOT TURN BACK

Only 5 Passengers Were In It

£5 EACH FOR CREW

Leading Fireman's Story of the Duff-Gordons

Surprising evidence was given at the Titanic inquiry yesterday.

Charles Hendrickson, a leading fireman, said that No. 1 boat left the ship with only twelve people on board. Lady Duff-Gordon was among them. The two women in the boat, he said, told the crew not to go back to attempt rescues, and the boat did not go.

On the Carpathia the boat's crew received £5 each.

Hendrickson was questioned by Lord Mersey about the gift. He swore that no money was offered by the Duff-Gordons when he wanted to go to the rescue of the drowning. The gift came as a pleasant surprise. Mrs Astor was not in this boat so far as he knew.

It was stated that women in two other boats expressed the fear that it would be dangerous to go to the rescue. These boats were in charge of officers.

In one case, Mr Scanlan, who is appearing for the Seamen and Firemen's Union, suggested that the officer showed a lack of discretion. He did not suggest cowardice.

SEARCHING QUESTIONS

Lord Mersey and the Gift to the Crew

Charles Hendrickson, a leading fireman, in his evidence said he saw a number of the boats lowered. A gentleman, whom he did not know, came up and told him to get the boats away as quickly as possible. The captain was then walking up and down the deck giving directions to the officers.

After the boats on the starboard side had been lowered Hendrickson went over to the port side. Just then the firing of rockets began. The officer who was lowering No. 1 boat (the emergency boat, and a smaller one than the others) called out for any of the seamen. There were none about, and he then told several firemen, including Hendrickson, to get in. The officer then called out for more passengers, but none came, so the boat was lowered, and the seaman in charge was told to keep close, and come back if called.

Asked why the boat did not go back to pick up some of the people struggling in the water, Hendrickson said: "I proposed going back, but the others objected. They would not listen to me – none of the passengers or anybody else."

Hendrickson thought they were about 100 to 200 yards away.

Lord Mersey: Am I to understand that when you were picked up by the Carpathia there were only twelve people on board? – Yes.

Of these twelve how many belonged to the crew? – Seven. There were five passengers – two women and three men. Two of the crew were seamen.

CRIES OF THE DROWNING

In reply to Lord Mersey, Hendrickson said that it was the women passengers who objected. The men passengers said nothing.

You had plenty of room for about a dozen more. Who was in charge of this boat? – A seaman named Simmons.

What were the names of the passengers? – I heard the name of one of the passengers.

What was that? – Duff-Gordon.

Did you hear the names of the others? – I think his wife was there, Lady Duff-Gordon.

Did his wife object? – Yes; she was scared to go back in case of being swamped.

The President: Was there, so far as you know, any danger of the boat being swamped if you had gone back? – It would certainly be dangerous.

Mr Scanlan: In the presence of the cries from the drowning were you the only one to propose to go back to the rescue? – I never heard anyone else.

Do you know the names of the other members of the crew on board this boat of yours? – Some of them.

The President: Let us have them.

Hendrickson: They included, I believe, Simmons, the cox, Collins, a fireman, Sheath, a trimmer, and Taylor, a fireman. That is all I know.

When Lady Duff-Gordon objected did her husband reprove her? – He upheld her.

He did not try to get her courage up to go back? – No. Hendrickson said that one reason why it would be dangerous to go back was that they had no lamp.

Lord Mersey: At the time the order was given to lower the boats how many people were on the boat deck? – I did not see anyone there. There were some people further along, but the boats there were being got out at the same time.

Did anyone call out for more people? – Someone in the boat did, and the officer called out: "Any more women and children?" No answer came.

NO ATTEMPT AT RESCUE

Lord Mersey asked Hendrickson what each of the other people in the boat said when he proposed that they should go back. Hendrickson replied: Duff-Gordon and his wife said it was dangerous, and that we should be swamped.

Did anybody else say it? – I did not hear anyone else. What did Simmons say? – He never said anything.

Am I to understand that because two of the passengers said it would be dangerous you all kept your mouth shut, and made no attempt to rescue anyone? – That is right, sir.

Mr Clem Edwards: When you were in New York did you see in the papers an article written by Lady Duff-Gordon? – No, I heard there was something printed about Lady Duff-Gordon calling everyone down.

Hendrickson said that on the Carpathia Duff-Gordon gave him and the other members of the crew an order for £5.

He could not say whether Mrs Astor was on board the boat, or Lady Duff-Gordon's maid.

Mr Lewis (for the British Seafarers' Union): You were prepared to go back? – Yes.

Lord Mersey: Did you know at the time you would receive the £5? – No.

Are you sure? – Yes. It came as a pleasant surprise? – Oh, yes; of course.

Mr Lewis: If there had been any arrangement between other members of the crew to do a certain thing for a certain price they would give the same price to all, and you would have known about it? – Yes.

Lord Mersey: I do not see why they should. (To Hendrickson): Who gave this money to you? – Mr Duff-Gordon.

WHEN THE GIFT WAS PROMISED

Did he call you all together? – Yes we all went up together on the Carpathia. Did you know what you were going for? – No.

WITNESSES FROM BELOW DECKS AT INQUIRY

| T. P. DILLON | C. Hendrickson | J. Johnson | T. Granger |
| trimmer | fireman | steward | greaser |

Four men called yesterday. Dillon was on the Titanic when she foundered, and was sucked under, but was picked up after swimming 20 minutes. *Daily Sketch* photographs.

What did you suppose you were going for? – He had promised us this present previous to this.

When did he promise it? – When we got aboard the Carpathia, but we did not know what it was.

What did he say when he promised you the present? – He said "I will make a small present to the members of the boat's crew."

You are quite sure there was no suggestion of any present before you got on board the Carpathia? – He told us in the morning before we were picked up that he was going to do something for us. He said he would make us a small present and would send a private telegram for each member of the crew telling his family he was safe.

When was this? – When we sighted the Carpathia.

Had anything been said before this? – Not to my knowledge.

Further questioned Hendrickson reiterated that he heard no mention of any promise of money until they sighted the Carpathia. He said that he saw Mr Duff-Gordon talking to another passenger, an American, apparently, but he did not know what they were saying. He did not think it was about the wreck.

Mr Laing was allowed to postpone his examination on behalf of the White Star Company, and the Court adjourned.

NO COMMOTION

Passengers Stood Quiet Till the Final Plunge

Thomas Patrick Dillon, a trimmer, said:-

"I went down with the ship, and was sucked down about two fathoms. Then I shoved myself off, and I seemed to get lifted up. When I came up again I saw the after-part of the ship come up. Then she went down again and finished."

After swimming for about twenty minutes he was picked up by one of the boats. He then lost consciousness. When he came to a sailor and a passenger were lying dead on top of him.

Asked how long he was waiting on the poop for the boat to go down, Dillon said "About sixty minutes" and an expression of terror passed over his face.

You could see the passengers. Was there any commotion? – No, none at all.

They were simply waiting for death? – Yes.

NINE LOST OUT OF SIX MILLIONS

Mr J. M. Robertson, M.P., (Parliamentary Secretary to the Board of Trade), speaking at the annual dinner of the Iron and Steel Institute last night, referring to the sinking of the Titanic, said in the ten years before that calamity the White Star Company's ships had actually carried six millions of passengers with a loss of only nine lives.

Mrs Bruce Ismay arrived Queenstown last evening by the Oceanic from Southampton, and disembarked with the intention of meeting her husband to-day on the Adriatic.

THE MANSION HOUSE FUND

The Mansion House Fund now amounts to £243,000.

ADVERTISEMENT

MADAME TUSSAUD'S EXHIBITION – THE LOSS of the TITANIC. Lifelike portrait model of the late CAPTAIN EDWARD J. SMITH. Realistic Tableau representing CHARLES DICKENS in his STUDY at GADS HILL. Free Cinematograph performances.

The model of Captain Smith was one of a number that were destroyed in a fire in the 1920s. I am indebted to Madame Tussaud's for their permission to reproduce here the only known photograph in existence of the model.

PORTRAIT MODEL OF CAPTAIN SCOTT

The collection of portrait models of celebrities at Madame Tussaud's has been enriched by a figure of Captain Scott. Our photograph shows the new model, which is placed near the figures of General Booth and Captain Smith, of the Titanic.

Picture Courtesy of Madame Tussaud's, London

BOAT NEARLY FULL OF MEN?

Steward's Sensational Evidence

WITNESSES DISAGREE

Lord Mersey Wants Evidence From Carpathia

A steward named Rule said at the Titanic Inquiry yesterday that the boat in which he left the ship was nearly full of men.

Women were called for, he said, but none came, and an officer ordered the boat to be lowered.

On the previous day another member of the crew said that this boat contained about sixty women. However, Rule adhered to his statement.

Lord Mersey expressed the hope that evidence on the point would be obtained from the Carpathia.

A graphic description of the last moments on the Titanic was given by John Joughin, the chief baker.

When the vessel lurched violently hundreds of people, he said, were thrown together in a heap.

Another witness, Frank Scott, a greaser, said that he saw some of the engineers on deck as the last boats were leaving.

According to Scott a number of the watertight doors were opened and were not closed again.

ANXIOUS MEN

"Scouts" Who Could Not Find Any Women

When the Titanic Inquiry was resumed yesterday Sir Robert Finlay, who appears for the White Star Line, said that the officers of the Titanic would arrive at Liverpool to-day, and he would like to adjourn his cross-examination of Charles Hendrickson, a leading fireman. Lord Mersey granted Sir Robert's application.

Hendrickson's evidence was that No. 1 boat (an emergency boat, and a smaller one than the others) left the ship with only twelve persons – seven of the crew and five passengers. Lady Duff-Gordon and Mr Duff-Gordon, he said, were among the passengers. The boat, which was in charge of a seaman, did not go to the rescue of the drowning because passengers objected. On the Carpathia Duff-Gordon gave the members of the boat's crew £5 each.

Samuel James Rule, a bathroom steward, was one of the witnesses yesterday. He said that Mr Ismay was helping to put people into No. 3 boat, and an officer – he thought it was Mr Lowe – was giving directions.

Boat No. 1 was already launched and the order was given to those in it: "Stand off from the ship's side and return when we call you."

"That, your lordship will remember," said the Attorney-General, "is the boat with five passengers and seven of the crew."

Was Mr Ismay dressed at this time? – No, he had on slippers, a light overcoat, and no hat.

Did you hear any passengers refuse to get in? – No.

Rule said he next helped at boat No. 5. As he was doing so some of the pantrymen came up with bread and biscuits. Every boat on the starboard side, except Nos. 1 and 3, which had then been launched, was provisioned.

BOAT NEARLY CAPSIZED

Later he was ordered into boat No. 15, the last boat on the starboard side. "We could find no more women and children to go," he said. "We sent 'scouts' round the decks but could find none." Sixty-eight people were in this boat, of whom four or five were women, three children and the rest men.

Lord Mersey: This is contrary to previous evidence.

The Attorney-General: Yes, I know. We will make it clear it was boat No. 15 he means. (To Rule): In lowering did you nearly capsize another boat? – Yes. We nearly came on top of No. 13.

Lord Mersey: How long were you waiting by boat No. 15? – About 10 or 12 minutes while the 'scouts' were looking for women and children. At that time no one got in. Then Mr Murdock (the first officer) said: "There are no more women or children, fill your boats and lower away." Rule thought the women in the boat were from the third class.

Lord Mersey pointed to the discrepancies between Rule's story and the evidence given by the man Cabell on the previous day. Cabell said that he was in boat No. 15 and that it took 60 women from one of the lower decks. However, Rule adhered to his statement that those in the boat were nearly all men, and that they were taken on board at the boat deck.

Lord Mersey: I hope the Carpathia may be able to give us evidence as to who got out of this boat.

The Attorney-General: I am not very sanguine, but we will try. (To Rule) Did you not think when you left that there were other women on board? – Yes.

WHERE THE "SCOUTS" LOOKED

Lord Mersey: Didn't it strike you, if these were all men, you were not doing what you ought to have been doing – taking away women and children? – We had all there were on that deck.

You knew there were hundreds elsewhere? – I imagine so.

Was there any rush of men? – No, not particularly. They were a bit anxious to get on board. The Titanic was then very much down by the head and had listed to port.

After the ship sank they rowed back to see if they could pick up anybody, but saw no one. Their boat was full and there was water up to the gunwales.

Lord Mersey asked Rule where the men who were sent to call women went. Rule said they went on the port side of the boat deck and on both sides of A deck. Did they go anywhere else? – I do not think so.

Do you think they wanted not to find the women? – No, for they were shouting pretty well all round. They were shouting "Any more women and children for the boat?" Anyone could hear them on the next deck.

The Attorney-General was pressing Rule as to the number of women on board when the Court was adjourned till Tuesday.

On Monday counsel engaged in the case will visit the Olympic.

OFFICER'S WARNING

"If Any Man Jumps I'll Shoot Him Like a Dog"

Frederick Scott, a greaser, who worked in the turbine department, said it was impossible to stop the engines at once without blowing the tops of the cylinders off.

When Scott got on deck he saw Mr Lowe, the fifth officer, fire his revolver and shout, "If any man jumps in the boat I'll shoot him like a dog."

Scott glided down the falls into the sea, and was picked up by a lifeboat that was undermanned.

He said that at twenty minutes past one, when all the boats but two had been lowered, some of the engineers and firemen were on deck.

He noticed Mr Farquharson, the senior second engineer among them. The circulating pumps were going at that time. Some of the engineers went on the boat deck, and when he last saw them they were looking over the side.

Mr Harbinson (for the third-class passengers) asked Scott if he saw any third-class passengers when he was taking a lifebelt from the third-class quarters.

Scott: No; some stewards were getting their belts there.

Mr Harbinson: They were looking after themselves also? – Yes.

Taking these third-class lifebelts? – Yes.

Was it not rather curious that you saw no third-class passengers at all? – I did not see any. You were not looking for passengers at all? – No.

Did you see any women or children about? – No. Scott added that he got to the boat deck from the third-class sleeping-rooms up the third-class staircase.

Answering Mr Laing (for the White Star Line), Scott said he did not know that lifebelts were provided for 1,000 third-class passengers, or that only 700 third-class passengers were carried on the voyage.

Following some questions by the Attorney-General in reference to the third-class lifebelts, Lord Mersey asked: "Were the doors of the third-class cabins open?" Scott said that he could not say.

While a steward was giving evidence Mr Cotter (who appears for the Stewards' Union) suggested that the German and Italian stewards on board might not understand some of the orders that were given after the collision.

HUNDREDS THROWN IN A HEAP

Baker Describes the Last Scene

PUSHED OFF A BOAT

A full account of what happened on the Titanic between the departure of the last lifeboat and the sinking of the ship was given by John Joughin, the chief baker.

When he got an order to provision the boats, Joughin sent thirteen men up with four loaves of bread apiece.

Joughin went to his boat station. "As we could not find sufficient women to fill the boat," he said, "two or three others went with me and forcibly brought the women to the boats."

He said he was supposed to be captain of the boat, but as there was not sufficient room he remained on the ship when the boat was lowered away.

"Then I went to my room again and had a drop of liqueur. When I went upstairs again all the boats seemed to have gone, and I threw about 50 deck chairs overboard.

"BUCKLING AND CRACKLING"

Why? – I was looking out for something to cling to.

"I went into the pantry for some water," Joughin went on, "and while there I heard a crash and a noise as though people were rushing along the deck. I looked out on deck and saw people rushing aft to the poop. There was a buckling and crackling as if the vessel was breaking. I kept out of the crush of people as long as I could. I went down to the well deck and just as I got there she gave a great list to port and threw everybody in a bunch. The people were piled up, many hundreds of them. I eventually got to the starboard side of the poop.

With the model in Court Joughin illustrated how the vessel listed. The angle was about 45 degrees.

Resuming his story Joughin said he hung on to the poop rail. "Just as I was wondering what to do next she went." Joughin said he was not dragged under water. He was a good swimmer, and he thought he was in the water about two hours. He did not attempt to get anything to hold on to. He was "just paddling" until daylight came. "Then I saw what I thought was some wreckage and started to swim towards it slowly. I then found it was a collapsible not properly afloat, but on its side, with an officer and, I think, about 25 men standing on the top, or rather the side of it.

The officer was Mr Lightoller."

SAVED BY THE HAND OF A FRIEND

They could not take you in? – Well, you see, there was no room for anymore. They were standing on it then.

Did you stay near it? – I tried to get on it, but I was pushed off, and I, what you would call, hung around. I eventually got round to the opposite side, and a cook on the collapsible recognised me and held out his hand, and I got the edge of my lifebelt hitched on to the side of the boat. Eventually a lifeboat came in sight. They got within 50 yards of us, and then they sung out that they could only take ten people on board. Then I said to the cook who was holding me, "Let go my hand, and I will swim to that boat. I am going to be one of the ten." I was taken into the lifeboat. I was hanging on to the collapsible boat about one and a half hours."

I suggest that the liqueur helped you to save your life. How much did you have? – Oh, about half a tumblerful.

Joughin said that when he got on to the lifeboat his feet were numbed, and he had to walk on his knees.

GUNS AS DISTRESS SIGNALS

The President of the Board of Trade is to be asked by Major Archer-Shee whether the Titanic was fitted with minute guns as laid down in the regulations for preventing collisions at sea; and, if so, whether the guns were fired to attract the attention of the ship stated to have been a few miles off.

THE MANSION HOUSE FUND

The Mansion House Titanic Fund yesterday reached £244,000.

MR ISMAY'S RETURN

Met by His Wife on the Adriatic's Arrival at Queenstown

Mr Bruce Ismay arrived at Queenstown yesterday on board the Adriatic, and was met by Mrs Ismay. Customs officers and officials of the White Star Line were the only people other than passengers allowed on board.

Sir J. Nutting, of Dublin, one of the passengers from New York, said Mr Ismay made no complaint as to the Senatorial inquiry into the Titanic disaster, but he expressed the opinion that some of the American newspapers were unjust to him without waiting to hear what statement he had to make.

Mr Ismay seemed to be suffering from nervous strain when he embarked, but his health has improved during the voyage. He kept much to himself, was never seen on the promenade deck, and used the lower deck very little.

Among the other passengers were Lowe, Boxhall and Pittman, officers of the Titanic, the look-out man Fleet, about forty other members of the crew, who were on their way to Liverpool, and an Englishwoman, Mrs Dean, with her two children, survivors of the disaster. The woman's husband was drowned, and a collection on her behalf among the passengers on the Adriatic realised £55.

A steward who saved himself by jumping into the sea when the forepart of the Titanic was under water as far as the bridge, told a cabin passenger on the Adriatic that in his opinion the majority of the passengers did not realise until the last ten minutes that the Titanic was going to founder. He heard many of them sympathising with those who were in the lifeboats in a freezing atmosphere thinly clad.

DAILY SKETCH SHILLING FUND

	Shillings
Per Mr and Mrs T. J. B.	2
Collected by Rowledge Brass Band	15
Springburn-road	1
Proceeds of a small Concert given by L. Marshall and G. Woods	5½
Collected by Blanch Evans	5
A Few Little Cheshire Girls	2
J. R. L.	2
W. C. and J. S.	2
A. P. (Bradford)	1
F. T. Waters	2
Customers of the Park Tobacconist, Cardiff	20
Padiham	2½
The May Queen, Barlow-road, Levenshulme	4
Elsie and Donald (aged 14 and 12)	7
E.C. (Birkdale)	2
Mrs Bowden (Blackpool)	5

Total, (including sums previously acknowledged) 17,481 and 3d.

It was common practice for all individual donations to appeals to be acknowledged in the pages of the newspapers. The largest example of this that I came across in my research was in The Times of Monday, 29th April, which devoted over two and a half pages to acknowledging receipt to the Mansion House Fund of over 5,200 donations, with sums ranging between £30,000 and £1.

DAILY SKETCH.

No. 991.—MONDAY, MAY 13, 1912. THE PREMIER PICTURE PAPER. [Registered as a Newspaper.] ONE HALFPENNY.

MR. BRUCE ISMAY WELCOMED HOME AGAIN WITH CHEERS.

Mr. Bruce Ismay received a warm welcome from a crowd assembled on the Liverpool landing-stage on Saturday when he came ashore from the White Star liner Adriatic, in which he returned to England from New York along with the surviving officers of the Titanic. (1) Mr. and Mrs. Ismay smiling in response to sympathetic cheers as they descended the gangway. (6) Crowd cheering Mr. Ismay (in car).—Daily Sketch Photographs.

Mrs. Ismay met her husband at Queenstown. Below is Sir John Hare returned from Canada. (2) Mr. H. G. Lowe, the fifth officer of the Titanic, with his father and sister. Mr. Lowe was the officer who fired his revolver. (3) Mr. H. J. Pitman, third officer, with relatives. (4) Mr. C. H. Lightoller (in bowler hat), second officer. (5) Mr. and Mrs. Ismay approaching motor.

MR BRUCE ISMAY

Cheered on Arrival at Liverpool

HEARTFELT THANKS

For Sympathy in the Trial of His Life

On his arrival at Liverpool on Saturday Mr Bruce Ismay was met by a crowd of sympathisers, who waved hats and handkerchiefs and loudly cheered the White Star chairman.

Mr Ismay, who was accompanied by his wife, greatly appreciated the reception given him, and raised his hat in acknowledgement. He was looking pale and haggard.

Through an official of the company, Mr Ismay sent the following request:-

"Mr Bruce Ismay asks the gentlemen of the Press to extend their courtesy to him by not pressing for any statement from him, first, because he is still suffering from the very great strain of the Titanic disaster and subsequent events; again, because he gave before the American Commission a plain and unvarnished statement of facts which has been fully reported, and also because his evidence before the British Court of Inquiry should not be anticipated.

He would, however, like to take the opportunity of acknowledging with a full heart the large number of telegraphic messages and letters from public concerns and business and private friends, conveying sympathy with him and confidence in him, which he very much appreciates in the greatest trial of his life."

The surviving officers of the Titanic – Messrs. Lightholler, Lowe, Boxhall and Pitman – reached Liverpool by the same ship as Mr Ismay – the Adriatic.

The fifth officer, Mr Lowe, who told the American Court of Inquiry that he asked Mr Ismay, while the boats were being lowered, not to let his anxiety to help hinder the men, attracted much attention from the crowd. It was Mr Lowe to whom Senator Smith, the chairman of the inquiry, apologised for having made – through a misunderstanding – an unfounded suggestion.

Mr Lowe was frank in his criticism of some of the newspapers on the other side.

ONE MAN ONE BOAT

Collapsibles Made to Fit Passengers' Pockets

INVENTING UNSINKABLES

One inevitable result of the Titanic disaster has been to hustle inventive genius into a fine frenzy of life-saving.

Patent agents and financiers who make a speciality of exploiting new ideas of a mechanical description are just now being snowed under by the piles of propositions that daily reach them from inventors of all ages and nationalities, professional and amateur alike.

Much attention is being directed to lifebelts and buoys, bulkheads and other technicalities which mainly interest naval architects and shipbuilders. But the majority of the inventive minds now tackling the questions raised by the loss of the Titanic seem to be concentrating on boats that won't sink.

One clever inventor, who has a dozen novelties to his name on the records of the Patent Office, showed the *Daily Sketch* his plans for a ship's boat that is both, he claims, collapsible and uncapsizable.

"I am convinced" he said "that the type of boat required must be a collapsible, folding away easily into very little space and needing no davits. I don't believe in davits. Now this boat which I have just invented will fold up into such small compass that you could almost stow it into your overcoat pocket, or keep it beside your bunk in your own cabin. It won't upset under any conditions. I've tested it severely and found it unsinkable and uncapsizable. All I want is a hundred pounds to see my boat through a public demonstration."

A Sunderland man's plan is the attachment of the water-tight compartments to the underside of the deck, and he claims that these could be attached without interfering with the loading and discharging facilities. The deck itself would be secured to the ship with specially designed bolts, which would be automatically released in case of the hull being filled with water. The deck would then become a floating raft, with enough weight underneath to prevent her being top-heavy.

TINIEST SURVIVOR OF THE TITANIC

Among the passengers rescued from the Titanic who returned to Liverpool by the Adriatic on Saturday was Mrs Dean with her two infants. Her husband was lost with the men in the steerage, and the Adriatic passengers collected £65 for the widow. The photograph shows the baby, six weeks old at the time of the disaster, in the charge of interested passengers.

I am happy to inform those readers who may be unaware, that the young baby pictured above, Miss Millvina Dean is a sprightly octogenarian who regularly enriches Titanic Conventions and associated events around the world with her presence. She is a delightful lady and now revels in her celebrity status. The picture below shows Debbie Danson, Miss Dean and myself at the 1994 Convention of the British Titanic Society held in Southampton.

VINCENT ASTOR CLAIMS HIS FATHER'S BODY

There were pathetic scenes in Halifax Harbour when the Mackay Bennett arrived and the sorrowing relatives of those who lost their lives in the Titanic disaster saw the boxes containing the bodies of the dead brought ashore. The photographs show (1) Hearses and undertakers wagons arriving at the Halifax morgue with the victims, (2) Vincent Astor arriving to claim his father's body.

WORLD'S BIGGEST BAND

Remarkable Memorial to Titanic Musicians

The most remarkable tribute to the memory of Wallace Hartley and his bandsmen who went to their death heroically fiddling the swansong of the Titanic will be the great memorial concert fixed to take place in the Royal Albert Hall on the afternoon of Empire Day.

The proposal was made by the Orchestral Association, and players in all of the most famous orchestras in London are heartily co-operating in the rendering of what should prove to be a programme of record interest.

The instrumental forces of the Philharmonic, the Queen's Hall, the London Symphony, and New Symphony orchestras, as well as the Beecham Orchestra and those of the two opera houses, will be united in a combination which will be the biggest band of its kind that has ever appeared at a single performance.

Sir Edward Elgar and Sir Henry J. Wood, as well as Mr Landon Ronald and Mr Thomas Beecham, will conduct in turn.

One of the looked-for results of the concert will be the erection of a suitable memorial to the Titanic bandsmen in the hall of the Orchestral Institute.

***

"The Messmates" Musical Society (whose motto is "Be Matey") are giving a big Bohemian concert at the Caxton Hall, Westminster, in aid of the Mansion House Titanic Fund, on Monday next. Tickets from Messmates, 27, Victoria-street, Westminster.

MR BRUCE ISMAY'S GIFT

£20,000 to Provide Pensions for Disabled Seamen

It is stated that Mr Bruce Ismay has decided to make a munificent gift to seafarers as a memorial to the heroism displayed by all sections of the crew of the Titanic, and as something of a thanksgiving offering for the safety secured to the surviving passengers and to himself.

This will take the form of an endowment fund of probably £20,000 to provide pensions for disabled men of all classes, whether engaged above or below deck, or for the widows of such men.

It is understood that details of the scheme will shortly be made known by the Lord Mayor of Liverpool.

The statement is made by the London correspondent of the *Liverpool Journal of Commerce.*

Sir Rufus Isaacs and others officially engaged in the Titanic Inquiry visited the Olympic at Southampton yesterday and made a thorough investigation of the vessel.

WITNESSES' WAGES GO UP

Mr Buxton, the President of the Board of Trade, stated in the House of Commons yesterday that the scale of pay for seamen witnesses at the Titanic inquiry had been increased.

PSYCHIC INTERVIEW WITH MR STEAD

Mrs Coates (wife of Professor Coates), Scotch medium, who claims to have had an interview with the spirit of Mr W. T. Stead. Mrs Coates is well known in psychic circles and was a personal friend of Mr Stead.

In the interview Mrs Coates says that Mr Stead affirmed that he had asked the band of the Titanic to play "Nearer, My God, To Thee".

The seance has naturally created the greatest interest. Mr Stead asked that his communications be published far and wide.

THE MANSION HOUSE FUND

The Mansion House Titanic Fund now amounts to £261,000.

DRAMATIC DAY AT THE INQUIRY

Did The Californian See the Titanic?

APPRENTICE'S STRANGE STORY

Ship With Glare of Light and Heavy List

Subtly yet surely the dramatic element in the Titanic inquiry is quickening.

From the region of dry technical details, vital, of course, but prosy enough, and of plain, unvarnished narratives such as have already been told to Lord Mersey and his five assessors by members of the Titanic's crew, the Court is passing to the knot of puzzles in which the whole tragedy still seems hopelessly tangled.

When the Commission resumed at the Scottish Hall yesterday there were many more eager listeners than at any previous sitting, though the ladies' gallery was sparsely tenanted. The spacious floor was well filled, from the back row of the seats assigned to counsel to the big red curtains which screen the entrances. Here women, in all the colours of bright summer frocks and millinery, were more conspicuous than men, though as the day passed men, too, turned up in ever-increasing numbers and contentedly took up standing places where they could at least see all that is to be seen though they could hear little.

Expectations of seeing Mr Bruce Ismay and the surviving officers of the Titanic had called together this larger muster of onlookers, and though these leading figures in the tragedy were not yet to be seen, the day's evidence was sufficiently exciting to hold the close attention of every man and woman in the hall.

It was exciting, and to that extent dramatic in a strangely suppressed sort of way, because one felt that at last one was reaching the heart of things, getting to an understanding of many points about which the world is curious.

MYSTERIOUS LIGHTS

The puzzle of the Californian, for instance. This was the particular question to which Lord Mersey, with the aid of the Attorney-General and other leading counsel, directed attention throughout the day, quite half of which was spent at the witness table by Stanley Lord, the captain of the Californian, the Leyland Line steamship which was somewhere in the neighbourhood of the Titanic on that fateful Sunday night.

As the master and men of the Californian told their story, an element not so much of the sensational as the sheerly inexplicable quivered the endless string of questions and answers. There were mysteries of lights seen across the waters, of rockets flashing into the sky, and other usual and unusual things to be explained. Somehow, in spite of the efforts of a keen questioner like Sir Rufus Isaacs, or of the quietly uttered but deep-searching interjections of Lord Mersey, the sense of the inexplicable remained and even deepened.

The Californian's captain is a well-built man of medium height, with high forehead and bronzed, clean-shaven face. He wore a blue suit and stood erect and at his ease as he answered crisply in tones that were plainly audible. Presently he leaned forward, with hands upon the table, as the questions gathered weight, while Sir Rufus Isaacs, having extracted preliminary facts, started upon a long and vigorous cross-examination.

CAPT LORD'S EVIDENCE

Other Californian Witnesses Ordered Out of Court

When the Titanic inquiry was resumed yesterday Sir Robert Finlay (for the White Star Line) referred to the evidence of the fireman Hendrickson, who has said that the emergency boat left the ship with seven of the crew and five passengers, and that Sir Cosmo and Lady Duff-Gordon were among the passengers. Sir Robert thought it was highly desirable that the cross-examination should be postponed until Friday, "in order that Sir Cosmo and Lady Duff-Gordon may be here and may have the opportunity of making their statement and of taking any steps they think proper."

Lord Mersey granted Sir Robert's application.

The Attorney-General, in announcing that he would call evidence from the Californian, said that whether the ship seen by the Californian was the Titanic or not was a question which could only be determined after the evidence had been heard.

Captain Stanley Lord, the master of the Californian, said that his wireless operator told the Titanic of the Californian's being stopped and surrounded by ice. About eleven o'clock on the Sunday night he saw a steamer's light approaching. The steamer was of medium size, and he remarked at the time that she was not the Titanic. He watched the vessel until 11.30, when it stopped. It was then about five miles away. One of the officers tried to communicate with it with a Morse lamp, but got no reply. Captain Lord retired to his chart room at 12.15. About a quarter past one the second officer informed him down the tube that the vessel had altered her bearings and that he had seen a white rocket from her.

After further questions Lord Mersey said to the Attorney-General: "You know, what is in my brain at present is this – that what they saw was the Titanic."

The Attorney-General said he would try to clear up the point.

"Can you tell us," he asked Captain Lord, "whether you saw one or two mast-head lights?"

Captain Lord replied that he only saw one. A day or two after the disaster he asked the third officer how many mast-heads there were, and he said "Two."

Lord Mersey: If you had seen only one, why did you ask him how many there were? – I was curious about the Titanic accident.

The Attorney-General: If he did see two lights it must have been the Titanic? – That doesn't follow. Other vessels, Captain Lord said, carried two lights.

Captain Lord said that he did not recollect that while he was in the chart-room the Californian's apprentice, Gibson, gave him a message about signals that he had seen. If he had spoken to the boy he must have done so in his sleep. Captain Lord said he went to bed about 1.30. At 4.30 the chief officer called him and said that the steamer was still to the southward. It was not until the morning that he was told that the steamer had fired several rockets after the one that went up at 1.15.

At this point the other Californian witnesses were ordered to leave the Court.

Lord Mersey: What do you think she was sending up the rocket for? – I thought she was acknowledging our signals. A good many vessels don't use Morse lamps.

Have you ever said that before? – That has been my story right through.

Captain Lord said that when the rocket was fired he asked the second officer: "Is that a Company signal?" He asked the officer to find out what the ship was and to send Gibson, the apprentice, with the reply. Some companies, Captain Lord said later, have white signals.

The Attorney-General: As far as you were concerned you did not know at all what the rocket was for? – No. And you remained in the chart-room and did nothing further? – I did nothing further.

The Attorney-General: Were you quite comfortable in your mind as to your own action when you heard that the Titanic had sunk? – I thought we ought to have seen her signal at nineteen miles. That was all that warned me. Captain Lord was positive the vessel he saw was not the Titanic, which could not have been mistaken.

Lord Mersey: The vessel you think you saw has not been heard of since? – Not to my knowledge.

Asked if it would not have been a simple thing to wake up the Marconi operator and try to get into communication with the ship, Captain Lord said, "I would have if it had worried me a great deal, but it did not." In his opinion the vessel they saw had no wireless.

Captain Lord said that even if they had received the Titanic's distress message he did not think they could have reached the scene of the disaster before the Carpathia.

"SHE LOOKS QUEER"

Apprentice Who Thought He Saw Morse Signals

The next witness was James Gibson (20), the apprentice who was sent to Captain Lord with a message.

He said that at 12.20 on the Sunday night he saw a white masthead light and a red side light. There was also a glare of white light on the after-deck. The ship was 4 to 7 miles away.

Did you see any second white light? – No, not distinctly.

A light was flickering, and he thought that they were trying to call them up by means of the Morse light. He went to the Morse keyboard and signalled to them, but came to the conclusion that the light was not a Morse light. Afterwards he saw three white rockets.

At 1.20, Gibson continued, the second officer said he saw the ship steam away to the south-west. The officer said to Gibson, as they were looking at her through glasses, "Look at her now. She looks very queer out of the water. The lights look queer."

"I looked at her through the glasses," Gibson said, "and the lights did not seem to be natural. When a vessel rolls at sea her lights do not look the same." There was no sea to cause any rolling. The ship seemed as if she had a heavy list to starboard.

Gibson said that later he was ordered by the second officer to report to the captain that the vessel had disappeared towards the south-west and that she had fired eight rockets. He carried out the order.

In answer to Lord Mersey, Gibson said that the captain was awake.

In reply to Lord Mersey he said that he did not take it that the second officer meant that the ship had sunk when he sent a message to the captain that it had disappeared to the south-west.

SECOND OFFICER'S EVIDENCE

Herbert Stone, the Californian's second officer, was the next witness.

After he had described how he saw white rockets go up Lord Mersey asked him several times what he thought the rockets meant. Mr Stone said he did not know.

Lord Mersey: Do be frank. You don't make a good impression.

Mr Stone said he told the captain on the tube about the rockets, and he asked "Are they Company signals?"

"I replied," Mr Stone said "I don't know, but they appear to me to be white rockets."

The captain instructed him to send any information he received by the apprentice.

Mr Stone said that the ship steamed away, and he did not think there was anything wrong with her. He and Gibson had no conversation at the time about the meaning of distress signals. Mr Stone suggested that the rockets might have come from a ship behind the one they saw.

The inquiry was adjourned.

PENSIONS FOR SAILORS' WIDOWS

Generous Gifts from Mr Bruce Ismay and His Wife

£11,000 TO START A FUND

Mr Bruce Ismay has offered to give £10,000, and Mrs Ismay £1,000, to a fund to provide pensions for the widows of those who have lost their lives at sea while engaged upon active duty in British mercantile vessels.

In a letter to Lord Derby Mr Ismay says:- The terrible disaster to the Titanic has brought prominently to my mind the fact that no permanent fund exists to assist the widows of those whose lives are lost while they are engaged upon active duty on the mercantile vessels of this country. The need for such a fund has been emphasised by some remarks made by your Lordship on the occasion of the Liverpool Blue Coat Dinner. The Mercantile Marine Service Association have administered with entire satisfaction the Liverpool Seamen's Pension Fund and the Margaret Ismay Fund which was established some years ago by my father and mother to provide pensions for Liverpool seamen and their widows, but neither of those funds covers the object I have in view.

If under the administration of the same body on the outlines of the enclosed memorandum a fund were initiated to meet the cause to which I refer I shall be happy to contribute £10,000 and my wife £1,000 thereto.

I need scarcely add that sufferers from the Titanic disaster would be eligible equally with others to the benefits of the proposed fund so far as it is necessary to supplement the generous assistance of the public.

The memorandum referred to states:- The object of the fund is to provide pensions for the widows of those who lose their lives at sea while engaged upon active duty in any capacity whatever upon a mercantile vessel registered in the United Kingdom.

No pension should exceed £20 per annum, and it will be continued or discontinued at the absolute discretion of the Committee.

The fund may be invested in the name of the Mercantile Marine Service Association, which will have complete discretion in selecting those who are to receive the pension and fixing the amount from time to time.

Lord Derby has written to Mr Bruce Ismay gratefully accepting his offer, and thanking Mr and Mrs Bruce Ismay for their generosity.

TITANIC WIDOW'S COMPENSATION

At Liverpool yesterday the widow of a bedroom steward on the Titanic was awarded £300 on behalf of herself and three children. The full amount has been paid into Court by the Titanic's owners.

HAROLD BRIDE SUBSCRIBES

Among the subscriptions received by the Mayor of Godalming towards the fund for providing a local memorial to Jack Phillips, the chief wireless operator on the Titanic (a native of the town) is one of £1 1s 0d from Harold Bride, the operator's colleague who was saved.

MEANING OF S.O.S.

Commenting at the Titanic Inquiry yesterday on the alteration of the distress wireless message, the Attorney-General said "The C.Q.D. signal means 'Come Quick – Danger' As far as I understand it, the new S.O.S. signal means 'Save our Souls,' and its advantage is that it is shorter.

MANSION HOUSE FUND TO BE CLOSED

The Mansion House Titanic Fund now amounts to £262,000. "It is probably desirable," says an official statement issued from the Mansion House, "that beyond bringing existing collections to a gradual conclusion, no further efforts should be initiated in support of the appeal, which has already met with such a splendid response."

ASTOR FAMILY IN DEEP MOURNING

Scenes at the funeral of Colonel J. J. Astor. The service was held at the Church of the Messiah on the Astor estate at Rhumbeck, on the Hudson, a few miles from New York. (1) Mrs J. J. Astor and little Miss Muriel Astor. (2) Mr and Mrs Cornelius Vanderbilt. (3) Mr Vincent Astor, who with Muriel shares the Astor millions, leave the church.

MYSTERY OF TITANIC'S SIGNALS

Captain Stanley Lord, the master of the Leyland Line steamer Californian, photographed outside the Scottish Hall, Buckingham Gate, yesterday. Below are a group of witnesses from the Californian. – G. Glenn (fireman), W. Thomas (greaser), C. F. Evans (wireless operator), G. Gibson (apprentice), H. Stone (2nd officer), W. Roass (A.B.), C. V. Groves (3rd officer) and G. F. Stewart chief officer.

CONVINCED HE SAW THE TITANIC

Californian Officer's Evidence

LORD MERSEY AND THE LOG

No Entries About the Distress Signals

Further surprising evidence from the Leyland Liner Californian was given at the Titanic inquiry yesterday.

Third Officer Groves, who was on duty on the Californian until midnight on the Sunday, declared he was now most decidedly of opinion that the ship he saw about midnight was the Titanic.

Groves said he knew at the time, from the number and brilliancy of her lights, that the ship was a large passenger steamer.

He stated that when he told Captain Lord that it was a passenger steamer Captain Lord, who saw the ship, said it was not, and said also that the only passenger ship near was the Titanic.

"ONLY THE TITANIC"

Midnight Incident In the Wireless Telegraphy Room

The first witness at the Titanic inquiry yesterday was Charles Victor Groves, the third officer of the Californian, who was on duty from eight o'clock until twelve on the Sunday night.

He said he saw a steamer with two white mast-head lights. (The Titanic had two white mast-head lights.) She had " a lot of lights," and was a large passenger steamer. About 11.30 he reported what he had seen to the captain, and told him the vessel was a passenger steamer.

As ordered by the captain, Groves tried to call the steamer up with the Morse lamp. Afterwards he saw a light and sent the message, "What?" That meant "What vessel are you?" The light on the steamer still flickered, and Groves concluded definitely that the steamer was not answering.

Captain Lord went on the bridge and said: "That does not look like a passenger steamer."

Groves said: "It is. When she stopped her lights seemed to go out, and I suppose they put them out for the night." The lights went out at 11.40.

In the course of their conversation about the steamer the captain said: "The only passenger steamer near is the Titanic."

Third Officer Groves

The court discussed the question of the apparent going out of the lights that Mr Groves noticed. Lord Mersey pointed out the Titanic's engines were stopped at 11.40, whereupon he was informed that the order from the bridge to stop the main engines would not result in the stopping of the engine that lighted the ship. It was pointed out the Titanic was stated to have made a turning movement when the iceberg was sighted, and Groves said that the lights might have been shut out by such a movement.

Groves said that when he went off duty he told Stone, the second officer, that he had seen a passenger steamer that stopped about 11.40.

"SPARKS" WAKENED

Between 12.15 and 12.30 Groves went to the Marconi room, woke up the operator, and said, "What ship have you got Sparks?" (Sparks is a ship nickname for the Marconi operator.) "Sparks" replied, "Only the Titanic." Groves then put the wireless instrument to his ear. He could read a message if it was sent slowly. He heard nothing.

How long did you listen? – I do not suppose it would be more than 15 to 20 seconds. I did it almost mechanically.

(The Marconi operator, who gave evidence later, explained that the "detector" stopped when he left off working. That being so any signals that the Titanic might have made afterwards would not be recorded.)

Groves then went to his bunk. Next morning the chief officer called him and said the Titanic had sunk. Groves then went to Stone, the second officer (who on Tuesday gave evidence that he saw several white rockets go up).

Groves said to Stone: "Is this right about the Titanic?" Stone replied: "Yes, it is right. Hurry up and get dressed; we shall be wanted in the boats. I saw rockets in my watch."

Lord Mersey: That conveys to me the notion that when he said he saw rockets in his watch he was referring to rockets which he believed came from the Titanic. Did he give you that impression?

Groves: It is rather difficult to say what impression I got. I was rather excited.

Lord Mersey: Knowing what you do now, do you think the steamer that you now know was throwing up rockets, that you thought was a passenger steamer, was the Titanic? – Most decidedly I do, sir.

Groves said that in the morning he saw a steamer whose name he did not know. It was smaller than the ship whose lights he saw the night before.

Mr Dunlop (for the owners and officers of the Californian) questioned Groves about the positions of the Titanic and the Californian, according to latitudes and longitudes that have been given. "If these figures are accurate," he suggested to Groves, "your opinion that this was the Titanic must be wrong." Groves replied, "If the figures are accurate."

Lord Mersey: And if his judgement is true it shows that the figures of latitude and longitude you refer to are not accurate.

George Frederick Stewart, the chief officer of the Californian, was the next witness.

NOT IN THE LOG

While he was giving evidence the Solicitor-General (Sir John Simon) pointed out that there was no entry about the distress signals in the Californian's log book. As he was questioning the officer about the position of the Californian on the day of the disaster, Lord Mersey asked, "Does your question suggest that the log has been doctored?" Sir John Simon replied that he wanted to know how a certain reckoning was made.

Asked why there was no reference to the distress signals in the log, Stewart was understood to reply that it might have been forgotten.

Do you think a careful man is likely to forget distress signals? No, my Lord.

Lord Mersey: Then don't talk to me about forgetfulness.

The chief officer added that he never questioned the second officer about the absence of any reference to the distress signals in the log.

Stewart was questioned about the unknown steamer seen in the morning. He said it had four masts and one funnel. He had been unable to find out her name.

Cyril Evans, the Marconi operator on the Californian, said that on the Sunday evening he told the captain that the Titanic was near. The captain told him to let the Titanic know that the Californian was stopped and surrounded by ice.

About 11 o'clock he called up the Titanic, but, as the Titanic operator was sending private messages to Cape Race, he was told to "keep out." The Californian's signals, Evans explained, would obliterate those from Cape Race.

Evans said he turned in about 11.30. He remembered Mr Groves visiting the Marconi room after midnight. Evans said he would have sent a call at any time during the night had he been asked.

All the witnesses from the Californian having been examined Lord Mersey allowed them to go.

The court adjourned till this morning.

246

MYSTERY OF THE ROCKETS

Captain Lord and Mr Stewart, chief officer   Charles Groves, third officer

The officers of the Californian who gave evidence yesterday before the Wreck Commission as to the lights and rockets they saw on the night when the big liner sank. The Court was crowded. Lord Mersey said he believed the rockets seen from the Californian were those of the Titanic.

247

CALIFORNIAN TELEGRAPHIST AND APPRENTICE

C. F. Evans, the telegraphist of the Californian, and James Gibson, apprentice, important witnesses as to the proximity of the Californian to the Titanic on the night of the disaster.

THIRD-CLASS DAY AT THE INQUIRY

Woman Who Were Left Down Below

REFUSED TO BE SAVED

Witness Breaks Down Whilst Giving Evidence

Evidence of members of the Titanic's crew who were in the third-class quarters was given yesterday.

A steward named Hart said that before he received the order to take women and children up to the boat deck he had told the passengers that he did not think there was any danger.

Afterwards, Hart said, "everything was made clear to them," but in spite of that, and notwithstanding the efforts of the stewards, some of the women in the third-class quarters refused to go on deck.

Of the sixty third-class stewards only eleven or twelve were saved, Hart said.

The Solicitor-General announced that to-day he would call evidence as to No. 1 boat, in which were Sir Cosmo and Lady Duff-Gordon, and with regard to which there was a special matter to be cleared up.

He also stated that Mr Ismay would be called as a witness.

CAPTAIN'S LAST WORDS

"Do Your Best for the Women and Children"

A steward named Rule was recalled at the Titanic inquiry yesterday, and was questioned about No. 1 boat, into which the Duff-Gordons got.

He said that when the order for lowering the boat was given Mr Ismay was at No. 3. Rule would not swear that an officer gave the order for No. 1 boat to be lowered, and he said that he did not know there were only five passengers in it.

Rule was in boat No. 15. Last week he said that the boat was nearly full of men. His evidence on the point yesterday was contradictory, and in the end he explained that his memory had been affected by the disaster. He had had many sleepless nights, and had been under the doctor.

John Edward Hart, a third-class steward, who was also in boat No. 15, was the next witness. Hart, who was complimented by the Solicitor-General upon the clear way he gave his evidence, said that there were about 70 in the boat – four male passengers, thirteen of the crew, and the rest women and children.

Hart said the collision did not wake him. Later someone roused him, but as he did not think there was anything serious the matter he went to sleep again. Then the chief third-class steward came along, and told him to get out the people he had charge of. Hart had charge of 58. Nine were men travelling with their wives, and the rest were women and children.

The chief steward's next order was "Get lifebelts placed on your people." Hart said the stewards went to each third-class room to rouse the passengers, and the majority were found to be already up. Some of Hart's people refused, he said, to have lifebelts on; they did not believe the ship was hurt.

From the chief steward came the order "Stand by your people; there will be further instructions." The chief asked whether all who were willing to have lifebelts on had had them put on, and Hart replied "Yes."

REASSURING THE PASSENGERS

Hart said he then went round among the passengers under his care, trying to reassure them that the vessel was not hurt to any extent, "as far as he knew." About half-past twelve the order came: "Pass your women and children up to the boat deck." That order reached all the third-class stewards, who were waiting in a bunch for orders.

Those who were willing to go to the boat deck were shown the way. Some were not willing and stayed behind. A number of those who went on deck returned to their cabins after seeing some of the boats lowered. Hart heard two or three of them say they would rather stay on the ship than be tossed about on the water like a cockleshell. Hart took two batches of passengers to the boat deck. The first consisted of about thirty women – all in his section who were willing to go. He was delayed on his way back for the

"There is no sorrow but will seek to lie
Within the stricken heart."

second batch because of the number of men going up to the boat deck. On reaching the third-class quarters he gathered together about 25 women and children. When he got to the boat deck with them there was only one boat left on the starboard side. One man who got into the boat had a baby in his arms.

When Hart left the third-class quarters for the second time passengers were still there. By that time he realised the position was serious, and he and other stewards tried to persuade the remaining passengers, some of whom were women, to go on deck, but they would not go. Of the 60 third-class stewards only eleven or twelve were saved.

Mr Harbinson (for the third-class passengers) asked Hart on whose authority he assured the passengers – until he realised the real state of affairs – that the vessel was not hurt. Hart replied that he did not do it on his own authority.

TO KEEP THEM QUIET

Mr Harbinson asked why, and Lord Mersey interjected, "To keep them quiet, of course."

Mr Harbinson (to Hart): I put it to you that it was in consequence of this assurance of yours that some of the people refused to leave their berths? – It was not so. If you pay a little attention you will find that some people were taken to the boat deck.

Mr Harbinson: Don't be impertinent.

Hart: I do not want to be impertinent.

Mr Harbinson was asking about the percentage of lives lost amongst the third-class passengers when Lord Mersey intervened and pointed out that a steward would not know anything about the question of percentages. Mr Harbinson then sat down.

Hart said that while he was in the lifeboat he saw two masthead lights of another ship.

TWO BABIES LYING ON DECK

Robert Victor Piercey, a young third-class pantryman, said he found two babies lying on the boat deck. He took them to a collapsible boat and Mr Murdock, the first officer, said to him, "Get inside with the babies and take charge of them." Piercey gave the babies to passengers and took an oar.

There was a painful scene when Piercey was asked to describe how the ship went down. He made several attempts and finally broke down with the words, "It upset me – I cannot describe it."

Edward Brown, a first-class steward, said he helped in the lowering of several boats, including one of the collapsibles. Mr Bruce Ismay was helping at the collapsibles, and was calling for women and children.

As the Titanic's bridge was nearly touching the water another collapsible boat was got out. Captain Smith, megaphone in hand, passed and said, "Well, boys, do the best for the women and children, and then look after yourselves." Captain Smith then went on the bridge. A very short time after that the vessel sank.

Just before the ship foundered the collapsible boat, which had been filled with people, was over-turned.

Brown was washed out with the rest, and he saw several women in the water. There was a whirlpool, and as he was battling to keep on the top of the water people struggling around him tore away some of his clothes. Brown was in the water till daylight – it seemed a lifetime, he said. He then came across a collapsible boat, on which were a number of passengers and crew. He, another man and a woman were taken aboard. When he was picked up his hands and feet were much swollen.

Brown said he heard the band playing just before he was thrown in the water. He could not swim, and was saved through having a lifebelt on.

Charles Donald McKie, a bathroom steward, was asked if he saw the Titanic go down. He replied: "Yes, we watched all the proceedings."

Asked if there were any complaints about the conduct of the men in his boat, he said, "yes, because we smoked."

The inquiry was adjourned till to-day.

COULD NOT DESCRIBE SCENE WHEN TITANIC SANK

(1) J.T. Wheat, a second-class steward; (2) John Hart, a third-class steward; and (3) Robert Victor Piercey, a third-class pantry hand, who gave evidence at the Titanic Inquiry yesterday. Piercey, who was ordered into the boats with two babies, almost broke down when asked to describe the last scene.

Daily Sketch Photographs.

DAILY SKETCH.

No. 996.—SATURDAY, MAY 18, 1912.   THE PREMIER PICTURE PAPER.   [Registered as a Newspaper.] ONE HALFPENNY.

SIR COSMO DUFF-GORDON GIVES EVIDENCE AT TITANIC INQUIRY

(1) Sir Cosmo Duff-Gordon on the witness stand answering the questions of Sir Rufus Isaacs at the Titanic Commission yesterday. Sir Cosmo said he was attending to his wife in the open boat on which he left the Titanic. He heard no suggestion that this boat should put back to help the drowning. (2) Seaman Symons, who was in charge of the boat, answering the questions of Lord Mersey, who said he was not satisfied with the witness's answers as to why the half-empty boat did not try to save some of the drowning Inset are portraits of Sir Cosmo and Lady Duff-Gordon.

SIR DUFF-GORDON'S EVIDENCE AT INQUIRY

Thought All the Women Had Left the Ship

EXPLANATION OF GIFT TO CREW

Heard No Suggestion That Boat Should Go Back

It was Ladies' Day at the Titanic inquiry yesterday.

Expectations of hearing more about the strange tales of "the Money Boat" had excited keen interest in the day's proceedings, and the prospect of seeing Sir Cosmo and Lady Duff-Gordon in Court relating their version of the incidents of that tragic vigil in mid-ocean was a compelling attraction to the fair and always curious sex.

From floor to topmost gallery the Scottish Hall was thronged. Mrs Asquith was an early comer, Miss Ismay, sister of the much-talked of chairman of the White Star Line, was an interested auditor.

The Duff-Gordons were in court at 10.30 a.m., and took their seats at the outer end of the first row of advocates. Sir Cosmo was wearing a black frock coat and light striped trousers, and Lady Duff-Gordon, who is, of course, familiar to the West End as Mme Lucille, the Court costumier, was in black with a cloak faced with purple. Just in front of them sat counsel who had been instructed on their behalf, Mr Duke, K.C., M.P., and Mr R. E. Vaughan Williams, while for Miss Francatelli, another lady passenger in the same boat who was frequently alluded to in the evidence as Lady Duff-Gordon's secretary-companion, there appeared Mr Ralph Sutton.

It was Mr Duke who lifted the curtain on this day's drama by cross-examining Hendrickson, the member of the Titanic's crew who had said that the passengers protested against their boat being rowed back to the wreck to save more lives lest they should be swamped. The circumstances in which £5 notes were given away by Sir Cosmo Duff-Gordon were described, and Hendrickson told how he and the other men afterwards wrote their names on Lady Duff-Gordon's lifebelt "in memory of the event," as counsel put it. He adhered to his story, and added that everybody in the boat ought to have heard what was said.

AN INGENUOUS WITNESS

Most of the morning was taken up, however, by the evidence of Symons, an able-seaman, who was in charge of the boat. He testified to having been seen, since he reached home at Weymouth, by a gentleman who called "on behalf of Sir Cosmo and Lady Duff-Gordon." The witness was closely pressed about this interview, and the Court rippled with laughter at hearing the sailor's ingenuous objection to saying anything at all about it because what took place in a man's home was no business of anybody.

All this enhanced the curiosity with which the last witness of the day was awaited. This was Sir Cosmo himself. With hair brushed well back, and wearing the clothes and the manner of a well-groomed, self-possessed Society man, he took his place at the table, where he leaned lightly on his hands and threw his head forward as he began, at the invitation of Sir Rufus Isaacs, to tell his story.

Crossing and recrossing his legs rather restlessly, now drawing himself up erect and then leaning forward again, the witness gave his evidence in a suave and somewhat high-pitched voice and in a manner that was at times elaborately explanatory. He would indicate where he stood on the deck by a half-turn to the ship's model behind him, waving his hand to the precise spot.

When the Court rose at four o'clock, adjourning till Monday, Sir Cosmo was still under examination, and the hall was filled by an audience that was straining its ears to catch every word. By this time it included princes and peers and diplomats. There were in Court Prince Leopold of Battenburg, Prince Albert of Schleswig-Holstein, the Russian Ambassador (Count Benckendorff), Lord Clarendon, and other prominent personalities.

EVIDENCE OF THE CREW

Statements Obtained From Them By Solicitors

Leading Fireman Hendrickson's statements as to why No. 1 boat did not go to the rescue of the drowning were investigated at the Titanic inquiry yesterday. No. 1 boat was known as the accident or emergency boat. It was much smaller than a lifeboat.

Last week evidence was given by Hendrickson that there were twelve people in it – two women passengers, three men passengers, two seamen and a fireman – that a seaman named Symons was in charge of the boat, and that the members of the crew received £5 each on the Carpathia.

Hendrickson was recalled and was cross-examined by Mr Duke. He declared that when the boat was about 200 yards from the spot where the ship went down he called out, "It is up to us to go back." That must have been heard by some, at any rate, of those in the boat, but nobody supported his suggestion. Lady Duff-Gordon was seasick during some of the time she was in the boat. Before leaving the Carpathia the crew signed their names on Lady Duff-Gordon's lifebelt.

The next witness was George Symons, an able seaman and a look-out man, who was in charge of the boat. He was asked why Mr Murdock, the first officer, ordered the boat to be lowered when it was not full. He said he could not say. There were no passengers in sight at the time.

Asked why he did not take his boat back when he heard cries Symons said: "I determined, as I was master of the situation, to go back when I thought that most of the danger was over. I used my own discretion, as being the master of the situation, that it was not safe to have gone back at that time until everything was over."

Lord Mersey: I want to know why it was not safe. What was it you were afraid of? – I was not altogether afraid of anything, only to endanger the lives of the people in the boat. Further questioned by Lord Mersey,

Symons said he was afraid that, with so many people in the water, the boat would be swamped.

Lord Mersey: I am not satisfied at all.

The Attorney-General: I want to know more about that. Was the question raised by anyone about going back to the people who were shrieking in the water? – No one whatever.

Symons said that someone called on him at Weymouth and obtained a statement from him. In regard to this Mr Duke explained that it was not done upon the instructions of Sir Cosmo, who was then at sea, but was done at the instance of a firm of solicitors who had been engaged by a relative and deemed it their duty, after Hendrickson's evidence, to get statements from others in the boat.

James Taylor, a fireman, who was also in No. 1 boat, said a suggestion was made that the boat should go back, but he did not know whether it was made by a man or a woman. There was a talk about it, and a lady passenger talked of the boat being swamped if it went back. Two gentlemen in the boat said the same thing.

Do you know which lady it was? – No. Did Sir Cosmo take any part in the conversation? – No.

In answer to Mr Scanlan (for the Seamen's and Firemen's Union), Taylor said he was willing to go back to the drowning, but he did not tell anyone then.

Sir Cosmo Duff-Gordon then went into the box. He said that sometime after the collision Colonel Astor pointed out to him that the ship had a list to port, and was getting lower at the head. Sir Cosmo then warned his wife, and with her and Miss Francatelli, who accompanied his wife as secretary, went on the boat deck, and saw three lifeboats lowered on the starboard side.

His wife and Miss Francatelli refused to leave him. They were asked two or three times to go. Some men got hold of his wife two or three times, asking her to get into No. 3 lifeboat, but she would not leave him. Later Lady Duff-Gordon remarked "I think we ought to do something." and he replied, "We had better wait for orders."

Sir Cosmo said he heard orders given with regard to the lowering of No. 1 boat. Later another officer told them they might as well get into the boat.

The Attorney-General: When the boat was lowered did you think the Titanic was in danger? – I thought it was in a very grave state.

You noticed there was room for more passengers? – There would have been if the oars and mast had been thrown out.

Do you suggest there was not room for more? – I suggest it wanted rearrangement.

Can you suggest why the boat was lowered with so few people in it? – There were no people visible, I am quite sure when I got into the boat.

Lord Mersey: But there were many people close at hand? – There was no one visible, certainly.

The Attorney-General: Did you think there was nobody on the vessel? – No, I thought that certainly all the women had got off.

How far do you think you were off when the Titanic sank? – I should have thought a thousand yards. It is true I have only one eye, and therefore am presumed not to be a judge of distance.

Did you hear the cries when the ship sank? – I heard an explosion first and then a prolonged wail. They were cries of persons drowning? – Yes.

Did it occur to you, there being room in your boat, that if you could get to these people you could save them? – It is difficult to say what occurred. I was minding my wife, and the conditions were abnormal, as you know, and there were many things to think about. It might well have occurred to one that they could have been saved by a boat.

And that there was room in your boat? – I do not think it was possible.

Lord Mersey: Did they begin to row away from the cries?

Sir Cosmo: They began to row. I do not know whether it was away or not. It was to stop the sound of the cries, I think.

You don't suggest they rowed back? – No. After the Titanic had gone down we lost all idea of where she had been.

As far as you are concerned, no notice at all was taken in your boat of those cries? – No.

And no thoughts entered your mind that you ought to go back? – No, I suppose not.

Lord Mersey: A witness said it would have been quite safe to have gone back. What do you say? – I do not know my Lord whether it would have been safe. I think it would have been hardly possible.

The Attorney-General: Why not possible? – I do not know to where we should have gone.

Lord Mersey: I mean to have gone back towards where the cries came from. – I do not know about that.

The Attorney-General: We have heard from two witnesses that the suggestion was made that your boat should go back and try to save some of the people. What do you say about it? – I did not hear any suggestion.

It is further said that one of the ladies identified by a witness as your wife was afraid to go back because she thought the boat would be swamped? – I know.

That was heard by a witness in the same thwart as you were? – Yes.

Did you hear your wife say that? – No, nor any person.

And did you hear either of the other men say that if they did go back there was a danger that the boat would be swamped? – I did not hear it.

You know now, don't you, that you might have saved a good many people? – I do not know that.

You know that your boat would have carried a good many more? – Yes, I know that is so. It is not a lifeboat.

Sir Cosmo then described how he came to promise presents to the men in the lifeboat. He said: "There was a man sitting next to me in the boat. Of course, in the dark I did not see anything. I could not see him, and I do not know yet who he is. I suppose it would be some time when they were resting on their oars, twenty minutes or half an hour after the Titanic had gone down.

The man said to me 'I suppose you have lost everything?' I said: Of course. He said 'You can get some more' and I said Yes. He said 'We have lost all our kit and they won't give us any more, and, what is more, our pay will be stopped from to-night, and all they will do will be to send us back to London'.

I said: You need not worry about that. I will give a fiver to start a new kit. That is all that there was said about the £5."

And when you got on the Carpathia? – There was a little hitch in getting one of the men up the ladders and Hendrickson took up my coat, which I had thrown in the bottom of the boat, for me, and I asked him to give me the men's names, and this, I believe, is his writing.

Lord Mersey (looking at the slip of paper): It is merely a list of names?

Sir Cosmo: Yes.

Did you say anything to the captain of the Carpathia about your intention? – I went to see him one afternoon and told him I had promised the crew of my boat a £5 note each. He said it was quite unnecessary, but I said I had promised and had got to give it.

At this stage the enquiry was adjourned until Monday.

WALLACE HARTLEY'S FUNERAL

The body of Wallace Hartley, the heroic bandmaster of the Titanic, was brought to Liverpool yesterday by the liner Arabic. The coffin was subsequently placed in a hearse to be conveyed by road to Colne, where the funeral with civic honours will take place to-day. The dead man's aged father met the liner, which also brought over two other Titanic victims, Allum, a passenger, and Lawrence, a steward.

PASSENGER'S REWARDS TO TITANIC SEAMEN

Photograph of an order handed by Sir Cosmo Duff-Gordon to J. Horswill, who was one of the crew of the lifeboat. Sir Cosmo handed a similar cheque to each member of the boat crew to enable him to buy a new kit to replace that lost when the Titanic sank.

DAILY SKETCH.

No. 997.—MONDAY, MAY 20, 1912.　　THE PREMIER PICTURE PAPER.　　[Registered as a Newspaper.]　ONE HALFPENNY.

30,000 MOURNERS AT BURIAL OF TITANIC BANDMASTER.

In keeping with the heroism of the man who led the Titanic's band as they stood on the deck of the doomed liner calmly playing "Nearer, my God, to Thee" while the last of the lifeboats pulled away from the sinking ship were the striking scenes witnessed on Saturday when the remains of Mr. Wallace Hartley were laid to rest in the cemetery of his native town of Colne, Lancashire. From all parts of the country, and especially from Lancashire and Yorkshire, flocked crowds, estimated at 30,000, to pay their last tribute of respect to the memory of the central figure of one of the most touching incidents in the history of the sea.

(1) A close friend (X) of the deceased musician at the graveside. (2) Mr. Hartley's father (on right) and the principal mourners. (3) Mr. Hartley (X) and the chief mourners approaching the grave. (4 and 5) The Bethel Choir and the Colne Orchestral Society, who sang the hymn "Nearer, my God, to Thee" as the body was being interred. (6) Leaving the Bethel Chapel, where Mr. Hartley was originally a choirmaster and his father was choirmaster for twenty-five years. Inset: The heroic bandmaster. –

Daily Sketch Photographs.

FATHER WELCOMES TITANIC'S RESCUED OPERATOR

A warm welcome awaited Harold Bride (in centre), the rescued Marconi operator of the Titanic, when he landed at Liverpool on Saturday from the White Star liner Baltic. Fully restored to health, he was cordially embraced by his father, Mr Arthur Bride, who is seen on the left of the picture

Daily Sketch Photograph

DAILY SKETCH.

No. 998.—TUESDAY, MAY 21, 1912.   THE PREMIER PICTURE PAPER.   [Registered as a Newspaper.]   ONE HALFPENNY.

LADY DUFF-GORDON TELLS HER STORY AT TITANIC INQUIRY

Sir Cosmo Duff-Gordon leaving the Scottish Hall after denying the allegation that he opposed the suggestion to rescue the drowning.

Lady Duff-Gordon answering questions on the witness stand.

Lady Duff-Gordon (on right) and Sir Cosmo Duff-Gordon (in the doorway) leaving the Titanic Inquiry for lunch yesterday.

Remarkable scenes were witnessed at the Titanic inquiry when Sir Cosmo and Lady Duff-Gordon gave evidence yesterday. The hall was packed. Rows of fashionably dressed women looked down from the galleries, and outbursts of applause were frequent when Lord Mersey stopped the counsel for the third-class passengers, Mr. Harbinson, from putting what his Lordship considered were unfair questions to Sir Cosmo Duff-Gordon.

LADY DUFF-GORDON'S DENIALS

Did Not Protest Against Going Back

PITCHED INTO BOAT

Made Up Her Mind She "Was Going To Be Drowned"

Feminine interest was again accentuated in yesterday's proceedings at the Scottish Hall when the evidence of the Duff-Gordons was concluded.

By the time Lord Mersey and the assessors took their seats the ladies' galleries were lined with spectators, while the floor-space was crowded, numbers of prominent Society people again putting in an appearance.

The ladies chiefly wore light costumes, flower-decked hats and white blouses being conspicuous, for the day, though dull, was warm. Many of those fortunate enough to secure places commanding uninterrupted views of the witness table settled down comfortably in their seats, took off their hats and jackets and coats, adjusted their opera-glasses, and looked fully prepared to see and hear every thing for the whole day without so much as bestirring themselves for lunch.

It was noticeable that the fashionable cerise colour which had prevailed among the fair listeners last week was now superseded by shades of purple and mauve. It was noticeable too that many clergymen took their places in the audience.

It was just a quarter before noon when Lady Duff-Gordon entered the box at the call of the Attorney-General. She was dressed in black, with a touch of white at her neck and bosom, and from her black hat fell a black veil over her shoulders.

Looking pale, but perfectly self-possessed, Lady Duff-Gordon put her narrative into a few crisp sentences, and was under examination for little more than twenty minutes altogether. Standing erectly at the table, she would turn her head slightly to Sir Rufus Isaacs to catch his questions, and then would turn to Lord Mersey to give her answers in a light, clear voice, which gave no hint of any emotional memories of the horror of shipwreck through which she had passed. There was just a little catch in the breath and a note of dismay as she told the Court that she had quite made up her mind she "was going to be drowned."

Nodding her head emphatically, Lady Duff-Gordon declared it was "not a case of one getting into the boat but of being pitched in." One smiled at the womanlike stress which the witness laid on the politeness of the ship's officer who had given permission to her husband and herself to board the boat.

Lady Duff-Gordon's was the briefest appearance of any material witness who had so far been called.

WHO GAVE DIRECTIONS?

Sir Cosmo Contradicts Another Passenger's Statement

Sir Cosmo Duff-Gordon concluded his evidence at the Titanic Inquiry yesterday.

After he had said that he knew Mr Ismay by sight on the ship, Lord Mersey asked whether Mr Ismay was giving a dinner party on the night of the disaster. Sir Cosmo replied in the negative. He said that Mr Ismay dined with Dr McLaughlin.

Lord Mersey: The reason I asked that question is that I have had sent to me by some lady, who says that her husband was drowned in this catastrophe, what is called a menu of a dinner given, it is alleged, by Mr Bruce Ismay. I do not believe it is the menu of a dinner given by him at all. It is quite possible that this thing was a list of dishes that can be had.

Sir Cosmo was questioned by Mr Harbinson, who represents the third-class passengers. Mr Harbinson suggested to Sir Cosmo, "These harrowing sounds could be distinctly heard by you?" – Sir Cosmo said that was not so.

Lord Mersey (to Mr Harbinson): It is very irregular to assume facts which are not proved. Your duty is to assist me to arrive at the truth, not to try to make out a case for this class against that class.

Mr Harbinson (to Sir Cosmo): You considered that when you were safe yourself all the others might perish? – No;

that is not the right way to put it.

Lord Mersey: The witness's position is bad enough. Do you think it is fair to put questions of that kind? Mr Harbinson: I will not press it. (Loud applause.)

Sir Cosmo having stated that a man in the boat made suggestions that it should be rowed this way and that Mr Harbinson asked, "Was it in consequence of what this man said that you offered them £5 each?" Sir Cosmo replied that the suggestions had no effect on anybody.

Lord Mersey (to Mr Harbinson): Why don't you put your questions plainly? What you want to ask is: Did you promise them £5 in order to induce the men in the boat to row away from the drowning people?

Mr Harbinson: That is the effect.

Lord Mersey: Why don't you put it in plain words? (Applause in the gallery, during which Mr Harbinson sat down.)

Mr Clem Edwards (for the Dockers' Union): Do you think it was natural not to think of rescuing the people? – I still think it was natural, I now see it would have been a splendid thing if it could have been done.

Sir Cosmo said there was no foundation for the suggestion that there was an arrangement between himself, the captain, and Mr Ismay that a boat should be put at Sir Cosmo's service.

In reply to the Attorney-General Sir Cosmo said that a Mr Stengel, a passenger in the boat, kept on saying "Let us go there" and "Boat, ahoy!" Sir Cosmo stated that he asked Mr Stengel to be quiet.

The Attorney-General: I asked you because he was examined in America. I want to call your attention to this statement of his. He was asked: "Do you know who gave directions?" and he said:

"I think between Sir Duff-Gordon and myself we decided which way to go." That is what Mr Stengel says.

Sir Cosmo: I think it is wrong.

The Attorney-General: What? – It is not the case. There was no question at all. I never spoke to the coxswain to give him any directions.

The remains of Mr Owen Allum, of Windsor, who was one of the victims of the Titanic disaster are to be interred at Clewes Parish Church, Windsor, to-morrow.

LADY DUFF-GORDON'S EVIDENCE

Lady Duff-Gordon was then called. She stated that she was pressed to get into two boats, but refused to leave her husband. "After three boats had gone down," she said, "my husband and myself and Miss Francatelli (her secretary) were left standing on the deck. There were no other people on the deck at all visible, and I quite made up my mind that I was going to be drowned. Then suddenly we saw this little boat in front of us – this little thing" – pointing to its model on the Titanic model at her elbow – "and we saw some sailors and an officer apparently giving them orders.

I said to my husband: Ought we not to be doing something? He said: Oh, we must wait for orders. We stood there quite some time while the men were fixing things up. Then my husband went forward and said: Might we get into this boat? and the officer said in a very polite way: Oh certainly do, I will be very pleased.

Somebody hitched me up from the back and pitched me into the boat, and I think Miss Francatelli was pitched in, and then my husband was pitched in. It was not a case of getting in at all, it was too high. They pitched us in this way into the boat." (Lady Gordon illustrated the method used to get her into the boat by placing her hand under her shoulders.) "Then two American gentlemen got pitched in." As far as Lady Duff-Gordon could remember the order given to the boat was "You will row away about 200 yards." She heard no order that the boat was to go back if called.

Lady Duff-Gordon said that she was terribly sea-sick in the boat.

She saw the ship go down. Before it sank she heard terrible cries. After it sank she never heard a cry. "My impression was," she said, "there was absolute silence."

You knew there were people in the Titanic, didn't you? – No, I was thinking nothing about it. Did you say it might be dangerous to go back; you might get swamped? – No.

With regard to an article under her signature in a newspaper Lady Duff-Gordon said that the signature was a forgery. She denied she had made many statements it contained and explained that it was written by a friend (who had supper with her in New York) from things that she had said.

"MY BEAUTIFUL NIGHTDRESS GONE"

Samuel Collins and Robert William Pusey, two firemen, who were also in the boat, said that they heard no suggestion that the boat should go back. Pusey told how the promise of a gift to the crew came to be made. He said: "I heard Lady Duff-Gordon say: There is my beautiful nightdress gone, and I said Never mind about your nightdress as long as you have got your life. Then a man said: We have lost our kit and our pay will be stopped, and then it was that the promise was made to give £5 each for a new kit."

When Pusey left the box Lord Mersey said: "And now we have finished with No. 1 boat, I hope."

MR LIGHTOLLER IN THE BOX

Conversation With Captain

NOTHING SAID ABOUT REDUCING SPEED

Mr Charles Herbert Lightoller, the Titanic's second officer who was on the bridge from six o'clock until ten on the night of the disaster, began his evidence at the inquiry yesterday.

Mr Lightoller, who is the senior surviving officer, dived from the ship as it was sinking. He was twice sucked under the water, and saved himself by clinging to an upturned collapsible boat.

He told the court that the night was clear, and an extra look-out was not required. Throughout her voyage the ship had been making her normal speed of 21½ knots.

The Solicitor-General: At 21 knots the ship travelled 700 yards a minute? – Yes.

Was it your view you could see a "growler" at a safe distance? – Yes, I could see a "growler" at a mile and a half or probably two miles.

Lord Mersey: Is this leading to a suggestion that the look-out men were to blame? Mr Lightoller: Not at all.

The officer then explained to the Court that with a slight swell (or a slight breeze) there was a phosphorescent line round an iceberg. That night there was no swell to be seen. It was the first time in 24 years experience that he had seen an absolutely flat sea.

Mr Lightoller said it was not his experience that the temperature fell as large bodies of ice were approached. It might even go up, he said.

WHAT THE CAPTAIN SAID

He then described, as far as he could remember, a conversation he had with Captain Smith on the bridge about nine o'clock.

"I said something about its being rather a pity a breeze did not get up, as we were going through the ice region. He would know what I meant. I was referring to the breeze making the waves break on the side of the berg.

Mr Lightoller continued:-

"We then discussed the indications of ice. I remember saying there would probably be in any case a certain amount of reflected light from the berg. He said: Oh, yes, there will be a certain amount of reflected light. He said probably even if the blue side of the berg was turned towards us the white outline would give us sufficient warning. He said: We shall be able to see it at a good distance."

Lord Mersey: Then you had both made up your minds at this time that you were about to encounter ice-bergs? – Not necessarily. We discussed it as a natural precaution.

Mr Lightoller said that Captain Smith was with him on the bridge until nearly 9.30. There was no discussion at all as to reduction of speed. As he left the bridge Captain Smith said: If it becomes at all doubtful call me at once. I'll be just inside. That, the officer said, had reference to the risk of ice. Mr Lightoller said he sent a message to the crow's nest shortly after the captain had left him telling the men to keep a sharp look-out for ice, especially growlers.

Asked what his view was as to the usefulness of glasses at night in detecting ice, he said that it was rather difficult to say. He should naturally think that glasses would be helpful. He himself had never seen ice through his glasses first. As a rule he preferred to rely on the naked eye.

The inquiry was adjourned.

"EVERYTHING AGAINST US"

Why the Berg Was Not Seen Sooner

SECOND OFFICER AND THE SPEED

He Will Not Admit The Ship Was Recklessly Handled

The question why the iceberg that struck the Titanic was not seen sooner was raised while Mr Lightoller, the second officer, was giving evidence yesterday.

Before that point came up Mr Lightoller said that he forgot to mention, while he was giving evidence on Monday, that during his conversation with Captain Smith about nine o'clock on the Sunday night the Captain said: "If it does become in the slightest degree hazy we shall have to go slow."

Mr Lightoller was on the bridge till ten o'clock, and during his watch the weather was clear. Neither was there any haze, he said, when he went on deck after the accident.

He heard nothing from his superior officers as to how it was the ship came to run into the berg.

Asked whether he could suggest why the iceberg was not seen sooner, Mr Lightoller said: "Everything was against us." There was a complication of circumstances which might not occur again for a hundred years. There was no moon and no wind, and most extraordinary of all, there was no swell. If there had been the slightest swell the berg would doubtless have been seen in plenty of time. Again, the berg was probably one that had capsized and had its black part above water.

Lord Mersey: Do these circumstances, in your opinion, account for the look-out men not seeing the ice sooner? – Yes.

In reply to Mr Scanlon (for the Seamen and Firemen's Union) Mr Lightoller said it was desirable that the look-out men should have binoculars.

NOT "BANGING ON"

Mr Scanlon then turned to the question of speed. Mr Lightoller adhered to the statement he made on Monday that it was his experience that if the weather was clear vessels did not reduce speed on account of reports of ice.

Mr Scanlon: If placed in the same circumstances would you bang on at 21½ knots? – I do not approve of the term "bang on" It suggests we would go on recklessly in disregard of everything.

I suggest it was utter recklessness in view of the conditions you have described, and in view of the knowledge you had from various sources, to proceed at 21½ knots? – Then all I can say is that that recklessness applies to almost every commander and every ship crossing the Atlantic.

Is it careful navigation in your view? – It is ordinary navigation, which embodies careful navigation.

Mr Lightoller declined to admit that the captain of a Transatlantic liner had a great many duties of a social nature to perform.

The White Star Line had no regulations with regard to ice, but there was a rule that everything was to be sacrificed for the safety of the ship.

Mr Lightoller, who was on the ship as she was foundering, said the behaviour of the passengers was excellent to the end.

Several men who got into a collapsible boat because at first there was no response to the calls for women, got out again when women came along.

BLOWN AWAY BY RUSH OF AIR

When the ship sank Mr Lightoller narrowly escaped being sucked down the ventilator by the rush of water. A rush of air blew him away from the ship. A forward funnel broke off and fell within a few feet of a collapsible boat he had seized after he had been swimming about for some time. The ship did not break in two as she sank. Mr Lightoller illustrated with a model how she went down.

Asked about the lowering and the filling of the boats in the roughest weather that a lifeboat could live in, Mr Lightoller replied: "It is extremely doubtful whether you could get them away from the ship because of the motion of the ship. This brings up the question of the size of the ship and the question of the height." In regard to the loading of the boats Mr Lightoller considered that he put as many people in them as they could safely be lowered with.

He gave orders to the boatswain to go below and open the gangway doors, so that passengers could be passed through them into boats not full. He did not think the order was carried out. Mr Lightoller heard the captain ordering boats on the water to come back, but he did not know whether the order was obeyed.

He was not in a position to say what steps were taken to see that third-class passengers had a fair chance.

When the question whether the ship was properly manned was raised, Lord Mersey pointed out that she was manned far in excess of the legal requirements.

Mr Scanlon said his contention was that the legal requirements were insufficient.

Mr Lightoller said he did not see much of Mr Ismay during the voyage. Mr Lightoller's examination had not concluded when the Court adjourned.

The Lord Mayor of Liverpool has received £1,000 from a Philadelphia citizens committee for distribution among the dependants of the lost members of the Titanic crew. The money has been sent to the Mansion House Fund.

SAFETY AT SEA

Board of Trade Attacked in House of Commons

MR BUXTON'S REPLY

The remissness of the Board of Trade, which, it was alleged, had failed to make proper provision for life-saving at sea, was the subject of debate in the House of Commons yesterday.

The subject was raised on the Board of Trade Vote of £226,862 by Major Archer-Shee, who moved its reduction by £100.

The fact that not sufficient lifeboat accommodation was provided for all carried on passenger steamers showed, said Major Archer-Shee, remissness on the part of those who framed the regulations. The Board of Trade had for ten years allowed these regulations to stand, and during those years the size of passenger ships had enormously increased.

The great complaint against the Board of Trade, said Lord Charles Beresford, was that they did not attempt to carry out their own regulations until after the Titanic inquiry.

Referring to the observations of previous speakers, he asked them not to overdo the question of the lifeboats. There were many days at sea when it would be impossible to launch them with safety.

Mr R. D. Holt said the object to be aimed at should be to keep the ship afloat as long as possible and get her into port. He preferred a bulkhead without a door at all.

PLACING THE BLAME

Mr Holt spoke of the great pressure exerted by passengers upon owners and captains to speed up. He said they were often to blame if disaster ensued. His firm was so impressed with the safety of the sea that it had not a single one of its ships insured.

Replying to the debate, Mr Sidney Buxton, President of the impeached Board, said all the matters raised were the subjects of anxious moment to himself and his department.

It was during the two years he had been head of the department the revision of the rules had been taken in hand, for the first time in many years. At present they were in consultation with the German Government with reference to an International Convention.

Mr Buxton agreed with what had been said about doorless bulkheads, and some time ago he had appointed a committee to report on the whole question. As to wireless telegraphy it was clear the time was ripe for extending the system, and he was considering the best method in which it could be done.

He had received assurances from 95 per cent of the owners of 661 vessels above 1,500 tons that they would provide boat accommodation for all on board.

MR ISMAY'S ANXIETY

Fifth Officer Lowe Gives Evidence

MORE ABOUT BOAT No. 1

How Lady Duff-Gordon Was "Bundled In"

Herbert John Pitman, the Titanic's third officer, told the Court of inquiry yesterday that when he went to the boat to which he had been ordered he saw Mr Ismay, who said, "We are uncovering the boat. There is no time to lose."

Pitman said he did not then know it was Mr Ismay who was speaking, and he took no notice.

When the boat was being got out Mr Ismay said "Get it filled with women and children." The officer replied that he would wait for orders from the captain. He then went and saw Captain Smith, and told him what Mr Ismay had said. Captain Smith said "Carry on." From the description given him Pitman then knew that it was Mr Ismay who had been speaking to him.

Mr Ismay helped to put women into the boat. After between thirty and forty women had been placed in it about half a dozen men got in. The men were allowed in because there were no women around except two who refused to go in the boat.

Further evidence about Mr Ismay was given when, later in the day, Harold Godfrey Lowe, the Titanic's fifth officer went into the box.

Lowe said he did not know to which boat he was assigned. He assisted in lowering several boats. He went in No 14 boat. No one ordered him to go in. He had seen five boats go away without an officer, and he said to Mr Moody, the sixth officer, that he thought an officer should go.

REVOLVER SHOTS

Asked why he used his revolver, he said: "Because while I was at the boat deck two men jumped into my boat. I chased one out and to avoid another occurrence of that sort I fired my revolver as I was going past each deck. The boat had about 64 persons in it and would not stand a sudden jerk."

You were afraid of the effect of other persons jumping in? – Yes. She had too many to lower safely.

Lowe said that he took charge of four other boats, lashed them together and transferred his passengers to them. Then he pulled back to the scene of the wreck and picked up four people. He found no others alive, but saw plenty of bodies.

Describing the rescues from the water, he said it took quite a long time to get one man out. They had to push their way through the dead.

Lowe said he afterwards came across a half-submerged collapsible boat, and took the living people off it. In reply to the question whether he knew the names of those on the collapsible he said, with a laugh, that he knew the name of the lady only.

Asked why No. 1 boat was allowed to leave the ship with only five passengers on board, Lowe said, "I don't know who was there. I cleared the deck."

Lord Mersey: When you put the people in it there were no other people left on the deck? – There were no people left on the starboard deck. Lowe added that he did not search the port side, as he wanted to get the boats away. He had no time to waste.

Lowe denied that when the passengers were put into No. 1 boat he said to Lady Duff-Gordon: "Are you ready, Lady Duff-Gordon?" He "simply bundled her in."

According to Lowe it was not the launching of the boats that took the time. He said that a boat could be got out and put in the water in ten minutes. It was getting the people there that took the time.

In reply to Mr Harbinson, he said he did not think any ship could have got her boats out better than the Titanic did. He did not go back at once when the ship sank. It would have been suicide to have done so, because the people would have swamped the boat.

Mr Cotter (for the Stewards' Union) asked whether Mr Bruce Ismay gave any orders. Lowe replied "No. He was trying all in his power to help the work, and was getting a little bit excited."

WHAT MR ISMAY SAID

What was he doing to help the work? – He was saying "Lower away, lower away!"

Do you consider any passenger on board ship has a right to give orders in that way?

Lord Mersey: You must not ask him that question. What he considers a passenger has a right to do has nothing to do with this inquiry.

Mr Cotter: What did you say to Mr Ismay?

Lowe (laughing): Well, I think you know. (Laughter.)

Did you see Mr Ismay go into a boat? – No. I told him – what I said – and I told the men to go ahead preparing No. 3 boat, and Mr Ismay went there and helped them.

Sir Robert Finlay (for the White Star Line): Mr Ismay did all he could? – He did everything in his power.

In regard to the collapsible boat Sir Robert Finlay asked Lowe if he was certain that the three people he left on it were dead. Lowe replied that he was. To make sure, he said, he made the men on the collapsible turn the bodies over.

The Solicitor-General yesterday made a striking statement in regard to ice warnings. He produced a number of wireless messages, which, he said, showed, if they were received by the Titanic, that she knew she was steaming with icebergs to the south of her as well as to the north.

The inquiry was adjourned

THE TITANIC RELIEF FUND

We are requested by the Lord Mayor of London and the Mansion House Committee to draw the attention of the relatives of the crew and passengers who were drowned in the Titanic disaster to the necessity of sending in their applications for relief without delay, and, at all events, before July 1. Letters should be addressed to the Secretary, Titanic Relief Fund, Mansion House, London.

Fifth Officer Harold Godfrey Lowe

Harold W.G. Lowe Collection

WIRELESS MYSTERY

Did Captain Smith Receive All The Warnings?

BRIDE'S EVIDENCE

How Phillips Dealt With The Lifebelt Thief

A mystery of wireless warnings about ice occupied the attention of the Titanic Court of Inquiry yesterday.

The question raised was whether the Titanic received all the warnings, and, if so, what was done with them.

To assist the Court the positions of ice reported in these messages have been marked on a chart, and an oblong enclosing them has been described on it. It was within the oblong that the ship sank.

The Court's attention was chiefly directed to two messages, sent from the Amerika and the Mesaba respectively. Both were sent on Sunday, and the Solicitor-General has stated that the Mesaba's message was sent about two hours before the collision.

Second Officer Lightoller, who was on the bridge from six o'clock till ten on the Sunday night, and Fourth Officer Boxhall said they knew nothing of these two messages. Lightoller said that had such a message as that from the Mesaba been received by the officers he had no doubt that the Mesaba would have been communicated with immediately.

Mr Turnbull, deputy manager of the Marconi Company, gave evidence to show that the message from the Amerika was sent to Cape Race through the Titanic.

CAPT SMITH'S KNOWLEDGE

This message, which reported the position of two large icebergs, was addressed to the Hydrographic Office at Washington. Mr Turnbull said that, though in the ordinary course a message passed on was regarded as private, it was the practice that messages important to navigation should be communicated to the captain.

The message from the Mesaba reported pack ice and a great number of bergs in latitude 42 to 41.25, longitude 49 to 50.30. (According to Fourth Officer Boxhall, who worked out the position, the Titanic struck the iceberg at lat 41.46 long. 50.14.) At the bottom of the message, said Mr Turnbull, there was an entry to the effect that a reply was received from the Titanic operator. It was not the answer of the captain.

At this point Lord Mersey said : "I am very anxious to know exactly what knowledge can be traced to Captain Smith. That is my anxiety." Later he remarked: "This message seems to me to justify the allegation made by the Solicitor-General that the Titanic must have known of the presence of ice in the oblong."

Sir Robert Finlay (for the White Star Line): It comes to this, of course, that the operator of the Titanic who received this message would know of it. I think it must have been Phillips. He has gone, of course, and it does not carry it a step further towards showing that the captain or any of the officers knew of it.

Lord Mersey: It would be a very extraordinary thing if a man in the Marconi room did not communicate a telegram of this kind to the captain.

BUSY WITH ACCOUNTS

Harold Bride, the junior operator on the Titanic, said that the only message he took about ice was one from the Californian. It was received on the Sunday afternoon, and it stated that the Californian had passed three large icebergs.

Bride said he overheard the message as it was being sent to the Baltic. Before that the Californian had called him up with the same message, but he could not take it then because he was busy making up accounts. Bride delivered the message to an officer on the bridge.

Bride described how Phillips sent out the distress calls after the collision, and said that the last time he went to the wireless room a man who was dressed like a stoker was trying to take off Phillips's lifebelt. "We stopped him," said Bride.

Mr Lewis (for the Seafarers' Union): You are supposed to have hit him? – Well, I held him and Phillips hit him.

Mr Lewis: That is rather different from what I read. Are you positive of this? – Yes.

"You are not likely to see him again," Bride added.

HAROLD BRIDE AT TITANIC INQUIRY

Harold Bride, the assistant Marconi operator of the Titanic (sitting next to the witness box) waiting to give evidence at the inquiry in London yesterday. In the box is Mr Turnbull (deputy manager of the Marconi Company).

Captain Smith told the wireless operators to leave the Marconi room as the ship was sinking.

When they got on deck they unloosed a collapsible boat. It fell into the sea and was overturned.

Bride was washed overboard, and was in the water about three-quarters of an hour. Once he found himself under the collapsible. How long he was there he did not know, but "it seemed like a lifetime."

After he had extricated himself he got on board the collapsible.

The inquiry was adjourned.

WHITE STAR LINE REPORT

The White Star Line report, issued in Liverpool yesterday, states that the year's working shows a profit of £1,074,752, and after deducting debenture, the general interest, and writing £414,140 off for depreciation, there is a balance of £551,035. During the year dividends amounting to £450,000 were paid to the shareholders.

Alluding to the Titanic disaster, the directors state the loss of this fine vessel is the source of deep regret, but is of minor importance compared with the terrible loss of so many valuable lives. Sincere and heartfelt sympathy is offered to all who suffered bereavement.

MR ISMAY'S BOAT

Why He and Another Man Got In

"JOKES" ABOUT ICE

New Story by a Look-Out Man

The chance circumstance by which the Titanic's distress signal was picked up by the Carpathia was related at the Court of Inquiry yesterday.

Harold Thomas Cottam, the Carpathia's operator, said that while he was waiting for a confirmation message from the Parisian before going to bed he asked the Titanic operator if he knew there was a big batch of messages coming from Cape Cod. "His only answer was 'Struck a berg, come at once'."

The Carpathia turned round immediately.

Cottam declared that the Titanic's signal did not become blurred. They were clear up to the end.

The Solicitor-General (Sir J. Simon) asked Cottam to read the following message from Captain Rostron of the Carpathia, to the captain of the Olympic: "Mr Ismay's orders, Olympic not to be seen by Carpathia. No transfer to take place." In reply to the Solicitor-General Cottam said that the Olympic was heading towards the scene of the wreck. Lord Mersey asked what the message meant.

The Solicitor-General: I suggest – though of course Mr Ismay will explain it – that it means he was giving instructions as to the respective courses to be taken by the two ships. They were not to come within range of one another.

Sir R. Finlay: I understand the Olympic is so very like the Titanic in appearance that if the survivors had seen the Olympic they might have supposed, "Here is the Titanic – not lost after all." At any rate it was with some idea of sparing the feelings of the survivors on board the Carpathia.

Frederick Fleet, one of the men in the crow's nest at the time of the collision, said that the sky was clear. A slight haze came on, but it did not interfere with the view ahead.

Sir Rufus Isaacs called attention to the following statement made by Lee, who was on the look-out with Fleet: "We had all our work cut out to pierce through it just after we started. My mate said 'If we can see through that we shall be lucky.'"

Fleet: I never said that.

Lord Mersey: I am not at all disposed to give credit to that man's (Lee) evidence on this point. It is inconsistent. My impression is this – that the man was trying to make an excuse for not seeing the ice-berg, and thought he could make it by creating a thick haze. Fleet declared that if he had had glasses he could have seen the ice-berg in time to get out of the way.

Mr Scanlon (for the Seamen's and Firemen's Union): So it is your view that if you had had glasses it would have made all the difference between safety and disaster? – Yes.

Lord Mersey: If you thought it necessary to have glasses why did not you go to the bridge, or telephone and say: "I am told to keep a sharp look-out and I haven't any glasses"? – They knew that.

Fleet seemed to be bored with the questioning he had to undergo, and some of his replies made the Court laugh heartily. He answered a question put by Mr Scanlon with what the Attorney-General described as an eloquent look.

Fleet said his eye-sight was tested at Washington and was found to be all right. It was a custom of the White Star Line to keep men specially for look-out work.

The Attorney-General having stated that the Board of Trade sight test was for masters and mates and had nothing to do with the men, Lord Mersey said it seemed very desirable that there should be some test for the look-out men.

Sir Robert Finlay (for the White Star Line) asked Fleet about the conversation he had with Lightoller (the second officer) on the Carpathia. Fleet replied, "I am not going to tell you my business."

Lord Mersey: You don't understand. That gentleman is not trying to get round you.

Fleet: No, but some of them are, though. (Laughter.) Lord Mersey told Fleet he had given his evidence very well.

Another look-out man, George Alfred Hogg, said that several times during the voyage the look-out men said when they were being relieved, "Nothing doing: keep a good look-out for small ice." He regarded it as a sort of joking password.

The Attorney-General: This is quite new.

Quartermaster George Thomas Rowe described how Mr Ismay left the ship. Rowe was in charge of the boat, which was a collapsible. Chief Officer Wilde called for more women and children, and as none came Mr Ismay (Rowe knew at the time it was Mr Ismay) and a Mr Carter got in. Rowe did not hear anybody tell them to get in.

Before the Court adjourned until June 4 Lord Mersey said that it was desirable that the Commission's report should be presented as quickly as possible. In reply to Mr Scanlon he said: "I do not think you need fear this tribunal will not inquire into the conduct of the Board of Trade previous to this disaster."

GIFT TO TITANIC OFFICER

In recognition of the gallantry of Harold Lowe, the Titanic's fifth officer, the inhabitants of Barmouth, his native town, are to present him with a gold watch. Lowe, it will be remembered, went back to the scene of the wreck and picked up four men.

**The gold watch was duly presented and was inscribed "Presented to Harold Godfrey Lowe, 5th officer R.M.S. Titanic by his friends in Barmouth and elsewhere in recognition and appreciation of his gallant services at the foundering of the Titanic 15th April 1912".

In addition, Mr Lowe's former school made their own presentation of a gold matchbox inscribed "Presented by the staff and pupils of Barmouth Intermediate School to Harold G. Lowe 5th Officer Titanic an old pupil of the school July 1912".

A further gift followed from America, of binoculars, telescope and sextant inscribed "To Harold G. Lowe 5th Officer Titanic. The real hero of the Titanic with the deepest gratitude from Mrs Henry B. Harris of New York".

I am grateful to Mr Lowe's son, Harold W.G. Lowe, now living in Australia, for his kindness in acquainting me with the above information.**

TITANIC'S BANDSMEN

Impressive Memorial Concert

10,000 SING FAMOUS HYMN

There was a deeply-moving scene at the Albert Hall yesterday afternoon at the concert in memory of the brave bandsmen who went down in the Titanic.

Quite 10,000 people, intense with emotion, sang in unison what is now one of the world's most famous hymns, and the effect was such that women wept and men had difficulty in mastering their feelings.

Seven of the world's leading orchestras, numbering together nearly 500 instrumentalists, combined to render a programme of classical music, such a treat as music-lovers never had before. The orchestra was the largest and most powerful that has ever appeared in the Albert Hall. It was led by composers and conductors whose names are household words. The royal box was occupied by Princess Henry of Battenberg.

The first item in the programme was Chopin's "Marche Funebre," played by the massed orchestras standing. Sir Henry J. Wood led, giving place later to Mr Percy Pitt, who conducted Sullivan's overture, "In Memoriam". Sir Edward Elgar, O.M., next conducted the combined orchestras through his "Variations," a dignified work that called forth rapturous applause. Mme Ada Crossley sang "O rest in the Lord," and there followed excerpts from the third movement in Tchaikovsky's "Symphonie Pathetique," led by Mr Landon Ronald.

The supreme moment of the day came when Sir Henry Wood led the orchestra through the first eight bars of Dyke's version of "Nearer, My God To Thee," and then, turning to the audience, he conducted the singing to the end. Ten thousand people, whose minds were filled with thoughts of one of the greatest sea tragedies ever known, sang the hymn with deep feeling.

To two ladies sitting in a box near the Royal party the hymn made special appeal, and their emotion was evident. The last time they had heard it was from a small boat laden to the water's edge and the band was playing the hymn on the boat-deck of the sinking Titanic.

BIGGEST ORCHEST
GRAND REQUIEM FO

RA EVER SEEN PLAY
R TITANIC BANDSMEN

Previous page: Sir Henry Wood conducting Chopin's Funeral March, played by 500 performers in the Albert Hall yesterday afternoon. The drums, the trombones and the double basses overflowed into the galleries. Such a huge band of musicians has never before been known at an orchestral concert, and a great audience gathered in the vast building. The majesty of the music was most imposing, and those present were profoundly moved, especially when the concert closed with the hymn "Nearer, My God, To Thee" sung by the whole audience.

Daily Sketch Photograph

TITANIC'S WAIFS RECLAIMED

LAST BOAT OF THE TITANIC

The last lifeboat of the Titanic found in mid-Atlantic on May 13 by the Oceanic. Three bodies in the boat were buried at sea.

Mne Navratil, who arrived at Cherbourg on Saturday on the Oceanic, and proceeded to Nice with her two little boys, who were saved from the Titanic. The mother went to New York to claim them.

274

SENATOR SMITH

Rhetorical Report On Titanic Disaster

GRAVE ALLEGATION

"All The Lives Might Have Been Saved"

WASHINGTON Tuesday

Senator Smith, in presenting the report on the inquiry, conducted by him into the loss of the Titanic, addressed the Senate to-day for upwards of an hour. Obviously he had spared no pains to produce an oratorical masterpiece, but the speech, though telling enough in places, was replete with extravagant rhetoric, the meaning of which was sometimes obscure.

Mr Smith prefaced his remarks with a justification of the inquiry and the lines on which it was conducted. "We have been guided," he said, "solely by the public interest and by the desire to meet expectations without bias, prejudice, sensationalism, or slander of the living or the dead. Our course was simply to gather the facts of the disaster while they were still vivid realitics.

"Without any pretension to experience or to special knowledge of nautical affairs, I am of the opinion that very few important facts escaped our scrutiny. Energy is often more desirable than learning."

Proceeding to apportion the blame for the disaster and its attendant loss of life, Mr Smith said:- "We shall leave to the honest judgement of England its painstaking chastisement of the Board of Trade, to whose laxity of regulation and hasty inspection of the world is largely indebted for this awful fatality."

DEMANDS CONTROL OF WIRELESS

Senator Smith laid stress on the following points brought out in evidence given before the Senatorial Commission:- Insufficient tests of boilers and bulkheads; no proper tests of gearing, equipment or signal devices; no drill or station practice. Further, he said, no helpful discipline prevailed, no "general alarm" was given and no organised system was undertaken for securing the safety of those on board.

After criticising the officials of the White Star Line for "battling with the truth" after receiving information from their Montreal office, he said he held Captain Lord, of the Californian, responsible for unnecessary loss of life, and declared in strong language that his failure to arouse the wireless operator after seeing signals was inexcusable.

The report makes the grave allegation that news of the disaster was suppressed by the White Star Company, and that misleading messages were sent to relatives. The wireless operator of the Carpathia is held to have withheld important news and to have "sold it for blood money in New York."

CAPTAIN SMITH

The Senator then went on to detail the incidents of the disaster, after which he delivered himself concerning Captain Smith as follows:- "He knew the sea, and his clear eye and steady hand often guided his ships through dangerous paths. For forty years storms sought vainly to vex him or to menace his craft, and but once before in all his honourable career was his pride humbled or his vessel maimed. Each new advancing type of ship built by his company was handed over to him as a reward for faithful services and as evidence of confidence in his skill.

"Strong of limb, intent of purpose, pure in character, and dauntless as a sailor should be, he walked the deck of this majestic structure as the master of his keel, Titanic though she was. His indifference to danger was one of the direct and contributing causes of this unnecessary tragedy, and while his own willingness to die was expiating evidence of his fitness to live, those of us who knew him well, not in anger, but in sorrow file one specific charge against him – over-confidence and neglect to heed oft-repeated warnings.

"But in his horrible dismay, when his brain was afire with honest retribution, we can still see in his manly bearing and tender solicitude for the safety of the women and children some traces of his lofty spirit. When dark clouds lowered all about him, and the angry elements stripped him of his command, his devotion to his craft, even as it writhed and twisted and struggled for mastery over the foe, calmed the fears of many of the stricken multitude who hung upon his words, lending a dignity to the parting scene as inspiring as it is beautiful to remember."

THE CALIFORNIAN

An Exchange message says the report contains 10,000 words, and makes the bold assertion that "all the lives might have been saved but for the 'negligent indifference' of the Leyland liner Californian to the Titanic's signals."

The report contains no personal criticism of Mr Ismay, and highly commends Captain Rostron, of the Carpathia.

The United States Senate has voted unanimously in favour of the award of a gold medal to Captain Rostron, who is given the privilege of admission to the floor of Congress.

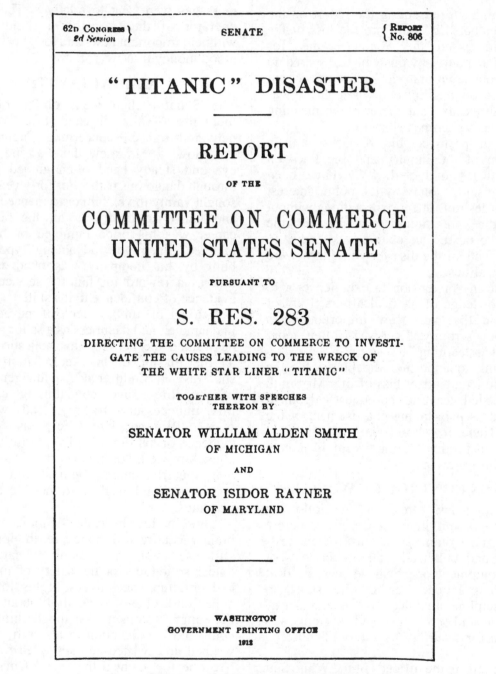

Cover Courtesy of 7C's Press Ludlow, MA USA

HONOUR FOR CARPATHIA'S CAPTAIN

Captain Rostron, of the Carpathia, whose conduct on the occasion of the Titanic rescue is so warmly praised by Senator Smith.

The senate has awarded the captain a gold medal – an honour which carries with it the privilege of admission to the floor of the Senate House.

The survivors of the Titanic disaster have presented Captain Rostron with a handsome loving cup on which is inscribed the story of the rescue of the survivors by the Carpathia.

They also presented medals to the liner's crew.

OUR TITANIC FUND

A Total of 18,361 Shillings Subscribed by Readers

The *Daily Sketch* Shilling Fund for the relief of sufferers through the disaster to the Titanic brought in a total of 18,361 shillings (£918 1s 3½d.). Some weeks ago the first instalment of 15,000 shillings (£750) was sent to the Lord Mayor of London, and yesterday the final cheque was dispatched.

To all who subscribed to and collected for the fund we tender our thanks.

WIDOWS OF THE WRECK

Mrs Astor Entertains Carpathia's Captain

NEW YORK Friday

Captain Rostron, of the Carpathia, and Doctor McGee, the liner's surgeon, were to-day the guests of Mrs Astor, the young widow of Colonel J. J. Astor, at luncheon. Mrs Bradley Cummings and Mrs Jacob Thayer, who were both widowed by the Titanic disaster, were present.

BERG FINDER

The game of chance was played by every big ship that sped through the ice-track at night or in a fog, said Professor Howard T. Barnes in a lecture on icebergs at the Royal Institution.

After pointing out that as a ship drew near a berg there was first a rise of temperature and then a rapid fall, he suggested that a sensitive self-recording instrument, such as the micro-thermometer, might solve the iceberg problem.

MR BRUCE ISMAY TELLS HIS STORY

Had Warning About Ice In His Pocket

"BE FRANK WITH US"

Attorney-General's Advice To White Star Chairman

All eyes were focused on the witness-stand at the Scottish Hall when, a little after noon yesterday, Mr Bruce Ismay, the head of the White Star Line, made his first appearance as a witness before the Titanic Commission.

The attendance of spectators was small in comparison with the crowds that had filled the hall during the many dramatic hours before the Whitsuntide holidays intervened.

Had there been any general expectation of seeing so prominent a survivor of the Atlantic tragedy as Mr Ismay, the court-room would doubtless have been packed with an eager throng. But no one guessed that so quickly after resuming the business of the inquiry the Commission would come to grips with points of absorbing interest. Only a few privileged visitors had any notion of the evidence that the day might bring forth.

Among those present was Mrs Lloyd George who, with her young daughter, early took a seat in one of the reserved rows just behind counsel and, wearing a large mauve-plumed hat, followed the proceedings with attentive interest. So did Mrs Asquith, who has been a frequent visitor to the inquiry.

Ladies, in fact, again formed the largest half of the spectators present when Lord Mersey took his seat with all five assessors beside him. Large and much-feathered hats provided a showy array of millinery, though with the considerateness of the really well-bred matinee girl many of the fair onlookers promptly removed their hats.

Several witnesses of minor importance preceded Mr Bruce Ismay in the box, but it was the advent of the White Star's chief that visibly quickened the interest of all in Court. Fashionably-dressed dames levelled lorgnettes and opera glasses at the simple green-carpeted dais close beside the big model of the Titanic.

They saw a quietly-dressed, rather youthful man of unassuming mien step up to take the oath. Speaking in a low, well-modulated voice that carried well in this hall of vocal difficulties, Mr Ismay proceeded to tell his own story in a series of crisp, direct answers to the Attorney-General's steady fire of questions.

No one looking at Bruce Ismay as he stood at the witness-table, now folding his arms before him, now clasping his hands behind his back, or occasionally slipping his left hand into his trousers-pocket with quite a boyish air, would have pictured this man as the head of one of the wealthiest and most powerful shipping corporations in the world. He looks and speaks so unlike the commonly accepted type of commercial monarchs as could well be conceived. A cultured cosmopolitan, if you like, but not a strong ruler of strong men.

But mere types are always misleading. Behind the quiet manner and low even tones one could detect the mental alertness of a man accustomed to handling large affairs on a large scale. He spoke of ordering the "finest ships that could be produced" and of spending a million and a half sterling on the building of the Titanic as a more or less everyday matter for a shipowner.

As a rule Mr Ismay gave his answers with easy deliberateness, though to a challenging question he would speak with rapid words. And a great many of the Attorney-General's queries were of a challenging character, and on one occasion he told Mr Ismay to be frank.

"SUPER CAPTAIN!"

Counsel's Suggestion About Mr Ismay

Mr Bruce Ismay told the Court that the Titanic cost a million and a half.

Coming to the voyage, Mr Ismay said he was on the ship as an ordinary passenger so far as the navigation was concerned.

Lord Mersey:- Did you pay your fare? – No. The Attorney-General: That rather disposes of the ordinary passenger theory.

Mr Ismay said that just before lunch on the

Sunday Captain Smith handed him a Marconigram from the Baltic reporting ice. Mr Ismay glanced at the message casually and put it in his pocket "in a fit of absent-mindedness" and kept it there for five hours.

It was intended, if the weather had been fine and the conditions suitable on the Monday or Tuesday, that the ship should be driven for a few hours at full speed. The only person to whom he had spoken about that was Mr Bell, the chief engineer. The conversation took place at Queenstown.

Mr Ismay said that there was no slowing down after ice had been reported.

The Attorney-General: You were the managing director, and the captain thought it of sufficient importance to bring the Marconigram to you. You of course appreciated that it meant you were approaching ice? – Yes.

If you were approaching ice at night it would be desirable to slow down?

Mr Ismay hesitated.

Lord Mersey: Answer the question.

Mr Ismay: I say no.

The Attorney-General: Mr Ismay, be frank with us.

Sir Robert Finlay (for the White Star Line): He is frank.

The Attorney-General: I don't think he is if you ask me.

Mr Ismay: If a man can see far enough to clear the ice he is perfectly justified in going at full speed.

The Attorney-General: You did not expect the captain to slow down? – Certainly not.

What is the object of continuing at full speed through the night if you expect to meet ice? – I presume the man would be anxious to get through the ice quicker. He would not want to slow down with the chance of fog coming on.

Mr Ismay was questioned as to the conversation that took place between him and Mrs Ryasson, of Philadelphia, one of the two ladies to whom he spoke about the Marconigram.

"Did she," asked counsel, "say to you 'Of course, you will slow down,' and did you answer 'Oh, no, we will put on more boilers to get out of it'?" Mr Ismay answered "Certainly not."

ASLEEP WHEN SHIP STRUCK

Mr Ismay said he was asleep at the time of the collision. The impact woke him. Going on deck to see what had happened he met Captain Smith and asked if the damage was serious. Captain Smith said he thought it was.

Mr Ismay said he assisted on the starboard side of the boat deck. There was no confusion, and he saw no attempts by men to force their way into the boats. All the women he saw on the boat deck got away in boats.

The Attorney-General: Did you realize that they were not all the women and children on board the ship? – I did not.

Mr Ismay said he did not get into the boat until the women and children who were on the boat deck had been got in. He did not inquire before entering the boat whether any women and children were left on the ship.

In regard to the light towards which his boat pulled, Mr Ismay said he thought it was that of a sailing ship.

Lord Mersey: Am I to understand you do not think it was the Californian?

Mr Ismay: I am sure of it.

Lord Mersey: I am sorry to hear it.

Mr Ismay explained that he did not mean to say that the vessel whose light was seen by others was not the Californian. He meant that the light his boat pulled towards was not the Californian's. The only light he saw was the one they rowed towards. The company to which the Californian belonged was under the financial control of his firm.

Mr Scanlan (for the Seamen's and Firemen's Union) recalled Mr Ismay's conversation with the chief engineer, and asked: What right had you, as an ordinary passenger, to decide the speed at which the ship was to go without consultation with the captain?

Lord Mersey: I can answer that – "None." It is no good asking him that. He has no right to dictate as to speed.

Mr Scanlan: He might answer as a super-captain.

Lord Mersey: What sort of person is a super-captain?

Mr Scanlan: As I conceive it, a man like Mr Ismay who can say to the chief engineer what speed the ship was to go.

Lord Mersey: The captain is the man to say that.

Asked why the number saved was not larger Mr Ismay said:- "It is due to the people not getting into the boats. I cannot blame anybody."

Answering Mr Clem Edwards (for the Dockers' Union) Mr Ismay said that the safety of the passengers and the ship was considered before luxury.

After Mr Ismay had said that he knew there were hundreds of people on the ship when he left her Mr Edwards suggested that, having regard to Mr Ismay's position, it was his duty to remain on the ship until it went down.

Mr Ismay: The boat was actually being lowered. There were no more passengers who could have been got into the boat.

Mr Ismay will continue his evidence to-day.

TITANIC VICTIMS' COMPENSATION

When the first batch of claims by dependants of lost members of the Titanic's crew were heard by Judge Gye at Southampton yesterday liability was not disputed by the White Star Company. They had already paid in to the Registrar the full amount of the claims. The maximum amount was £300 for stewards, £294 was paid for leading firemen and greasers, £237 for firemen, and £223 for trimmers.

COUNTESS OF ROTHES

"Much Concerned" About Titanic Statements

Evidence was given at the Titanic inquiry yesterday about the boat in which the Countess of Rothes (who was known on the Carpathia as "the plucky little Countess") left the Titanic.

Alfred Crawford, a first-class steward, said the Countess was at the helm, and she steered very well indeed. From time to time she reported to him the position of the lights they were rowing towards. Shortly before daybreak they came to the conclusion that the vessel whose lights they saw was "turning round and leaving them."

Lord Mersey, reading from a witness's deposition, said it was stated that when it was suggested that the boat should go back to the Titanic the ladies objected. The Attorney-General said it might be taken from his lordship's reading that Lady Rothes objected.

Lord Mersey said he ought to have said, "Most of the ladies." The Attorney-General: I know from her statement that it was not her view. She is rather concerned about it.

Crawford said he did not hear Lady Rothes object to the boat's going back.

MR ISMAY ENJOYS POST-PRANDIAL SMOKE

Mr Bruce Ismay enjoys a cigarette after lunch while returning to resume his place in the witness stand at the Titanic inquiry. *Daily Sketch* **Photograph**

MR BRUCE ISMAY & THE ICE

Mr Bruce Ismay leaving the Court with Mrs Ismay after giving evidence at the resumed Titanic Inquiry yesterday. Asked why the Titanic went at high speed through the night Mr Ismay said he presumed the men wanted to get through the ice quickly.

WHERE WERE THE OTHERS

When Mr Bruce Ismay Left the Ship?

SIR RUFUS ISAACS' QUESTION

Lord Mersey Hears of Liners Dashing Through Fog

Mr Ismay yesterday concluded his evidence at the Titanic inquiry. He was in the box nearly six hours.

In reply to Sir Robert Finlay (for the White Star Line) Mr Ismay said that on the occasions on which he had crossed the Atlantic he had never attempted to interfere with the captain in regard to navigation.

Lord Mersey: Will you ask him why Captain Smith handed him the Marconi message about ice?

Mr Ismay: I think he handed it to me simply as a matter of information – a matter of interest.

In regard to the Californian, Lord Mersey asked: "Have you any doubt that the Californian did see the rockets from the Titanic?" Mr Ismay replied: "Judging from the evidence I should say not."

Sir Robert Finlay: You were asked about a conversation which was held at Queenstown. It was suggested that you gave some orders to Mr Bell (the chief engineer) as to speed? – I gave no order. Bell came to my room, and I spoke to him in regard to the coal on board the ship. I also said there was no chance of the ship arriving in New York on Tuesday and that we had very much better make up our minds to arrive on Wednesday morning at 5 o'clock, and that, if the weather was fine and bright in every respect on Monday or Tuesday, we could then take a run out of the ship. That could not have been done without communication with the captain.

Mr Ismay was again questioned about the circumstances in which he left the ship.

"NOT THINKING ABOUT IT"

The Attorney-General: You knew you had not boats sufficient on the Titanic to accommodate all the passengers and crew? – Yes.

And, indeed, your boat accommodation was not sufficient to take off all the passengers without the crew, was it? – I believe not.

The object of these questions is to draw your attention to this: That at any rate when the last boat left the Titanic you must have known that a number of passengers and crew were still on board the vessel? – I did.

And you have told us you did not see any on the deck? – I did not. There were no passengers on the deck.

You said also that you did not see any as the boat was lowered? – I did not.

Where were the passengers? – I can only assume the passengers had gone to the after end of the ship.

And you would not be able to see them as your collapsible boat was just before the foremast funnel? – I presume they went there. I was really not thinking about it.

MANAGER'S OPINION

"Not Wise or Necessary to Have Boats For All"

The next witness was Mr Harold Saunderson, the manager of the White Star Line.

Mr Saunderson said that, having regard to the extraordinary nature of the accident that happened to the Titanic, he still did not feel that it would be wise or necessary to provide boats for everybody on board.

One reason why he did not think it wise to have boats for everybody was that the boat deck would be so crammed that the efficiency of the crew's work would be impaired. However, he admitted that the lifeboat accommodation might be increased.

The company were looking forward to the

Court of Inquiry's recommendation on the matter. "In the meantime, in order to satisfy the public, on whom we are dependant for our living, we are putting on the ships more boats than I think is wise to do so."

Lord Mersey handed to Mr Saunderson a plan on which fourteen additional lifeboats were provided for. His Lordship asked Mr Saunderson whether such additional boats could be conveniently placed on a vessel like the Titanic. Mr Saunderson replied that he thought they might be. If the fourteen boats were lifeboats they would accommodate about 910 people.

Asked if it was at one time contemplated to double the boats of the Titanic, Mr Saunderson said he never heard of it until after the accident.

Mr Saunderson said that if they were to increase the number of lifeboats appreciably, and if it was ordered that they must be manned by able seamen, he did not think there would be enough A.B.s in the country.

So far as his knowledge went vessels did not, so long as the weather was clear, reduce speed on account of ice.

Lord Mersey: I have been told that Atlantic liners pay no attention to fog, but steam just as quickly through it.

Mr Saunderson: Any man who told you that was a very ignorant man or very vicious man. It is absolutely untrue.

Since the disaster the company had ordered binoculars to be given to all the look-outs. "There is," said Mr Saunderson, "a popular cry that they shall have glasses and we have to satisfy them."

The inquiry was adjourned.

This day's edition of the Daily Sketch was to be the last on which coverage of the Titanic story extended to a full column length.

THE FALLEN PILLAR

Within a multitude of memories, some things are readily forgotten. It is not pleasant to behold the death's head at the feast, or to hear one saying within the heart of the pleasure hour, that "In the midst of life we are in death." Life is so beautiful to many, that the very thought of death is peace-destroying; while, to others, life is a burden, and death a welcome visitor.

It is the duty of the living to venerate existence, and to find all joy in the heart of being. It is but right that healthy minds should seek to live, and the healthy life becomes the key to the healthy death. Nevertheless, death cannot be forgotten, and in the day of calamity we are drawn towards the consideration and sympathy of Nature's law. Calamity has its lessons, but is too readily forgotten, and it is with the hope that the Titanic wreck will be remembered, that these lines have been written.

The rich and the poor, the weak and the strong, are swept into one common grave, for death respects none, and the democracy of death is stronger than all the thought manifestations and class separations of the living. In the hour of disaster all that is noblest and best sacrifices self that others may be saved, and the spirit of the hero is enshrined in the song and thought of the living.

Let us remember the loss of the Titanic, and venerate the memory of the heroic dead, by a cultivation of that selflessness within which all heroism is nourished in the dark hour of being. Let us remember the afflicted, and look upon humanity as the passengers of a huge Titanic, each of which must be saved before self is carried into the boat. If the weak are first led to safety in the hour of disaster, why not remember them now as worthy of our attention? In this spirit I pray that the weak and afflicted be not forgotten, and that the widows and orphans will be fathered and honoured.

SYLVANUS

BOLD VIEWS ON BOATS

Risk of Titanic Situation Must Be Taken

MANAGER'S OPINION

A bold view in regard to boat accommodation was put before the Titanic Commission yesterday by Mr Harold Sanderson, the general manager of the White Star Line.

Mr Clem Edwards (for the Dockers' Union) asked him: Do you believe you should still have less boat accommodation than the passengers carried, although you have not faith in the unsinkability of the ship?

Mr Sanderson replied: I do. There are certain risks in connection with going to sea which is impossible to eliminate, just as there are risks in travelling on land.

Mr Edwards: And you think those risks ought to be borne by at all events a proportion of the passengers and crew on every one of your ships.

Lord Mersey: You mean ought to be divided amongst them; not borne by a portion but divided amongst them generally. It appears to me Mr Sanderson is quite right. Every person who goes to sea or, for that matter, walks on land, must accept some risk.

Mr Sanderson added that in his judgement boats should be carried purely for transfer purposes – that was to say for transferring the people, in the event of disaster, from ship to shore or from ship to ship.

Mr Edwards: And in the case of being in such a situation as there are no ships to which to transfer that is a risk which must always be taken? – Yes, and it is a very small one.

Mr Edwards: We all thought it was.

It came out during Mr Sanderson's evidence that the Olympic has not now enough boats for everybody on board when she carries her full complement.

To allay public feeling after the Titanic disaster the company put enough lifeboats on the Olympic to carry everybody. "But we saw that was absurd," said Mr Sanderson, "so we reduced them."

MILLIONAIRES' SUITES

Having his attention drawn to the fact that the proportion of women and children saved in the third-class was smaller than the proportion saved in either the first or second class, Mr Sanderson said he thought the explanation was that the best position for launching boats happened to be nearer to the first and the second class quarters than to the third-class quarters.

Mr Harbinson, who represents third-class passengers, asked Mr Sanderson if he did not think some of the space given up to millionaires' suites and deck promenades might not have been better used to ensure the safety of passengers.

Mr Sanderson: If there were anything more we could do to ensure the safety of passengers millionaires' suites would not stand in the way.

Evidence regarding the construction of the Titanic was given by Mr Wilding, a naval architect in the employment of Harland and Wolff. Mr Wilding described the means by which passengers could get from their quarters to the boat deck. The third-class passengers had to pass through the second-class quarters. There was nothing to impede them except the rails, which could be easily lifted by hand.

Mr Wilding said the ice must have penetrated the ship to the extent of three feet six inches.

The inquiry was adjourned.

CARPATHIA'S CREW THANKED

The Liverpool Shipwreck and Humane Society has awarded the Society's gold medal and an illuminated certificate of thanks to Captain Arthur Henry Rostron, of the Carpathia, and the thanks of the committee to his officers and crew for their services in rescuing the survivors of the Titanic.

RAFTS ON LINERS: NEW LIFE-SAVING METHODS AT SEA

Liners leaving Liverpool are now carrying boats for all. The extra accommodation is provided by means of rafts, which take up less space than lifeboats. The rafts are built of wood, floated on four long cylindrical tanks to make them buoyant, and have sufficient space for 30 persons, while ropes hang from the side to which many more could cling. The photograph shows the two types of raft on the boat deck of the Cunard liner Carmania.

OLYMPIC'S BOATS

Mr Sanderson's Explanation at the Titanic Inquiry

At the Titanic inquiry yesterday Mr Sanderson the general manager of the White Star Line, said that the policy pursued now by him was to provide lifeboat accommodation for every passenger and member of the crew on board the Olympic.

This was not sufficient for every person that the vessel could carry.

Paul Maugre, who said he was secretary to the chef of the restaurant on the Titanic, stated that the staff of the restaurant, about sixty in all, were prevented from going on deck by the stewards, and were all drowned. He escaped by jumping into a lifeboat eight feet below. The chef was with him, but he did not jump because he was too fat.

Mr Edward Wilding, a naval architect, of Harland and Wolff's, said he thought that if the Titanic had struck the iceberg a fair blow she would have got to harbour, although the impact would have telescoped her bows for about 100 feet and everybody within that space would have been killed. If the helm had not been starboarded the Titanic might have been saved.

Mr Wilding calculated that about 16,000 tons of water entered the Titanic before she sank.

In reply to Lord Mersey, Mr Wilding said he believed his firm had supplied motor lifeboats to some vessels, but not to the White Star line.

Lord Mersey said he was thinking about the Californian and he expressed the opinion that motor boats might have towed the lifeboats to the light seen by those in the Titanic's boats.

Mr Wilding agreed that in these circumstances it would be an advantage to have motor-boats.

The inquiry was adjourned till Monday.

LOVING CUP FOR CAPTAIN ROSTRON

Presentation at New York

Captain Arthur H. Rostron, commander of the Cunard liner Carpathia, which rescued more than 700 survivors from the ill-fated Titanic, being presented with a handsome loving cup by Mrs J. J. Brown of Denver, the lady president of the committee of survivors organised for the purpose of raising the testimonial. Captain Rostron also received a gold medal and his officers and crew silver and bronze medals.

TITANIC'S BOATS

Startling Evidence at the Inquiry

HOW BOARD OF TRADE COMMITTEE WAS WARNED

Some startling evidence was sprung upon the Titanic Commission yesterday by the Right Hon. A. M. Carlisle, who until 1910 was chairman of managing directors and general manager of works for Harland and Wolff, the builders.

He said that plans were worked out and submitted to the White Star Company providing for four boats under each set of davits on the Titanic and Olympic.

Mr Carlisle said he considered there were not enough boats on the Titanic. Before she sailed he told the Merchant Shipping Act Committee (appointed by the Board of Trade), of which he was a member, that she was inefficiently boated. She should have had at least 48 lifeboats on board instead of 16.

Mr Carlisle said he took the plans with him to the committee meeting at the Board of Trade offices.

Lord Mersey said that the Court would procure the minutes of the committee's meetings.

Mr Carlisle was closely questioned as to two interviews that took place between representatives of the White Star Line.

Asked who was present when plans showing facilities for increased boat accommodation were submitted, Mr Carlisle named Mr Bruce Ismay and Mr Sanderson, the manager of the White Star Line. He could not say whether Mr Sanderson realised what the plan was, as he did not speak.

Mr Carlisle continued, "I came especially from Belfast in October 1909, with those plans, and also the decorations, and Mr Ismay and Mr Sanderson, Lord Pirrie, and myself spent about four hours together."

LONG TALK ABOUT DECORATIONS

Did Mr Sanderson stay for four hours without speaking? (Laughter) – No, that was over the whole of the decorations. We took up that day the entire decorations of the ship.

Never mind the decorations. We are dealing with the lifeboats. – The lifeboat affair took five or ten minutes.

"I showed them the plans," Mr Carlisle went on, "and said it would put them to no expense or trouble in case the Board of Trade came on them to do anything at the last minute."

Mr Carlisle replied that the builders had a very free hand, but he did not think they could possibly have supplied any more boats for the ship without getting the sanction of the White Star Line.

Did you try? – You must remember I retired before the ship was launched.

"I MUST HAVE BEEN SOFT"

In reply to further questions Mr Carlisle said he was a party to the Board of Trade's Advisory Committee's report last year, the recommendations in which required a less boating capacity than there was on the Titanic. He was asked to join the committee two days before it finished its report, and when it had come to certain conclusions he did not consider them satisfactory, and told the committee so. But he signed the report.

Mr Laing: That seems extraordinary.

Mr Carlisle: I confess it looks very extraordinary, but if you had been at the meeting and heard what I said you would understand.

Answering the Attorney-General on the same subject, Mr Carlisle said, "I am not usually soft, but I must have been soft when I signed that."

The inquiry was adjourned.

CARPATHIA'S SERVICES FREE

The White Star Company state that the Cunard Company have declined to accept remuneration for the Carpathia's salvage services respecting the Titanic.

The White Star Company will present Captain Rostron with 100 guineas, and the surgeon purser and the chief steward with 50 guineas each. All other members of the crew will receive a month's wages.

287

MR STEAD'S WILL

"Automatic Writing Diaries" & a Missing Codicil

Mr W. T. Stead left estate valued at £13,000 (so far as can at present be ascertained).

His will is written in his own hand on both sides of a sheet of notepaper. It was made on the day of his departure for Constantinople in July, 1911. Mr Stead names as executors "my beloved wife, Emma Lucy Stead" and his eldest daughter, Emma Wilson Stead, "commonly called Estelle." He left all his property to his wife. His manuscripts, letters, "automatic writing diaries" and everything of an autobiographical or private personal interest are left to his eldest daughter to be dealt with at her discretion.

Mr Stead mentioned in the will that he intended to append a codicil, but the codicil has not been found.

THE FALLEN PILLAR

In Memoriam

W.T.S.

The ended task remembers me of him
  Whose soul, caught up to God, still leads us
  on
Towards the Cherubim and Seraphim,
  When life is lost and won.
O Noble life: Great heart that faced the world
  With noblest courage in the gloomy days,
The flag of peace thy spirit has unfurled,
  Flies, where no good decays.
Enshrined within our memory, though fled
  Beyond earth-strife, to us thou art not dead –
Heav'ns gates are opened, love with love
  repays,
  The love bloom still unshed,
Still, still art thou, God's noble servant,
  Stead.

MR BRUCE ISMAY

Sir Isaacs Calls Attention to an "Extraordinary Thing"

Captain Hayes, a White Star commander, told the Titanic Commission yesterday that Mr Ismay had frequently sailed on boats commanded by him and had never interfered with the navigation of the ship.

Lord Mersey: As far as I know there is no evidence that he did interfere. The evidence tends the other way.

The Attorney-General: I agree that there is no evidence that he interfered in the navigation of the vessel. I do not agree that he was an ordinary passenger. We have always to bear in mind that the ice report was given to him for a specific purpose.

Sir Robert Finlay (for the White Star Line) said he did not know what the Attorney-General's suggestion was.

The Attorney-General: Then I have no objection to telling you. The object of giving him the telegram was because he, as chairman of the company, was there; that it was looked upon as a very serious report; that it was given to him because it was a serious report – it was given to him to consider and appraise himself of the facts; and that it was then handed back, as we know, later on to the captain after a request to do so, and that the object of giving it to him, I certainly shall suggest, was that if he had any directions to give with regard to the Titanic, that was the time to give them.

Lord Mersey: The real point of the matter is that he did not give any directions.

The Attorney-General: Except that to my mind an extraordinary thing is that the captain, instead of pinning that thing up in the chart room, as I should have thought he ought to have done, handed it to Mr Ismay or anybody. That is a very extraordinary thing. I cannot help thinking it is very extraordinary that there never was a word exchanged about it.

Sir Robert Finlay: There most certainly would be if you were right. The Attorney-General: I am not certain that there was not, if you challenge me to say it. Sir Robert Finlay: If Mr Ismay's word on that point is impeached it is another matter.

The inquiry was adjourned.

"LIVES A SECONDARY CONSIDERATION"

How The Board of Trade Made Lifeboat Rules

DRAMATIC INCIDENT AFTER TITANIC DISASTER

The Board of Trade was on its trial at the Titanic inquiry yesterday.

Sir Walter Howell, chief of the Marine Department of the Board of Trade, was in the witness box.

Sir Walter said that the governing principle on which the scale for life-saving appliances had been fixed was gross tonnage, not the number of passengers carried.

Lord Mersey wanted to know why the Board of Trade's Advisory Committee (a committee consisting of shipowners, shipbuilders, representatives of seamen's associations and of other bodies) excluded the number of lives from their consideration and took only into consideration the size of ships.

Sir Walter replied that the main basis was the tonnage of the ship. The minor consideration running through the whole thing was the number of lives on board.

Lord Mersey again asked "Why?"

Sir Walter replied, "The reason was that they were told to divide the ships into classes, and, if they were told so, why should they say the basis of the rules should be lives? That would not require division into classes."

Asked why there had been no alteration in the regulations for eighteen years, Sir Walter said that he was not competent to answer the question.

In April, 1911, the Board of Trade's Advisory Committee was invited to advise on the question of increasing the scale of the life-saving appliances.

NOT SATISFIED

After the committee had made its report experiments were made at the ports, and as the Board of Trade were not altogether satisfied with the results the matter was sent back to the Advisory Committee.

Sir Walter then described a dramatic incident that occurred at the Board of Trade offices on the day after the news of the Titanic disaster was received.

On April 4 Sir Walter directed that a letter should be sent to the Advisory Committee as to the alteration of the scale. The letter was not sent out until April 16. The delay was due to the Easter recess. Before the letter was sent out it was brought to him with the observation: "This disaster has happened. Is this letter to go?" and he replied, "Certainly, without the smallest alteration."

Before Mr Scanlan (for the Seamen's and Firemen's Union) cross-examined Sir Walter, Lord Mersey said that there had been a considerable outcry against the Board of Trade, and he should like to know whether Mr Scanlan intended to suggest charges of neglect.

Mr Scanlan said he suggested that there had been negligence in not bringing the regulations in regard to life-saving appliances up to date. Again, the rules for the manning of ships were defective.

Lord Mersey, who earlier in the day had remarked that, so far as lifeboats were concerned, a man was safer on a cargo boat than an emigrant ship, now said that he had serious doubts as to whether it would be wise to provide lifeboat accommodation for everyone on board. The loss of the Titanic showed that it might be wise to increase the number of lifeboats.

"Public opinion," Lord Mersey said later, "is of very little value in the view of the experts."

The inquiry was adjourned.

DECLINE OF THE SAILOR

Board of Trade Expert Blames Hustling Methods

Captain Young, who became nautical adviser to the Marine Department, Board of Trade, last year, told the Titanic Commission yesterday that in the course of his duties he had seen methods of putting out boats that were disgraceful to the merchant service.

It was not the fault of the deckhands themselves; it was simply due to the hustle of the passenger service at the present day, which precluded the men from getting the training they ought to have. He did not think a test for deckhands would hurt the men.

In reply to Lord Mersey he said that the question whether there should be boats for all depended on the structure of a vessel. He thought the Titanic might have carried boats for all. As to the Board of Trade's lifeboat scale it should have been extended so that the Titanic would have carried 26 boats. The delay in extending the scale was due to the fact that experiments were carried out with various types of lifeboats. Though it was not the case with the Titanic, the lifeboats on many ships were ill-formed and only able to carry a full complement in a calm sea.

Sir Alfred Chalmers, Captain Young's predecessor as nautical adviser to the Marine Department of the Board of Trade, said that one reason why the Board of Trade lifeboat scale had not been altered for 18 years was that travelling across the Atlantic was the safest mode of travelling in the world. Even in view of the disaster he did not think the lifeboat scale should be extended.

In the view of Sir Alfred Chalmers the Germans were so encumbering their decks with boats that in case of disaster the consequences might be serious. It was stated that under the German law the Titanic would have carried boats for over 3,000.

DAILY SKETCH IN CALIFORNIA

Mrs Jane P. Rowe, of Farallone, San Mateo County, California, who has the *Daily Sketch* forwarded to her by her sister, Mrs Bell, of Fermoy, County Cork, Ireland, sends us a cutting from a San Francisco paper about a precious item of the Titanic's cargo.

This was a consignment of rare orchids, 500 of them, that were bound from India for California. They were of a variety not yet introduced on the Pacific coast, and the orchid growers there were laying great store on them till word reached San Francisco the other day that they had been shipped on the Titanic.

THE DUFF-GORDONS

Attorney-General Will Not Criticise Them

LORD MERSEY AND MR ISMAY

The conduct of Mr Bruce Ismay and Sir Cosmo and Lady Duff-Gordon was alluded to at the Titanic inquiry yesterday, when counsel intimated the line they purposed to take in their speeches in regard to some of the points raised before the Court.

The Attorney-General (Sir Rufus Isaacs) said that he did not intend to make any further comment or criticism on Sir Cosmo and Lady Duff-Gordon. Their conduct, whatever it was, was immaterial to this inquiry, and the only point in calling them was to throw some light on the suggestion that appeared to underlie a statement by one of the crew about the boat not going back. The only way he proposed to use their evidence was in reference to the conduct of the man in charge (Simon) of the boat. "That boat must form the subject of a good deal of comment and a good deal of criticism," the Attorney-General said.

Lord Mersey: I am of opinion that I ought not to express an opinion on the conduct of individuals in the position of passengers. Different considerations may arise with regard to Mr Ismay, but I will say nothing about that at present.

Mr Laing (for the White Star Line) said that the Attorney-General had suggested that he was going to put forward some charge against Mr Ismay and was going to ask the Court not to accept his evidence. "It would be very desirable," said Mr Laing, "that we should know what is going to be said."

The Attorney-General: If my friend wishes it I have no objection to putting a specific question with regard to Mr Ismay, but it does not seem necessary.

Lord Mersey: After all, the question of the conduct of Mr Ismay is only material to the extent to which it may be said to have improperly influenced the captain.

The Attorney-General: I am not going to make any comment with regard to Mr Ismay's conduct in leaving the ship upon a boat at that particular moment. It is always a very difficult thing to determine in special circumstances whether or not he took the right course, and I should rather suggest also that it involves considerations which are not quite those which ought to guide the Court in determining this inquiry.

Lord Mersey: I absolutely agree with you.

Addressing the other counsel representing various interests his lordship said: "I regard you, Mr Scanlan, and others as the accusers." Mr Scanlan represents the Seamen's and Firemen's Union.

In regard to the "Californian incident" Lord Mersey said: "I do not suppose I have any jurisdiction to direct that the captain's certificate should be interfered with in that case."

The Attorney-General: I think that only arises in a collision.

Lord Mersey: Assume that I take a view adverse to the conduct of the Californian, all I can do is to express it.

The Attorney-General: What we were going to ask your lordship to do was to express your conclusions, and those we shall have to consider.

While evidence was being given Lord Mersey said that the extraordinary thing was that the iceberg that struck the Titanic was not seen sooner.

Captain Cannon, for twenty years an Atlantic commander, said that, supposing it was a clear night, with no haze, the look-out men on the Titanic ought to have seen the berg at least two miles away, and so ought the men on the bridge.

THE TITANIC FUNDS

Lord Derby, the Lord Mayor of Liverpool, having seen an announcement by Mr Sydney Buxton to the effect that the whole of the funds raised for sufferers from the Titanic disaster were to be amalgamated and administered by a joint board, telegraphed to Mr Buxton to know whether Liverpool's fund was meant to be included, and what authority there was for the statement.

His lordship has received a reply from Mr Buxton stating that reference to Liverpool was made under a misapprehension.

TITANIC'S CONSTRUCTION

Counsel Suggests Board of Trade Rules Were Broken

At the Titanic inquiry yesterday, Mr Edwards, who represents the Dockers' Union, suggested that if there had been more stringent tests the bulkheads of the ship might not have given way.

He claimed that the ship was not constructed according to Government Rules, that either the builders had defied the Board of Trade or there had been extraordinary laxity on the part of the officials.

William Archer, principal ship surveyor to the Board of Trade, said he made recommendations last year that would have given boating accommodation on the Titanic for nearly 3,000 persons.

The inquiry was adjourned.

**DAILY SKETCH
WEDNESDAY 19 JUNE 1912**

MARCONI'S LATEST

Wireless Distress Signal That Rings a Bell

TITANIC COMMISSION HEARS OF NEW INVENTION

Mr Marconi, the inventor of wireless telegraphy, gave evidence at the Titanic inquiry yesterday.

He has another invention on the way. The idea is to have a wireless distress signal that shall ring a bell.

He explained the idea in the course of a reply to a question by the Attorney-General (Sir Rufus Isaacs), whether it would be possible to devise, for ships that only have one wireless operator, a simple distress signal that could be detected by a person who was not an operator.

At present if the operator is off duty there is little chance of a distress signal being picked up.

To overcome this difficulty Mr Marconi suggested that the distress signal should be accompanied by a sequence of waves that would cause a bell to give a prolonged ring.

Mr Marconi said that tests had been made with the bell-ringing apparatus, and he had considerable confidence that it could be employed. Meantime the only reliable plan was to have two operators.

Sir Ernest Shackleton, the explorer, was called to give evidence about the distance at which icebergs could be seen.

Ships ought not to go at full speed in an ice zone, Sir Ernest declared.

Lord Mersey: So you think all these liners are wrong in going full speed in regions where ice is reported? – I think the possibility of accident is greatly enhanced by the speed at which the ship goes. I was in a ship specially built for ice, but I took the precaution to slow down. You can never tell the condition of ice; there may be projecting spurs.

There was some laughter when Sir Ernest, in reply to a question, said that the speed of his ship was six knots.

Lord Mersey: Do you mean to say you slowed down with a vessel of six knots? – Yes, I always did.

Then where did you get to? – We got very near the South Pole. (Laughter.)

I mean what speed did you get down to? – We slowed to about four knots.

The inquiry was adjourned.

CAPTAIN SMITH

"Not Usual to Find Dead Men Guilty of Negligence"

LORD MERSEY AND THE TITANIC COMMANDER

At the Titanic inquiry yesterday Lord Mersey said he should like to know what liners were traversing the same region as the Titanic about the time of the disaster and at what speeds they were travelling.

"My reason is this," he said. "I shall have to consider whether Captain Smith was guilty of negligence or merely an error of judgement, and I think my opinion on that matter would be greatly influenced by the conduct of other experienced navigators traversing the same district at the same time."

The Attorney-General said that inquiries had been made, but several of the steamship lines had not answered. The information that has been received would be laid before the Court.

Lord Mersey: The absence of a reply would have a significance in my mind.

Lord Mersey added that he should be inclined to say that a man who had followed the practice of twenty years was guilty of an error of judgement rather than of negligence. He was told, he said, that it was not the practice to find negligence against a dead man. He asked Mr Aspinall, an Admiralty counsel of long experience, if that was so.

Mr Aspinall (who is one of the counsel for the Government in this inquiry): I know of no rule, but the Courts have always shown great reluctance to find negligence against a dead man.

Lord Mersey: That is what I feel. I feel the greatest reluctance in finding negligence against a man who cannot be heard, but if there is a fixed practice which binds me, well, of course, I am relieved of the difficulty altogether.

Mr Aspinall: I cannot say it has been laid down as a fixed practice, but I have never known a case in which the Court has found a dead man guilty of negligence, and I do not know of a case in which it has been invited to do so, even by adverse interests.

Whilst evidence was being given Lord Mersey said he had come to the conclusion that it was not desirable for the men in the crow's nest to have binoculars.

Mr Wilding, naval architect to the builders of the Titanic, said that there was no foundation for the suggestion that the Board of Trade's rules were violated in the construction of the vessel.

The inquiry was adjourned till to-morrow, when the captain of the Carpathia will be called. He is the last witness.

DAILY SKETCH
SATURDAY 22 JUNE 1912

TITANIC'S WOMEN

Counsel Suggests They Should Have Been Forced Into Boats

Captain Rostron, of the Carpathia, gave evidence at the Titanic inquiry. When the Attorney-General (Sir Rufus Isaacs), on behalf of the Government, thanked the captain for his services, there was loud applause in court.

Before counsel's speeches were begun, the position of the Duff-Gordons was considered.

The Attorney-General said it was clear from the evidence that there was no promise of money to induce the men in the Duff-Gordons' boat not to go back to the place where the ship sank.

Lord Mersey said the Court had to consider to what extent the conduct of the Duff-Gordons might be said to explain why the boat was not full.

"I do not propose," his Lordship said, "to make any reflection upon the conduct either of the gentleman or his wife; and I want to add that, if I do not, my silence is not to be taken as any adverse reflection on him at all. I shall be silent simply because it has got nothing to do with what I have before me."

Mr Scanlan, M.P., in his address on behalf of the Seamen's and Firemen's Union, contended that the disaster was due to neglect on the part of the officers to take precautions against ice. Evidence had been given that made Mr Bruce Ismay, as well as the captain, responsible for the navigation of the ship.

While Mr Scanlan was speaking on the custom that prevailed among commanders of going full speed in ice regions, Lord Mersey asked: Have you ever considered who are really responsible for this practice, if it is a wrong practice? Is it not the passengers?

Mr Scanlan: I agree that it is the demand of the public and the taste for high speed that lead to a disregard of precautions which one would think ordinary common sense, apart from seamanship, would dictate.

In regard to the women, Mr Scanlan said that the stewards should have been instructed to use force, if necessary, to get them into the boats.

Lord Mersey: I cannot imagine anything more alarming than for stewards to be dragging women by force. It would be a most terrifying thing.

Mr Scanlan: It is very alarming, but it is not quite so terrible as being left behind on a ship that is doomed.

The inquiry was adjourned.

DAILY SKETCH
TUESDAY 25 JUNE 1912

ALL EYES AND EARS

Addressing the Titanic Commission, Mr Harbinson, who appears for the third-class passengers, said that the Board of Trade had many eyes and many ears, but it did not seem to have any brains.

Mr Edwards, who represents the Dockers' Union, alleged negligence against the navigators of the Titanic. It was important to know how far Captain Smith was influenced by Mr Ismay. Mr Edwards thought that Mr Ismay was anxious that there should be a record passage.

The inquiry was adjourned.

EVERY LITTLE HELPS

(To the Editor of the *Daily Sketch*)

Sir, – I am sending a contribution to your Titanic Relief Fund as soon as I receive my pay. Being a married man I can't send much, but I suppose every little will help.

Umtali, Rhodesia   ROB AUCHTERLONIE

DAILY SKETCH
WEDNESDAY 26 JUNE 1912

MR ISMAY'S HONOUR

Addressing the Titanic Commission yesterday Sir Robert Finlay (for the White Star Line) said that there was not the slightest ground for suggesting that any other life would have been saved if Mr Ismay had stayed on the ship. Mr Ismay violated no point of honour, and had he thrown away his life those who now attacked him would have said that he did so to avoid inquiry.

DAILY SKETCH
THURSDAY 27 JUNE 1912

FLYING LINERS

Do Captains Race to Win Owners Approval?

Sir Robert Finlay continued his speech for the White Star Line at the Titanic inquiry yesterday, and had not finished when the Court adjourned.

He criticised some of Sir Ernest Shackleton's evidence. Sir Ernest stated that he believed Atlantic captains only obeyed the instructions of their owners in going at full speed. "That," said Sir Robert, "only illustrates Sir Ernest's complete ignorance of the conditions prevailing in the North Atlantic trade. When he is near the South Pole Sir Ernest is supreme; but when he gets near the North Atlantic he is only an ordinary man.

Lord Mersey: It certainly is by no means an uncommon impression that a good passage improves the captain's position in the eyes of the employer.

Sir Robert Finlay: But not a good passage involving risk, because nothing is more serious to a company than for the impression to get abroad that risks are run.

CAPTAIN ROSTRON'S GOLD MEDAL

At Liverpool yesterday Captain Rostron was presented with a gold medal and an illuminated address for rescuing the Titanic survivors. Lord Derby, the Lord Mayor of Liverpool, handed the medal to Captain Rostron.

DAILY SKETCH
FRIDAY 28 JUNE 1912

MR ISMAY'S POSITION

Lord Mersey Says There Is No Evidence of Interference

Continuing his address on behalf of the White Star Line at the Titanic inquiry, Sir Robert Finlay repeated that the collision would not have occurred had the ice message from the Mesaba been received on the Titanic's bridge.

Lord Mersey remarked that the dead wireless operator Phillips neglected the direction that messages dealing with the navigation of the ship should take precedence of all others.

With regard to Mr Ismay's position, Lord Mersey said there was no evidence that he interfered with the navigation of the vessel.

The Attorney-General (Sir Rufus Isaacs) agreed.

Lord Mersey replying to Sir Robert Finlay, said he was satisfied that no record passage was attempted.

When the question of discipline and organisation was raised the Attorney-General said that he should contend that if there had been better preparation for such an event a number of people would have been saved in the boats who were lost. He was not going to say there was anything in the nature of panic. Speaking generally, the crew behaved extremely well.

Lord Mersey: I think so as well.

The Attorney-General: In the circumstances order was maintained to an extraordinary degree, and with one or two exceptions the passengers seem to have behaved with extraordinary calmness, not to say heroism.

The inquiry was adjourned until to-day.

FILMING "THE MIRACLE"

Reinhardt's Great Show to be Seen in Kinemacolor

Rheinhardt's great show, "The Miracle" is presently to be played to larger audiences than even Olympia could accommodate. It is to be reproduced on the cinematograph and in kinemacolor.

Next month Professor Reinhardt is calling his host of actors and actresses and supers together in Vienna, where he proposes to rehearse the famous wordless play anew for the benefit of an audience of camera, and early in August the filming will take place.

An enterprising development of this undertaking is being made by Mr Charles Urban, who has acquired the sole rights to reproduce "The Miracle" in kinemacolor. This he hopes to have ready for presentation in London some time early in the autumn.

I can find little further information about these early versions of Max Reinhardt's story. It was however re-filmed in 1959 by Warners, also titled 'The Miracle' and was set in Spain during the Peninsular War. It was the story of a nun who broke her vows in order to follow a British soldier – a statue of the Virgin Mary steps down to take her place. This version starred Carroll Baker & Roger Moore.

TITANIC DISASTER

"One of the Things That Must Happen Now and Then"

It is expected that the Titanic Inquiry will be finished on Monday, Sir Robert Finlay, who appears for the White Star Line, yesterday concluded his address for the White Star Line. He began it on Tuesday.

Winding up, he said that the accident was due to an extraordinary concatenation of circumstances, and that no blame could be attached to the company or to those responsible for the ship.

It was one of those things that must happen every now and then, and does happen without any fault on the part of anyone.

When Mr Dunlop rose to make his speech on behalf of the Californian Lord Mersey asked: "How long will it take you to convince us that the Californian did not see the Titanic's lights?"

Mr Dunlop said he should take about two hours. He contended that the lights seen by the Californian were not those of the Titanic.

To-day the Attorney-General (Sir Rufus Isaacs) will address the Court.

THE TITANIC RELIEF FUND

A SCHEME TO BE DRAWN UP

A meeting of the Committee of the Mansion House Fund for the relief of the sufferers by the loss of the Titanic was held yesterday in the Venetian Parlour. The LORD MAYOR presided.

The Fund was reported to amount to £307,500, which is exclusive of the funds in the hands of the Lord Mayor of Liverpool, the Mayor of Southampton, and the *Daily Telegraph*.

The MAYOR of SOUTHAMPTON stated that, of the 673 members of the crew who were lost, 535 appeared to belong to Southampton and 138 to other places. Of the Southampton crew, 403 relatives had been traced there, and 132 had removed and were being traced. The list showed 227 widows, 363 children under 14; 75 over 14; and 2,250 (?) dependants.

SIR WILLIAM SOULSBY said that of 819 passengers reported as lost, the families of 411 had, so far, made claims. Of these 223 were British, 14 Austro-Hungarians, 18 Belgians, 33 Bulgarians, three Danish, one French, one Italian, 15 Norwegian, 19 Russian, 71 Swedes, five Swiss, and ten Syrians. The families represented by these 411 claims were 113 widows, 202 children, 397 parents, and 460 other relations – 1,172 persons in all. In addition, from 60 to 70 applications were expected from other Syrians and from 30 to 40 other Austro-Hungarians. There were still over 300 passengers in respect of whom no claims had as yet been made.

The cases of American sufferers were being adequately dealt with in New York and elsewhere.

Large numbers of claims had also come from survivors – both crew and passengers – who had lost property in the disaster.

Mr Farrell, M.P., and Mr Herbert Deane, a solicitor, attended on behalf of the dependants of a considerable number of young unmarried Irish emigrants.

The COMMITTEE in reply, said they would deal with each case on its merits and in a generous way, but the fund was not a medium for granting permanent compensation for the loss of future benefits from relatives.

It was referred to the Public Trustee, the Hon. Harry Lawson, M.P., and the Town Clerk of Southampton to bring up a scheme, after obtaining actuarial assistance, for dealing with the cases of the crew. It was hoped that this might be forthcoming within a fortnight.

It was decided to extend the time for receiving claims in respect of passengers until September 1. Meanwhile the committee will be prepared to go on affording immediate relief to all cases needing it, and applications in that respect, if addressed to the Mansion House, will have instant attention.

WHEN · OTHER · HELPERS · FAIL

"Much love is hidden till death comes our way,
To tell us what is best."

CLOSE OF THE TITANIC INQUIRY

PROPOSAL FOR INTERNATIONAL CONFERENCE

The Court of Inquiry into the loss of the Titanic finished its investigation, which has occupied 36 days, yesterday morning. In the course of the inquiry 98 witnesses have been called, and over 25,600 questions asked. The Attorney-General thanked the President for his patient attention, and Lord Mersey dismissed the subject for the present by promising that he would endeavour to report "in reasonable time."

The ATTORNEY-GENERAL, resuming his speech, explained the reasons why new rules had not been brought forward by the Board of Trade since the Titanic disaster. He mentioned that it was desired that any recommendation by the Court should be considered, and, further, that an international conference was proposed to deal with the question of life-saving appliances at sea, including boat accommodation, so that regulations might be made which would apply to the vessels of all countries.

THE CALIFORNIAN

The last question with which he proposed to deal was that relating to the Californian. So far from being desirous of bringing home to the captain of the Californian or to any of her officers that they saw distress signals and took no steps afterwards he was most anxious to find some excuse for the inaction of the Californian. It was a matter of great regret that he had to make the submission that there was no excuse, but he thought that all the President was asked to do was to give the view of the facts he had formed after hearing the evidence.

The PRESIDENT – If Captain Lord saw distress signals and he neglected a reasonable opportunity to go to the relief of the vessel in distress it may very well be that he is guilty of a misdemeanour. Am I to try that question?

The ATTORNEY-GENERAL – Certainly not.

The PRESIDENT – I think not.

The ATTORNEY-GENERAL – But nevertheless the facts which you are asked to find, whether they reflect upon him or not, are material to the inquiry. I ask you to find the fact that they did see distress signals and that they were distress signals from the Titanic, and that the distance to the Titanic from the Californian was only a few miles.

The PRESIDENT – How many?

The ATTORNEY-GENERAL thought it was difficult to say, but put the distance at seven or eight miles. He added that Captain Lord's evidence on the point was most unsatisfactory.

The PRESIDENT – I think we are all of the opinion that the distress rockets seen from the Californian were the distress rockets of the Titanic.

The ATTORNEY-GENERAL said that was the material fact, and once established, a state of things was reached which was really quite inexplicable – the more extraordinary as the rule which everybody going to sea never failed to observe was that if a vessel were seen in distress the utmost must be done to get to her. He did not think it was altogether wise to speculate upon the reasons which might have guided Captain Lord, but that this vessel might have got to the Titanic in time to save the passengers was, he feared, the irresistible conclusion to be drawn from the evidence.

TWO CAUSES OF DISASTER

In concluding his speech the ATTORNEY-GENERAL said that the Court might recommend most useful precautions for saving life, the Board of Trade and Parliament might take the amplest care that proper precautions should be prescribed, and that there should be sufficient protection given to those who were sailing on the seas against loss of life in the event of disaster; but no human wisdom of this character, however great, would be able to prevent the recurrence – he would not say of such a disaster as this, but the recurrence of disaster at sea, for the simple reason that everything depended upon the exercise of judgement and care by those responsible for navigation. As a result of this inquiry it was to be hoped that no vessel would ever take such utterly unnecessary risks as, it was his submission, were taken on this voyage, and that it would always be borne in mind by those responsible for navigation that for passengers to pass a few more hours on board would be very much better in the interests of everybody than to press on at a great rate of speed when there had been some indication given of danger ahead. Speaking generally, the two causes of disaster to vessels at sea were failure to keep a good look out and proceeding at too great a rate of speed; and this disaster had impressed upon all those whose duty it was to consider such questions how important it was that in both those matters the greatest care should be taken when the possibility of meeting ice was reported. It only remained for him to say that the latitude his Lordship had allowed during the inquiry had narrowed the range of controversy at the end. In any event, as far as the Board of Trade was concerned, all the material which could be of any value had been placed before the Court. He thanked his Lordship in all sincerity for the patience with which he had listened to this long inquiry.

The PRESIDENT – Very well, Mr Attorney; I will try to get my report out in reasonable time.

The inquiry then closed.

Notice will be given in the Press of the next sitting of the Court.

THE TITANIC REPORT

LOSS DUE TO EXCESSIVE SPEED

MASTER'S "GRIEVOUS MISTAKE"

LORD MERSEY AND THE BOARD OF TRADE

The report on the loss of the Titanic was presented at a final sitting of the Court of Inquiry held at the Scottish Hall yesterday morning. The Report, a long printed document, occupying 74 pages, was read by the Wreck Commissioner, Lord Mersey. The finding of the Court is as follows:-

The Court, having carefully inquired into the circumstances of the above-mentioned shipping casualty, finds, for the reasons appearing in the annex hereto, that the loss of the said ship was due to collision with an iceberg, brought about by the excessive speed at which the ship was being navigated.

This finding, and the Report itself, are concurred in by the five Assessors:-

Rear-Admiral the Hon. S.A. Gough-Calthorpe, R.N.

Captain A.W. Clarke.

Commander F.C.A. Lyon, R.N.R.

Professor J.H. Biles D.Sc., LL.D.

Mr E.C. Chaston, R.N.R.

The full contents of the Court's report are detailed in a number of other publications. It is sufficient for our purposes here to confine ourselves to extracts from THE TIMES' coverage on the Section dealing with Sir Duff-Gordon and Mr Ismay, and also their concluding paragraphs.

SIR C DUFF-GORDON AND MR ISMAY

The Report refers to the attack made in the course of the inquiry on the moral conduct of Sir Cosmo Duff-Gordon and Mr Bruce Ismay. The Commissioner says:-

It is no part of the business of the Court to inquire into such matters, and I should pass them by in silence, if I did not fear that my silence might be misunderstood. The very grave charge against Sir Cosmo Duff-Gordon, that having got into No. 1 boat he bribed the men in it to row away from drowning people is unfounded. I have said that the members of the crew in that boat might have made some attempt to save the people in the water, and that such an attempt would probably have been successful; but I do not believe that the men were deterred from making the attempt by any act of Sir Cosmo Duff-Gordon's. At the same time I think that if he had encouraged the men to return to the position where the Titanic had foundered they would probably have made an effort to do so and could have saved some lives.

As to the attack on Mr Bruce Ismay, it resolved itself into the suggestion that, occupying the position of managing director of the Steamship Company, some moral duty was imposed upon him to wait on board until the vessel foundered. I do not agree. Mr Ismay, after rendering assistance to many passengers, found "C" collapsible, the last boat on the starboard side, actually being lowered. No other people were there at the time. There was room for him and he jumped in. Had he not jumped in he would merely have added one more life, namely, his own, to the number of those lost.

I have always agreed with the Court's vindication of Mr Ismay, but now, since starting this project, I must add my own personal rider: I had not been aware before that Mr Richard Fry, valet to Mr Ismay, had travelled on the Titanic with his employer (see Times article 22 April 1912). Mr Fry, a married man with two children, had been in Mr Ismay's service for 10 years. I can find no record of any attempt by Mr Ismay to have Mr Fry informed of the impending disaster, or was it a case, even after such long service, that Mr Fry was just an "ordinary employee" as Mr Ismay was an "ordinary passenger" ?

The Commissioner, having concluded the reading of the Report, said he desired to express his thanks for the assistance which the Court had received from those who had been engaged in collecting and preparing evidence in relation to the Inquiry. He would mention particularly the White Star Line, Messrs. Harland and Wolff, and the Board of Trade. The owners and builders of the Titanic placed all the information in their possession or which was procurable by them at the disposal of the Court, and enabled the Court to make a thorough investigation into the matter submitted to it. Sir Ellis Cunliffe and his assistants at the Board of Trade had been indefatigable in preparing evidence so that it might be presented in an intelligible form for the consideration of the Court. He should also mention Mr Marconi, who when asked to do so instantly placed at their disposal the resources of his office, and tendered his own evidence and that of his officials. Lastly, he thanked the gentlemen who had appeared for the different parties. They had done very much to lighten the labours of the Inquiry, and to guide the Court into the various issues involved.

Mr SCANLAN raised the question of costs.

The ATTORNEY-GENERAL said as this was a special case they should treat it in a special manner. Speaking on behalf of the Board of Trade, on the distinct understanding that it was not to be taken as a precedent, he said the Board of Trade would deal with it in an exceptional manner, and pay such costs to those parties whom his Lordship thought ought to be paid. They left that entirely in his Lordship's hands.

The COMMISSIONER – That removes my difficulty. The ATTORNEY-GENERAL – Of course, I have not yet heard who it is who is applying for costs.

The COMMISSIONER said the Attorney-General need not imagine that there was anybody not applying for costs. (Laughter) He indicated that he was disposed to allow costs to the Stewards' Union, the National Sailors' and Firemen's Union, the British Seafarers' Union, the Imperial Merchant Service Guild, certain third-class passengers, the Dockers' Union, and the Marine Engineers' Association.

RELIEF OF THE SUFFERERS

The Mansion House Fund for the relief of the sufferers now amounts to over £321,000. The Lord Mayor yesterday received from the editor of the *Daily Mail* the balance of the "Women's Fund" collected by that paper – £9,632 9s 2d – making in all £59,632 9s 2d. Included in the sum remitted yesterday was £400 – being half the profits of a concert at the Albert Hall on May 24, which Mr R. Fergusson McConnell, the secretary, requested should be ear-marked for the benefit of the families of the musicians who perished in the disaster. The *Daily Mail* Women's Titanic Fund is now closed.

The eventual sum donated to the Mansion House Fund was to reach a total of £412,000, the equivalent of £17,613,000 in today's money. The Fund was officially closed on completion of its duties in 1958.

WIRELESS OPERATOR'S MEMORIAL

Over £330 has been subscribed towards the memorial at Goldalming to Mr Jack Phillips, the chief Marconi operator on board the Titanic, who was a native of the town. It is hoped to raise at least £400, and intending subscribers are asked to send their contributions as soon as possible to the Town Clerk. The memorial committee have decided to ask Miss Gertrude Jekyll to design a drinking fountain. About an acre and a half of land will be set apart, and round the fountain will be a lily pond and a small playing ground for children.

I have deliberately saved the following article to the end. Although it was written at the height of media coverage of the Titanic story, its simple message rings every bit as true today as it did then. I trust the reader will agree . . .

THE KEEPSAKE

It may be urged that the time has come to cease writing and speaking of the Titanic, and there is some justification for the plea. It is over. We may have confidence that the lessons so terribly taught will be remembered. It is certain that ships will be furnished in future with boats enough for all they carry. It is more than probable that the peril of the ice will receive the fullest attention of those who are qualified to deal with such matters, and there are some grounds for hoping that steps will be taken to check the extravagances of private wireless installations. Is it not time, then, to turn the tear-stained page, and to set the mind free for the service of other and happier things?

Almost, perhaps, it is time. But before we put it aside there is something which must be done by all who have any respect for life and for their own hearts. First we must make sure of our harvest. When we have done that, and when we have done our duty to those who have been made destitute by the wreck, we may, if we choose put the matter aside.

And what is this harvest we must reap? If you will search your memory and recall the great events – whether sad or joyful – which you have known and which you remember, you will, I think, understand. Each of them holds its place in your mind, does it not, by virtue of some single incident, some vivid, striking thing which seemed to you at the time to contain in itself the essence of the whole business, and serves now to bring back to you all those happenings of which it was only a part – perhaps an insignificant part.

If you have grasped my meaning you will be able to supply your own illustrations of this. If you have not, I must ask you to consider some of mine. Three, taken altogether at random, will suffice.

At times there comes across the mind the picture of the nave of one of our provincial cathedrals as I saw it on a February day eleven years ago. It was packed with people, and, standing above them, the extraordinary blackness of that vast crowd was a thing that took the mind and held it. And whenever the memory of that sombre gathering comes, there comes with it the memory of the unity of grief which was wrought by the death of Queen Victoria.

Some years later it was reported – whether truthfully or not I cannot tell – that a certain telegraph operator closed a message in which he had described the ruin of the very building in which he was working with the words: "It's me for the simple life!" That phrase – the reckless courage which is next door to panic, and the slangy, terse efficiency of it – serves for a reminder and a token of the San Francisco earthquake.

Not a year ago I saw a lorry being dragged round a village at the tail of a procession of happy people. Upon it were two long benches. One was occupied by a number of very old men and women, and the other by some tiny children, and all of them were very joyful. That is my picture of the coronation of King George.

So now, what about the Titanic? Have you found your picture, your keepsake of this that was so terrible, and so great in its terror? If you have not, you must seek for one, for this is a thing which must not be forgotten. Read all you can about it until you reap your harvest.

For many of us the token will be just the thought of the bandsmen who, when they had heartened all who could be saved on their way to the boats, stood there and played "Nearer, My God, to Thee" while the ship took them down to death.   H.L.

"A berg in her bottom would make her drink
Enough in a couple of hours to sink"

INDEX

To this day some confusion exists regarding the correct names, and spellings, of a number of the passengers and crew of ss TITANIC. This index has been compiled from entries as they appeared in the *Daily Sketch*, which itself contains a number of differing versions, and the index therefore should not be taken as the definitive guide. Surnames printed which are believed to be incorrect have been enclosed in brackets. A number of them cannot be tallied with other sources of Titanic information. Entries in bold print indicate photographs or illustrations.